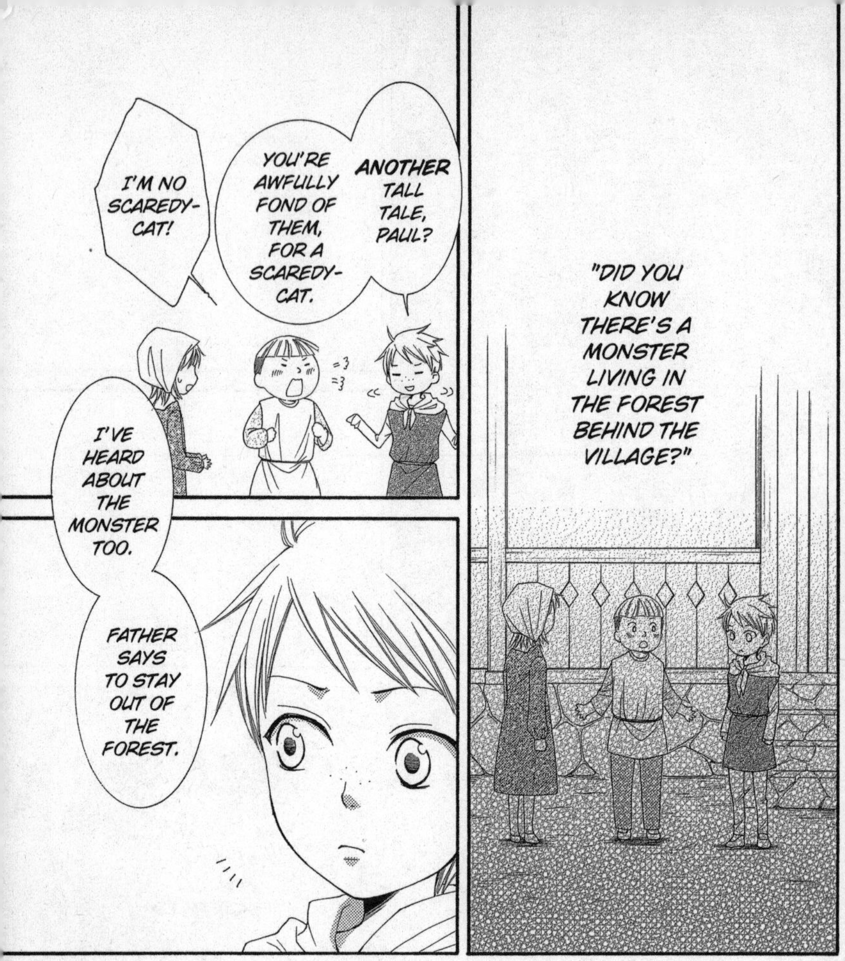
"DID YOU KNOW THERE'S A MONSTER LIVING IN THE FOREST BEHIND THE VILLAGE?"
ANOTHER TALL TALE, PAUL?
YOU'RE AWFULLY FOND OF THEM, FOR A SCAREDY-CAT.
I'M NO SCAREDY-CAT!
I'VE HEARD ABOUT THE MONSTER TOO.
FATHER SAYS TO STAY OUT OF THE FOREST.

Dawn of the Arcana

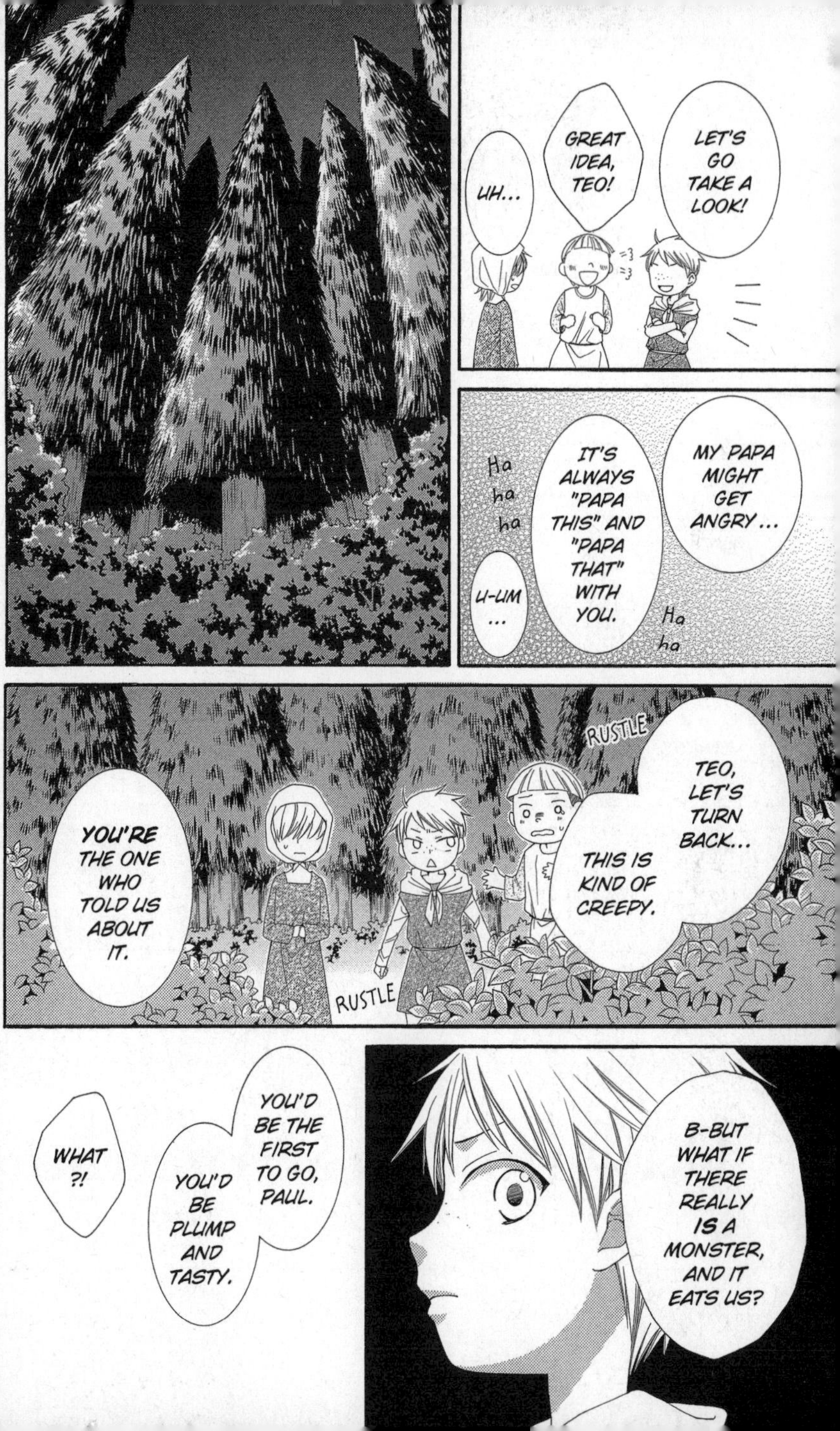
LET'S GO TAKE A LOOK!
GREAT IDEA, TEO!
UH...
MY PAPA MIGHT GET ANGRY...
IT'S ALWAYS "PAPA THIS" AND "PAPA THAT" WITH YOU.
Ha ha ha
U-UM...
Ha ha
RUSTLE
TEO, LET'S TURN BACK...
THIS IS KIND OF CREEPY.
YOU'RE THE ONE WHO TOLD US ABOUT IT.
RUSTLE
B-BUT WHAT IF THERE REALLY IS A MONSTER, AND IT EATS US?
YOU'D BE THE FIRST TO GO, PAUL.
YOU'D BE PLUMP AND TASTY.
WHAT?!

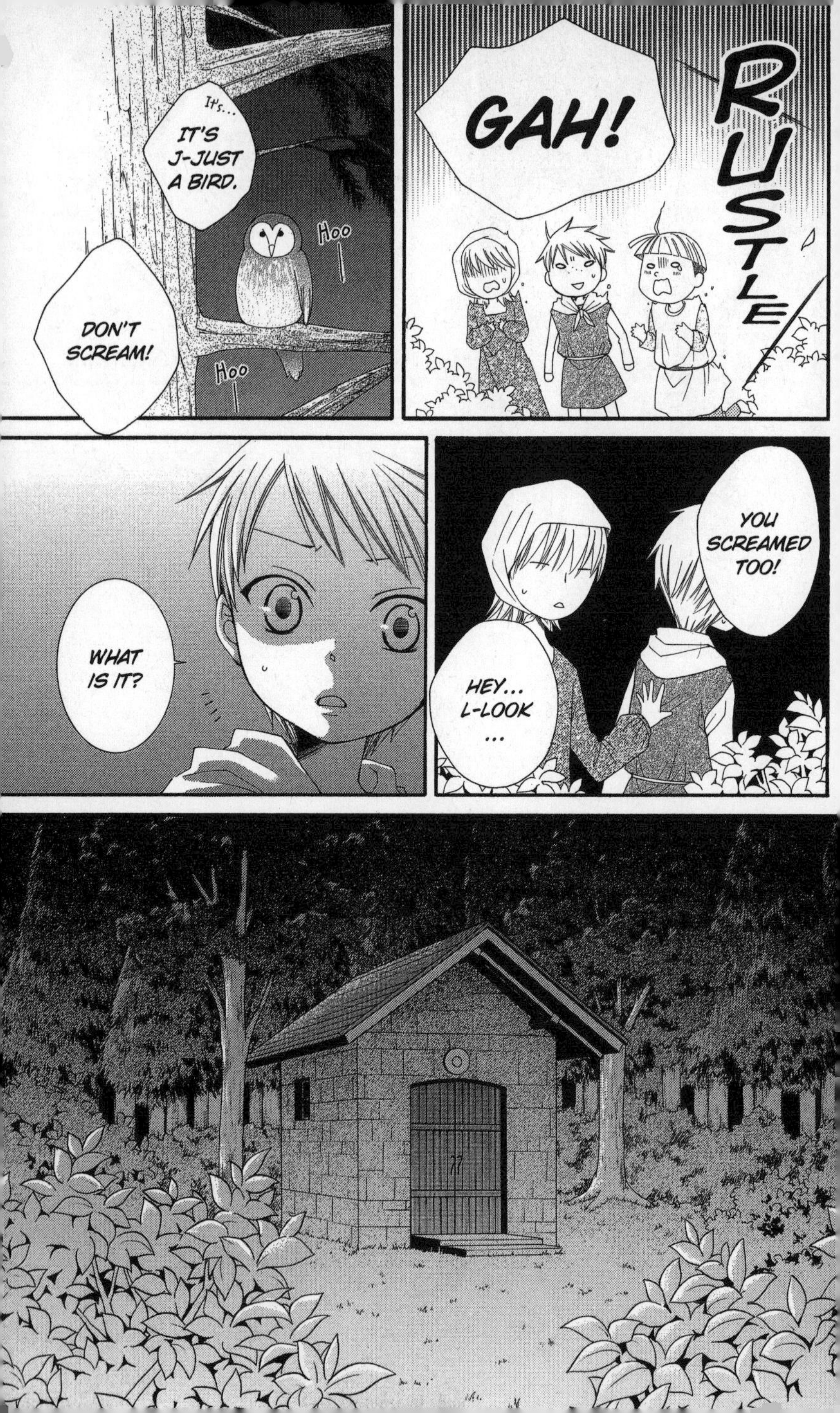
GAH!
RUSTLE
It's...
IT'S J-JUST A BIRD.
Hoo
DON'T SCREAM!
Hoo
YOU SCREAMED TOO!
HEY... L-LOOK ...
WHAT IS IT?

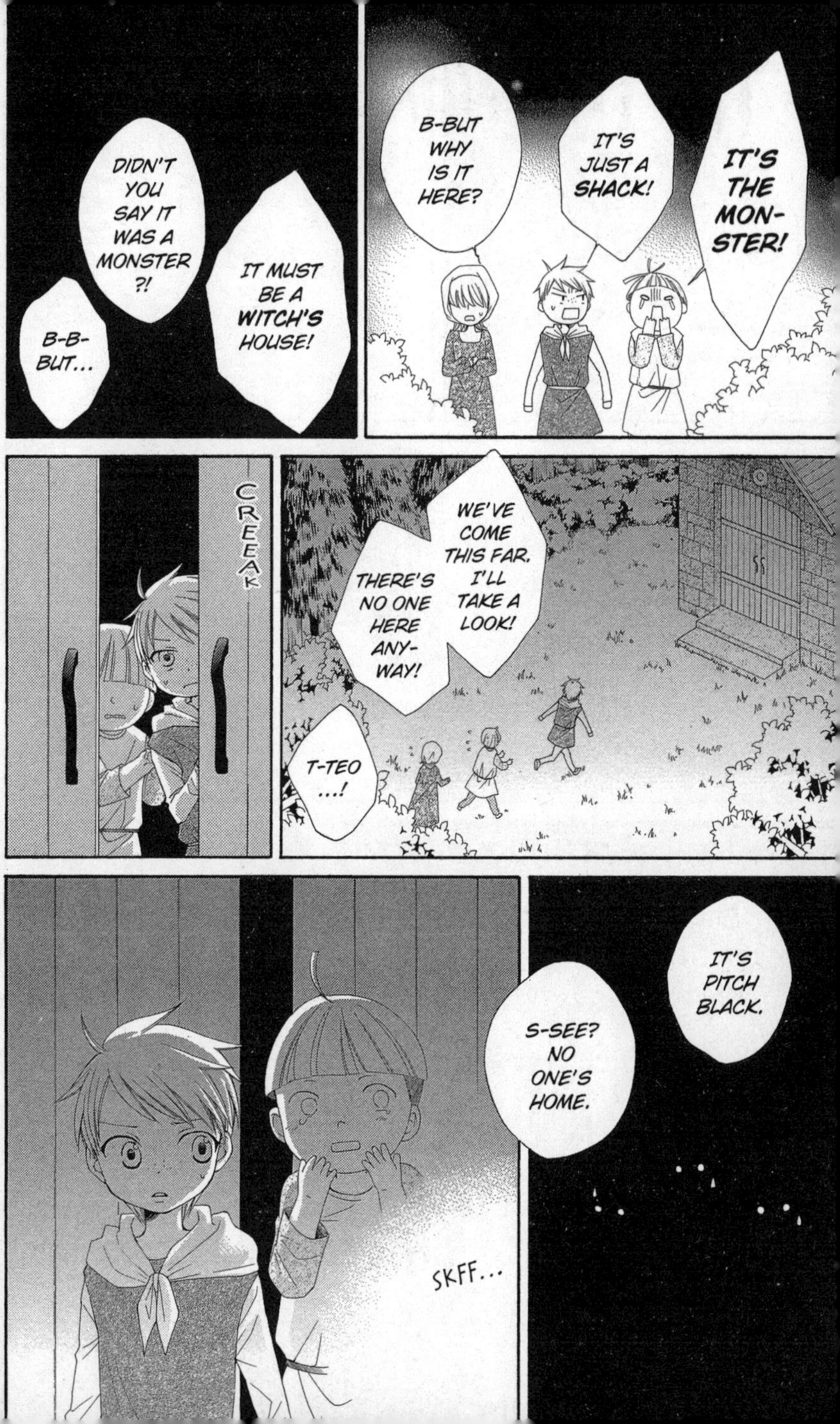
IT'S THE MON-STER!
IT'S JUST A SHACK!
B-BUT WHY IS IT HERE?
IT MUST BE A WITCH'S HOUSE!
DIDN'T YOU SAY IT WAS A MONSTER?!
B-B-BUT...
WE'VE COME THIS FAR. I'LL TAKE A LOOK!
THERE'S NO ONE HERE ANY-WAY!
T-TEO...!
CREEAK
IT'S PITCH BLACK.
S-SEE? NO ONE'S HOME.
SKFF...

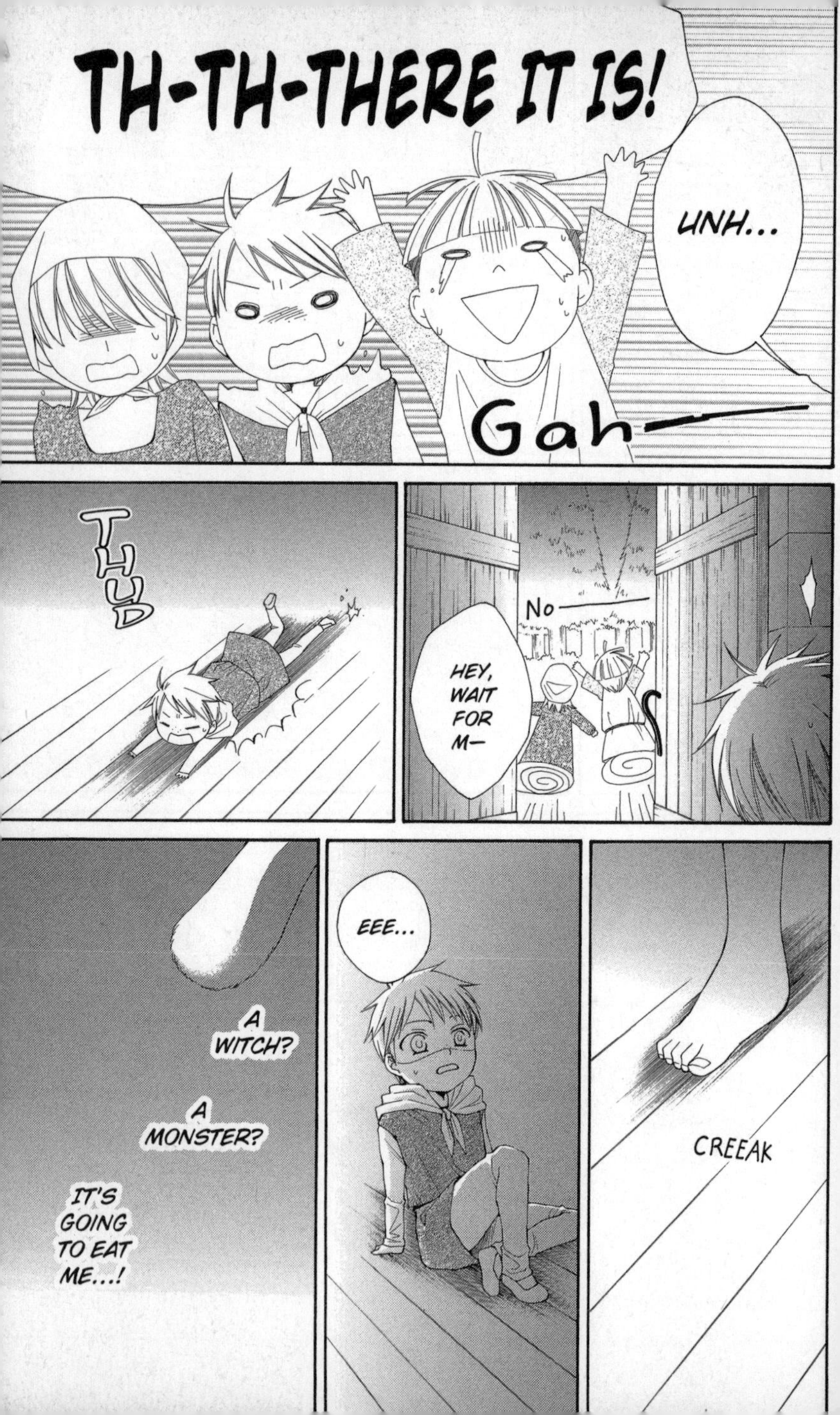
TH-TH-THERE IT IS!
UNH...
Gah
No—
HEY, WAIT FOR M—
THUD
CREEAK
EEE...
A WITCH?
A MONSTER?
IT'S GOING TO EAT ME...!

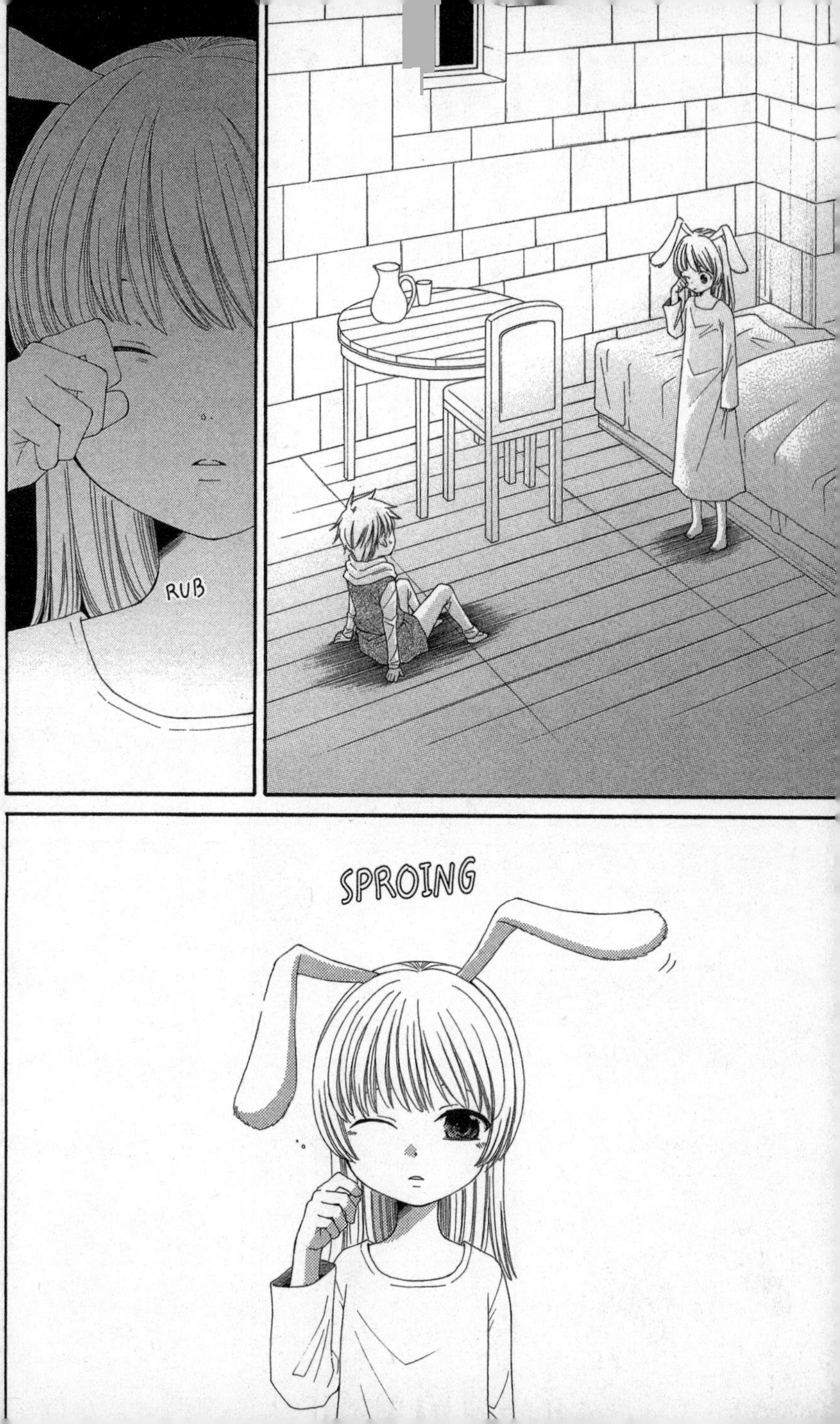
RUB
SPROING

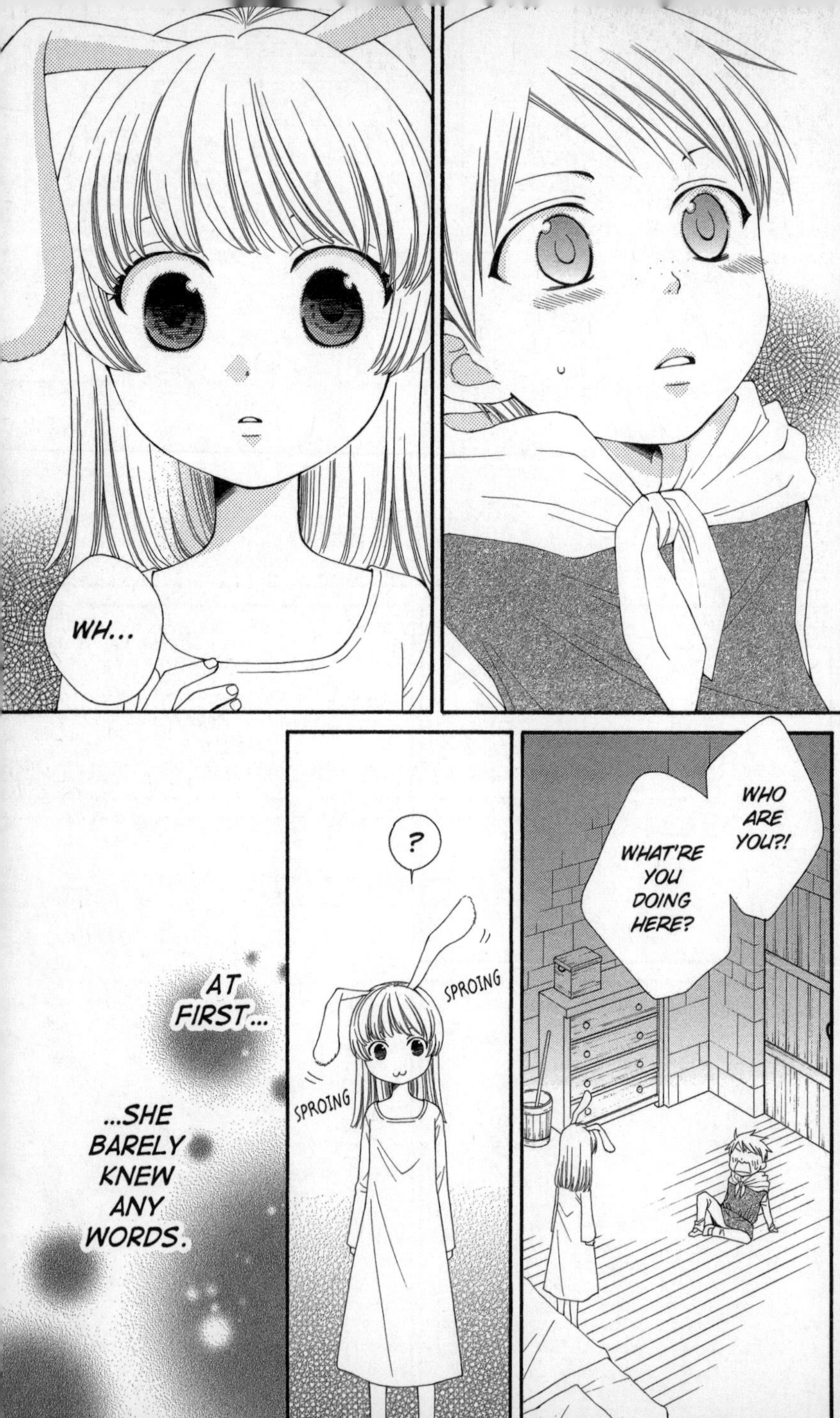
WH...
WHO ARE YOU?!
WHAT'RE YOU DOING HERE?
?
SPROING
SPROING
AT FIRST...
...SHE BARELY KNEW ANY WORDS.

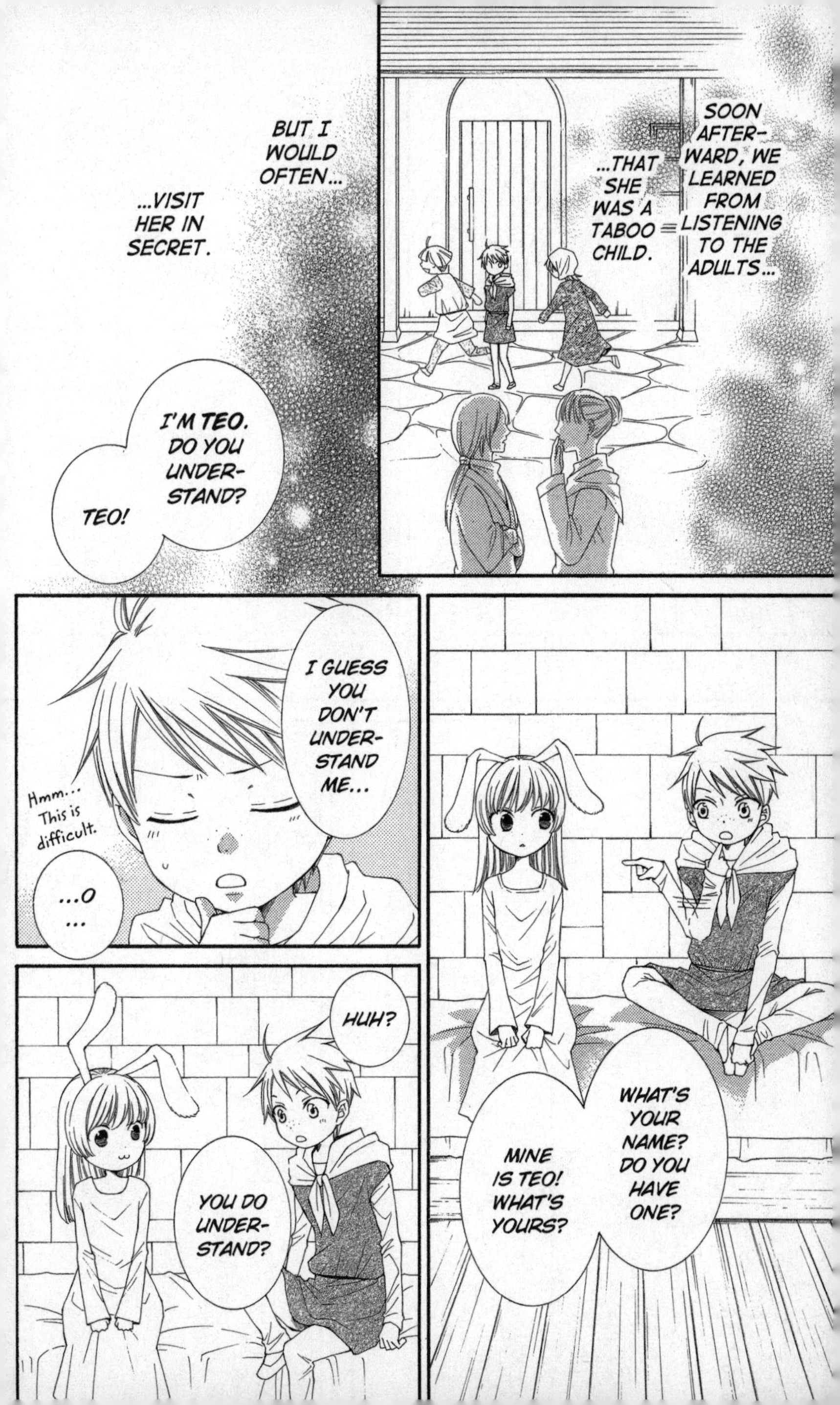
SOON AFTER-WARD, WE LEARNED FROM LISTENING TO THE ADULTS...
...THAT SHE WAS A TABOO CHILD.
BUT I WOULD OFTEN...
...VISIT HER IN SECRET.
I'M TEO. DO YOU UNDER-STAND?
TEO!
WHAT'S YOUR NAME? DO YOU HAVE ONE?
MINE IS TEO! WHAT'S YOURS?
I GUESS YOU DON'T UNDER-STAND ME...
Hmm... This is difficult.
...O ...
HUH?
YOU DO UNDER-STAND?

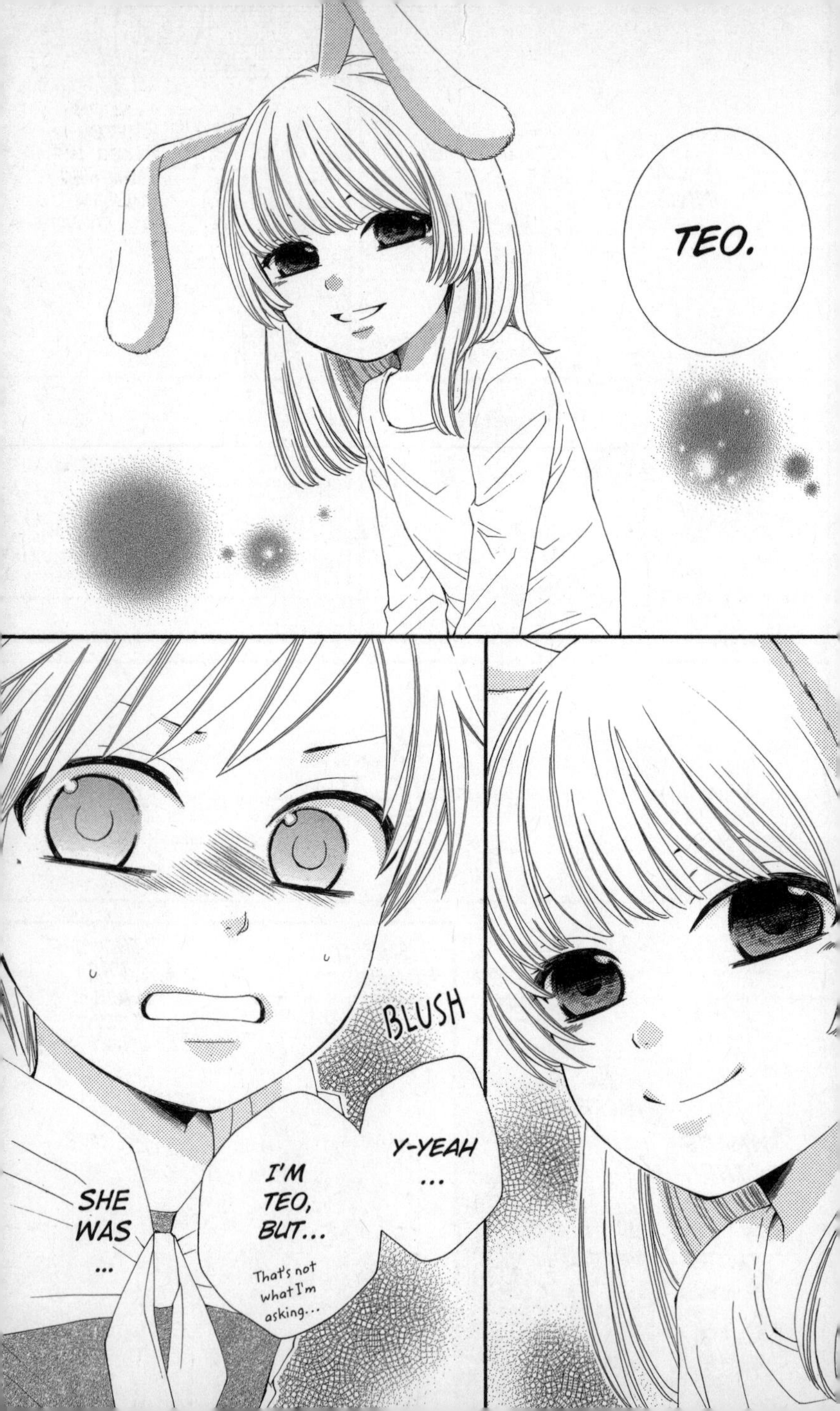
TEO.
BLUSH
Y-YEAH...
I'M TEO, BUT...
That's not what I'm asking...
SHE WAS...

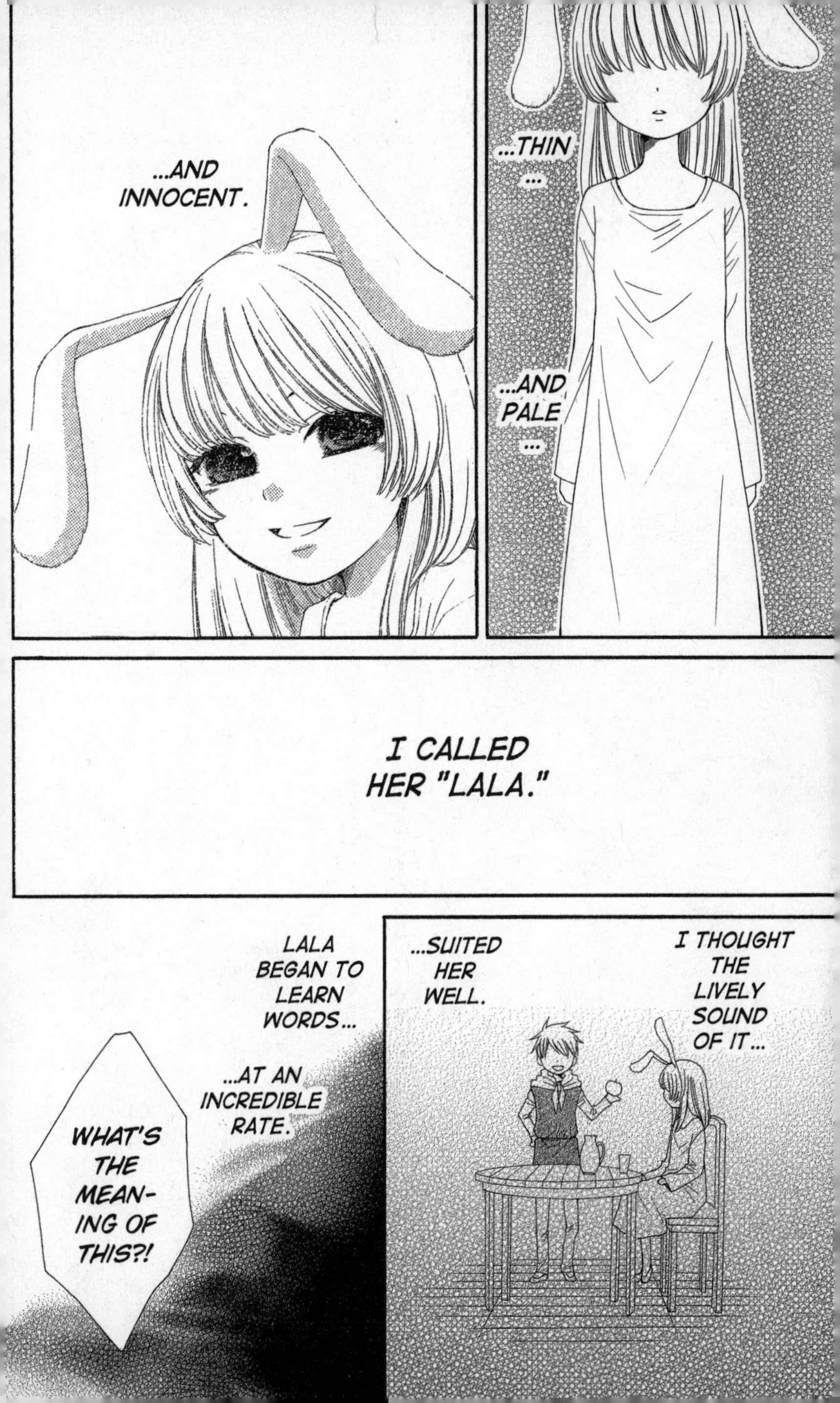
...THIN ...
...AND PALE ...
...AND INNOCENT.
I CALLED HER "LALA."
I THOUGHT THE LIVELY SOUND OF IT...
...SUITED HER WELL.
LALA BEGAN TO LEARN WORDS...
...AT AN INCREDIBLE RATE.
WHAT'S THE MEAN-ING OF THIS?!

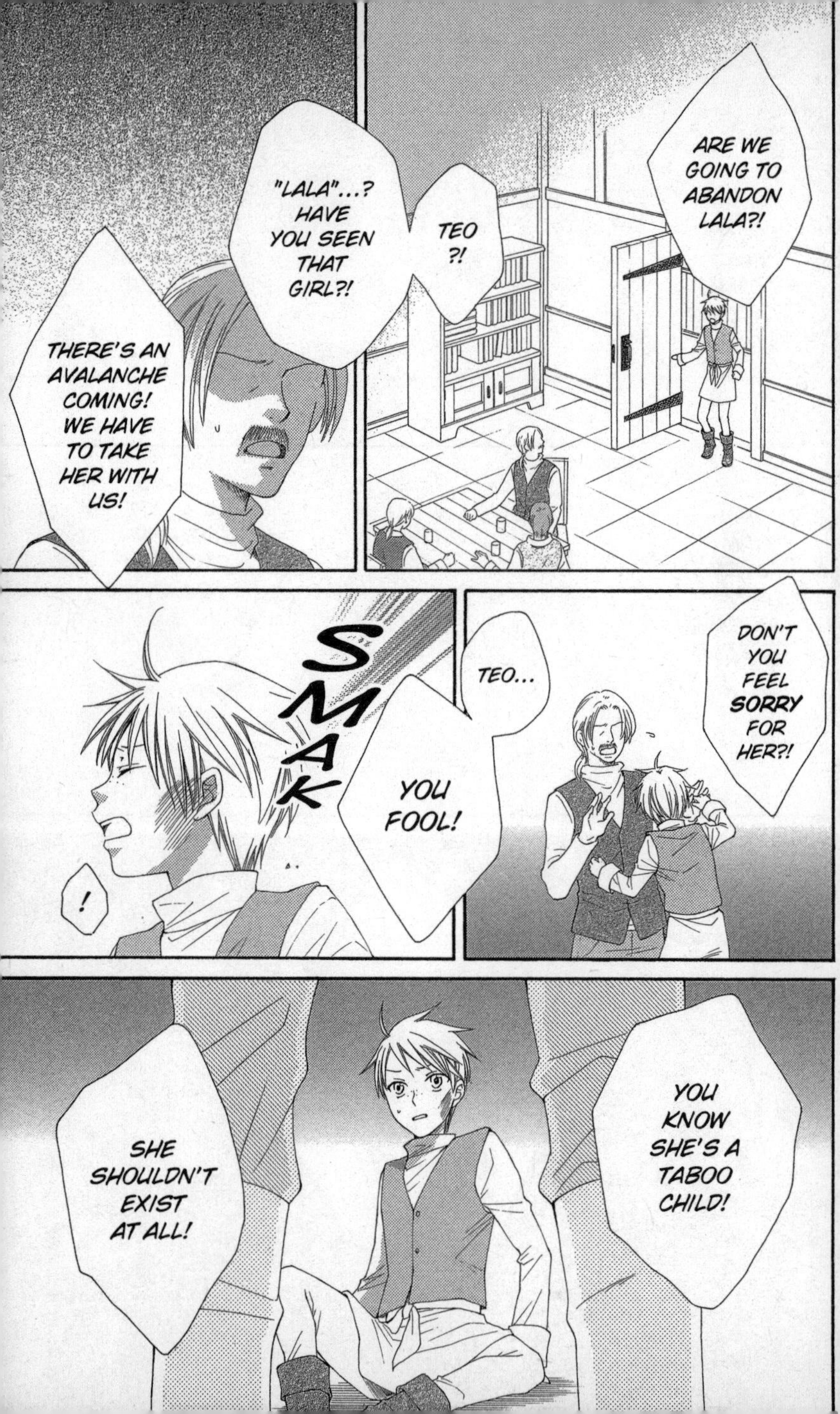
ARE WE GOING TO ABANDON LALA?!
TEO ?!
"LALA"...? HAVE YOU SEEN THAT GIRL?!
THERE'S AN AVALANCHE COMING! WE HAVE TO TAKE HER WITH US!
DON'T YOU FEEL SORRY FOR HER?!
TEO...
YOU FOOL!
SMAK
!
YOU KNOW SHE'S A TABOO CHILD!
SHE SHOULDN'T EXIST AT ALL!

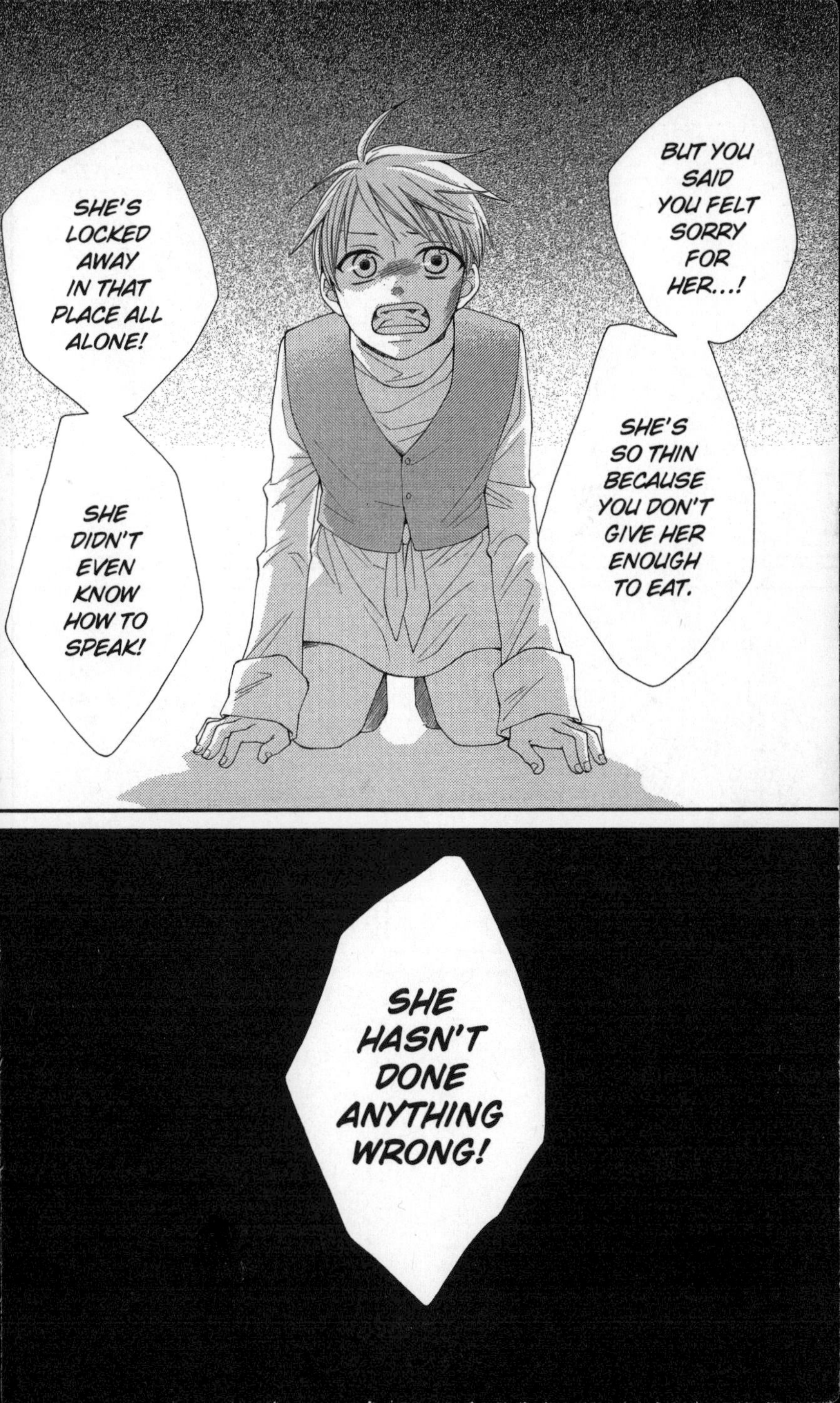
BUT YOU SAID YOU FELT SORRY FOR HER...!
SHE'S SO THIN BECAUSE YOU DON'T GIVE HER ENOUGH TO EAT.
SHE'S LOCKED AWAY IN THAT PLACE ALL ALONE!
SHE DIDN'T EVEN KNOW HOW TO SPEAK!
SHE HASN'T DONE ANYTHING WRONG!

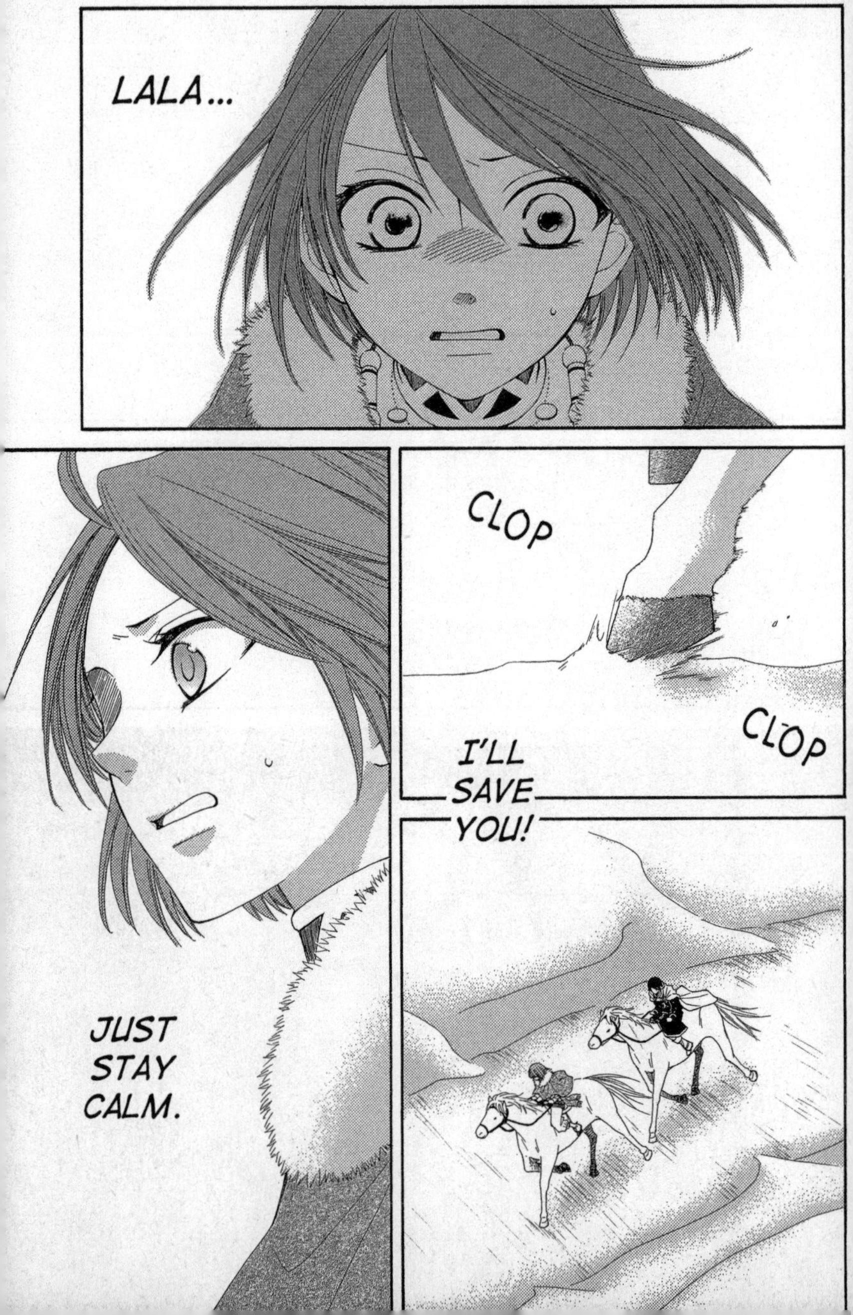

LALA...
CLOP
CLOP
I'LL SAVE YOU!
JUST STAY CALM.

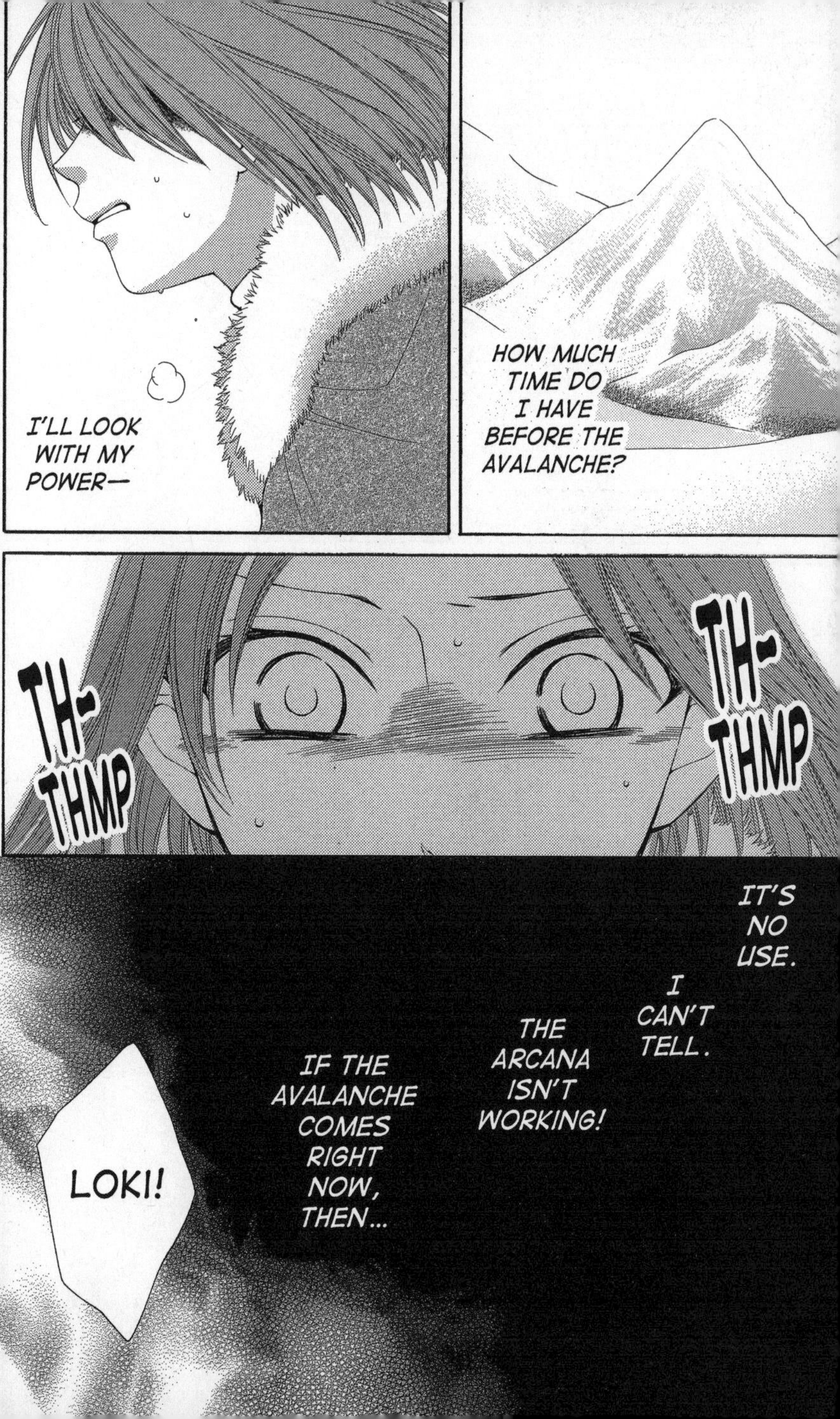

HOW MUCH TIME DO I HAVE BEFORE THE AVALANCHE?
I'LL LOOK WITH MY POWER—
TH-THMP
TH-THMP
IT'S NO USE.
I CAN'T TELL.
THE ARCANA ISN'T WORKING!
IF THE AVALANCHE COMES RIGHT NOW, THEN...
LOKI!

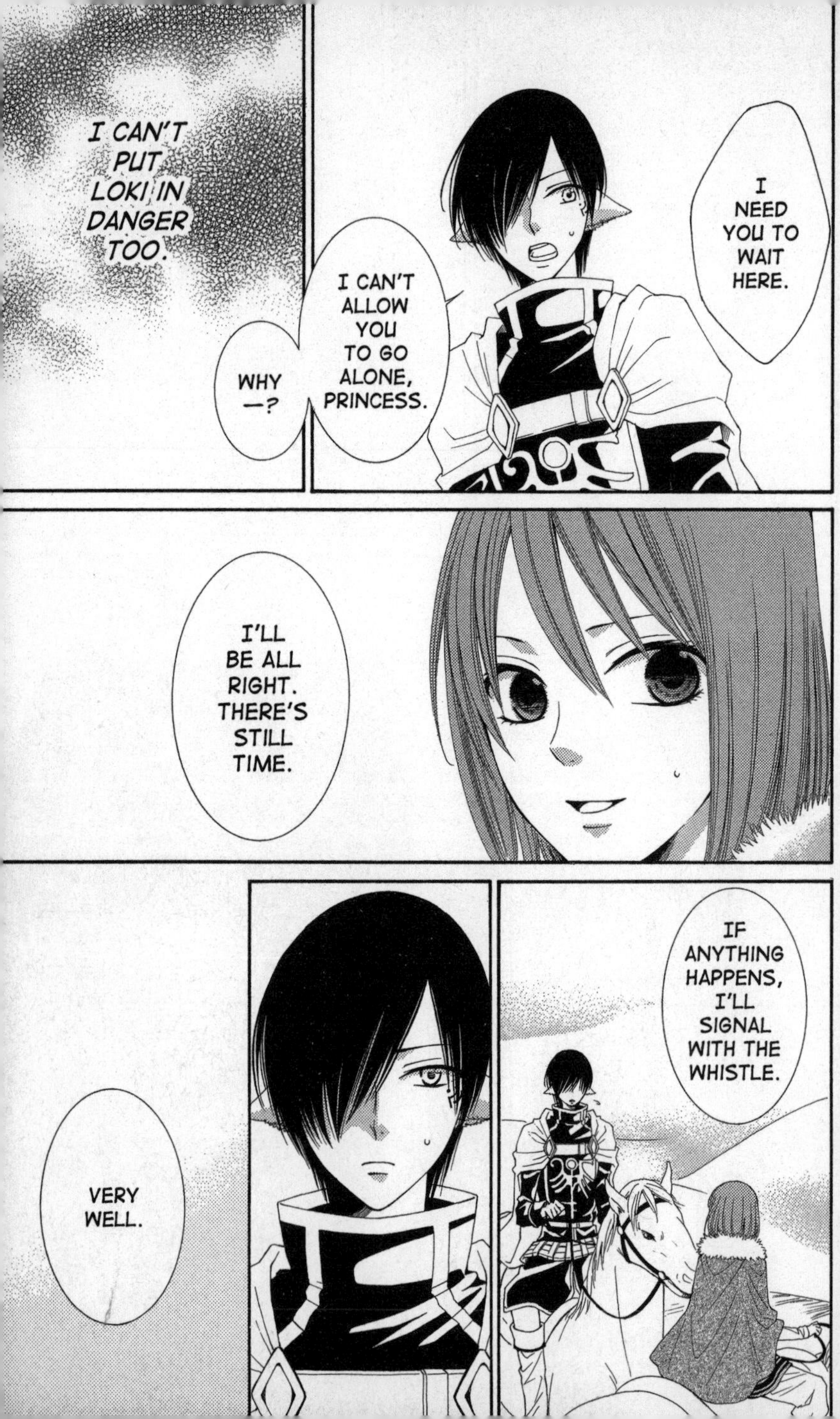
I NEED YOU TO WAIT HERE.
I CAN'T ALLOW YOU TO GO ALONE, PRINCESS.
WHY—?
I CAN'T PUT LOKI IN DANGER TOO.
I'LL BE ALL RIGHT. THERE'S STILL TIME.
IF ANYTHING HAPPENS, I'LL SIGNAL WITH THE WHISTLE.
VERY WELL.

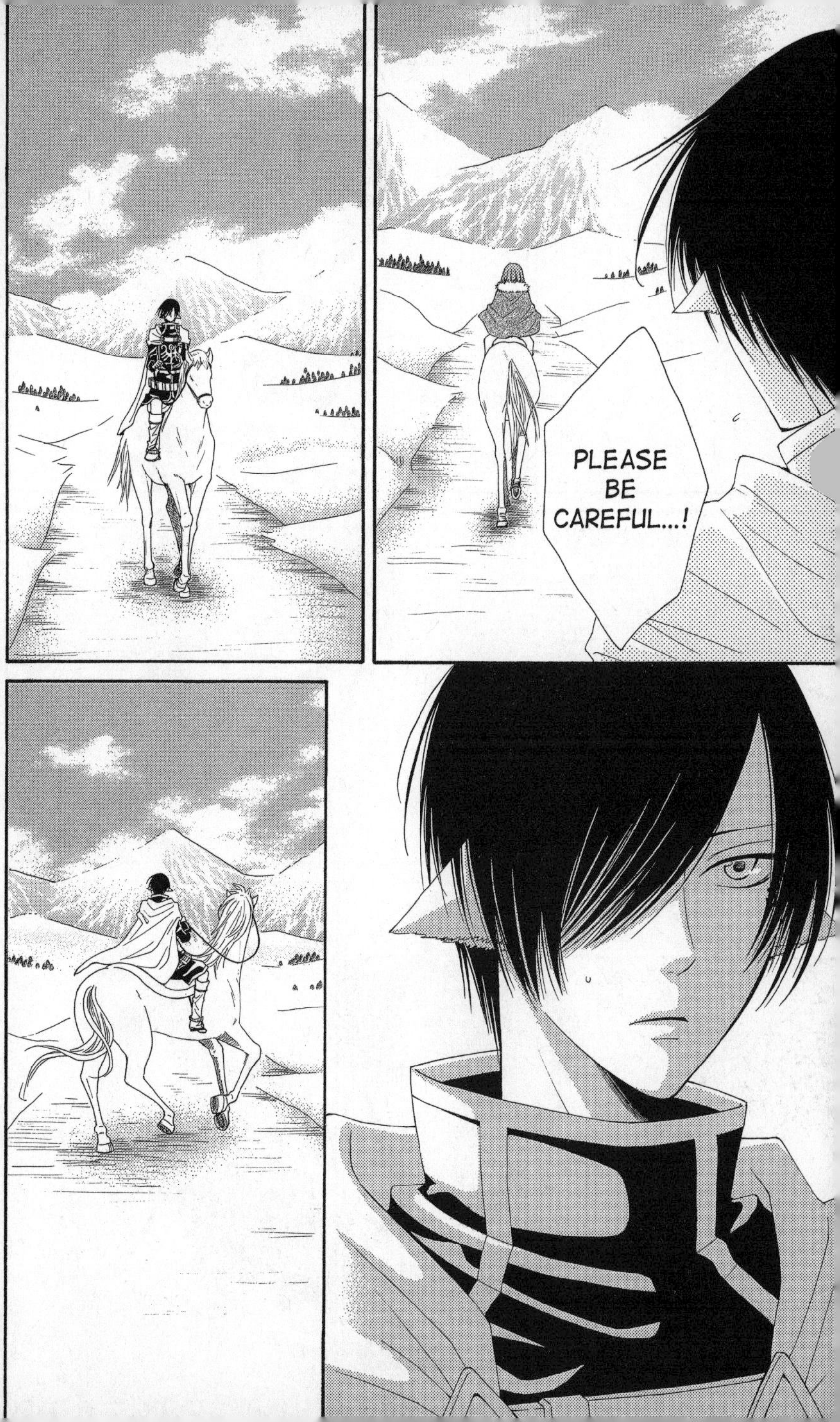
PLEASE BE CAREFUL...!

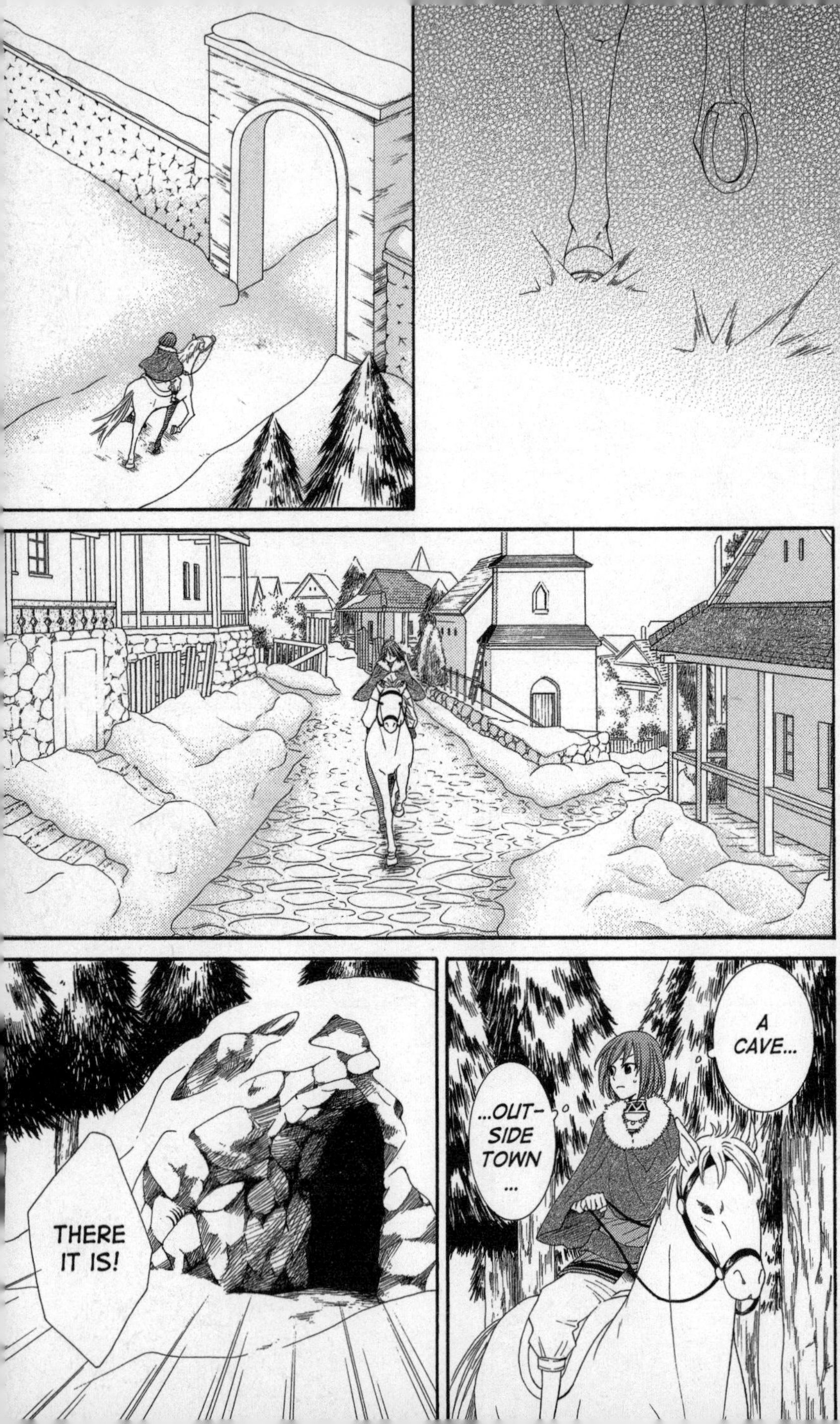
A CAVE...
...OUT-SIDE TOWN ...
THERE IT IS!

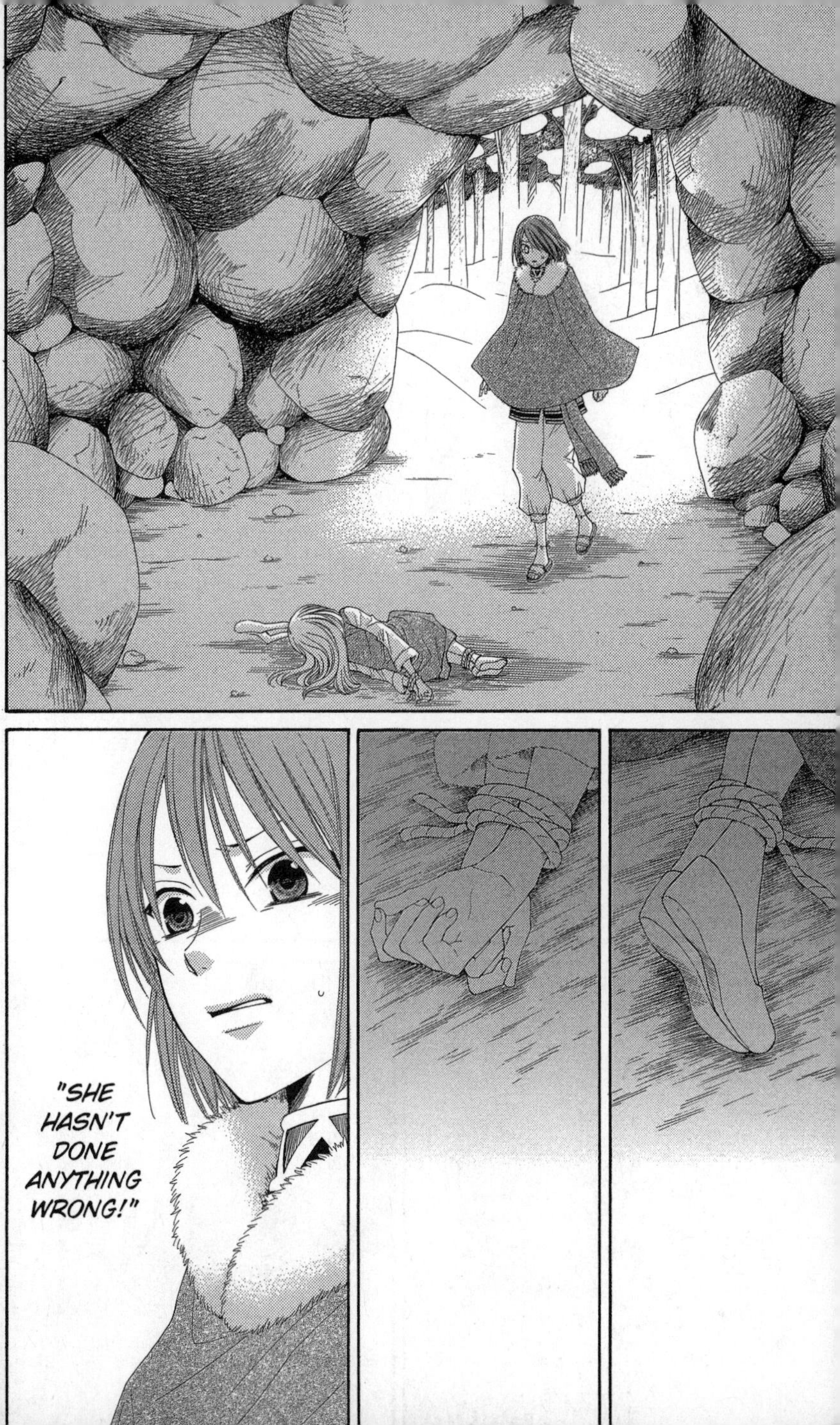
"SHE HASN'T DONE ANYTHING WRONG!"

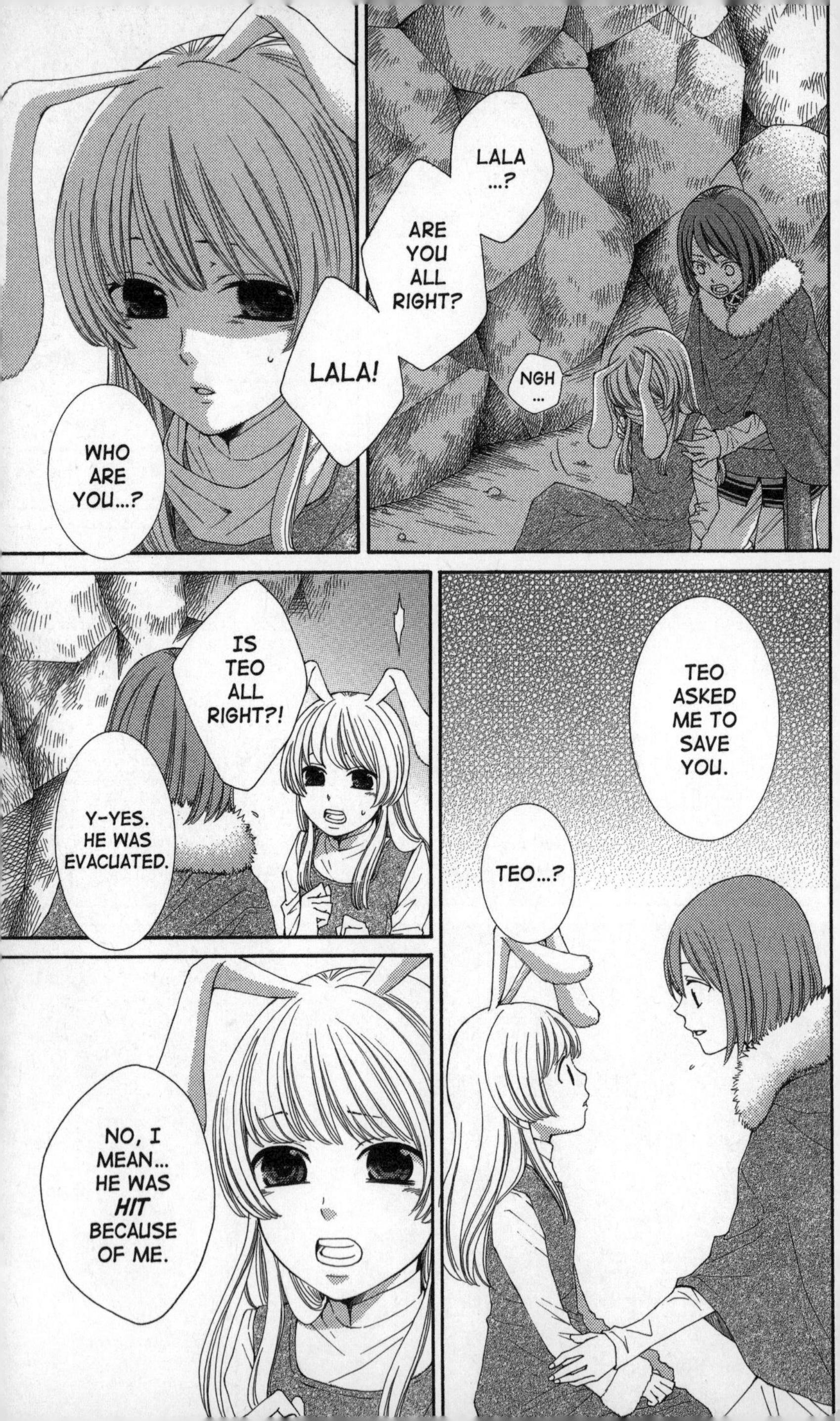
LALA ...?
ARE YOU ALL RIGHT?
LALA!
NGH ...
WHO ARE YOU...?
TEO ASKED ME TO SAVE YOU.
TEO...?
IS TEO ALL RIGHT?!
Y-YES. HE WAS EVACUATED.
NO, I MEAN... HE WAS *HIT* BECAUSE OF ME.

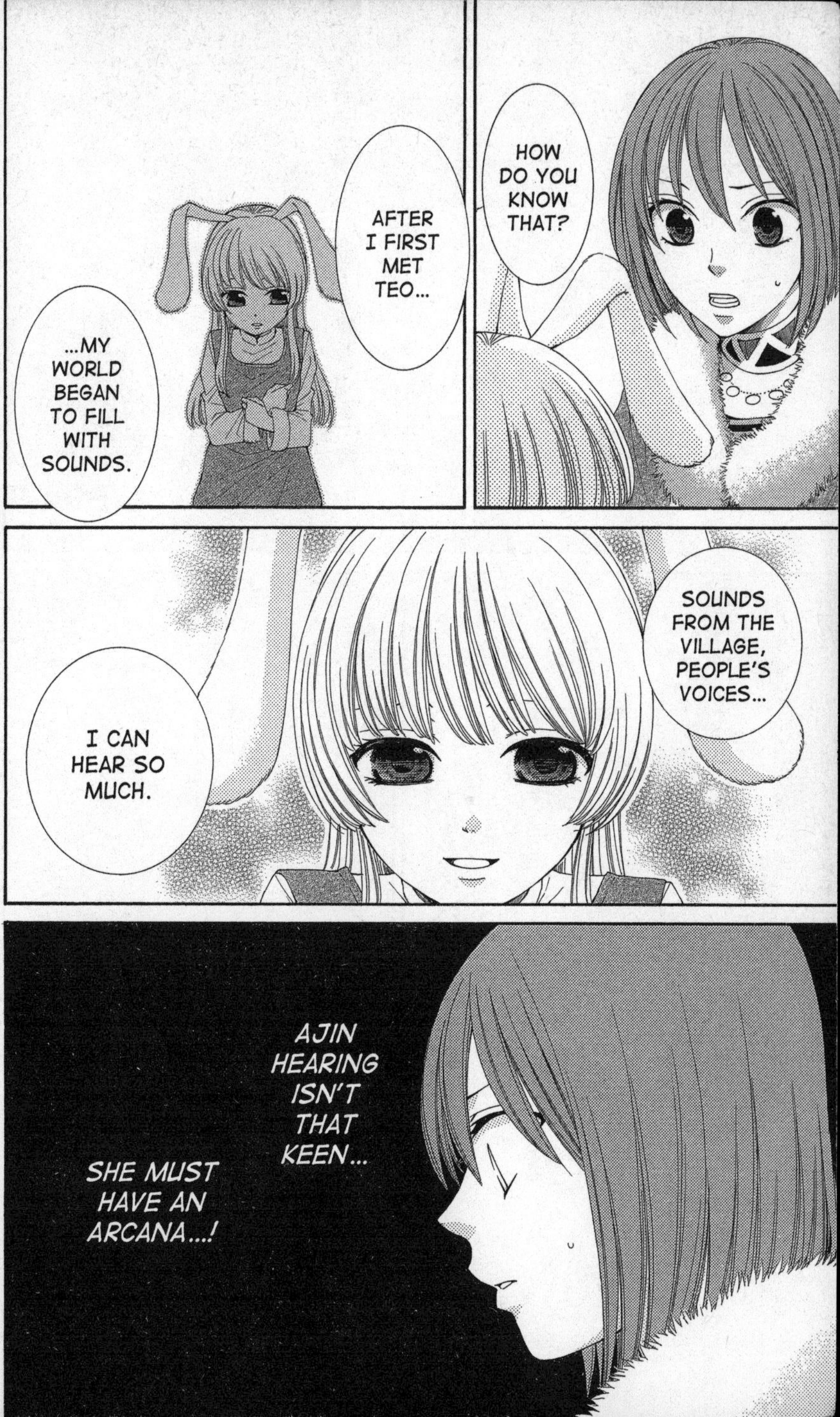
HOW DO YOU KNOW THAT?
AFTER I FIRST MET TEO...
...MY WORLD BEGAN TO FILL WITH SOUNDS.
SOUNDS FROM THE VILLAGE, PEOPLE'S VOICES...
I CAN HEAR SO MUCH.
AJIN HEARING ISN'T THAT KEEN...
SHE MUST HAVE AN ARCANA...!

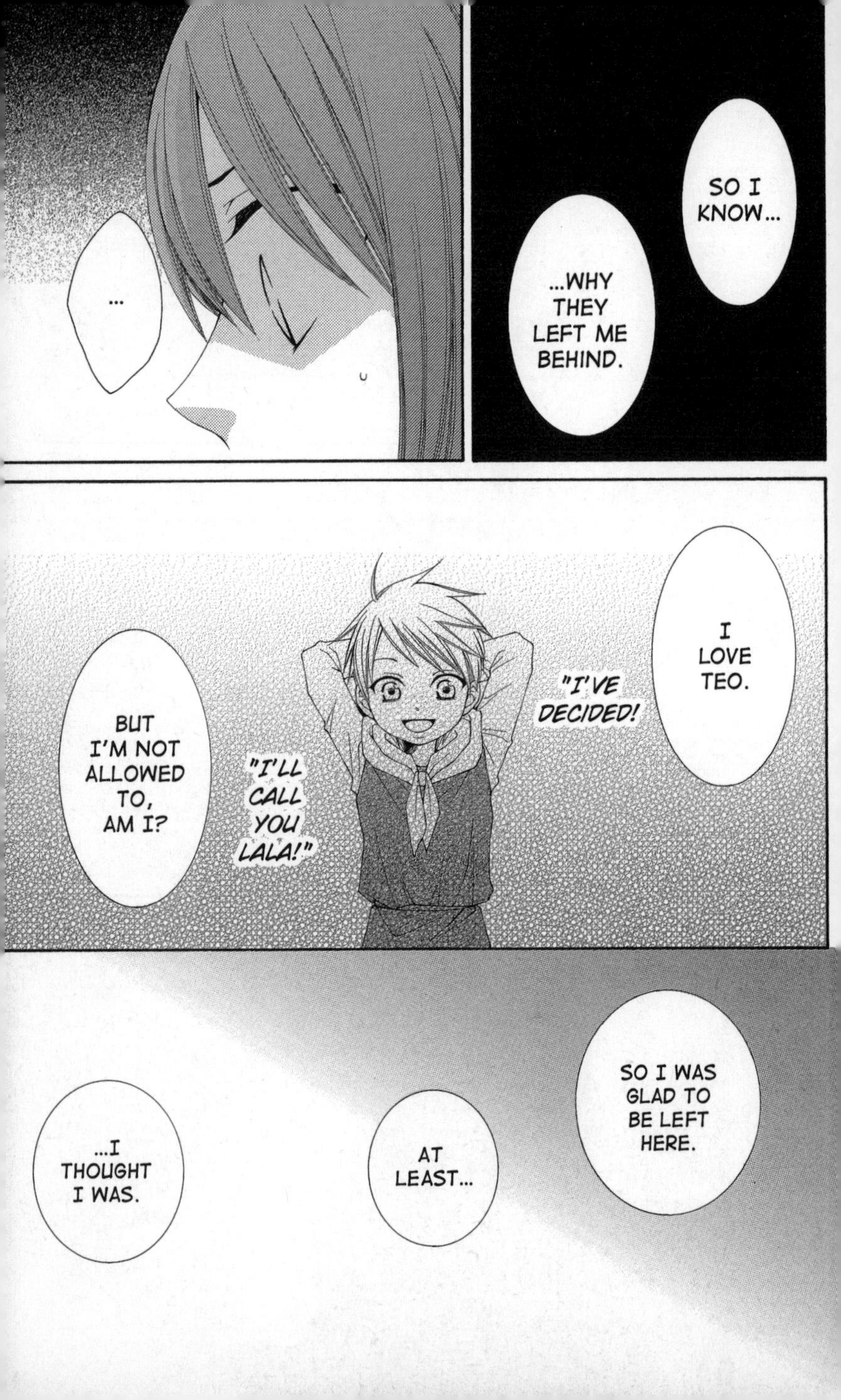
SO I KNOW...
...WHY THEY LEFT ME BEHIND.
...
I LOVE TEO.
"I'VE DECIDED!
"I'LL CALL YOU LALA!"
BUT I'M NOT ALLOWED TO, AM I?
SO I WAS GLAD TO BE LEFT HERE.
AT LEAST...
...I THOUGHT I WAS.

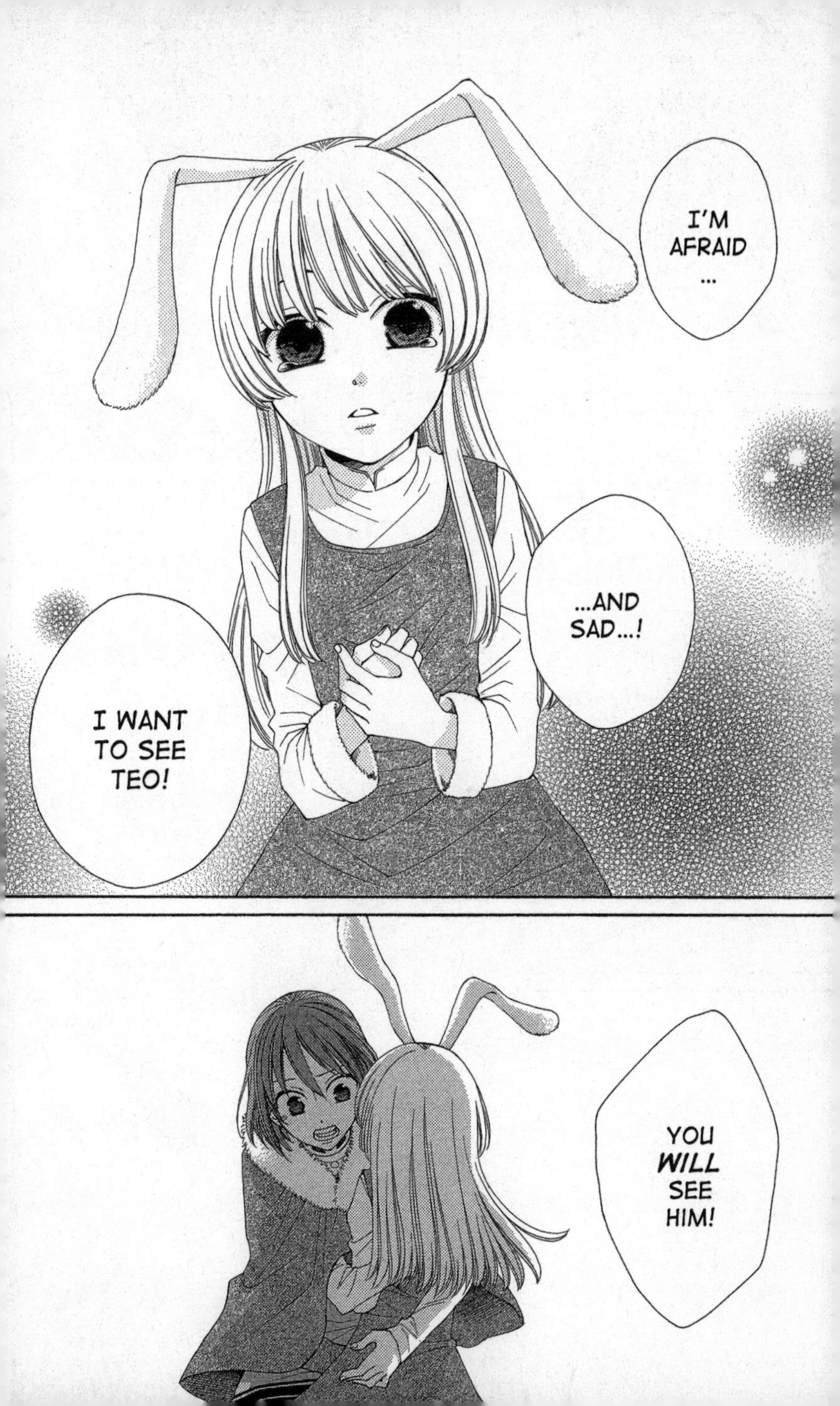
I'M AFRAID ...
...AND SAD...!
I WANT TO SEE TEO!
YOU *WILL* SEE HIM!

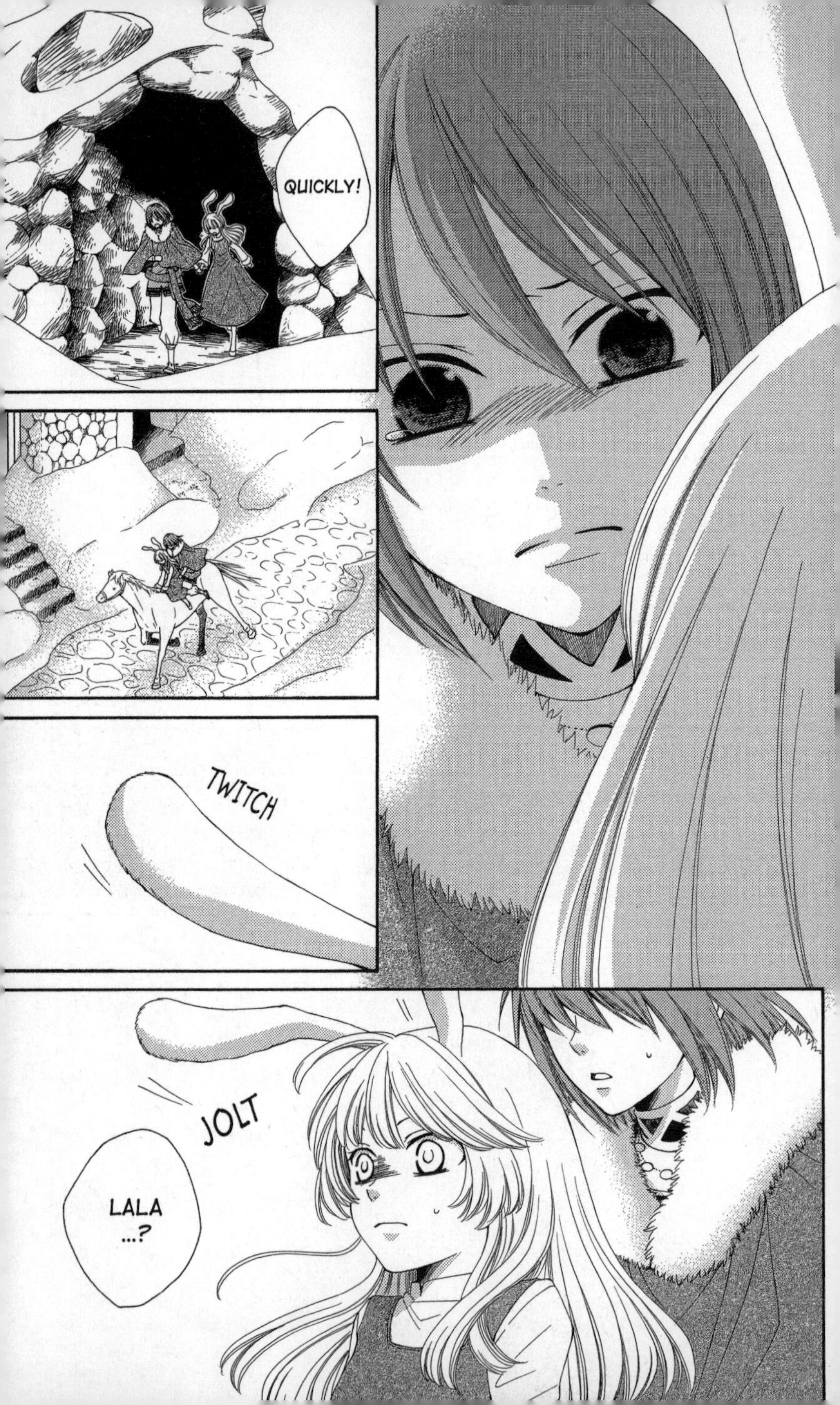
QUICKLY!
TWITCH
JOLT
LALA ...?

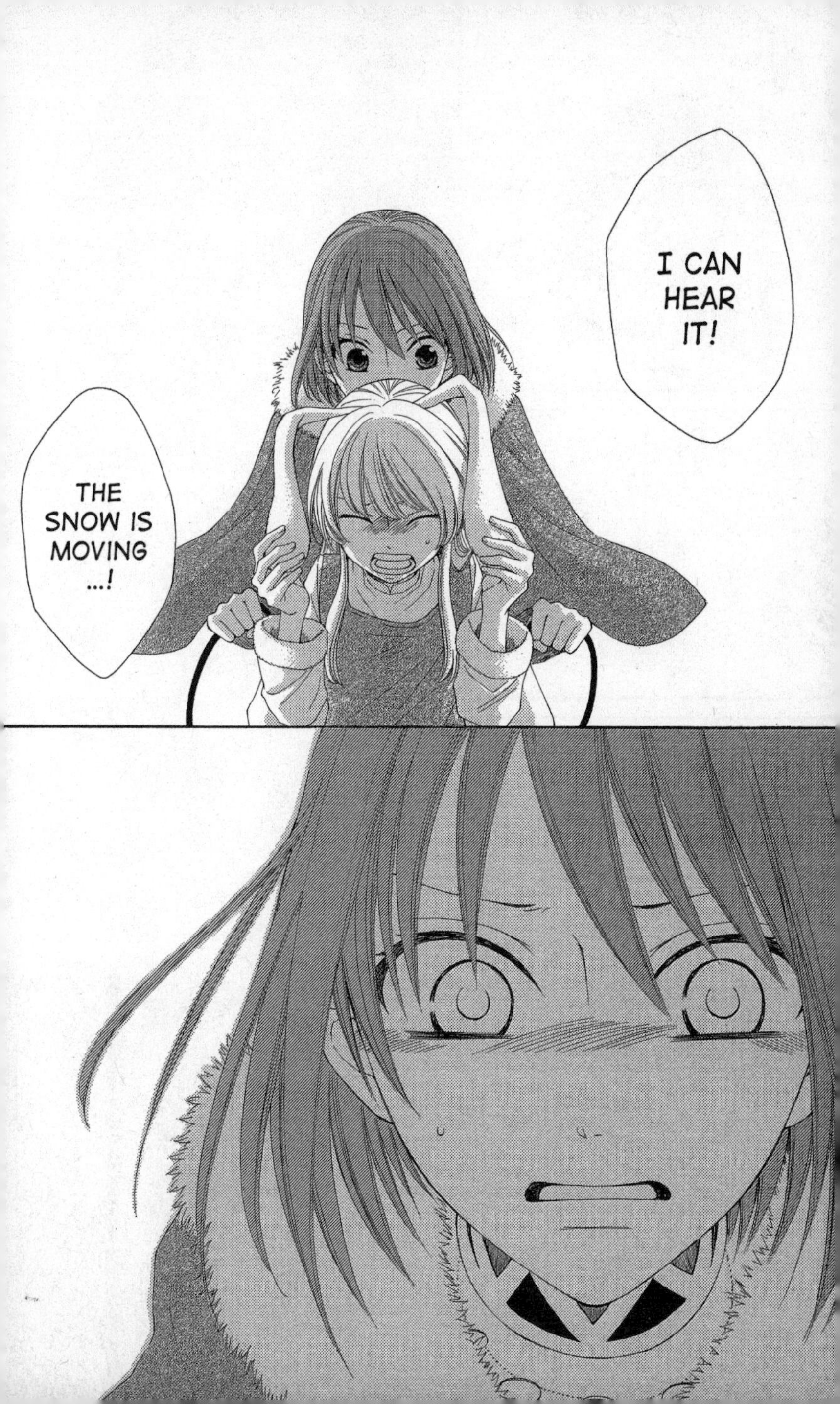
I CAN HEAR IT!
THE SNOW IS MOVING ...!

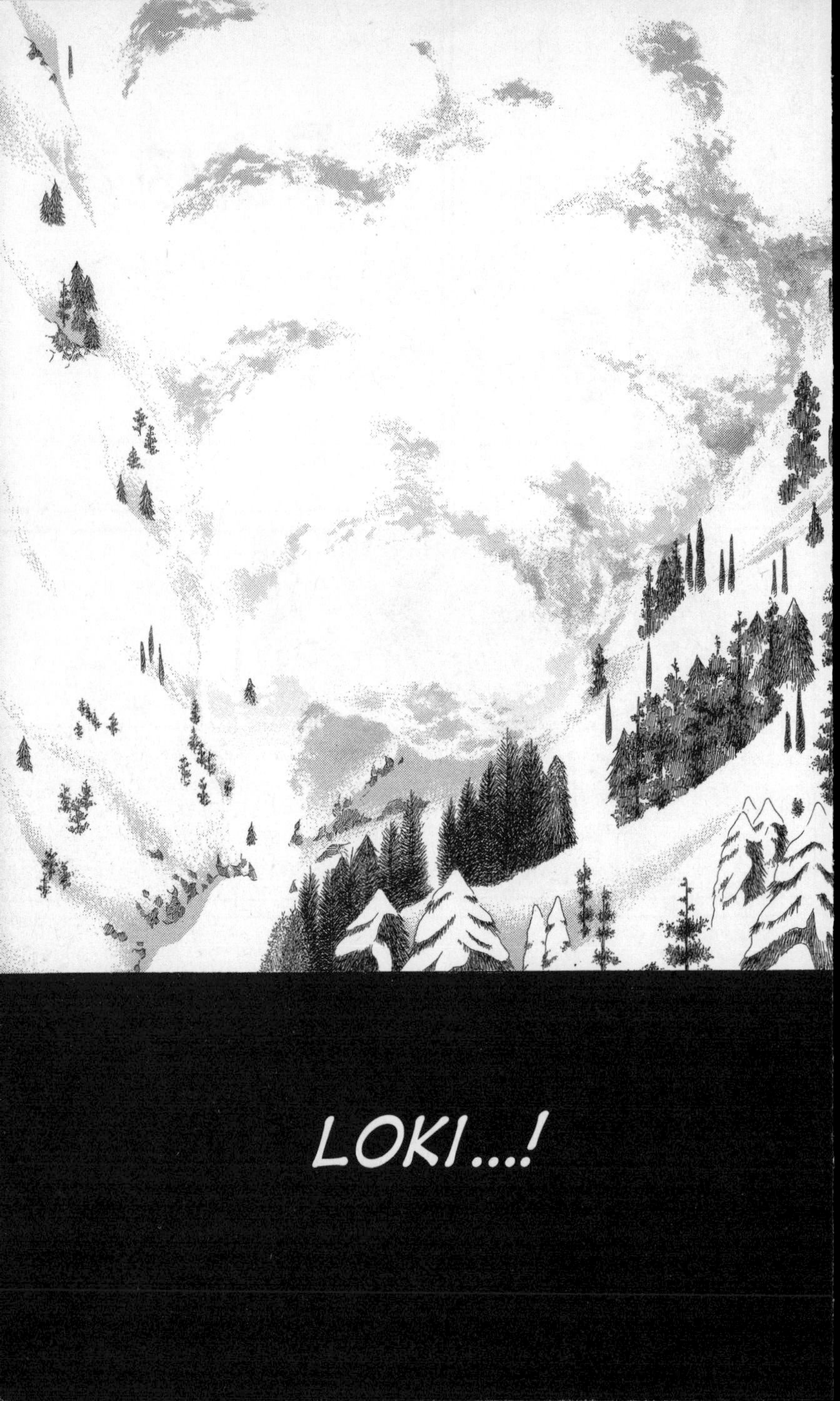
LOKI...!

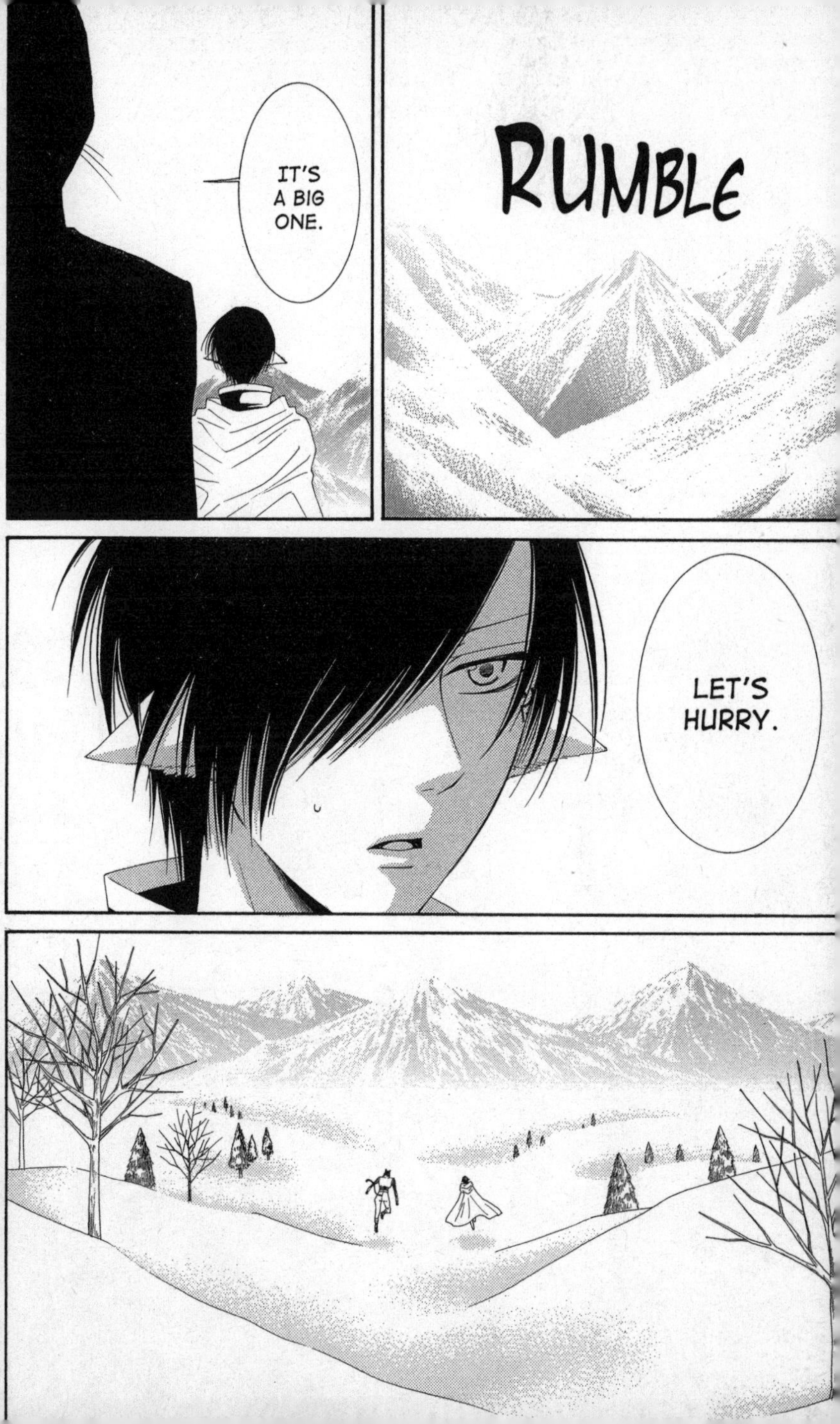
RUMBLE
IT'S A BIG ONE.
LET'S HURRY.

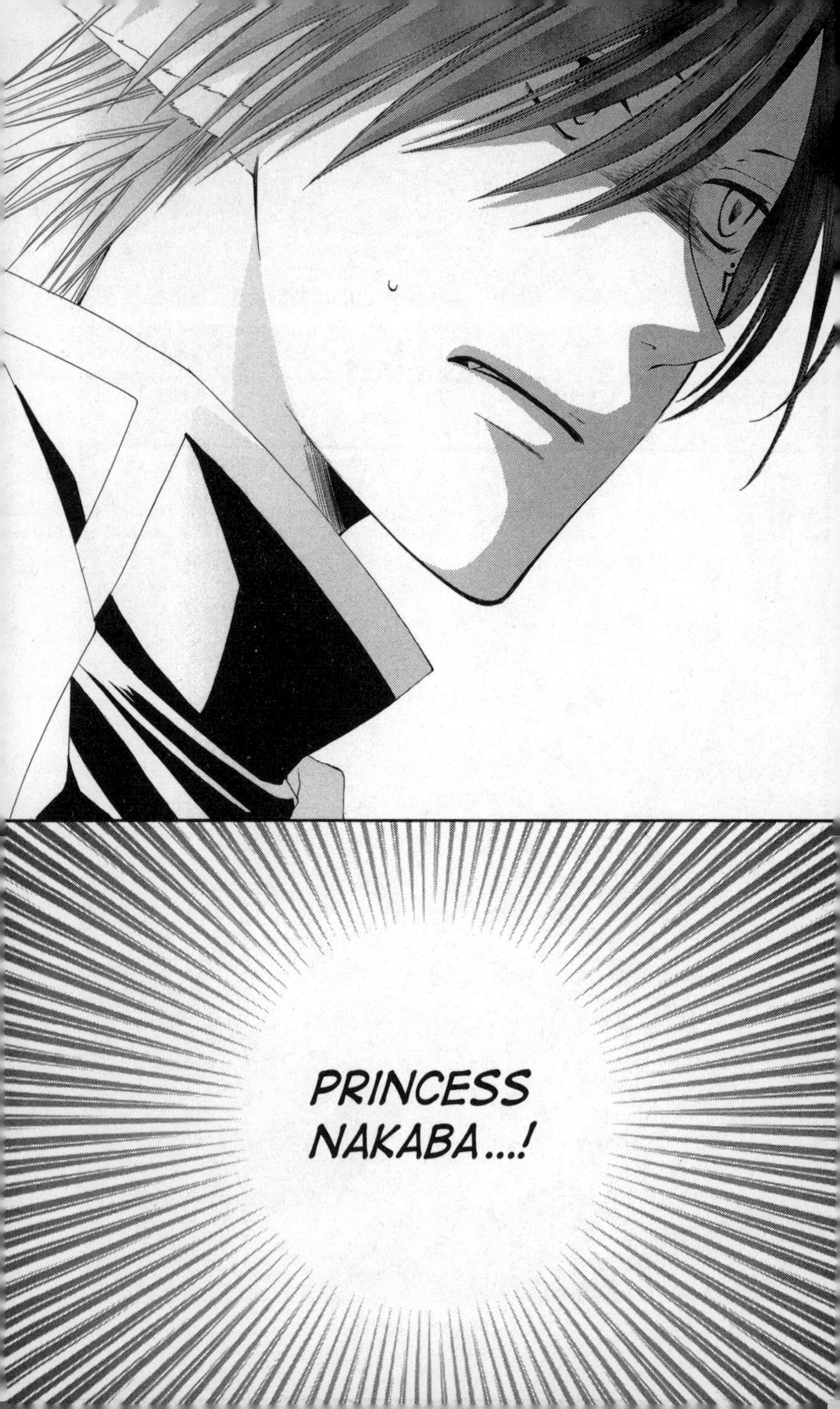
PRINCESS NAKABA...!

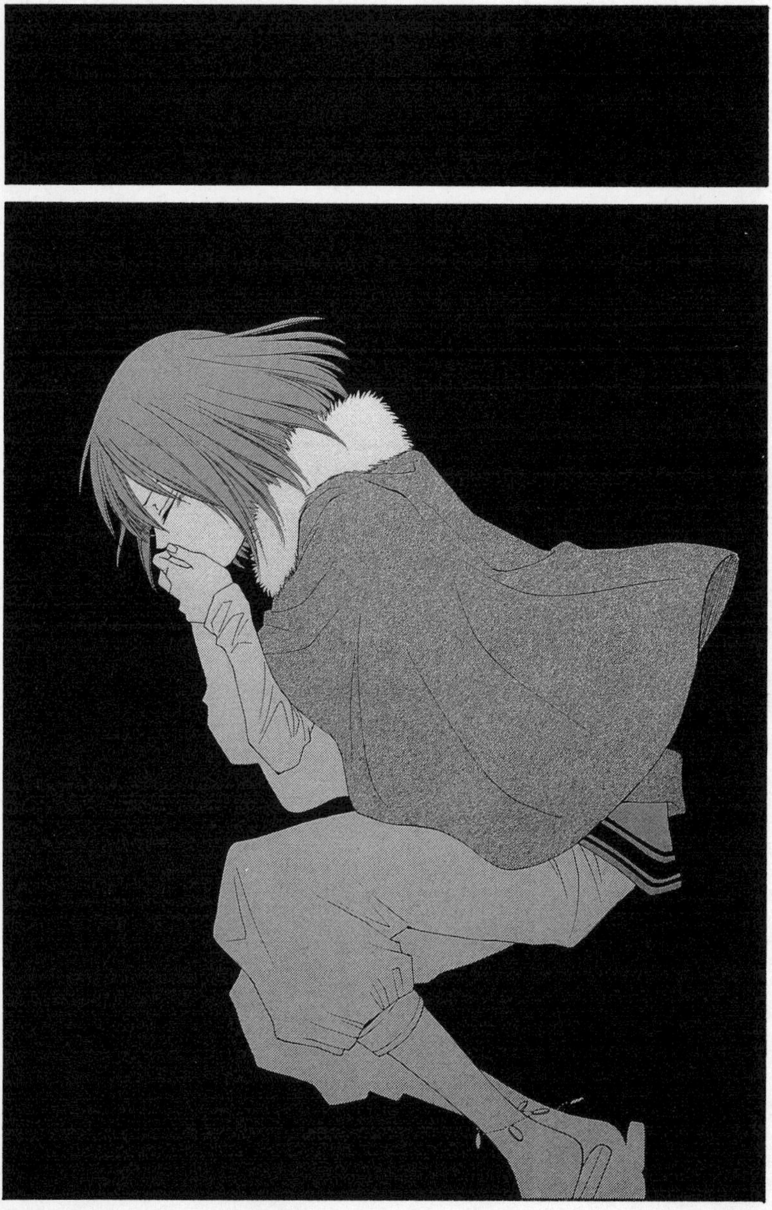

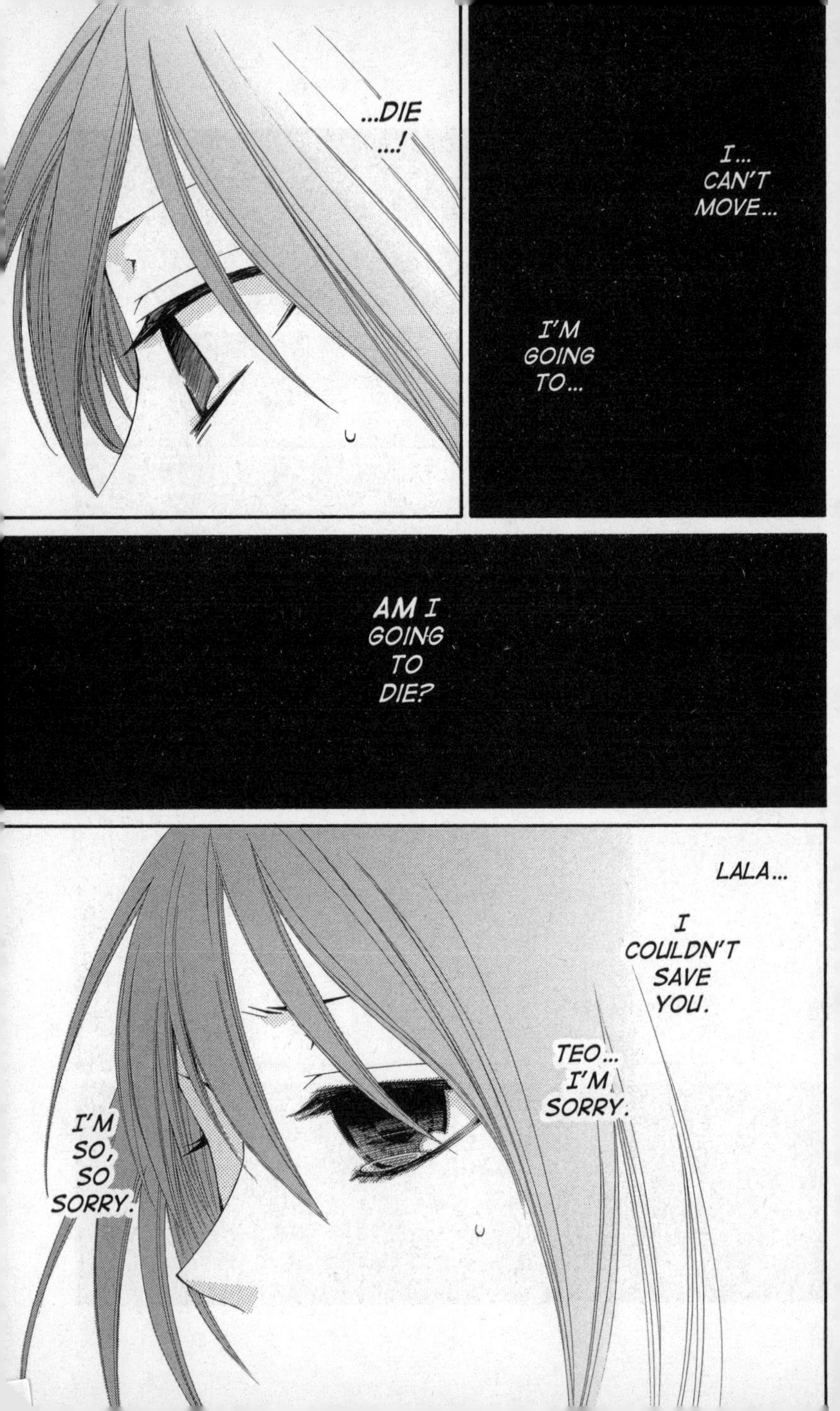
I... CAN'T MOVE...
I'M GOING TO...
...DIE ...!
AM I GOING TO DIE?
LALA...
I COULDN'T SAVE YOU.
TEO... I'M SORRY.
I'M SO, SO SORRY.

CAESAR...

...ONE
LAST
TIME...

I
WANTED
TO SEE
YOU...

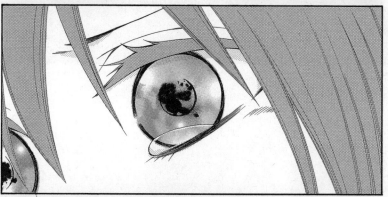

IF THIS IS
THE END, I
WANT TO...

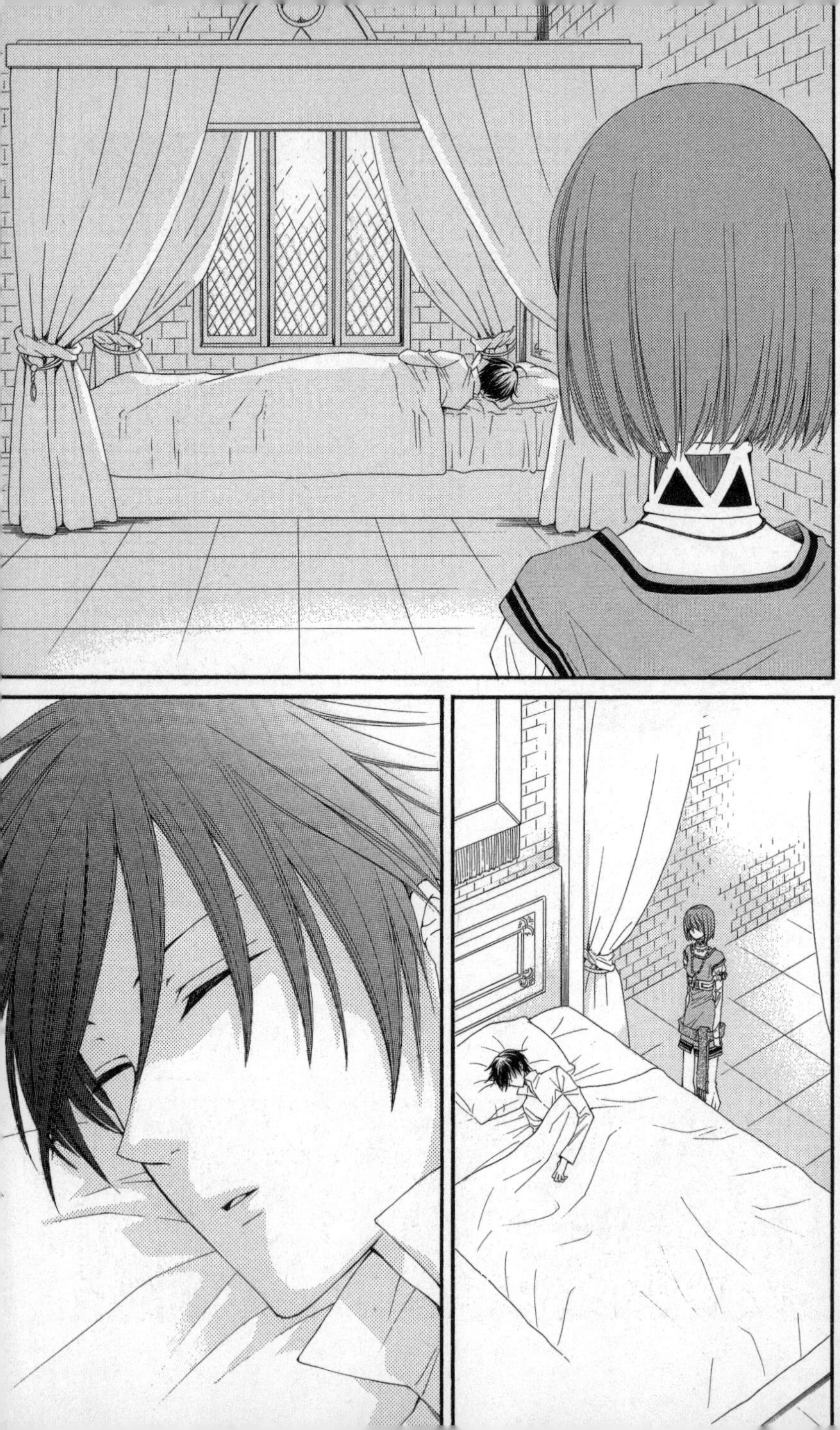

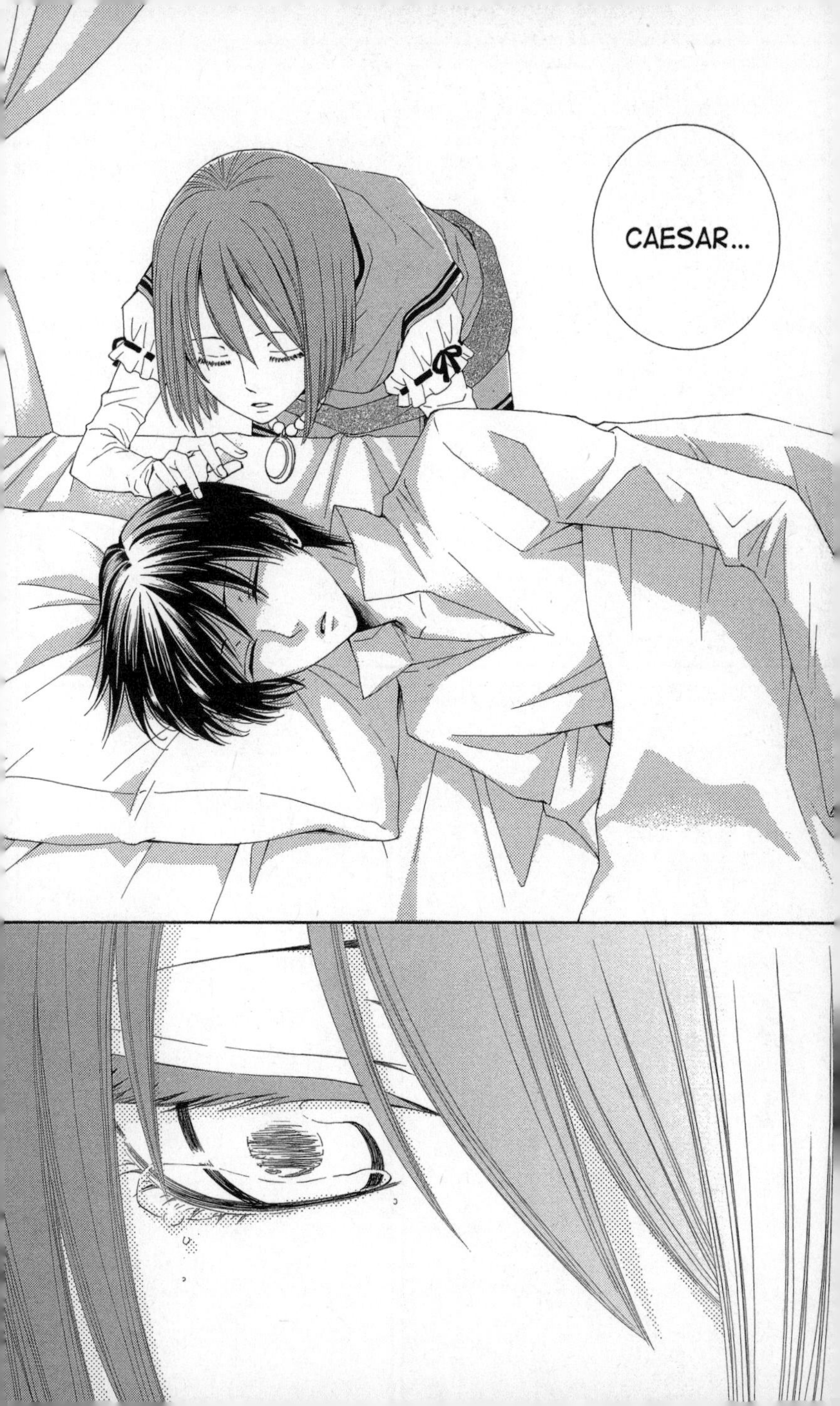
CAESAR...

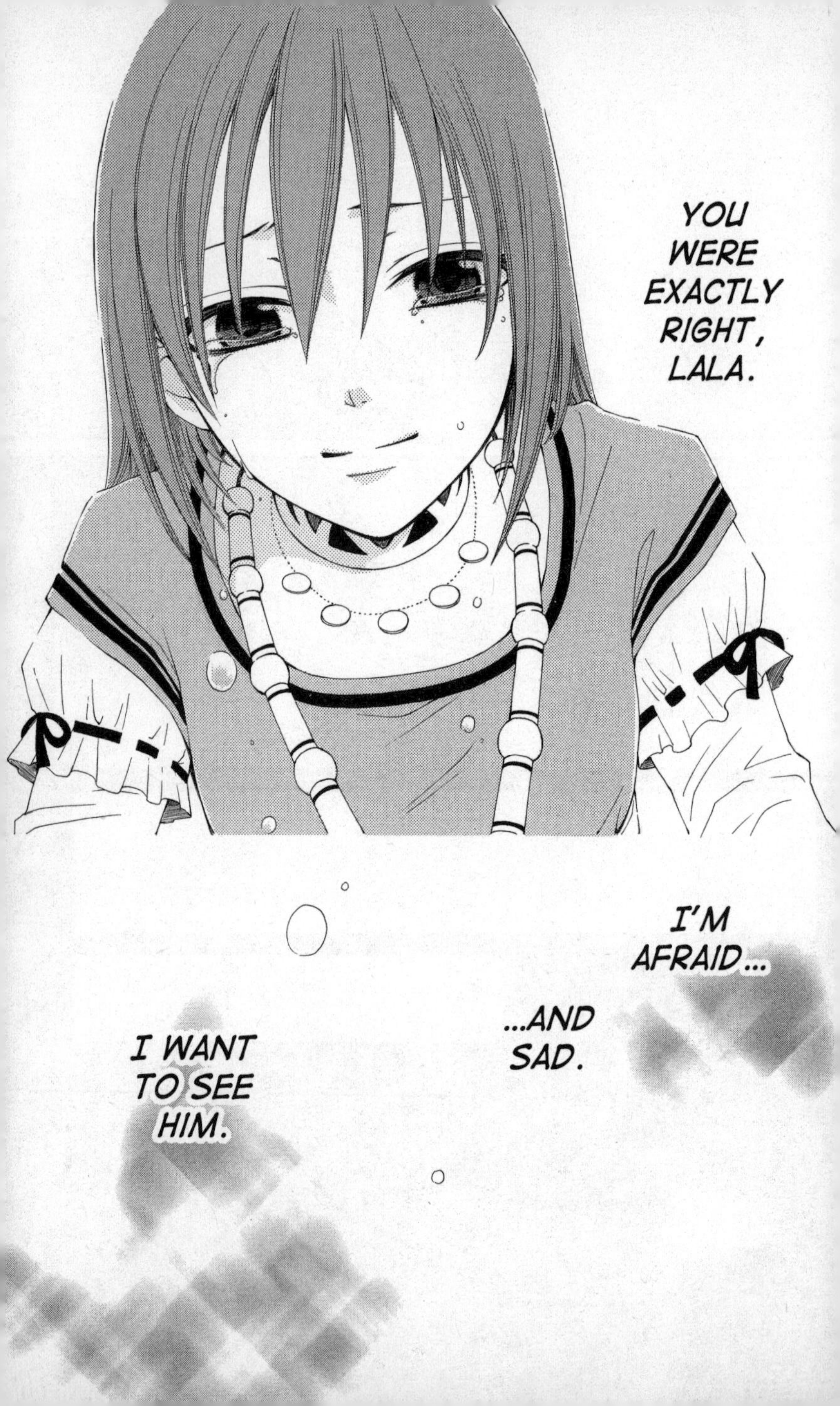
YOU WERE EXACTLY RIGHT, LALA.
I'M AFRAID...
...AND SAD.
I WANT TO SEE HIM.

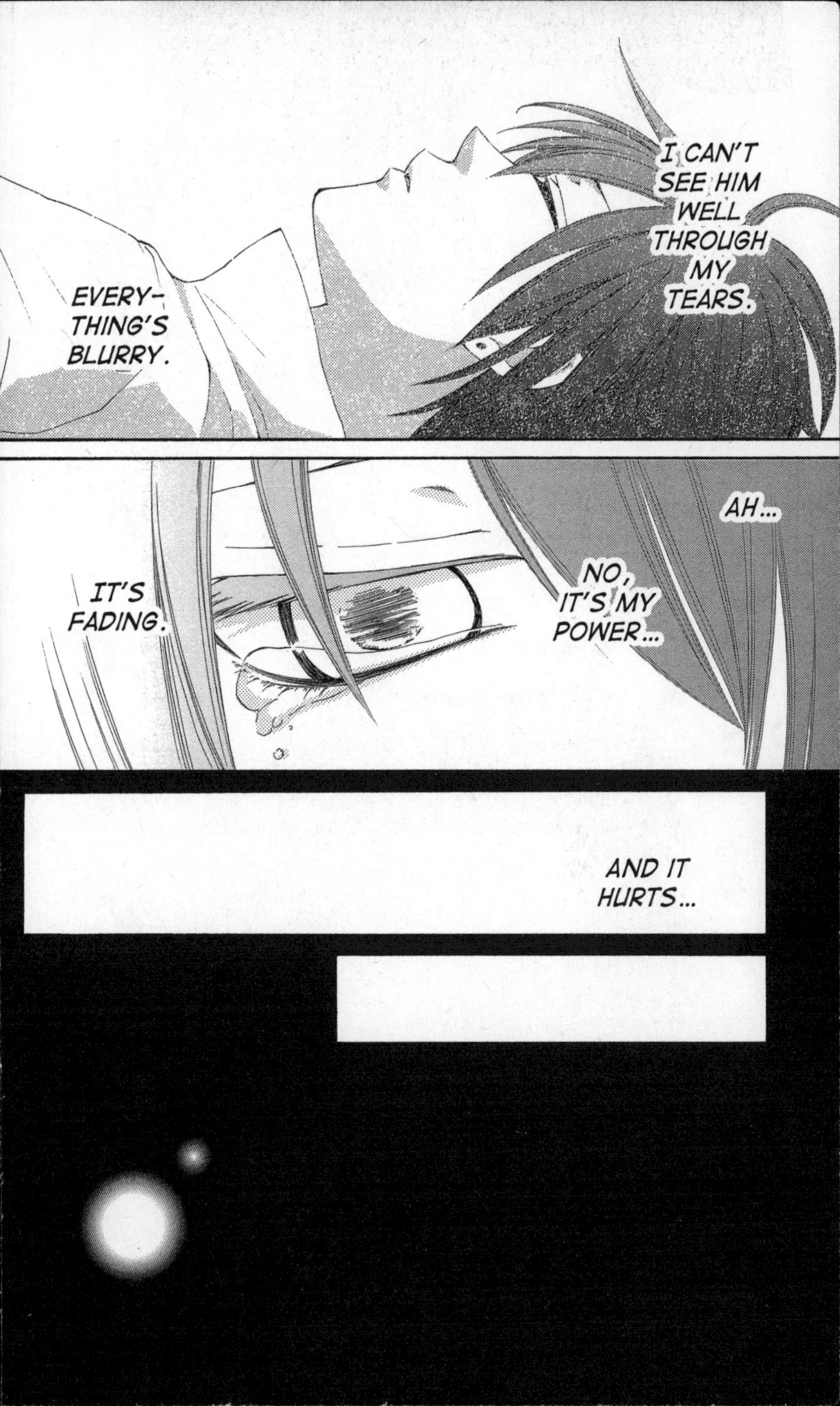
I CAN'T SEE HIM WELL THROUGH MY TEARS.
EVERY-THING'S BLURRY.
AH...
NO, IT'S MY POWER...
IT'S FADING.
AND IT HURTS...

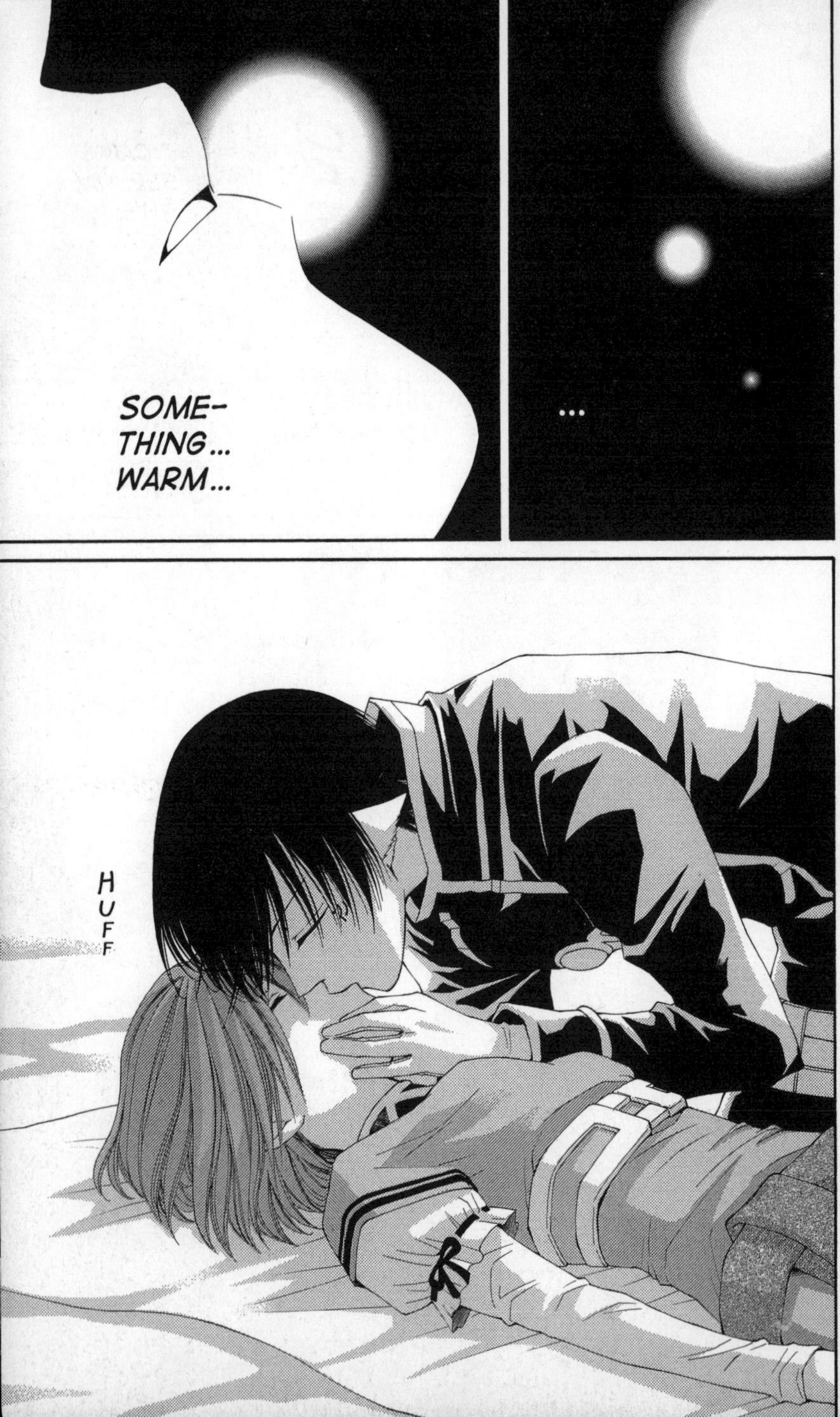
...
SOME-THING... WARM...
HUFF

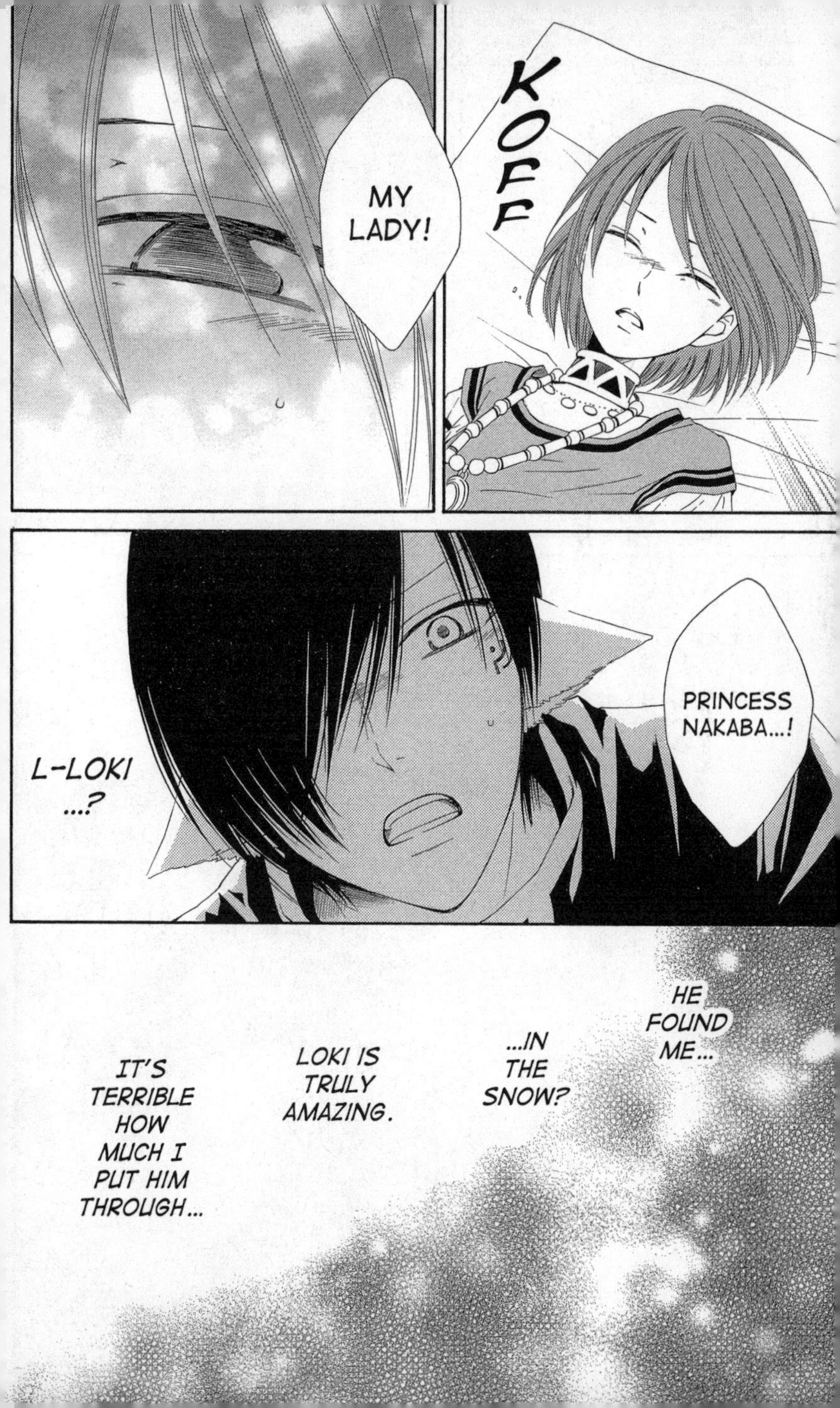
KOFF
MY LADY!
PRINCESS NAKABA...!
L-LOKI ...?
HE FOUND ME...
...IN THE SNOW?
LOKI IS TRULY AMAZING.
IT'S TERRIBLE HOW MUCH I PUT HIM THROUGH...

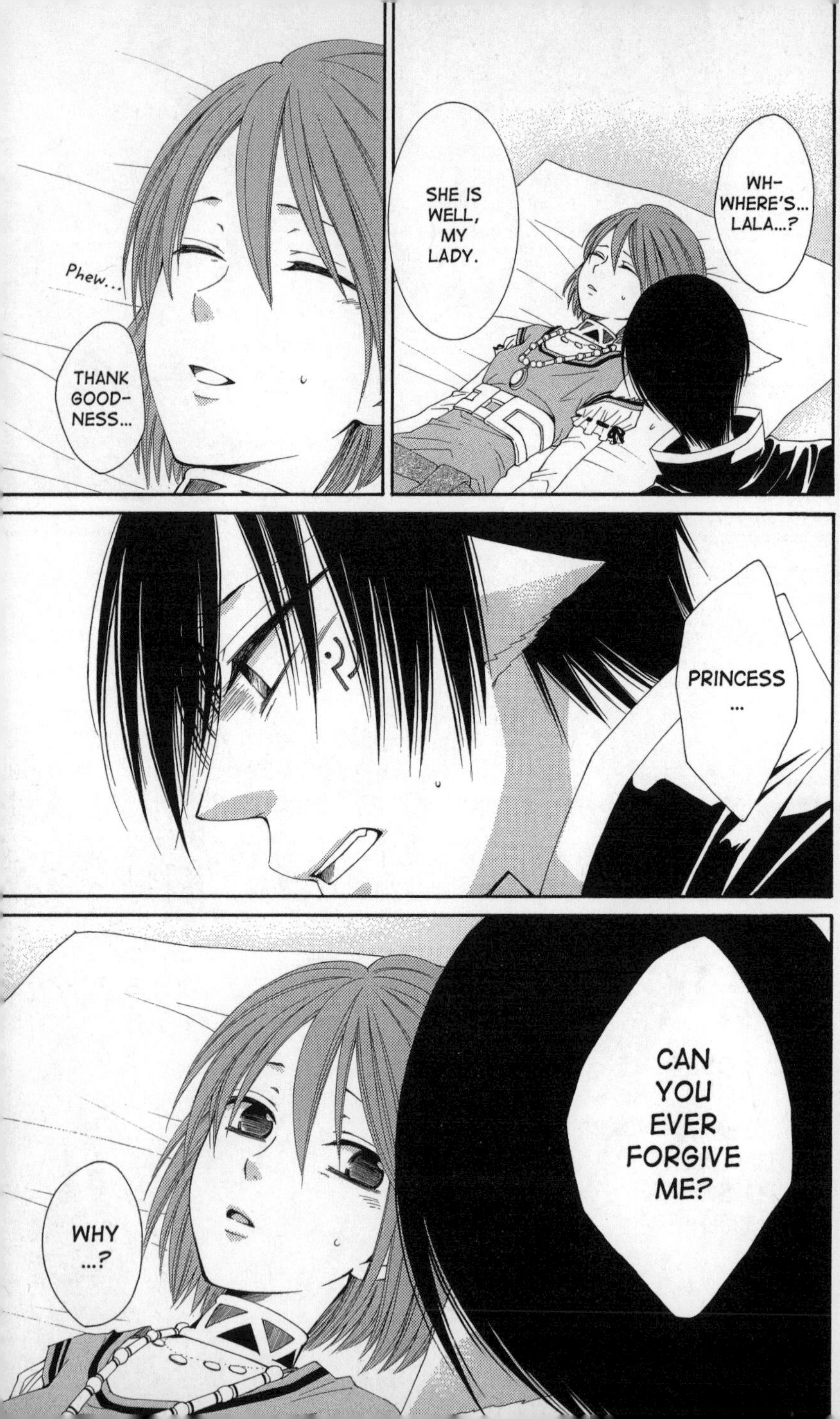
WH- WHERE'S... LALA...?
SHE IS WELL, MY LADY.
Phew...
THANK GOOD-NESS...
PRINCESS ...
CAN YOU EVER FORGIVE ME?
WHY ...?

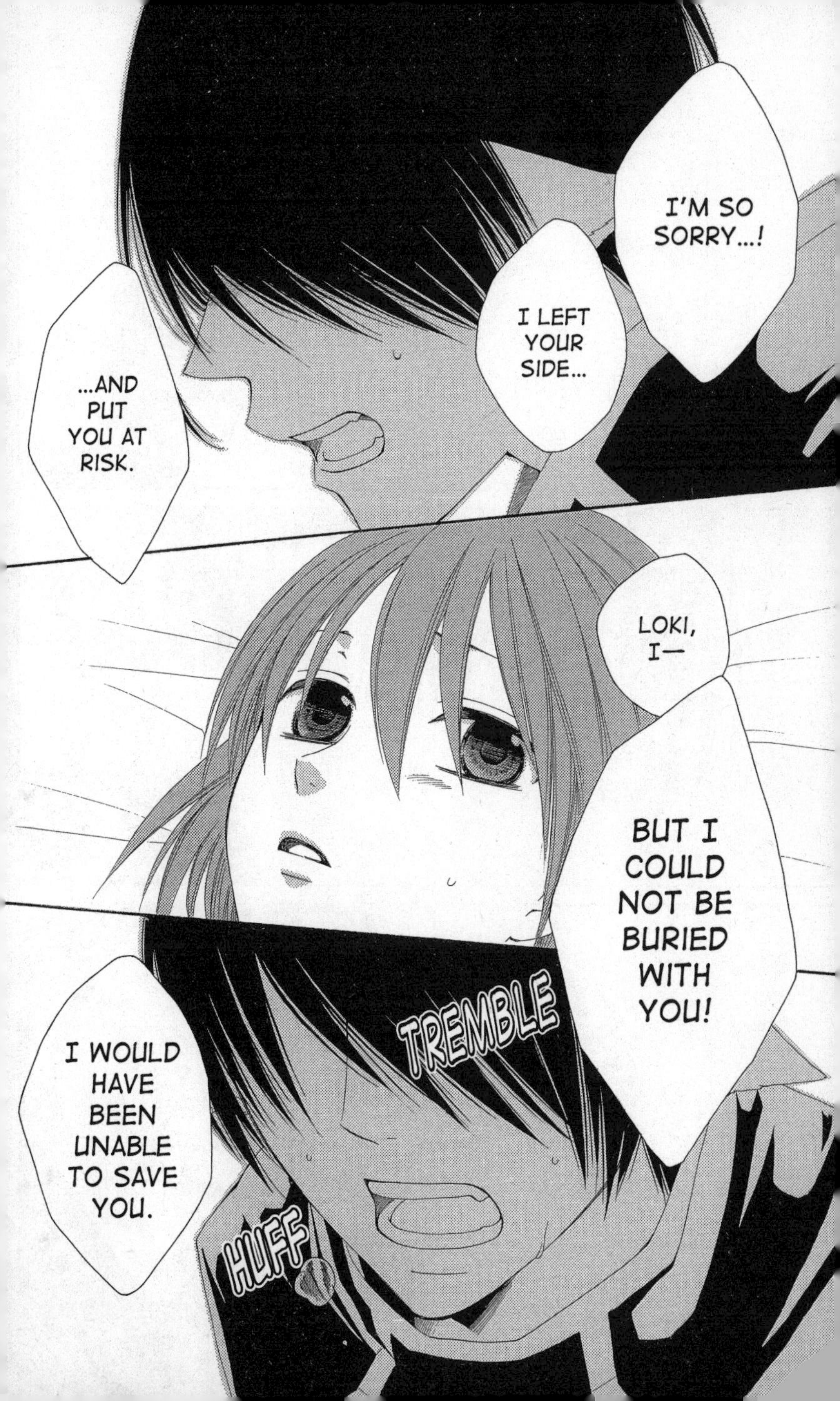
I'M SO SORRY...!
I LEFT YOUR SIDE...
...AND PUT YOU AT RISK.
LOKI, I—
BUT I COULD NOT BE BURIED WITH YOU!
TREMBLE
I WOULD HAVE BEEN UNABLE TO SAVE YOU.
HUFF

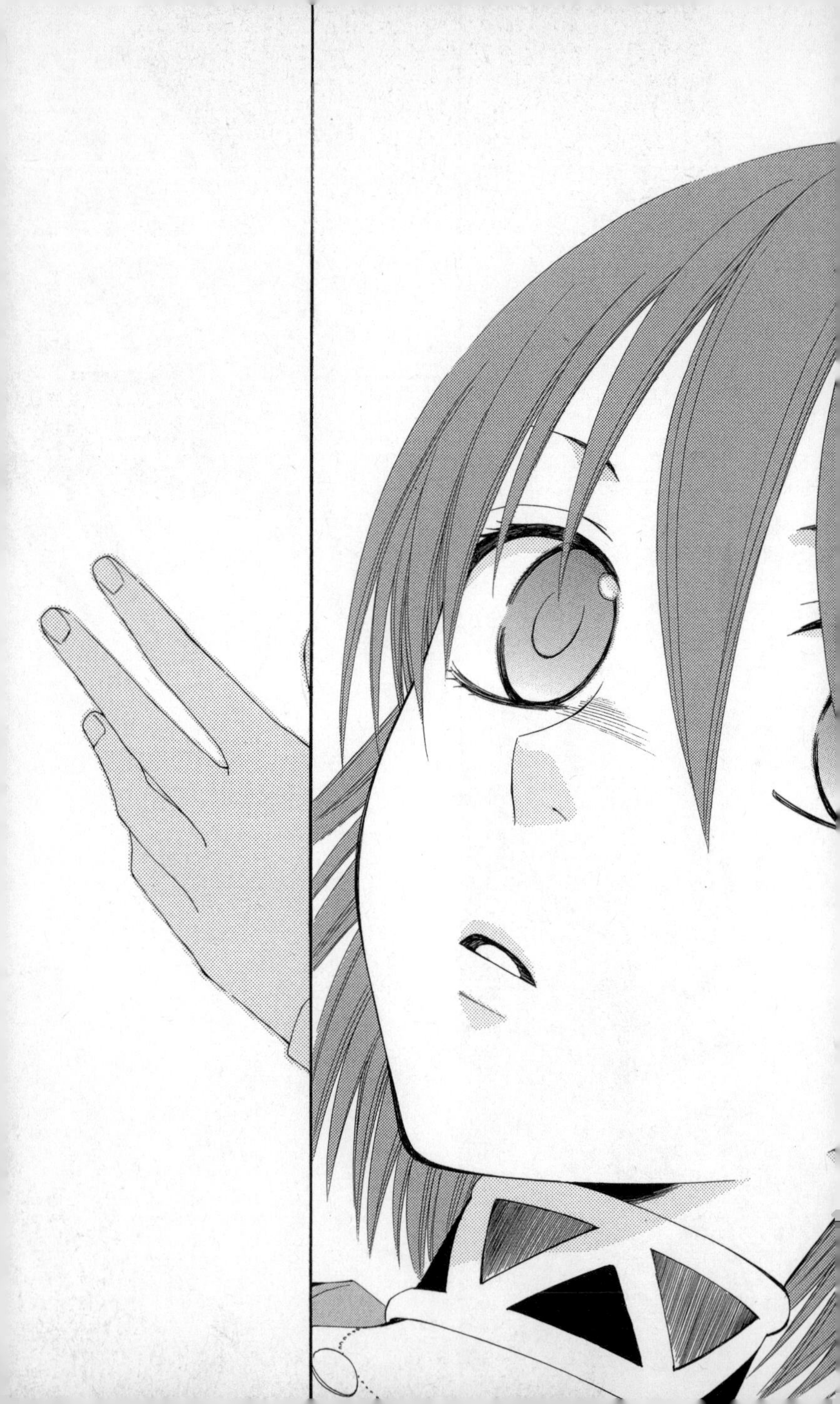

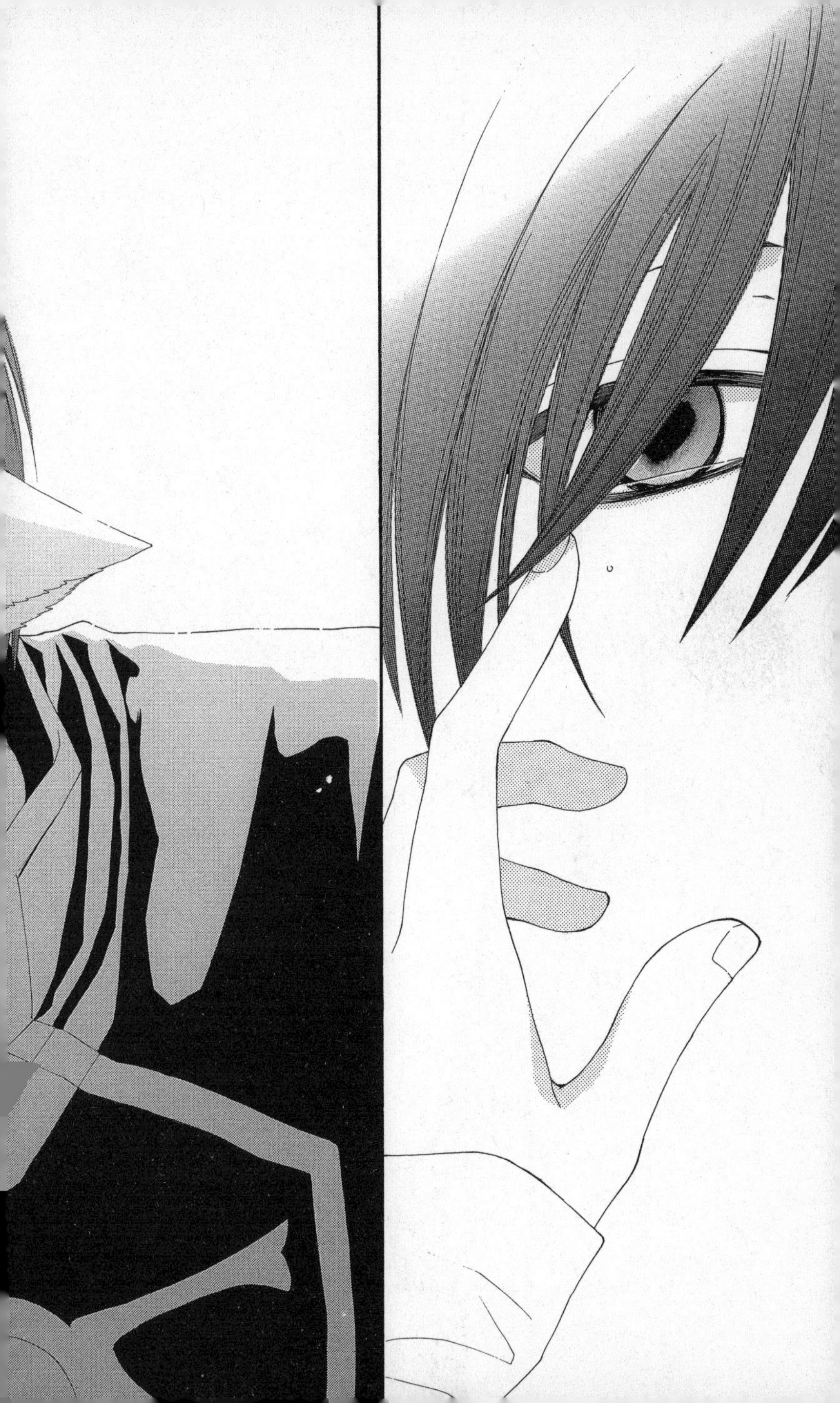

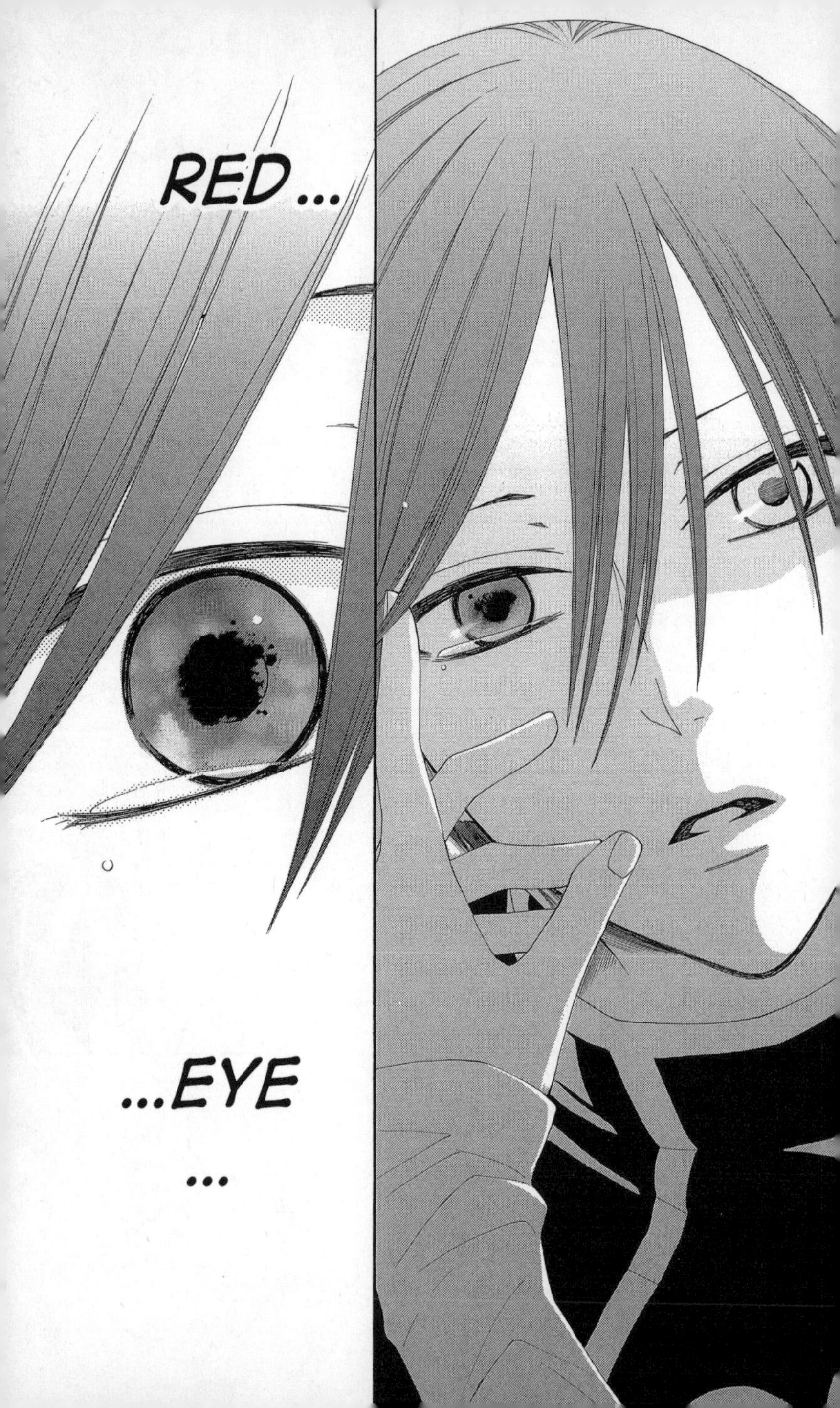
RED...
...EYE
...

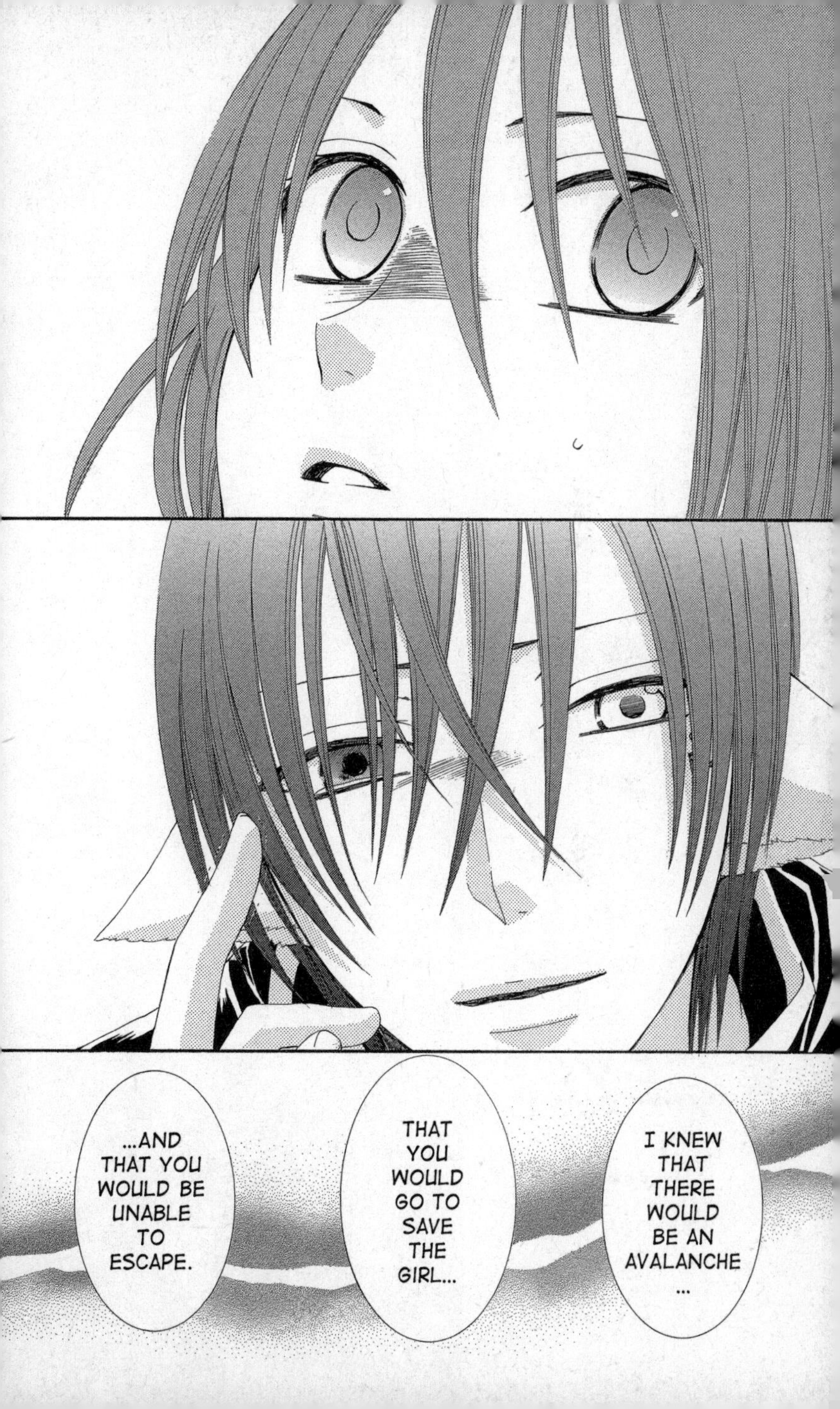
I KNEW THAT THERE WOULD BE AN AVALANCHE ...
THAT YOU WOULD GO TO SAVE THE GIRL...
...AND THAT YOU WOULD BE UNABLE TO ESCAPE.

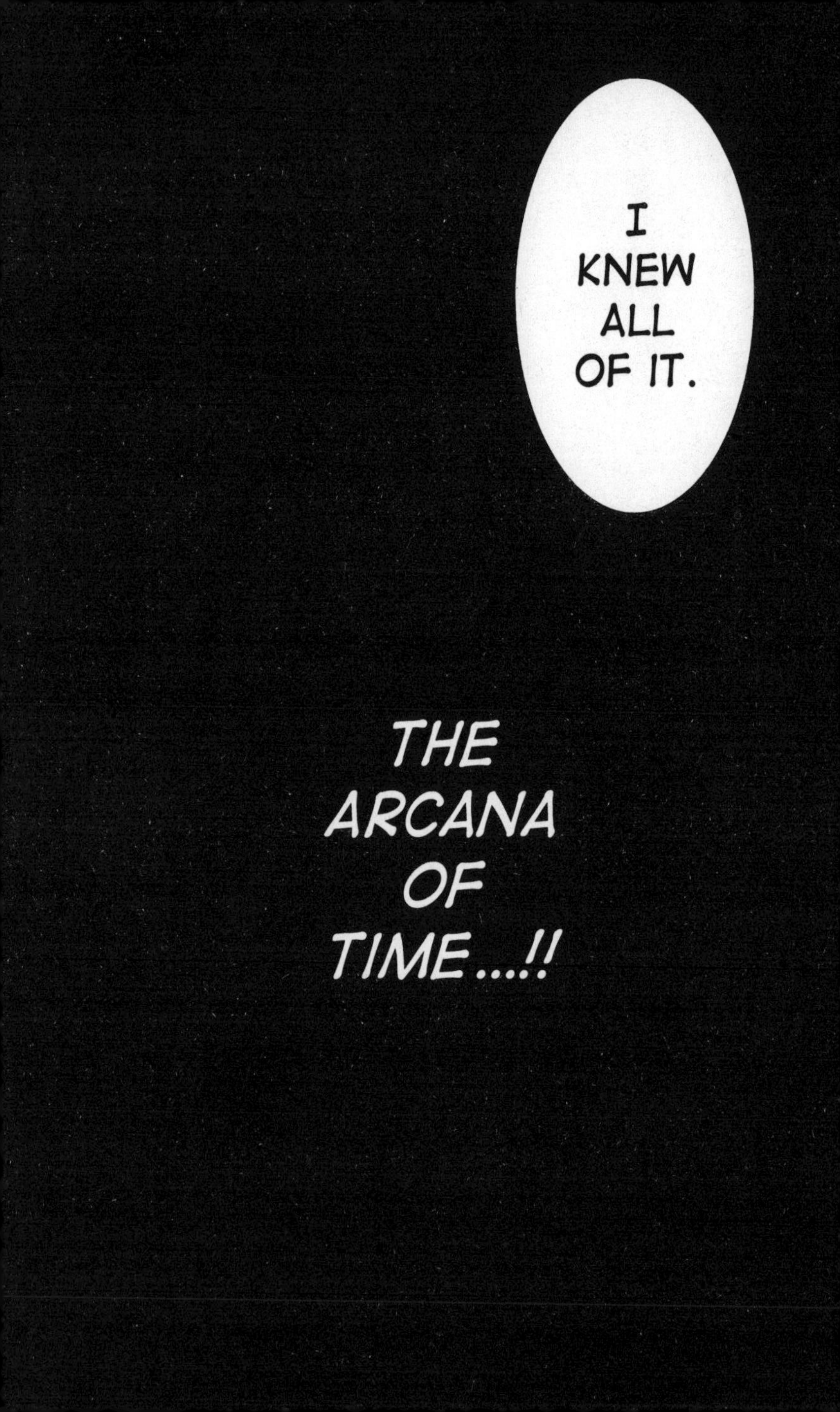
I KNEW ALL OF IT.
THE ARCANA OF TIME...!!

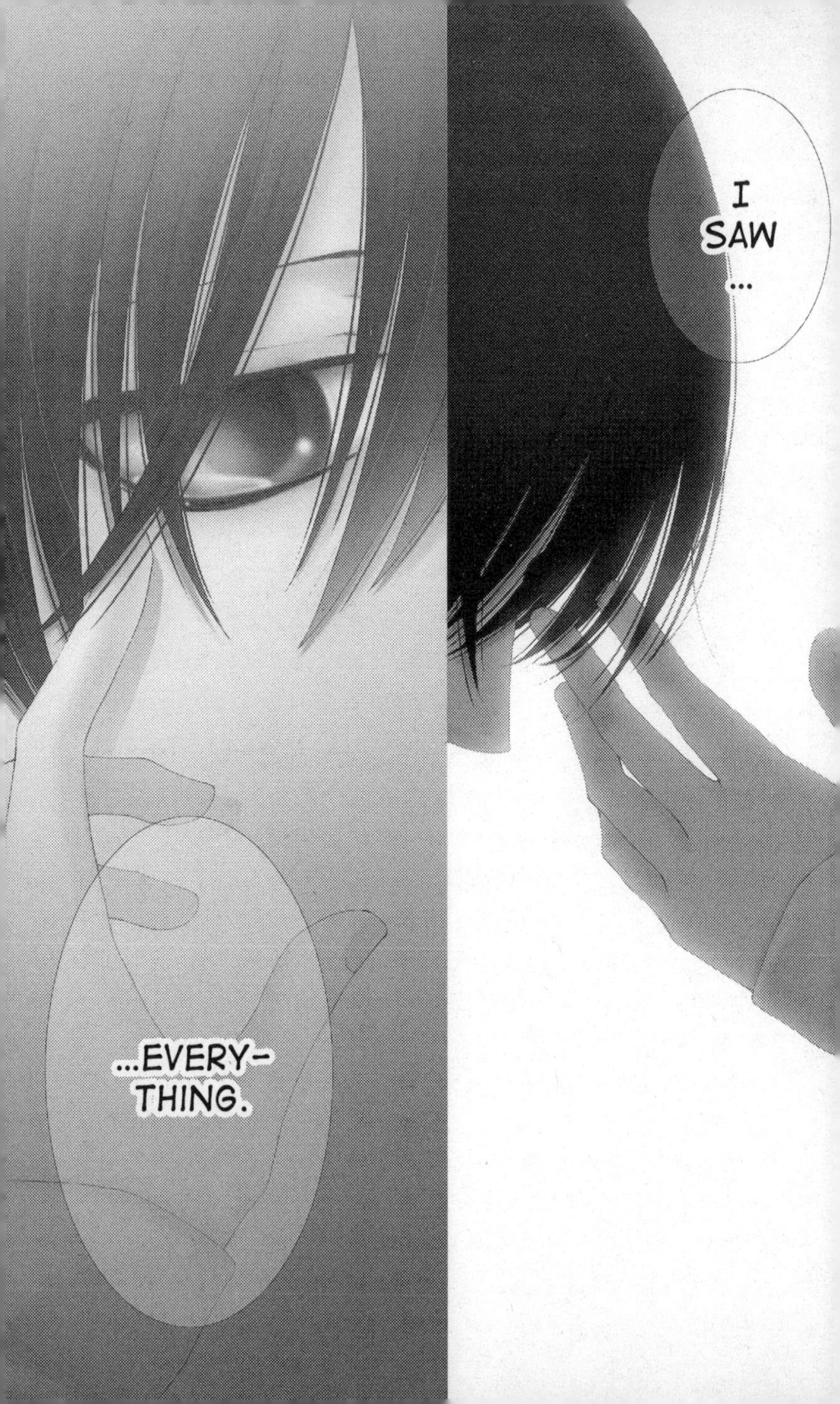
I SAW ...
...EVERY-THING.

Chapter 42

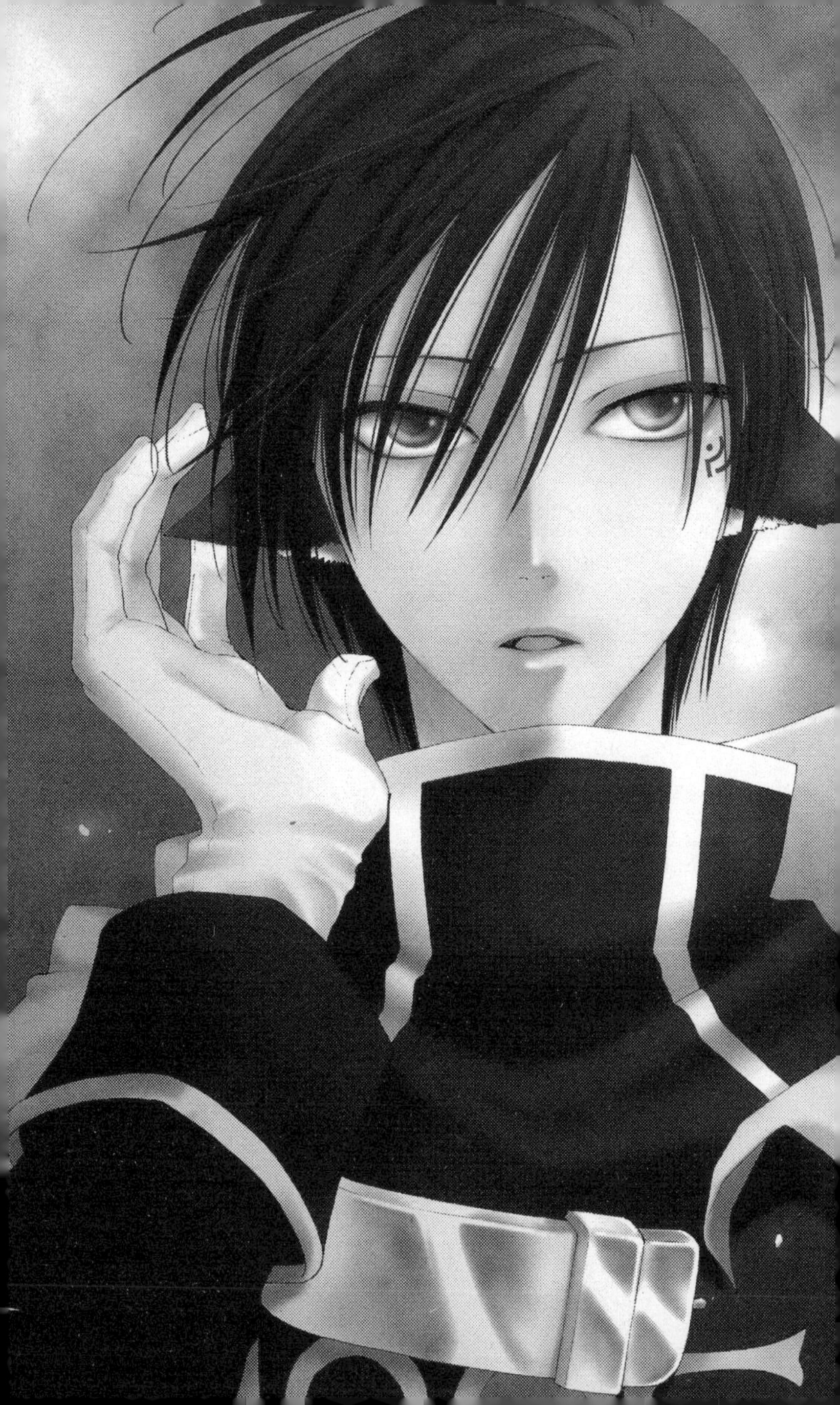

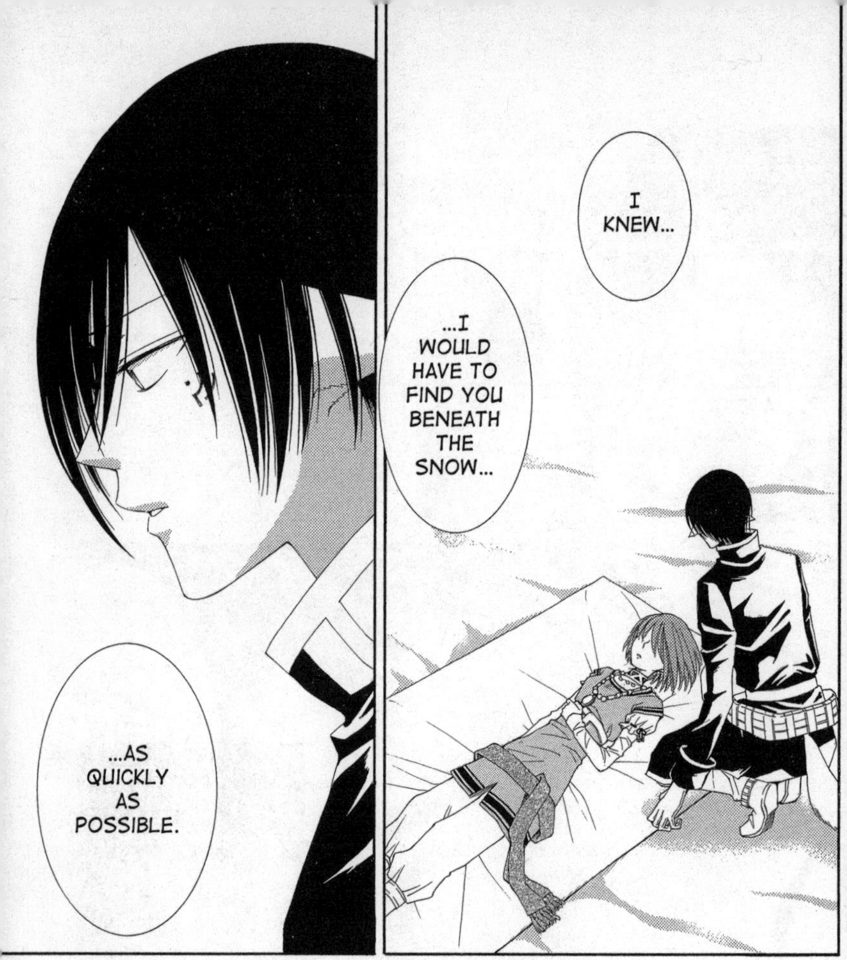
I KNEW...
...I WOULD HAVE TO FIND YOU BENEATH THE SNOW...
...AS QUICKLY AS POSSIBLE.

Dawn of the Arcana

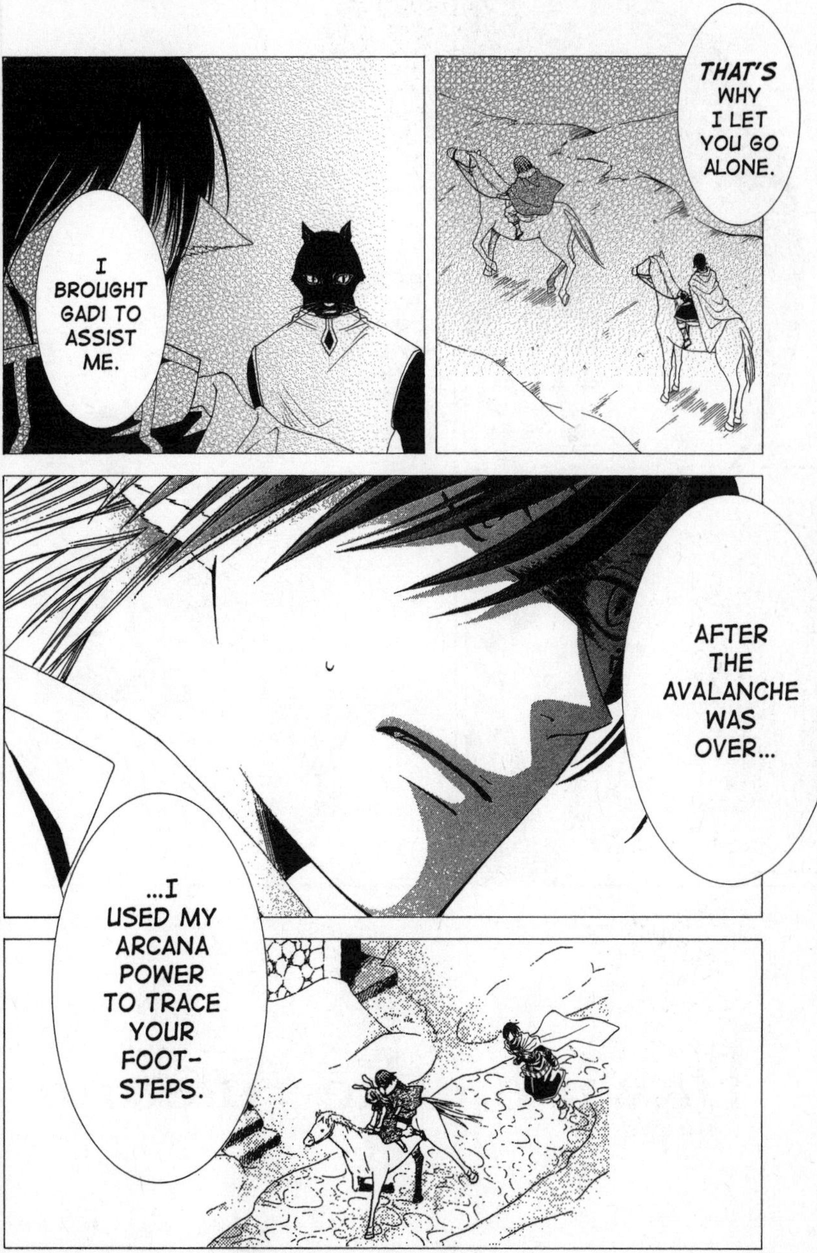
THAT'S WHY I LET YOU GO ALONE.
I BROUGHT GADI TO ASSIST ME.
AFTER THE AVALANCHE WAS OVER...
...I USED MY ARCANA POWER TO TRACE YOUR FOOT-STEPS.

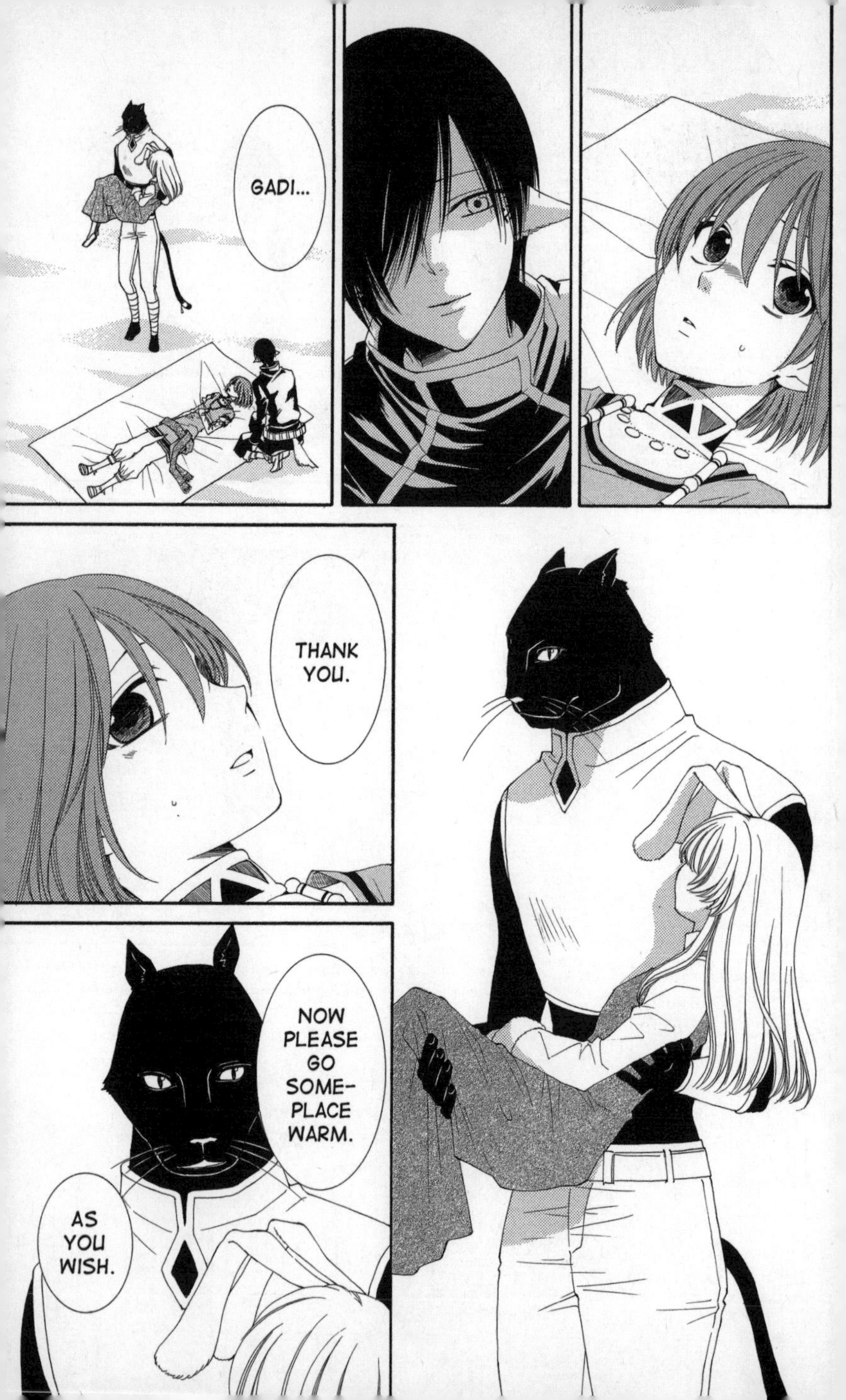
GADI...
THANK YOU.
NOW PLEASE GO SOME-PLACE WARM.
AS YOU WISH.

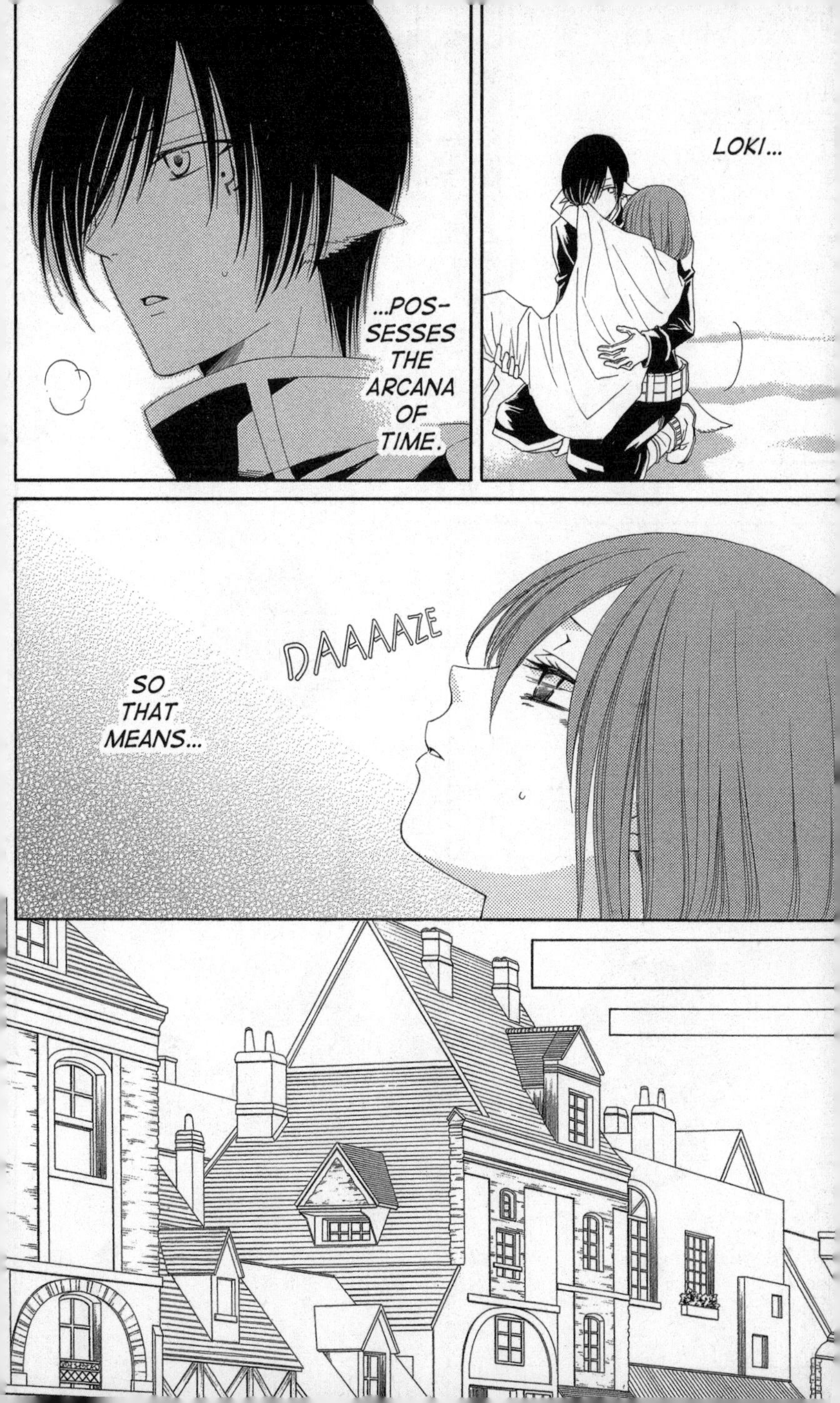
LOKI...
...POS-
SESSES
THE
ARCANA
OF
TIME.
DAAAAZE
SO
THAT
MEANS...

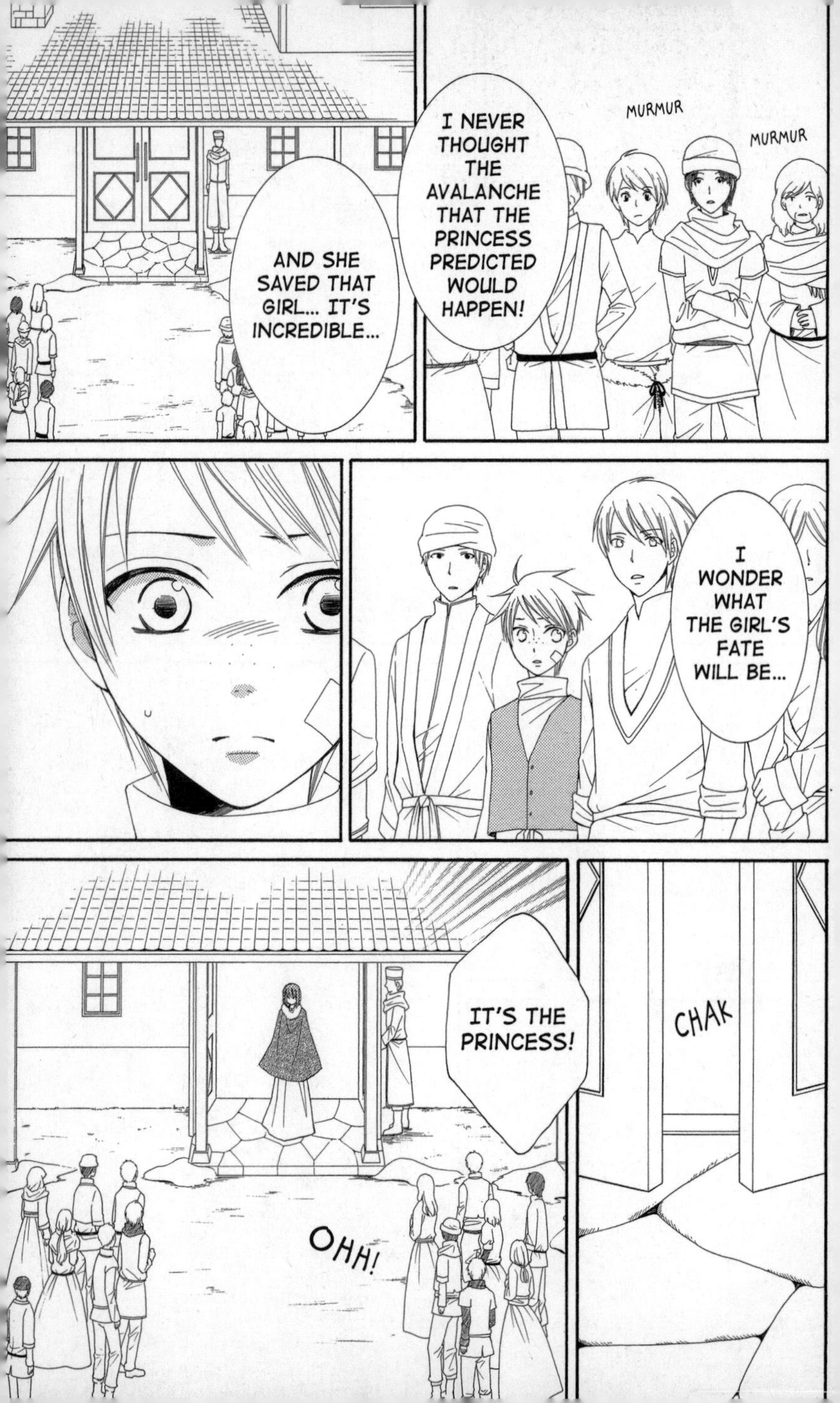
MURMUR
MURMUR
I NEVER THOUGHT THE AVALANCHE THAT THE PRINCESS PREDICTED WOULD HAPPEN!
AND SHE SAVED THAT GIRL... IT'S INCREDIBLE...
I WONDER WHAT THE GIRL'S FATE WILL BE...
CHAK
IT'S THE PRINCESS!
OHH!

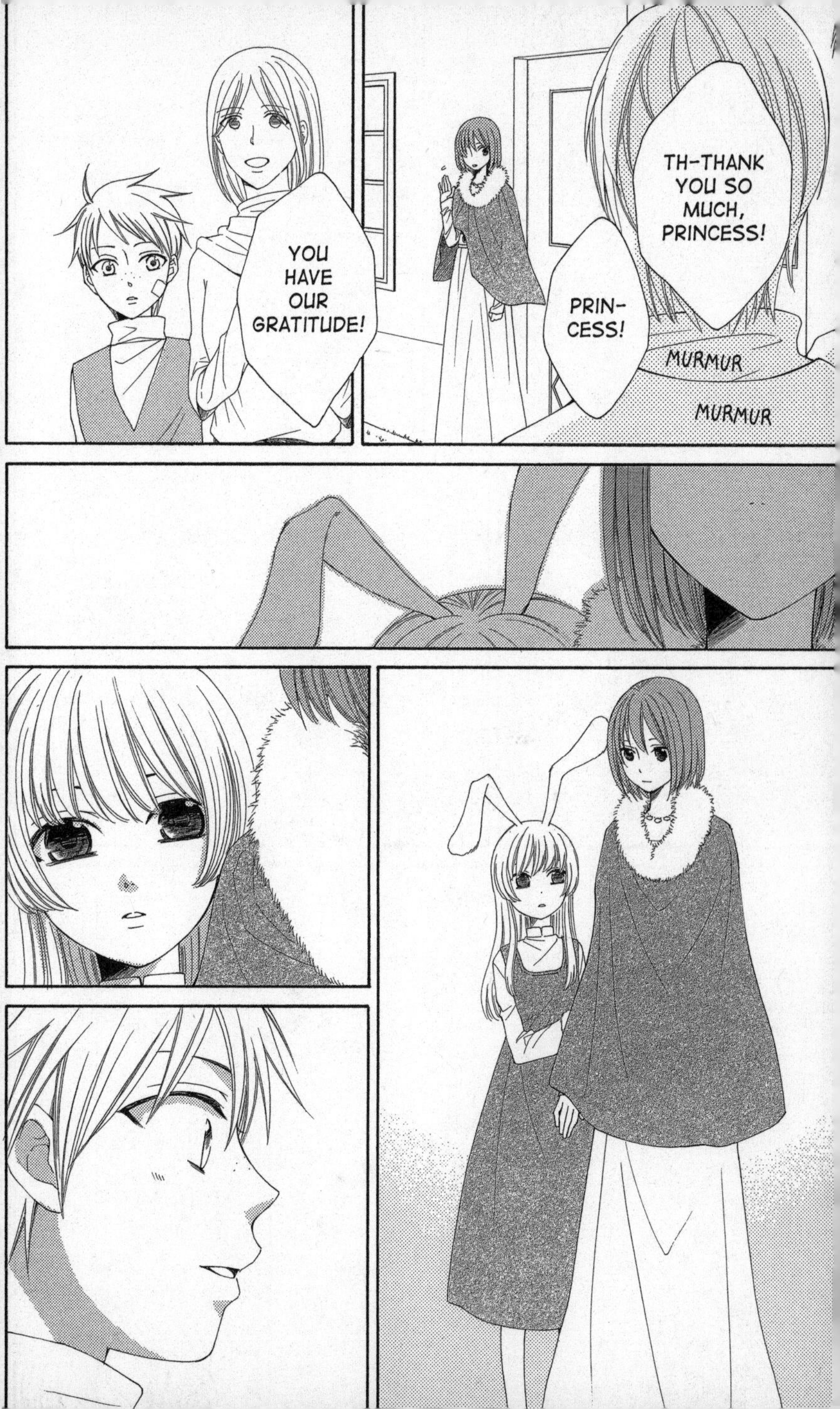
TH-THANK YOU SO MUCH, PRINCESS!
PRIN-CESS!
MURMUR
MURMUR
YOU HAVE OUR GRATITUDE!

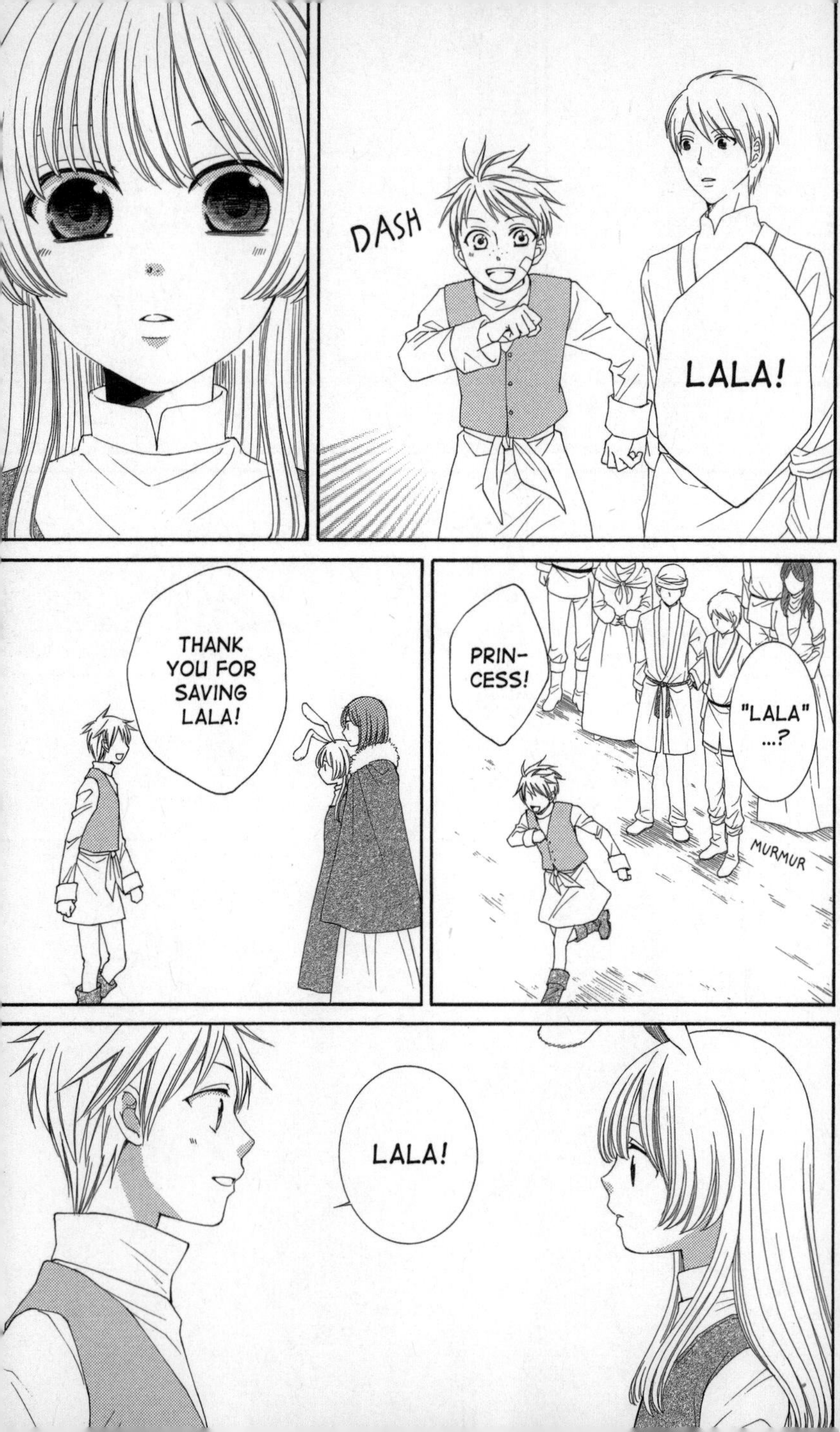
LALA!
DASH
PRIN-CESS!
"LALA" ...?
MURMUR
THANK YOU FOR SAVING LALA!
LALA!

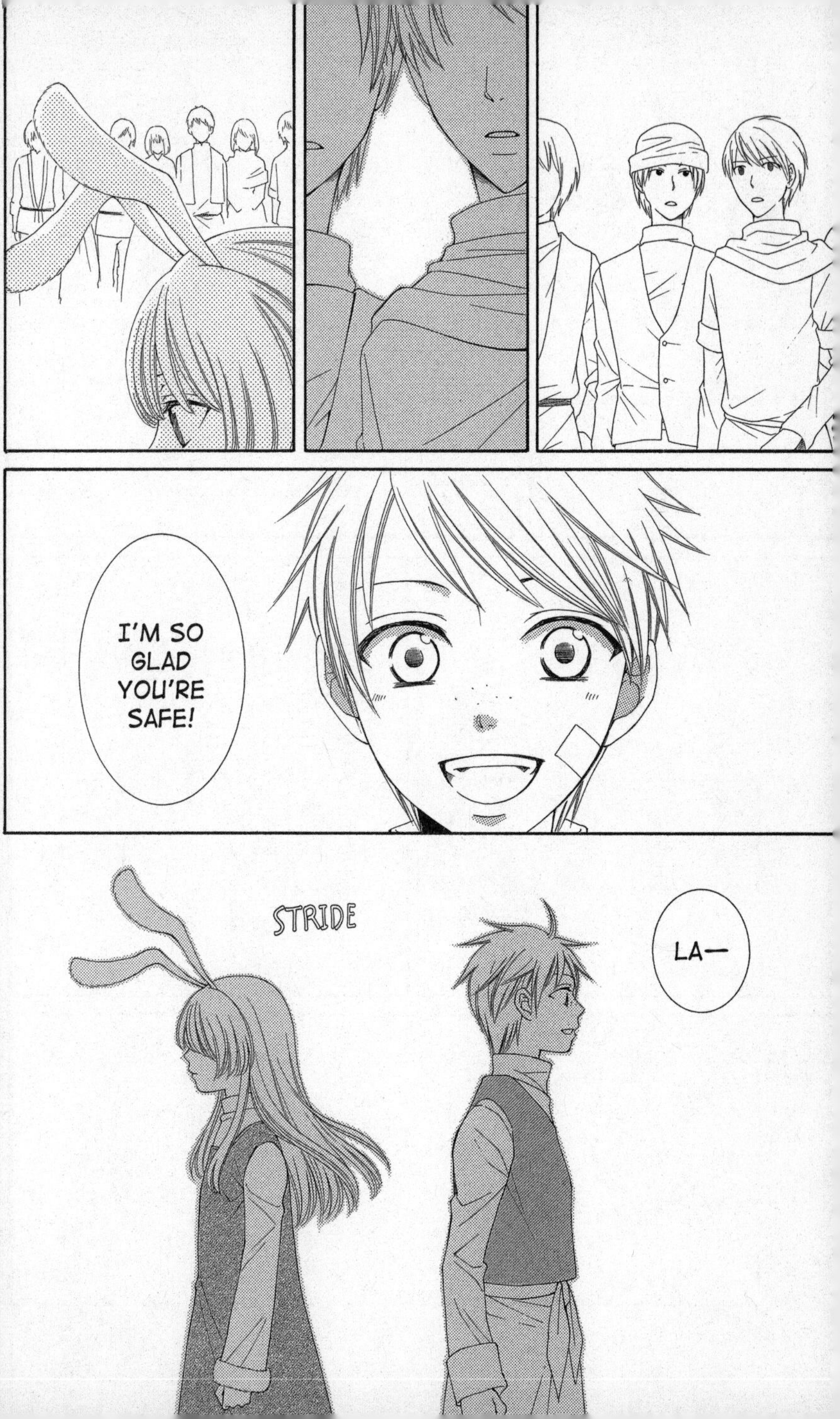
I'M SO GLAD YOU'RE SAFE!
LA—
STRIDE

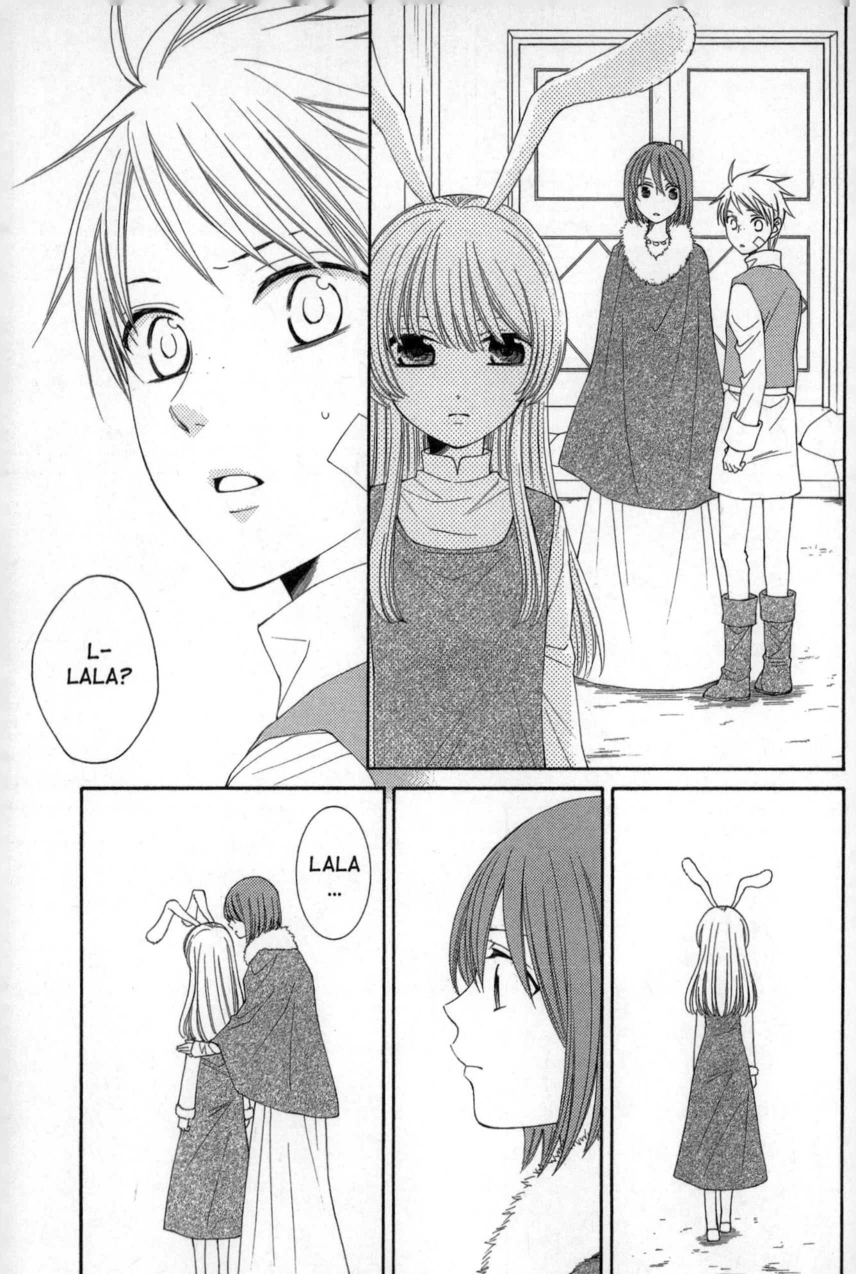
L-
LALA?
LALA
...

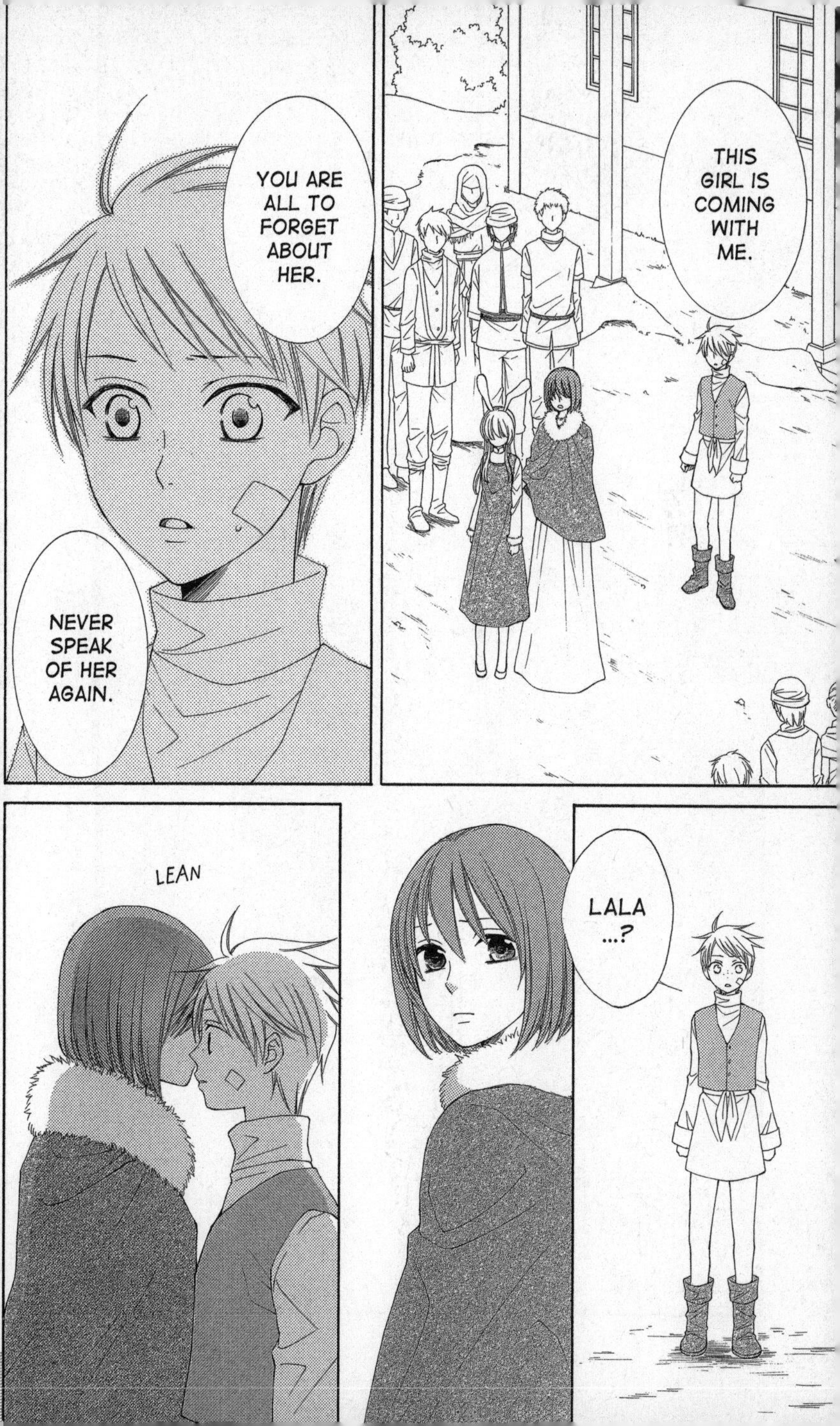
THIS GIRL IS COMING WITH ME.
YOU ARE ALL TO FORGET ABOUT HER.
NEVER SPEAK OF HER AGAIN.
LALA ...?
LEAN

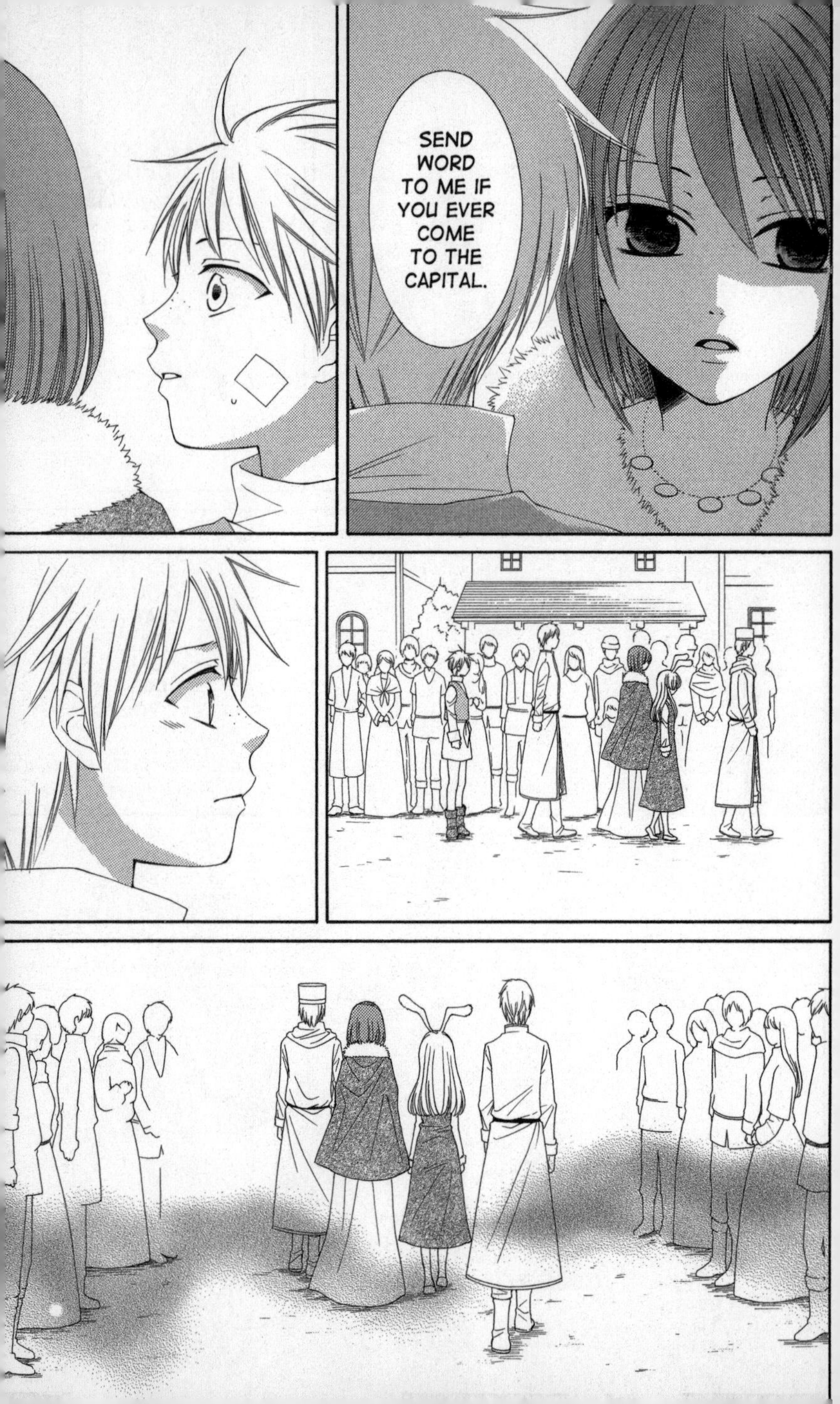
SEND WORD TO ME IF YOU EVER COME TO THE CAPITAL.

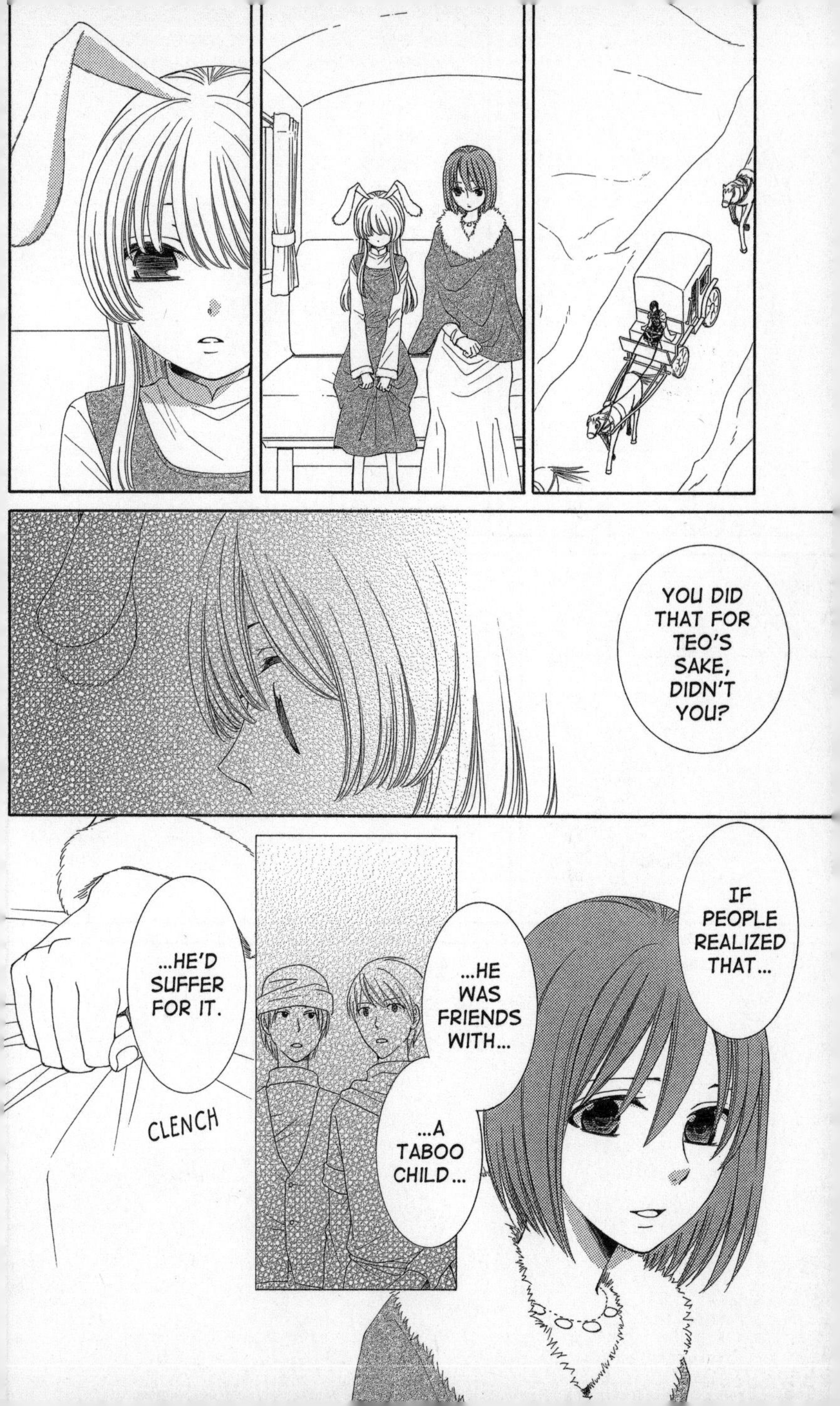
YOU DID THAT FOR TEO'S SAKE, DIDN'T YOU?
IF PEOPLE REALIZED THAT...
...HE WAS FRIENDS WITH...
...A TABOO CHILD...
...HE'D SUFFER FOR IT.
CLENCH

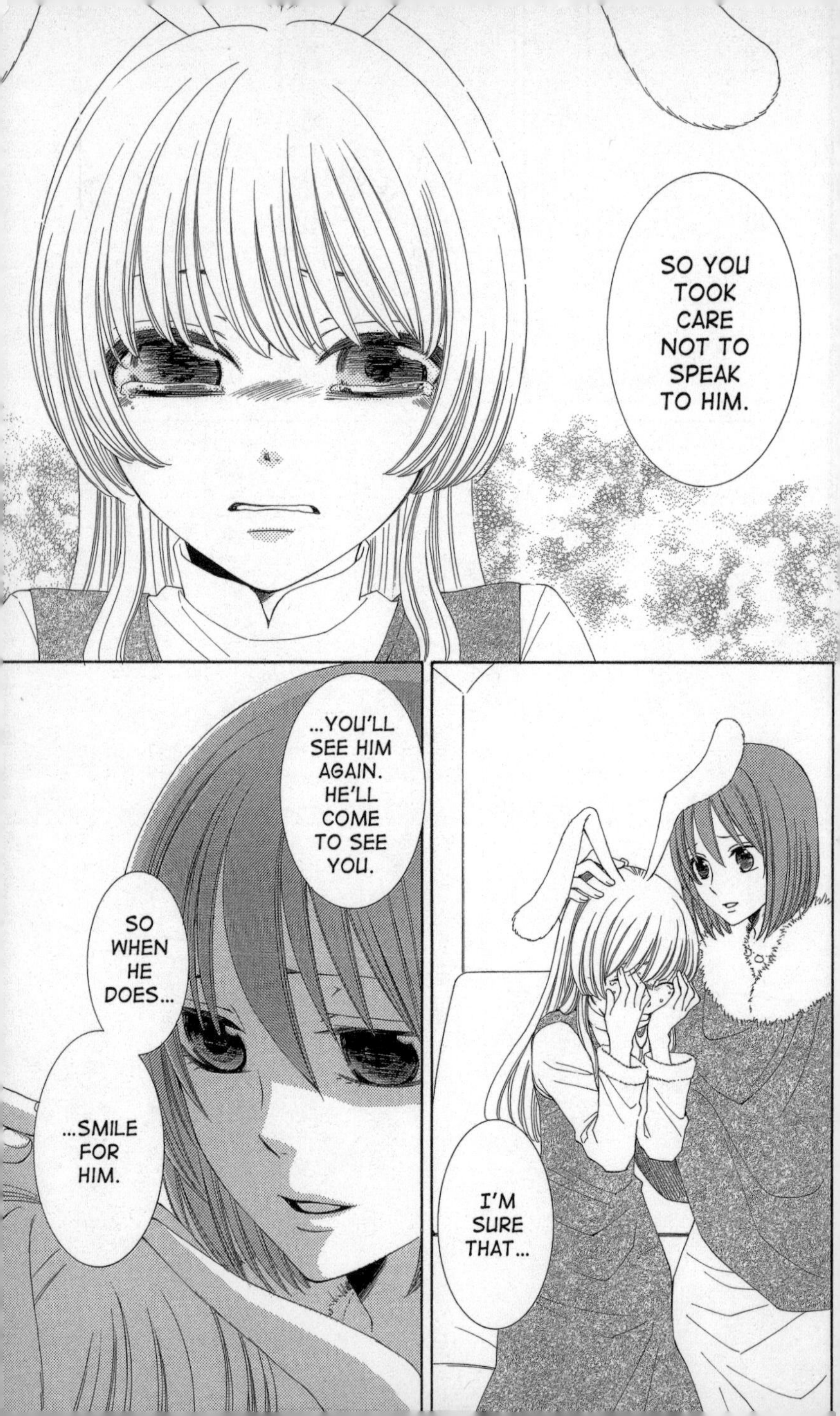
SO YOU TOOK CARE NOT TO SPEAK TO HIM.
I'M SURE THAT...
...YOU'LL SEE HIM AGAIN. HE'LL COME TO SEE YOU.
SO WHEN HE DOES...
...SMILE FOR HIM.

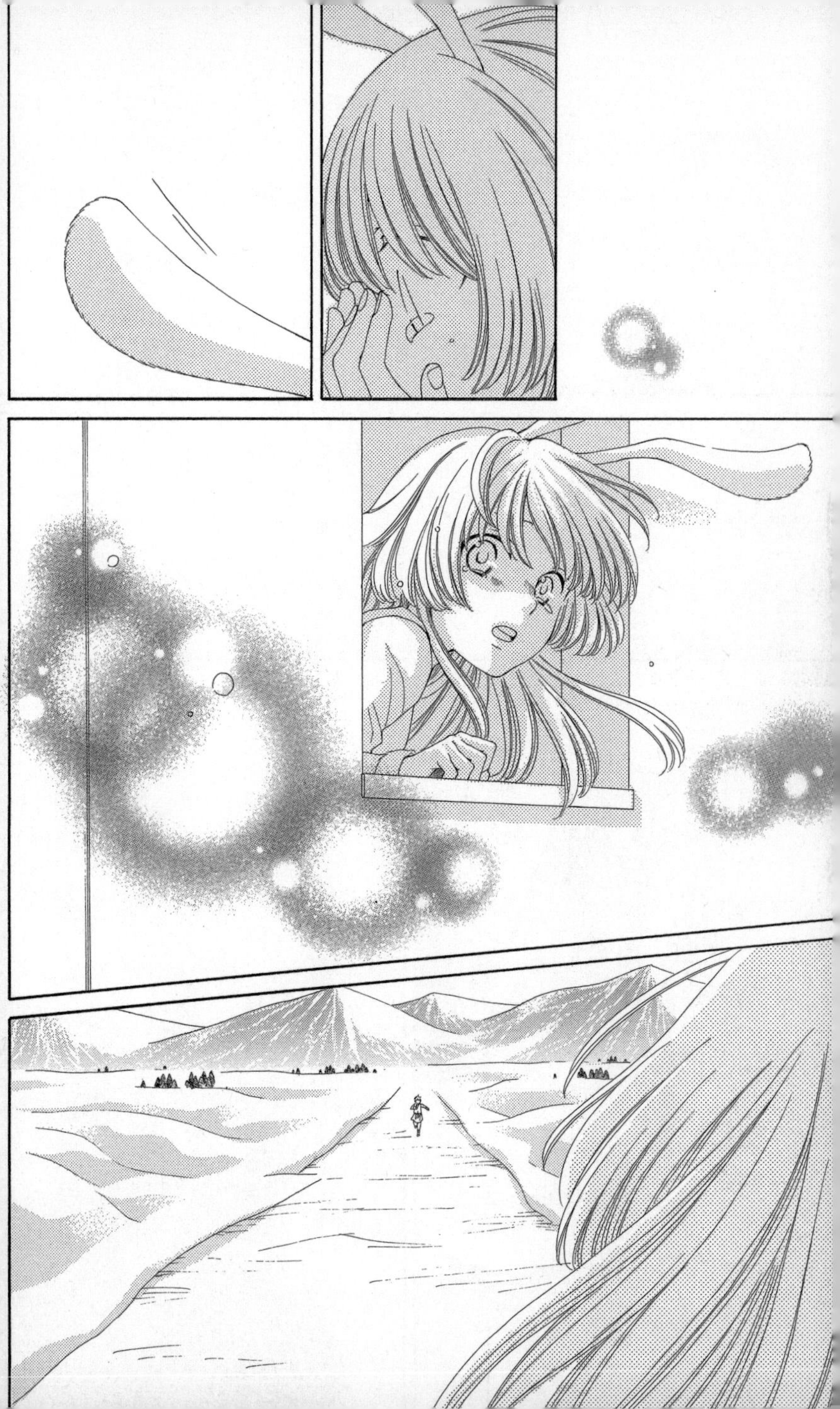

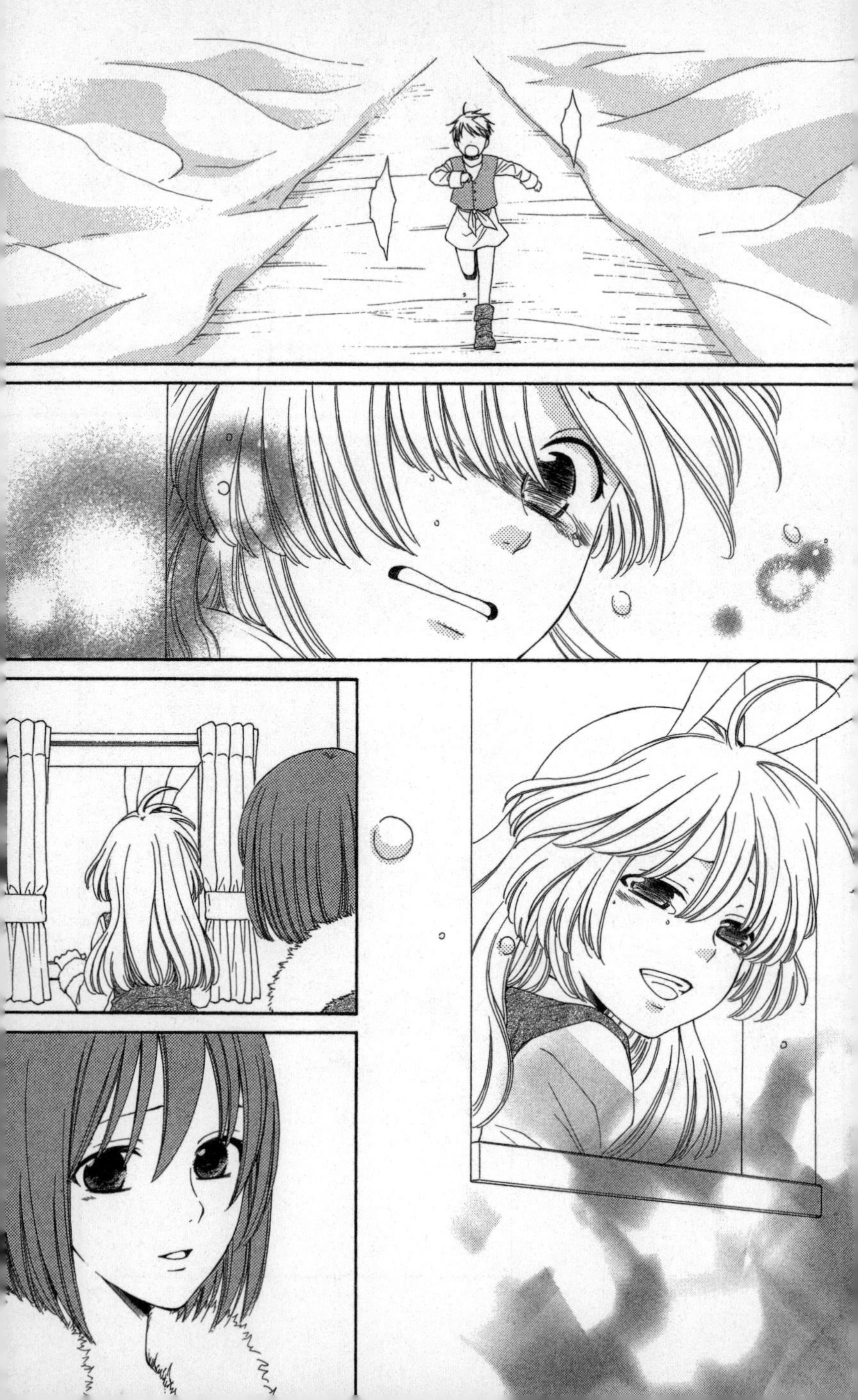

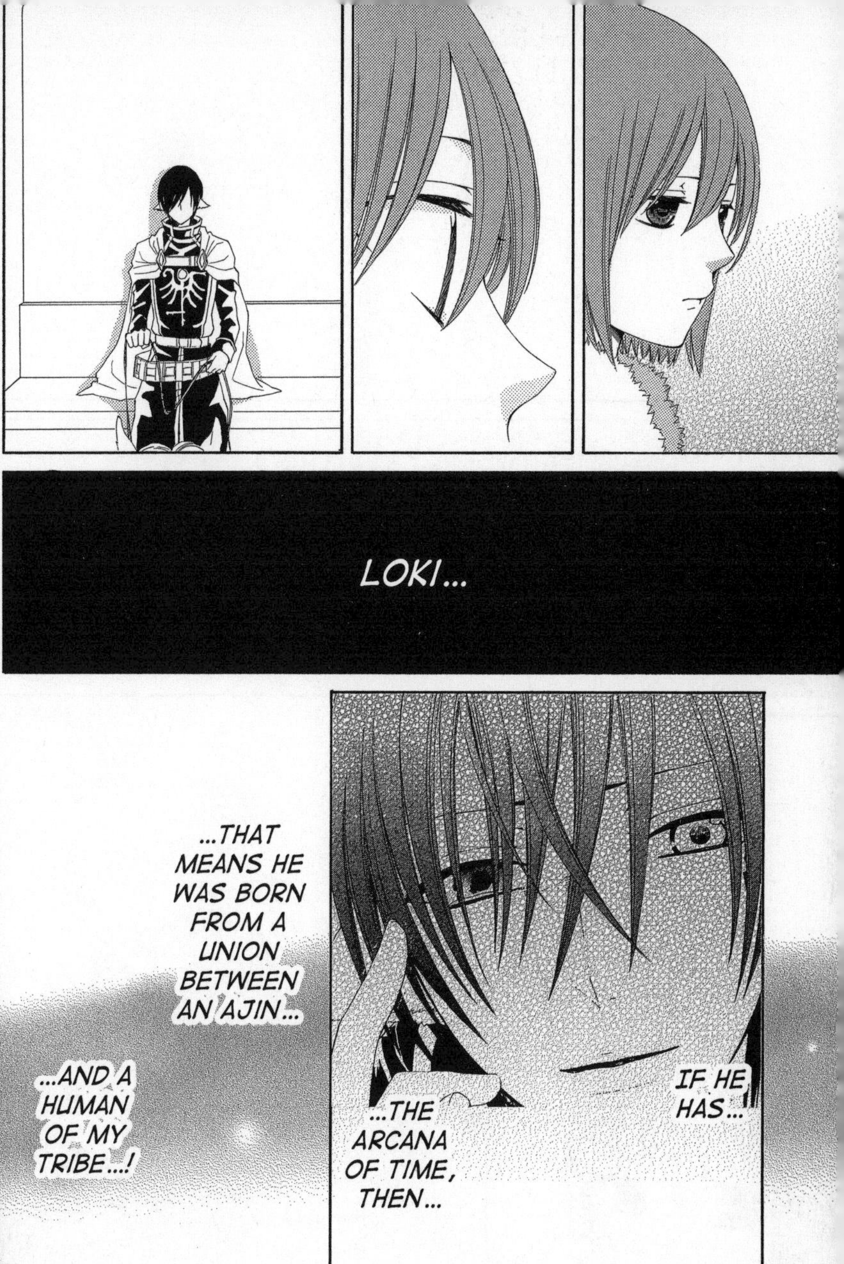
LOKI...
IF HE HAS...
...THE ARCANA OF TIME, THEN...
...THAT MEANS HE WAS BORN FROM A UNION BETWEEN AN AJIN...
...AND A HUMAN OF MY TRIBE...!

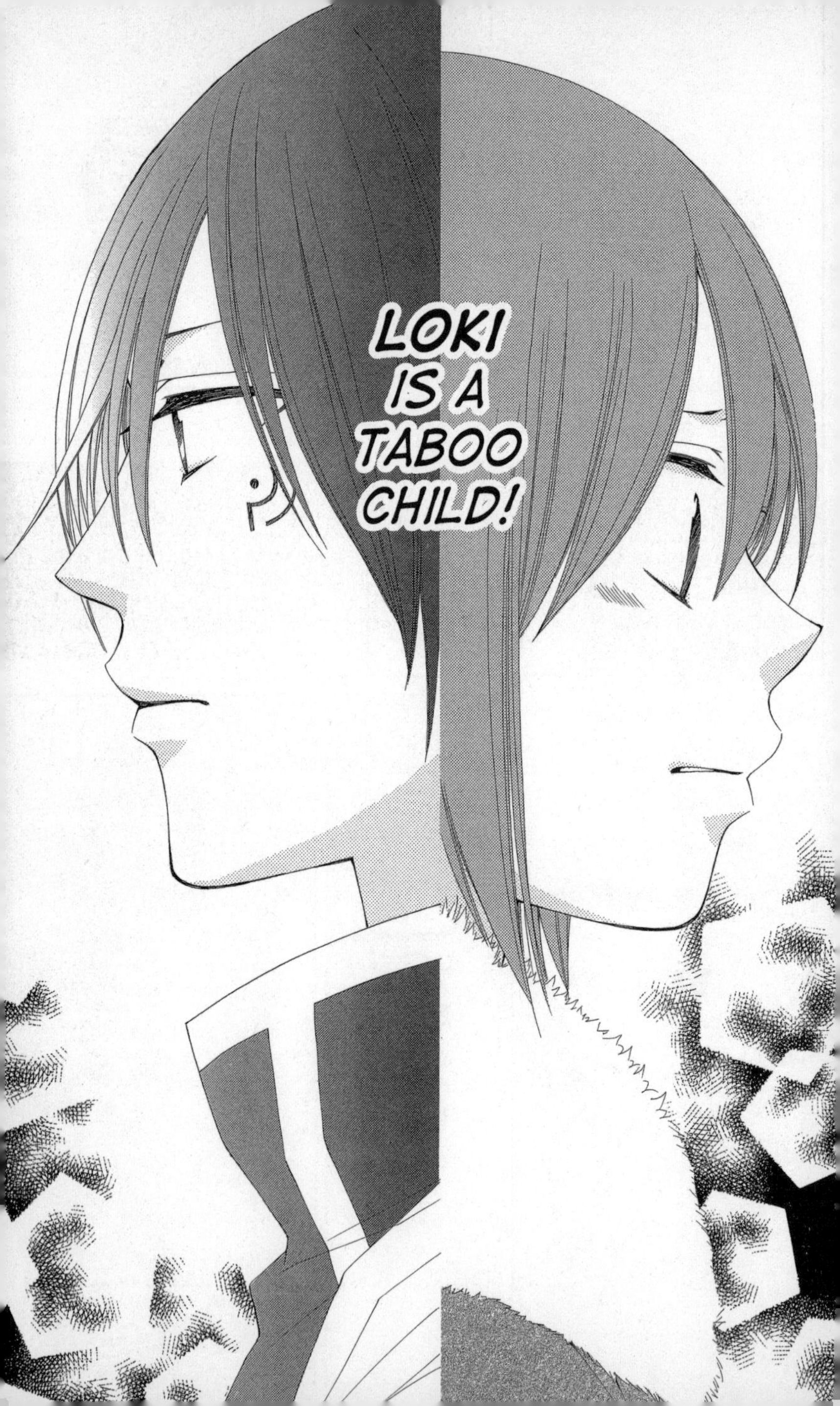
LOKI IS A TABOO CHILD!

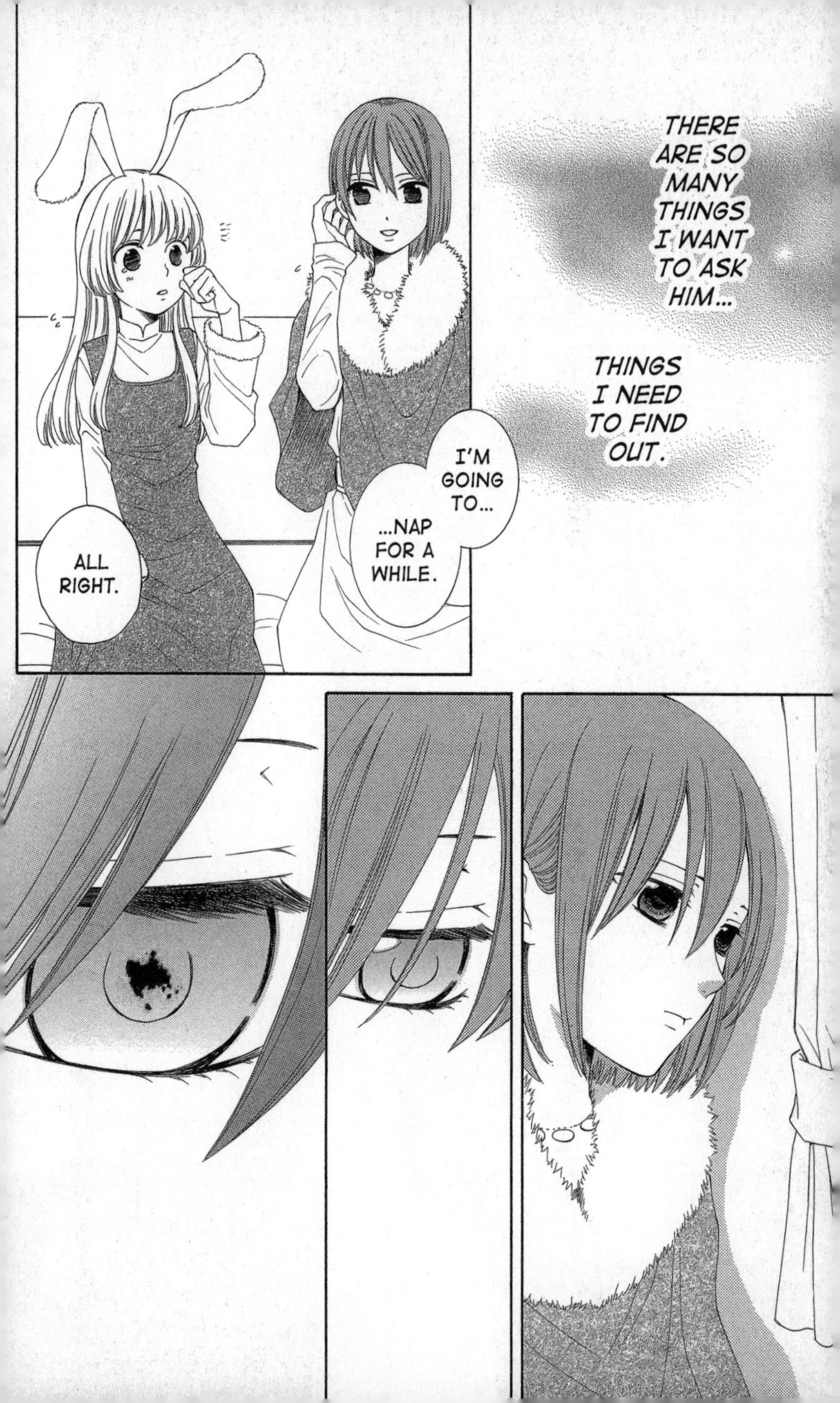
THERE ARE SO MANY THINGS I WANT TO ASK HIM...
THINGS I NEED TO FIND OUT.
I'M GOING TO...
...NAP FOR A WHILE.
ALL RIGHT.

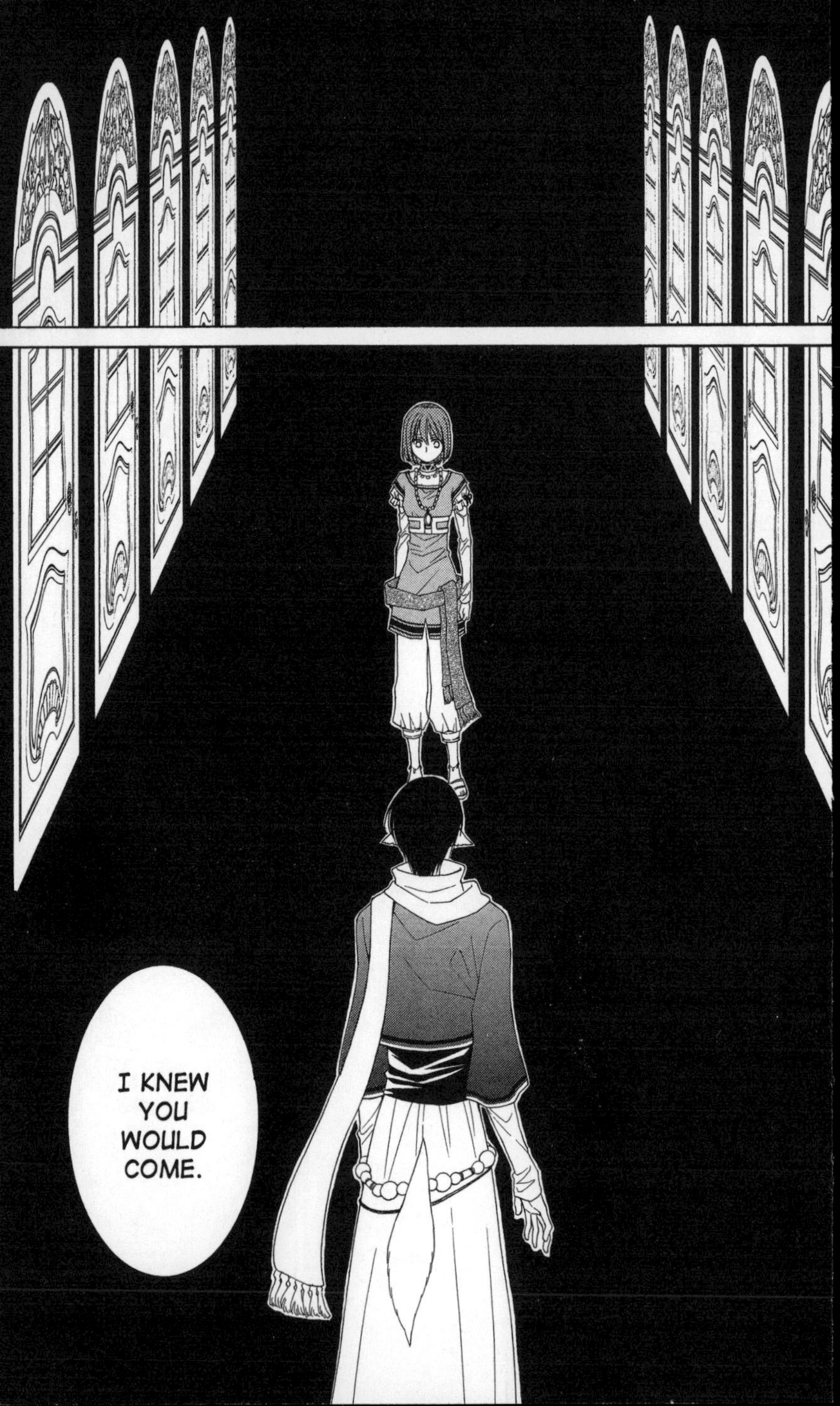
I KNEW YOU WOULD COME.

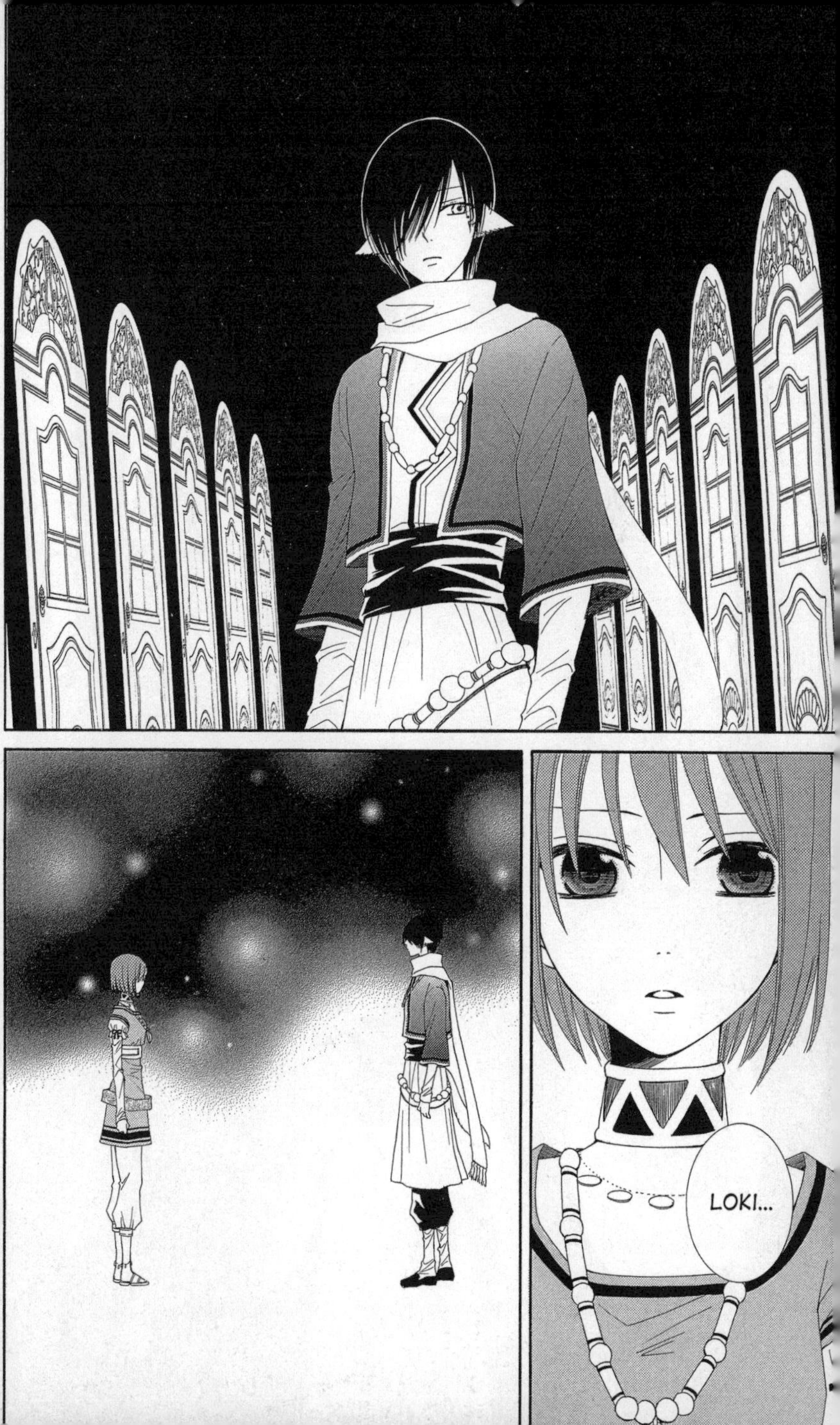
LOKI...

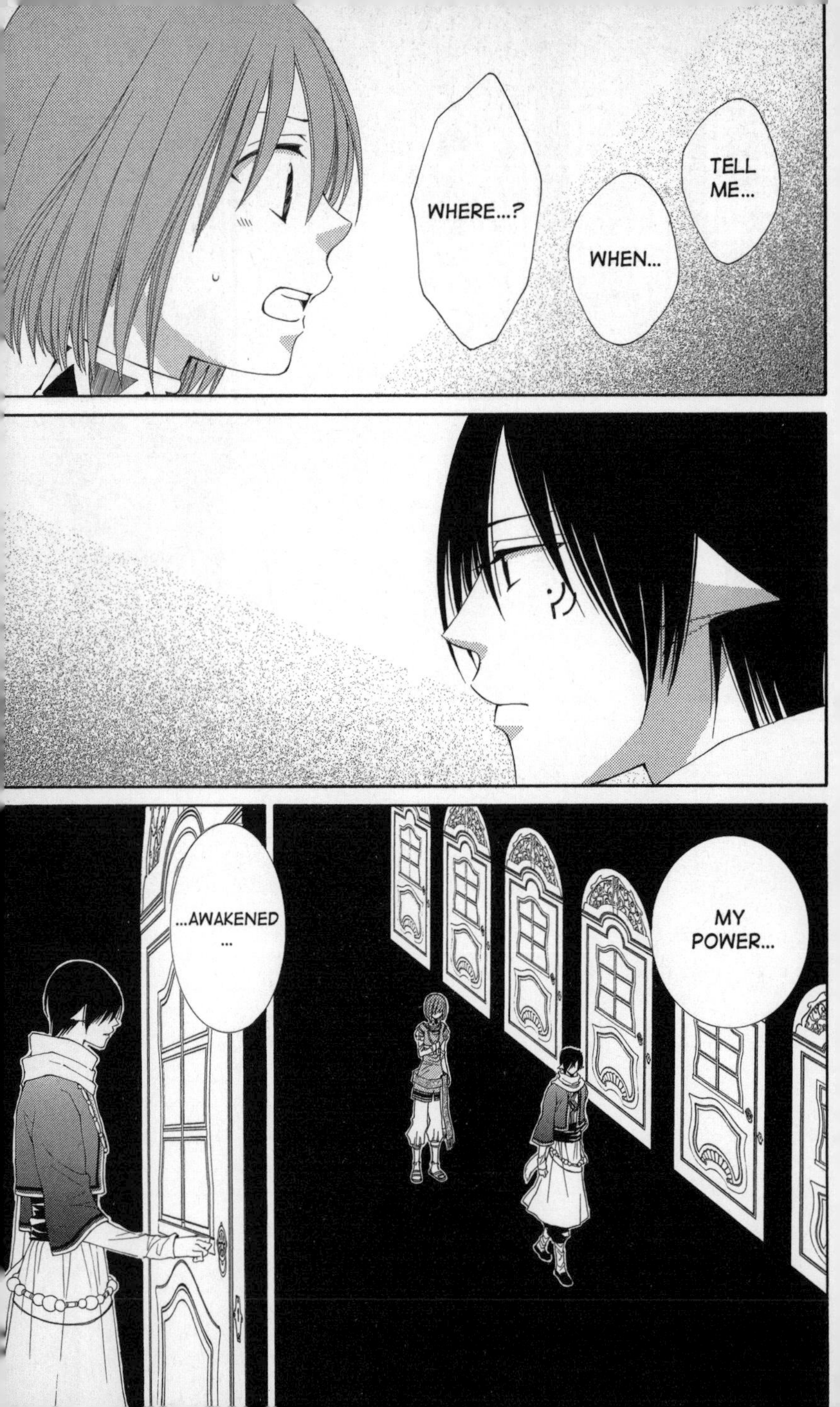
TELL ME...
WHEN...
WHERE...?
MY POWER...
...AWAKENED ...

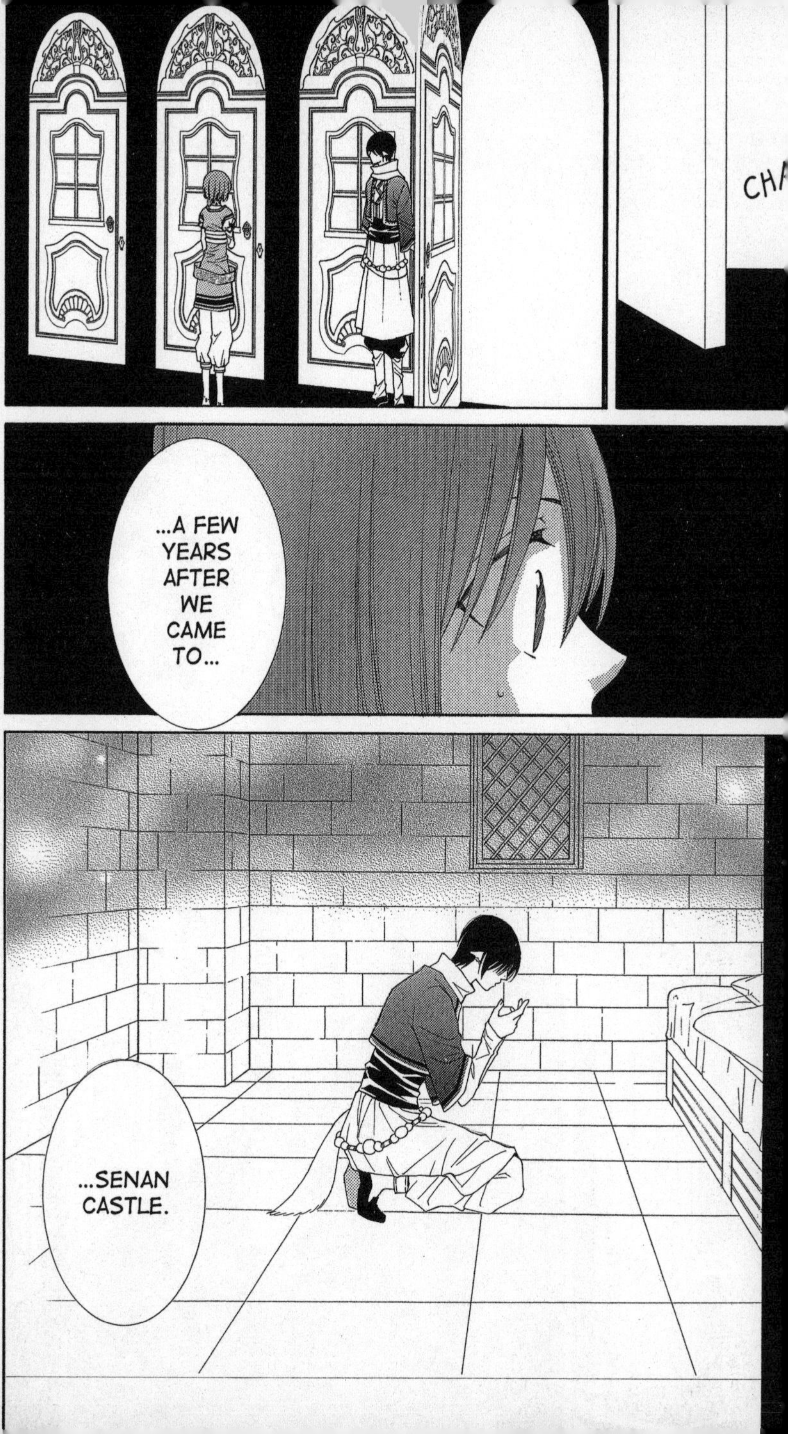

CHA
...A FEW YEARS AFTER WE CAME TO...
...SENAN CASTLE.

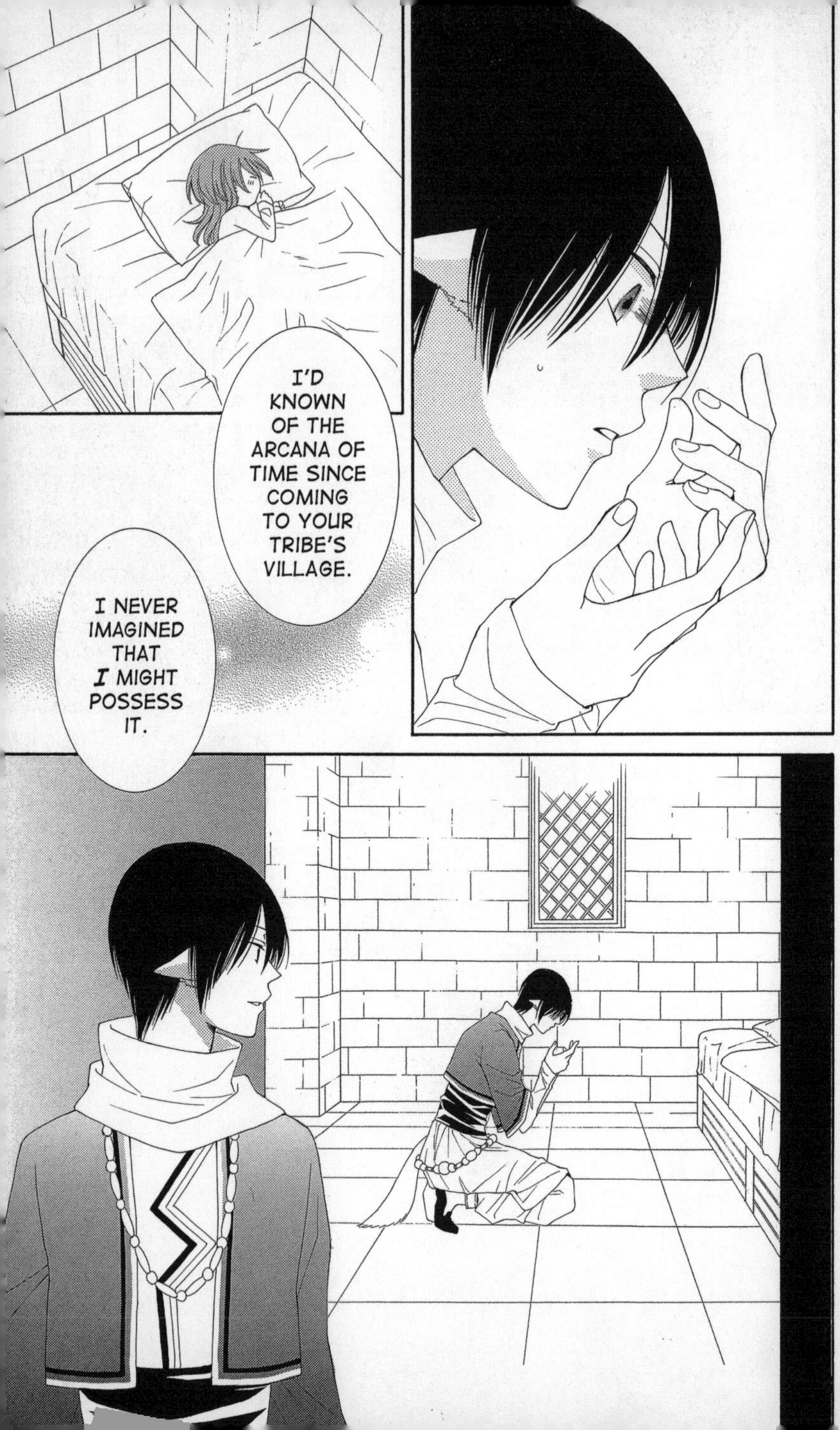

I'D KNOWN OF THE ARCANA OF TIME SINCE COMING TO YOUR TRIBE'S VILLAGE.
I NEVER IMAGINED THAT *I* MIGHT POSSESS IT.

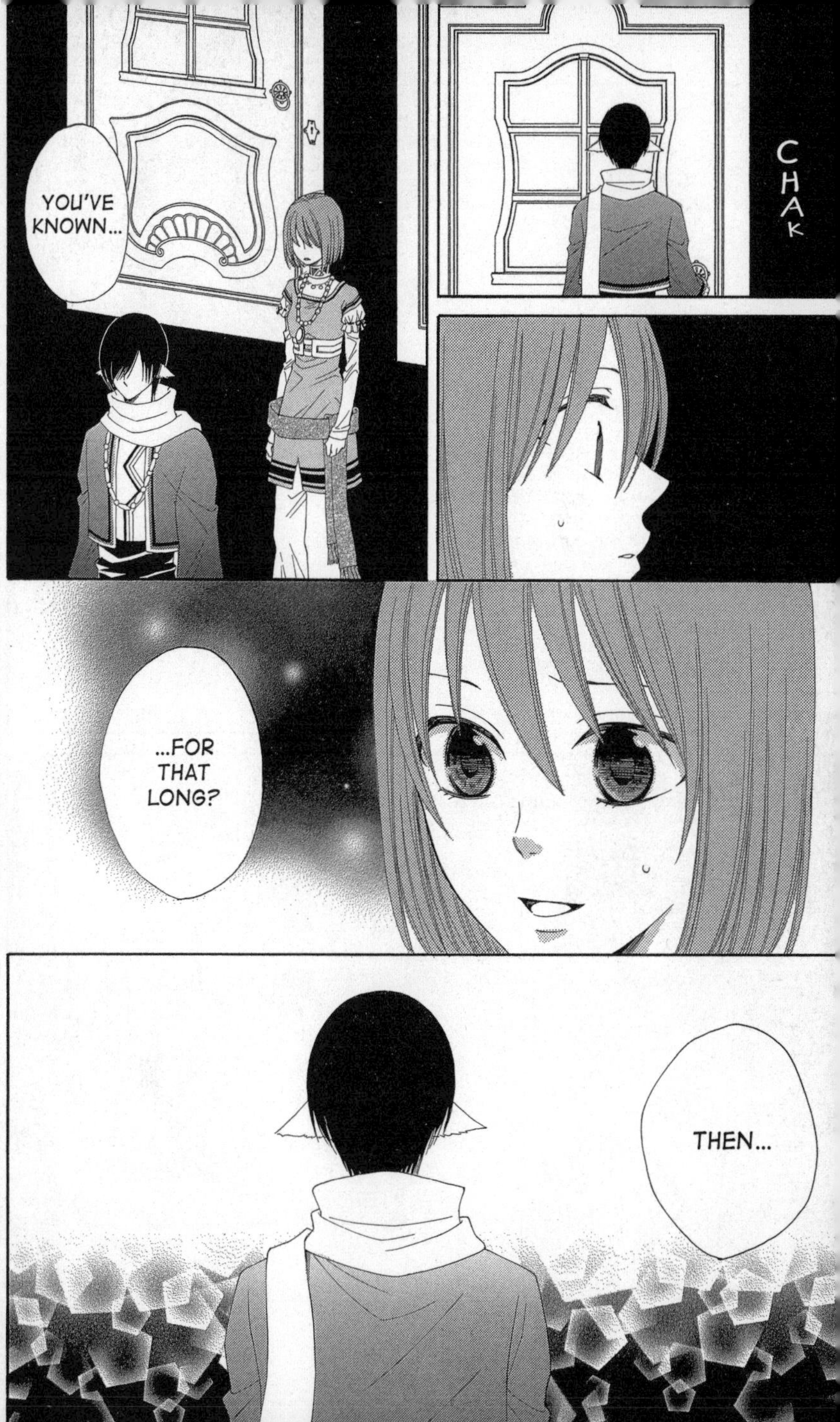
CHAK
YOU'VE KNOWN...
...FOR THAT LONG?
THEN...

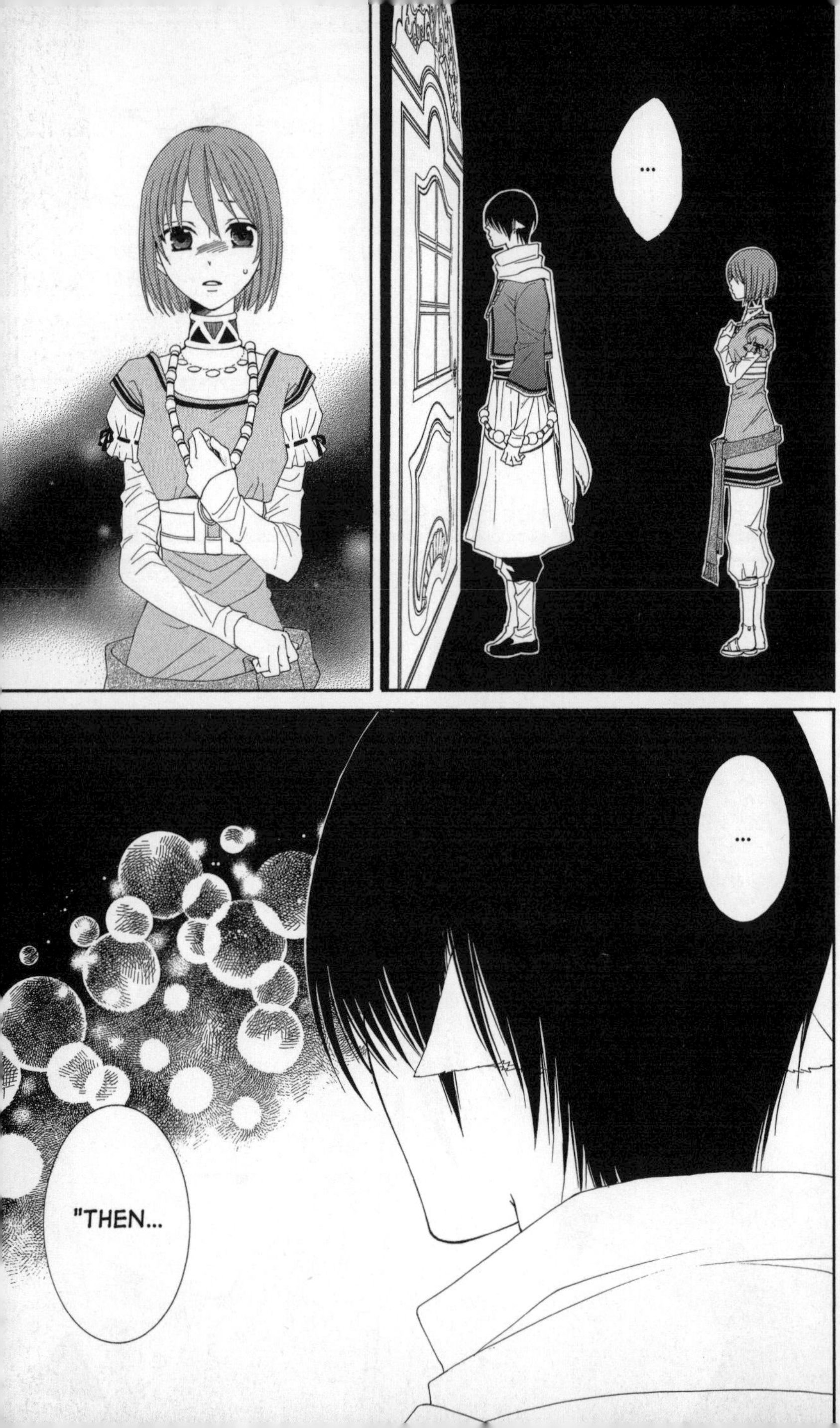
...
...
"THEN...

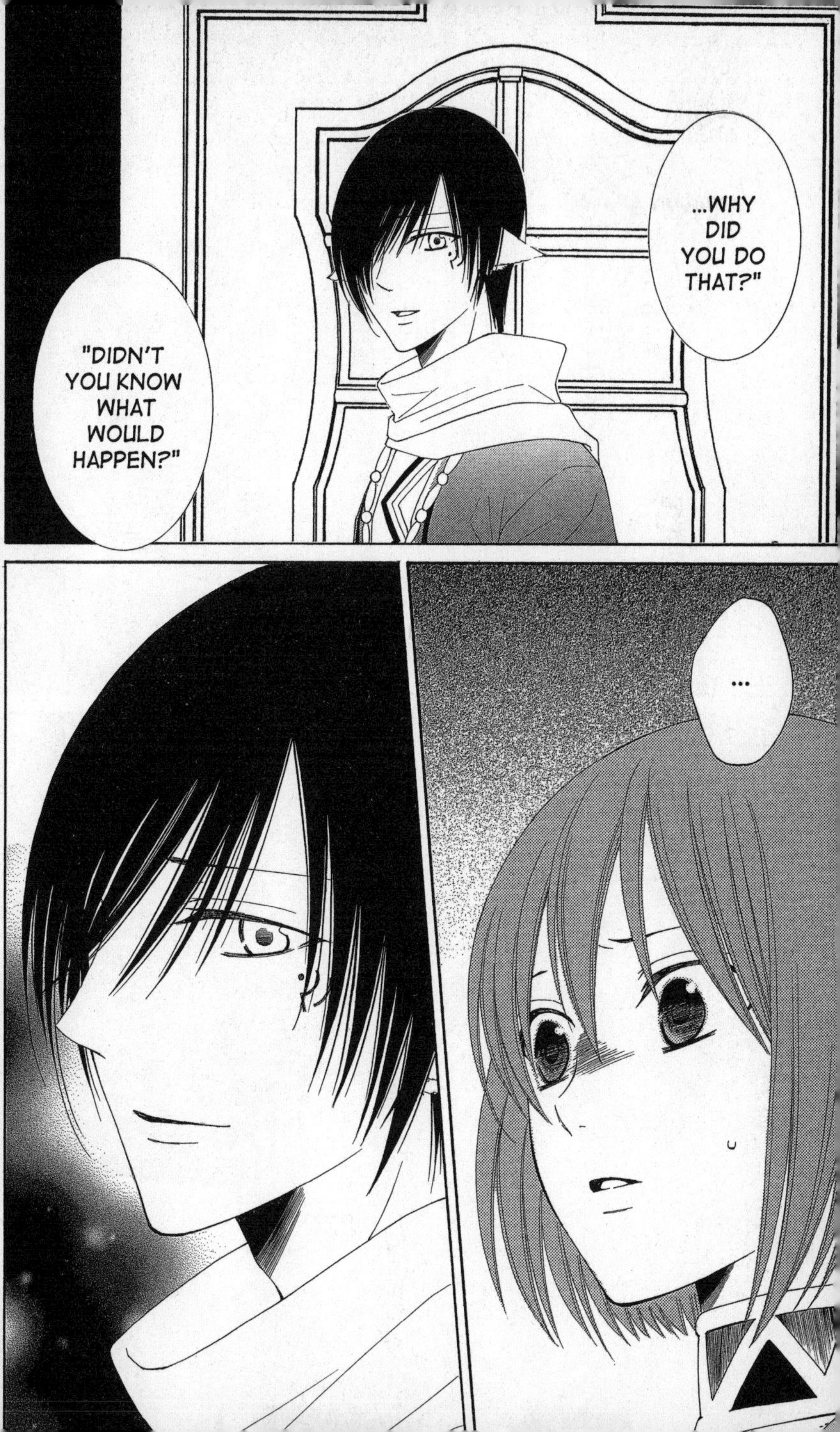
...WHY DID YOU DO THAT?"
"DIDN'T YOU KNOW WHAT WOULD HAPPEN?"
...

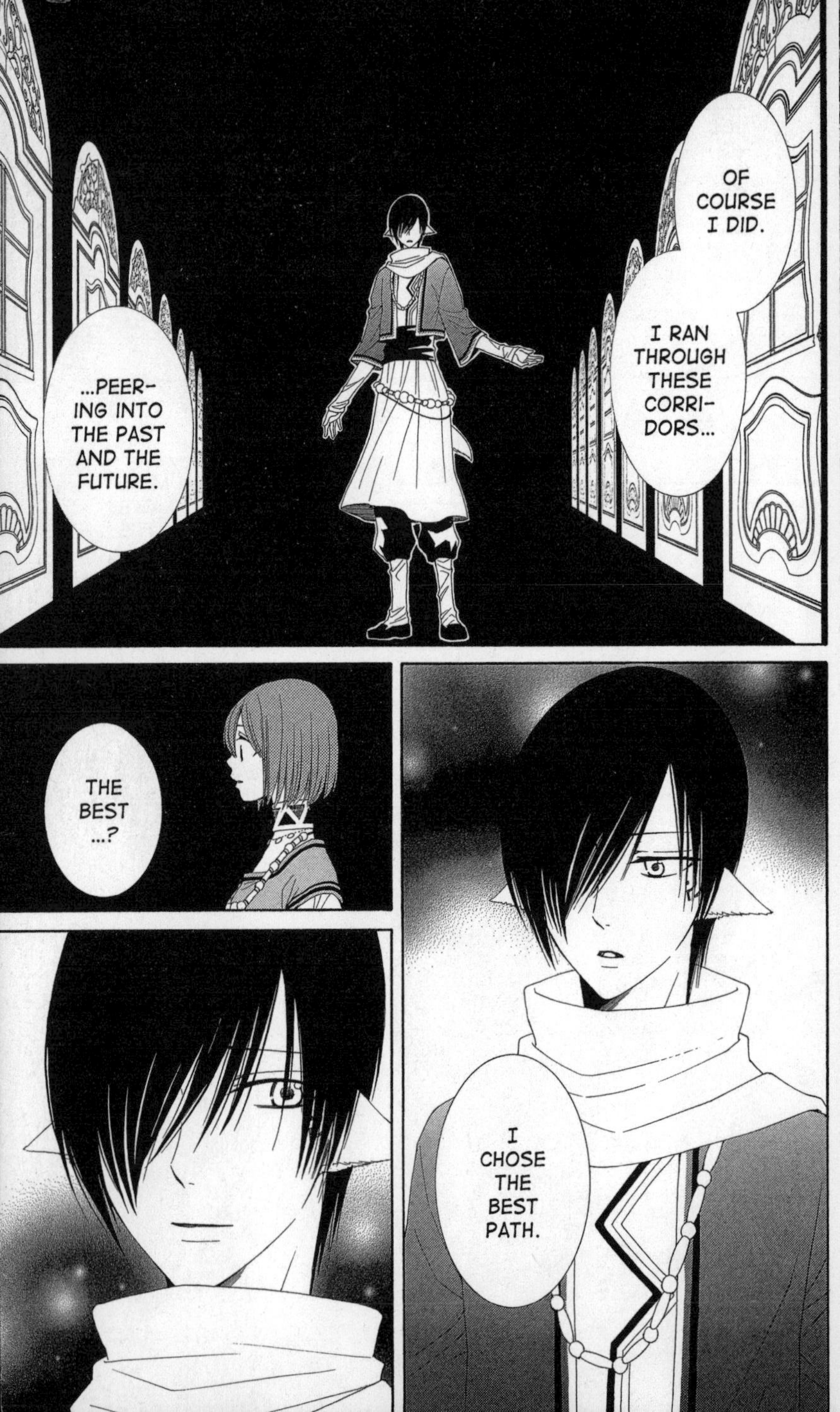

OF COURSE I DID.
I RAN THROUGH THESE CORRIDORS...
...PEERING INTO THE PAST AND THE FUTURE.
I CHOSE THE BEST PATH.
THE BEST ...?

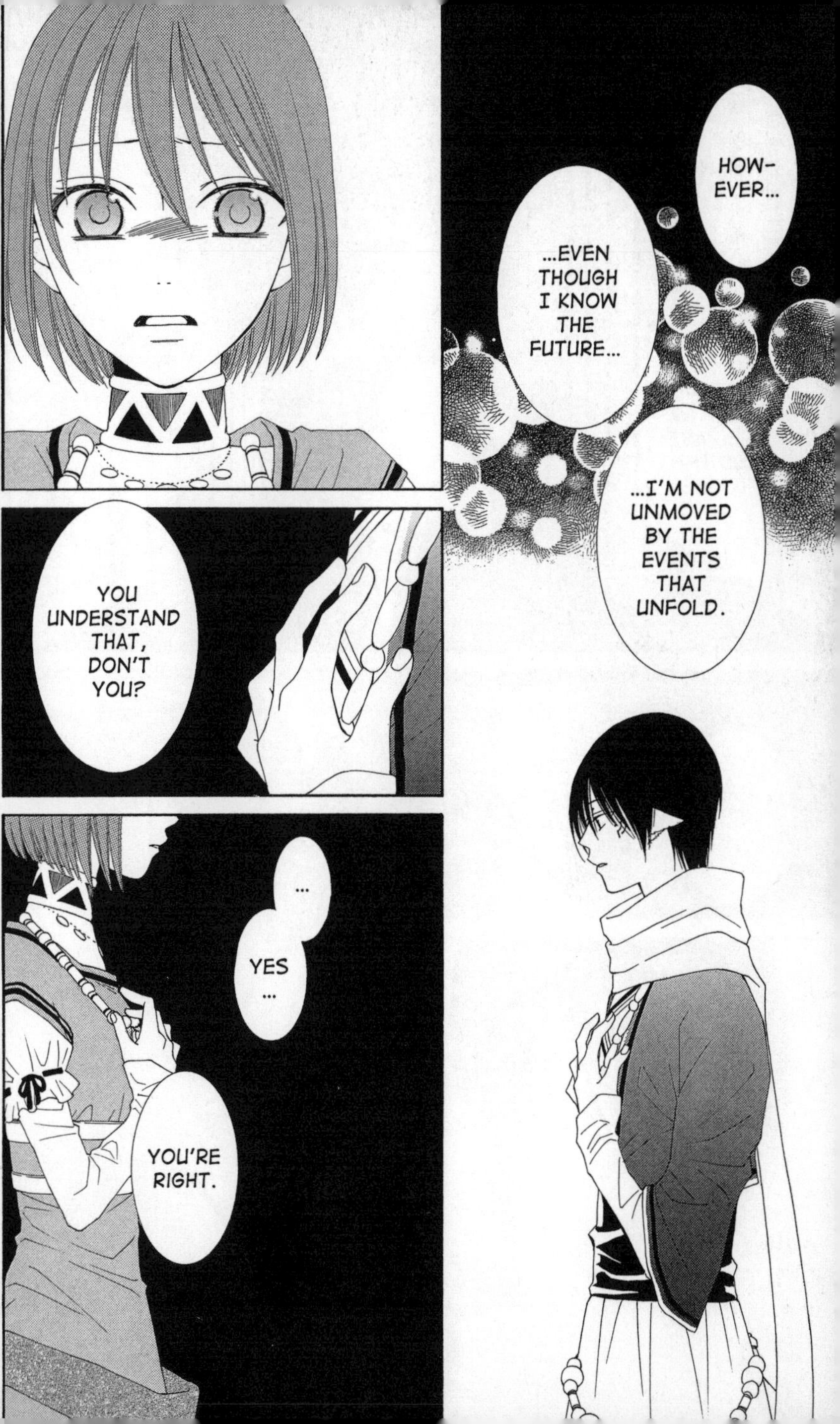
HOW-EVER...
...EVEN THOUGH I KNOW THE FUTURE...
...I'M NOT UNMOVED BY THE EVENTS THAT UNFOLD.
YOU UNDERSTAND THAT, DON'T YOU?
...
YES ...
YOU'RE RIGHT.

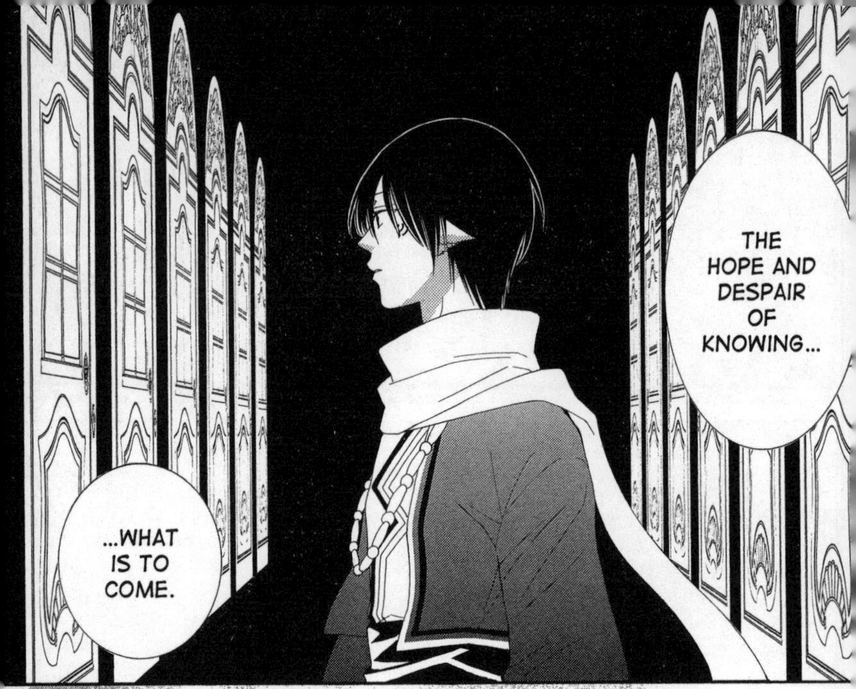
THE HOPE AND DESPAIR OF KNOWING...
...WHAT IS TO COME.
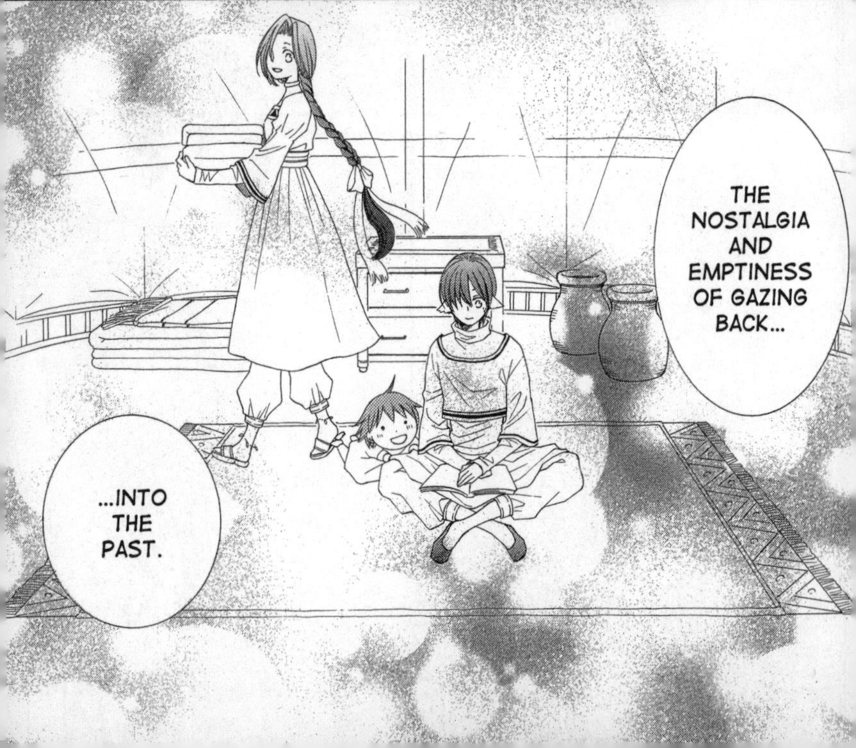
THE NOSTALGIA AND EMPTINESS OF GAZING BACK...
...INTO THE PAST.

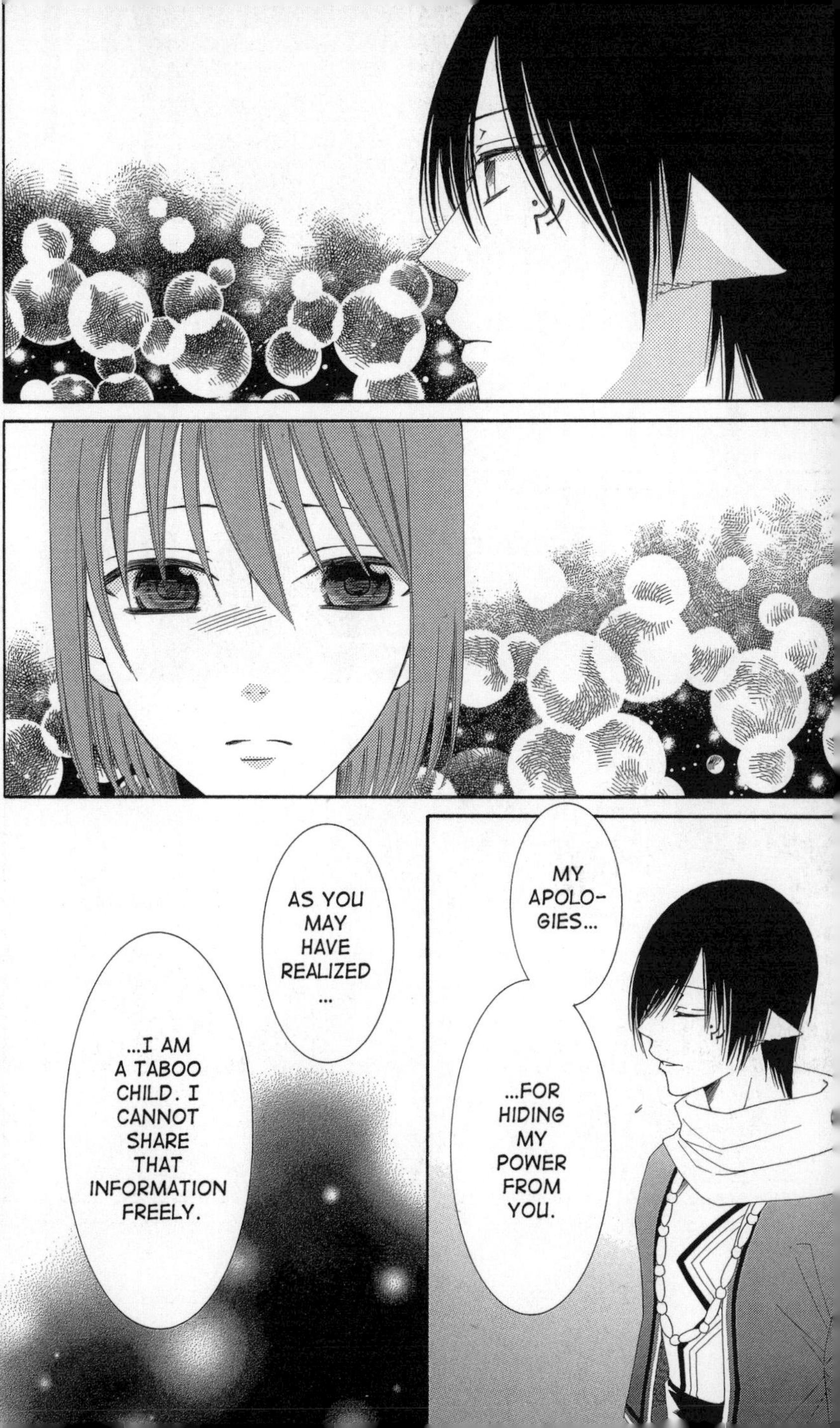
MY APOLOGIES...
...FOR HIDING MY POWER FROM YOU.
AS YOU MAY HAVE REALIZED...
...I AM A TABOO CHILD. I CANNOT SHARE THAT INFORMATION FREELY.

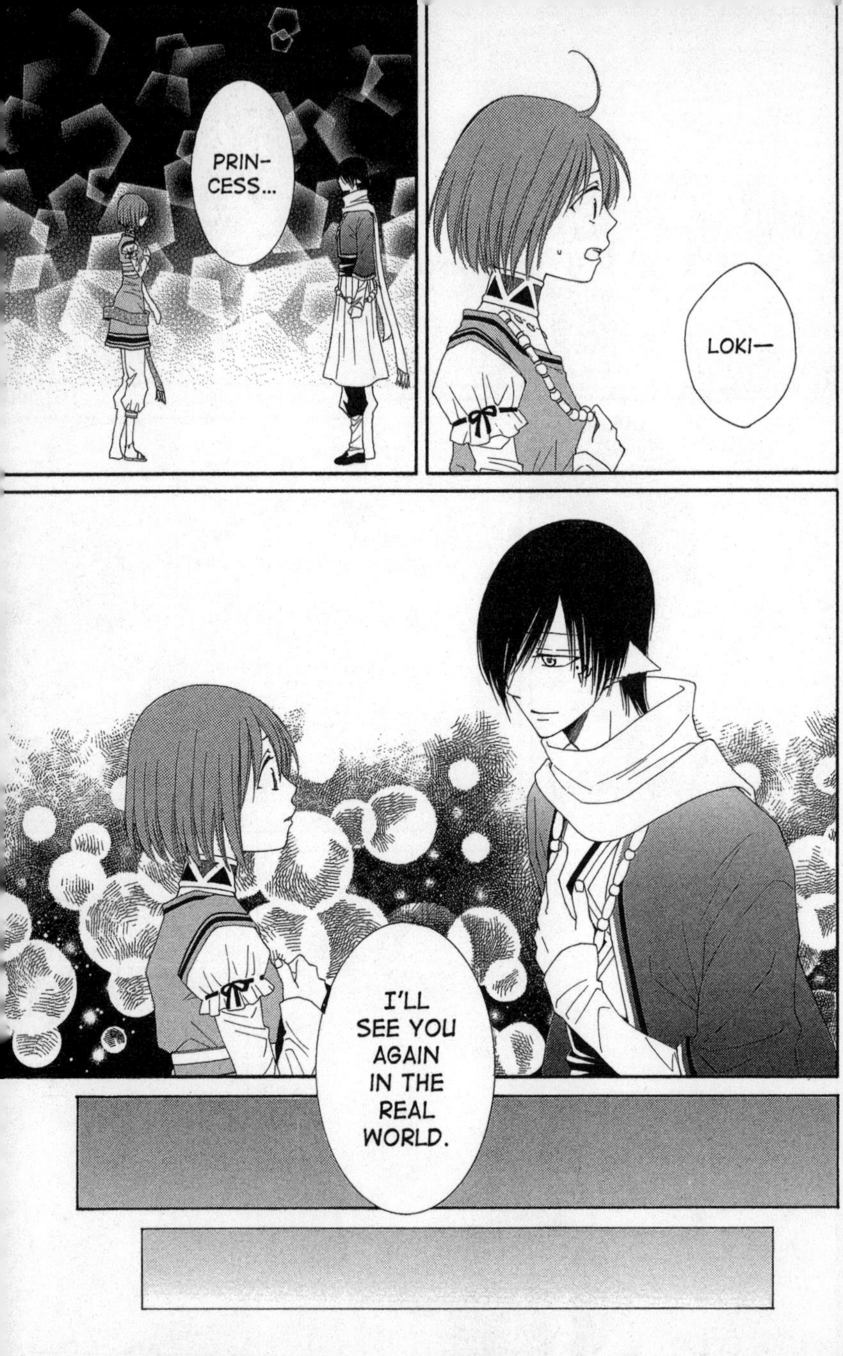
LOKI—
PRIN-CESS...
I'LL SEE YOU AGAIN IN THE REAL WORLD.

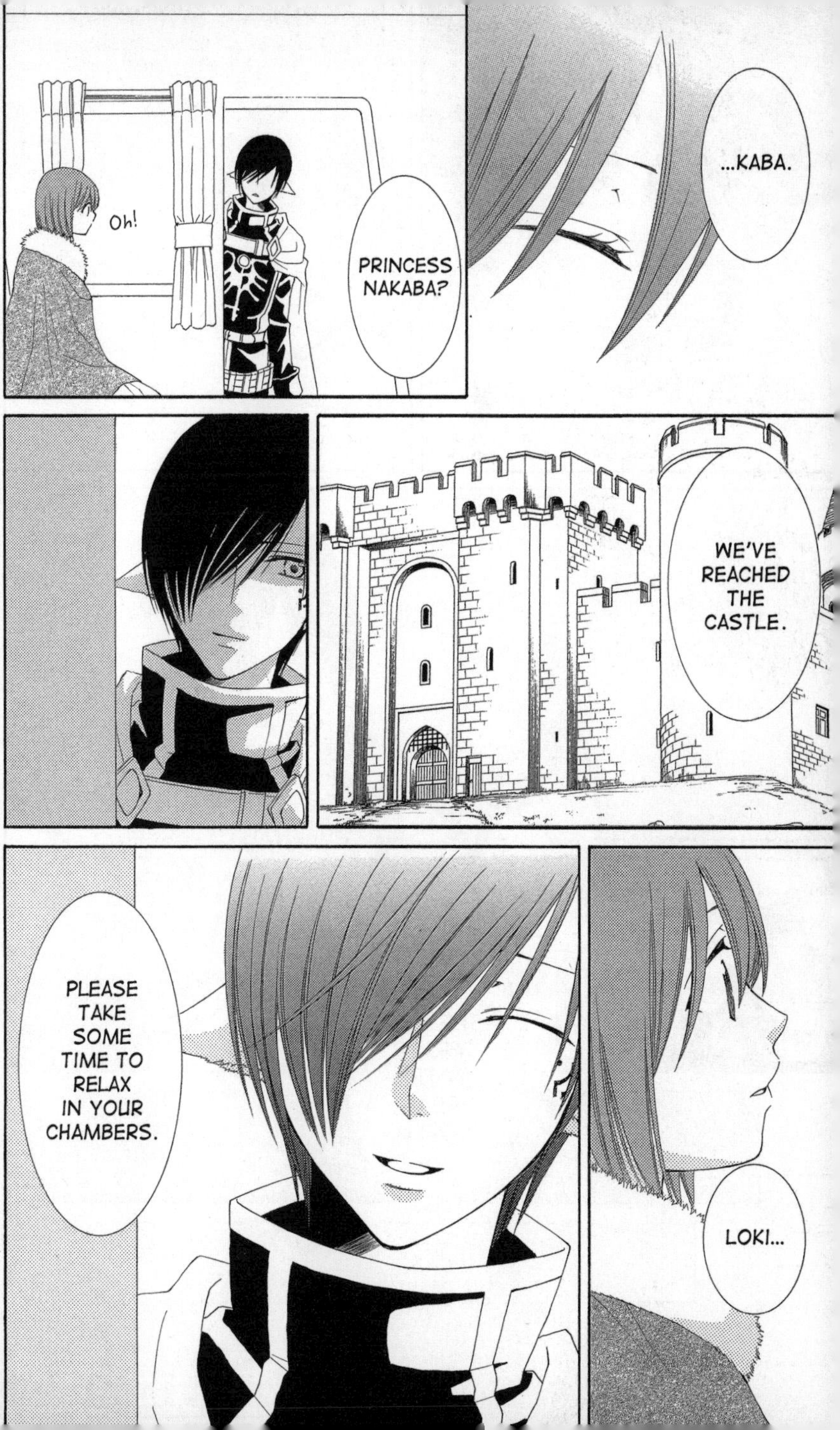
...KABA.
PRINCESS NAKABA?
Oh!
WE'VE REACHED THE CASTLE.
LOKI...
PLEASE TAKE SOME TIME TO RELAX IN YOUR CHAMBERS.

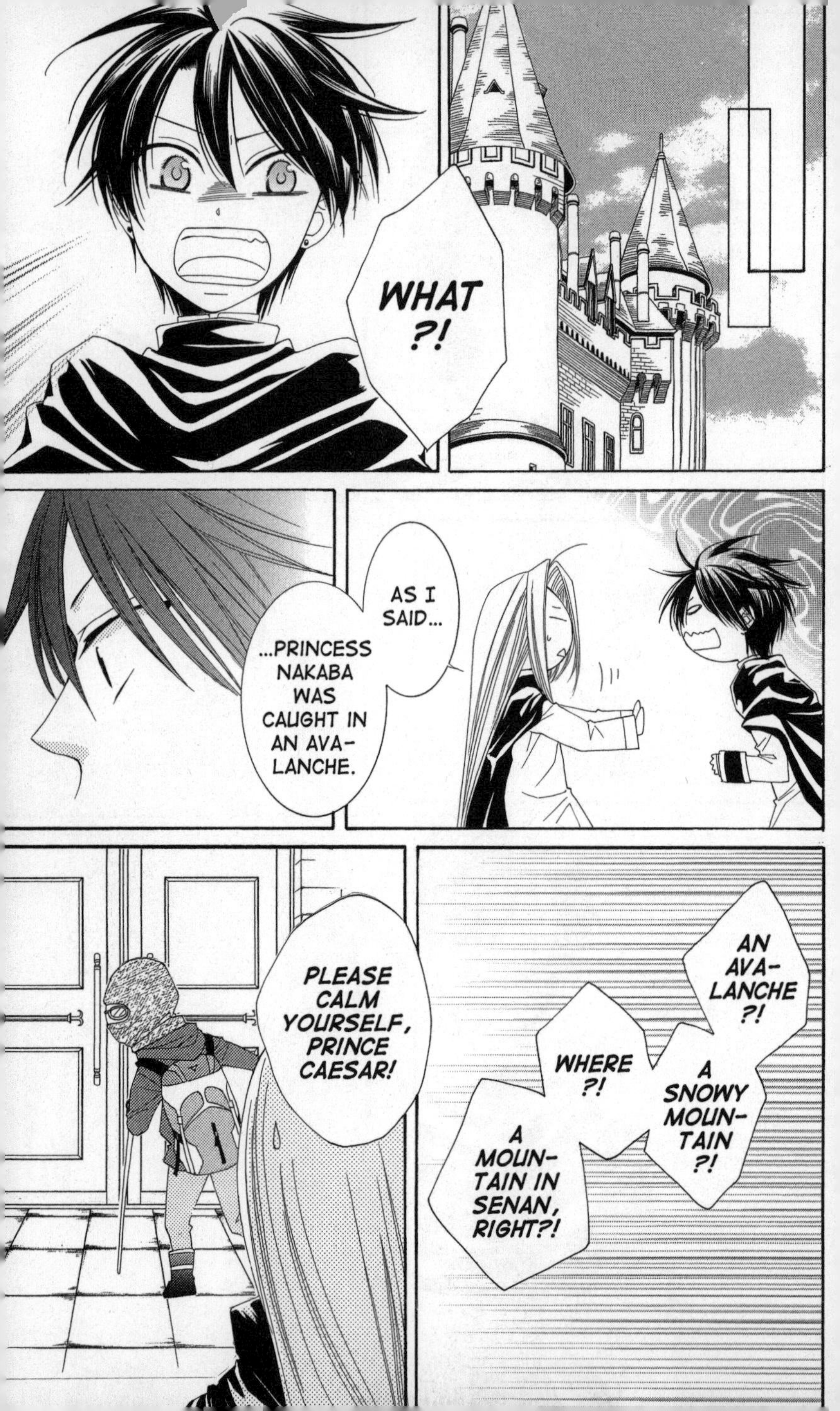
WHAT ?!
AS I SAID...
...PRINCESS NAKABA WAS CAUGHT IN AN AVA-LANCHE.
AN AVA-LANCHE ?!
A SNOWY MOUN-TAIN ?!
WHERE ?!
A MOUN-TAIN IN SENAN, RIGHT?!
PLEASE CALM YOURSELF, PRINCE CAESAR!

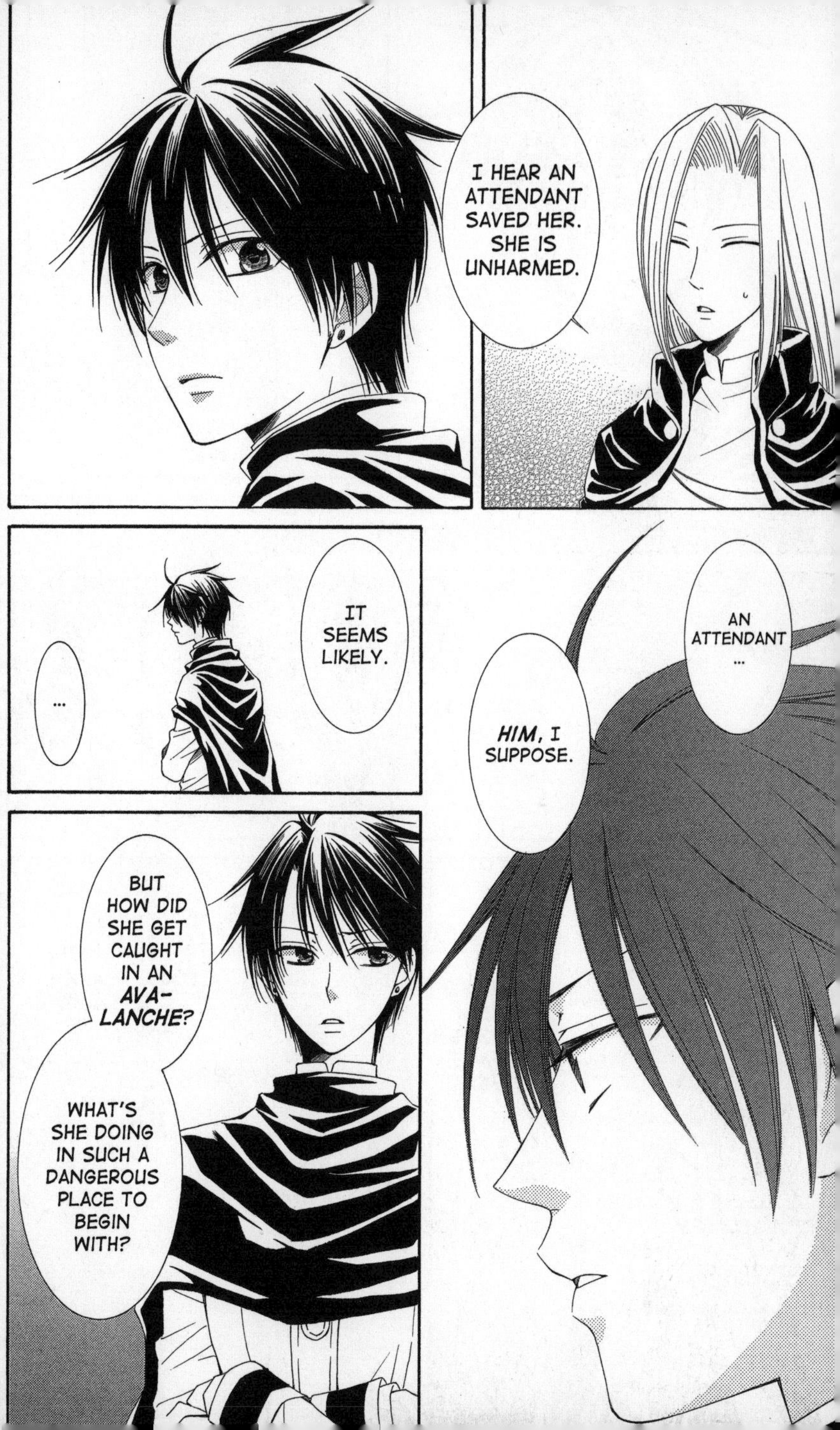
I HEAR AN ATTENDANT SAVED HER. SHE IS UNHARMED.
AN ATTENDANT ...
HIM, I SUPPOSE.
IT SEEMS LIKELY.
...
BUT HOW DID SHE GET CAUGHT IN AN *AVA-LANCHE*?
WHAT'S SHE DOING IN SUCH A DANGEROUS PLACE TO BEGIN WITH?

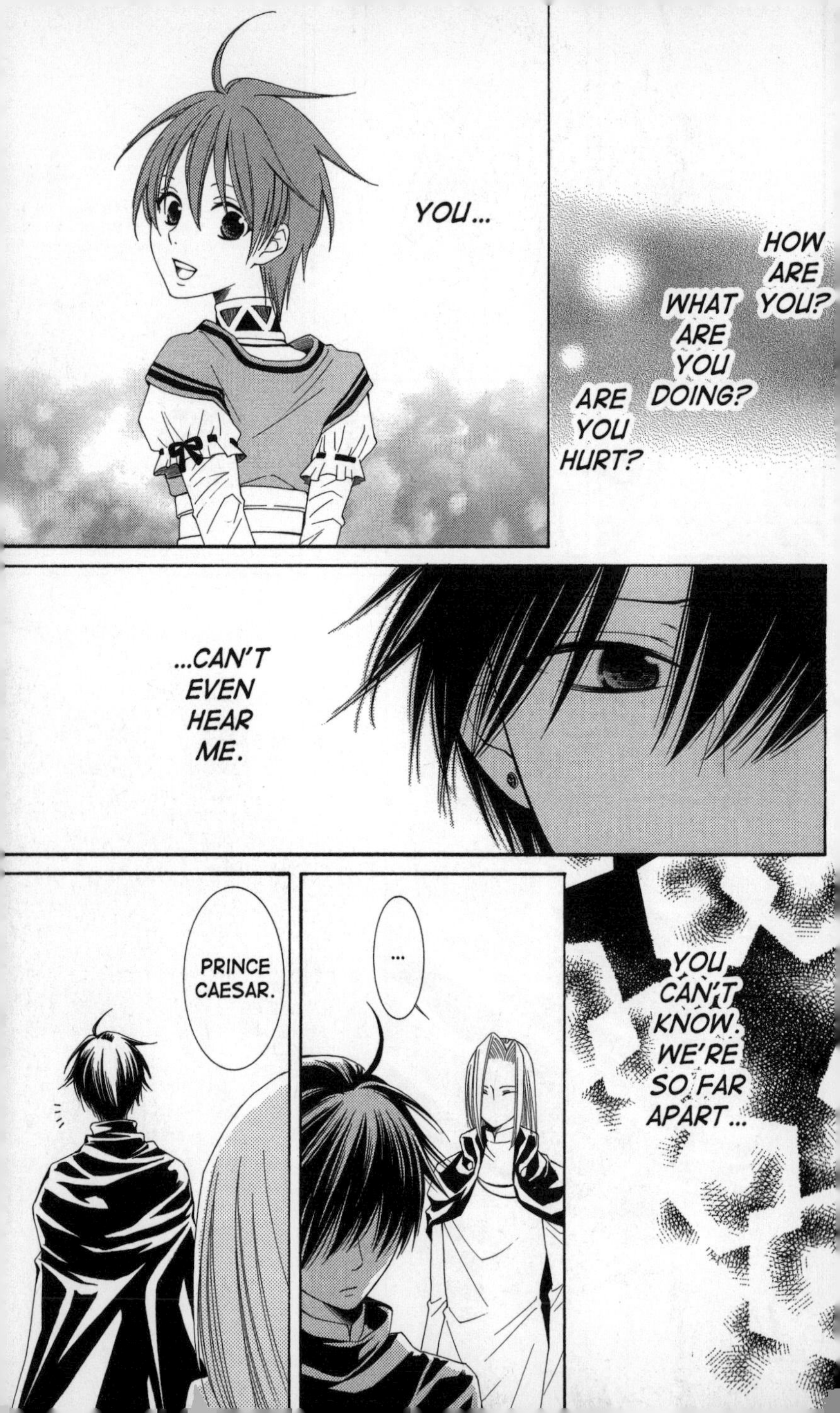
HOW ARE YOU?
WHAT ARE YOU DOING?
ARE YOU HURT?
YOU...
...CAN'T EVEN HEAR ME.
YOU CAN'T KNOW. WE'RE SO FAR APART...
...
PRINCE CAESAR.

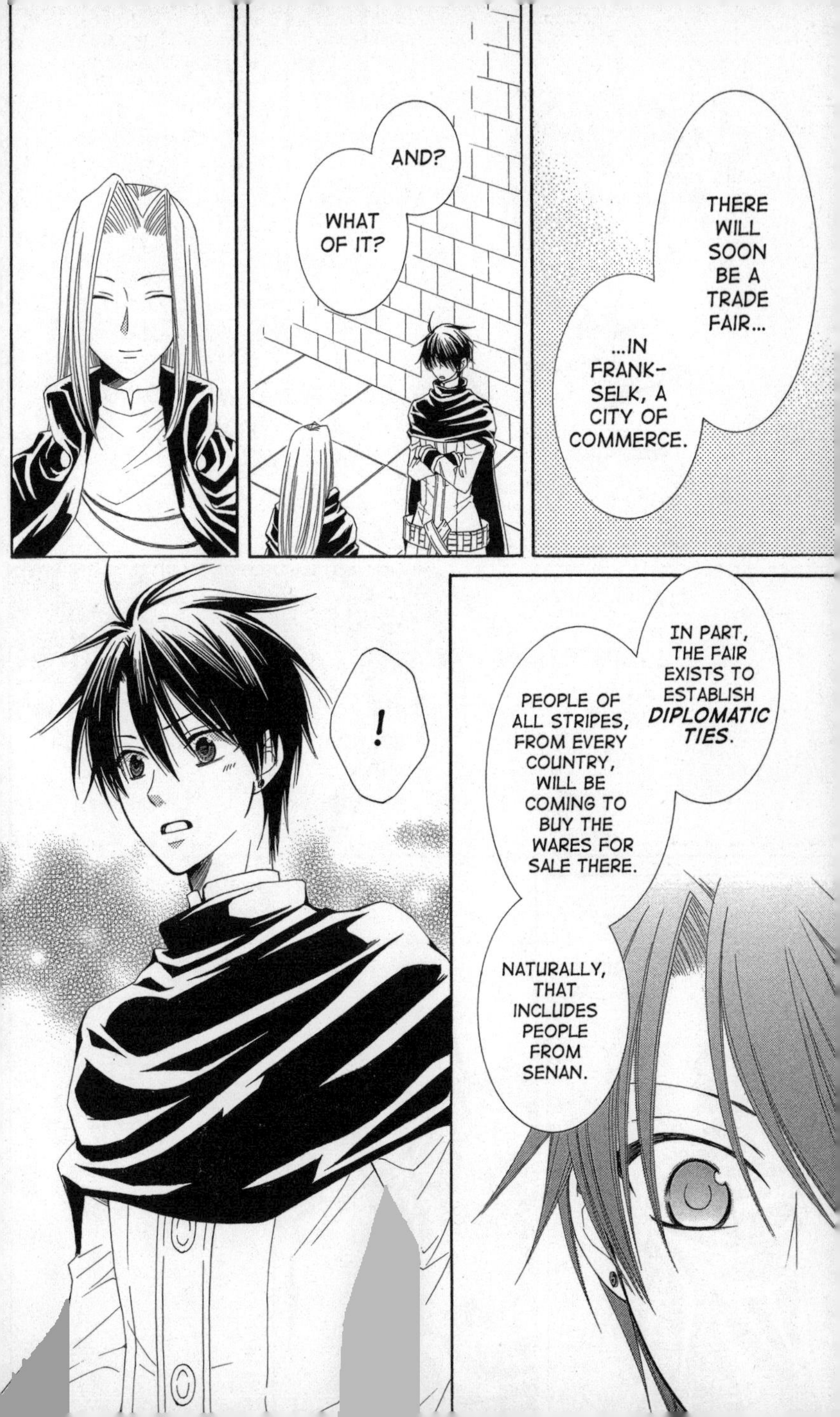
THERE WILL SOON BE A TRADE FAIR...
...IN FRANK-SELK, A CITY OF COMMERCE.
AND?
WHAT OF IT?
IN PART, THE FAIR EXISTS TO ESTABLISH *DIPLOMATIC TIES*.
PEOPLE OF ALL STRIPES, FROM EVERY COUNTRY, WILL BE COMING TO BUY THE WARES FOR SALE THERE.
NATURALLY, THAT INCLUDES PEOPLE FROM SENAN.
!

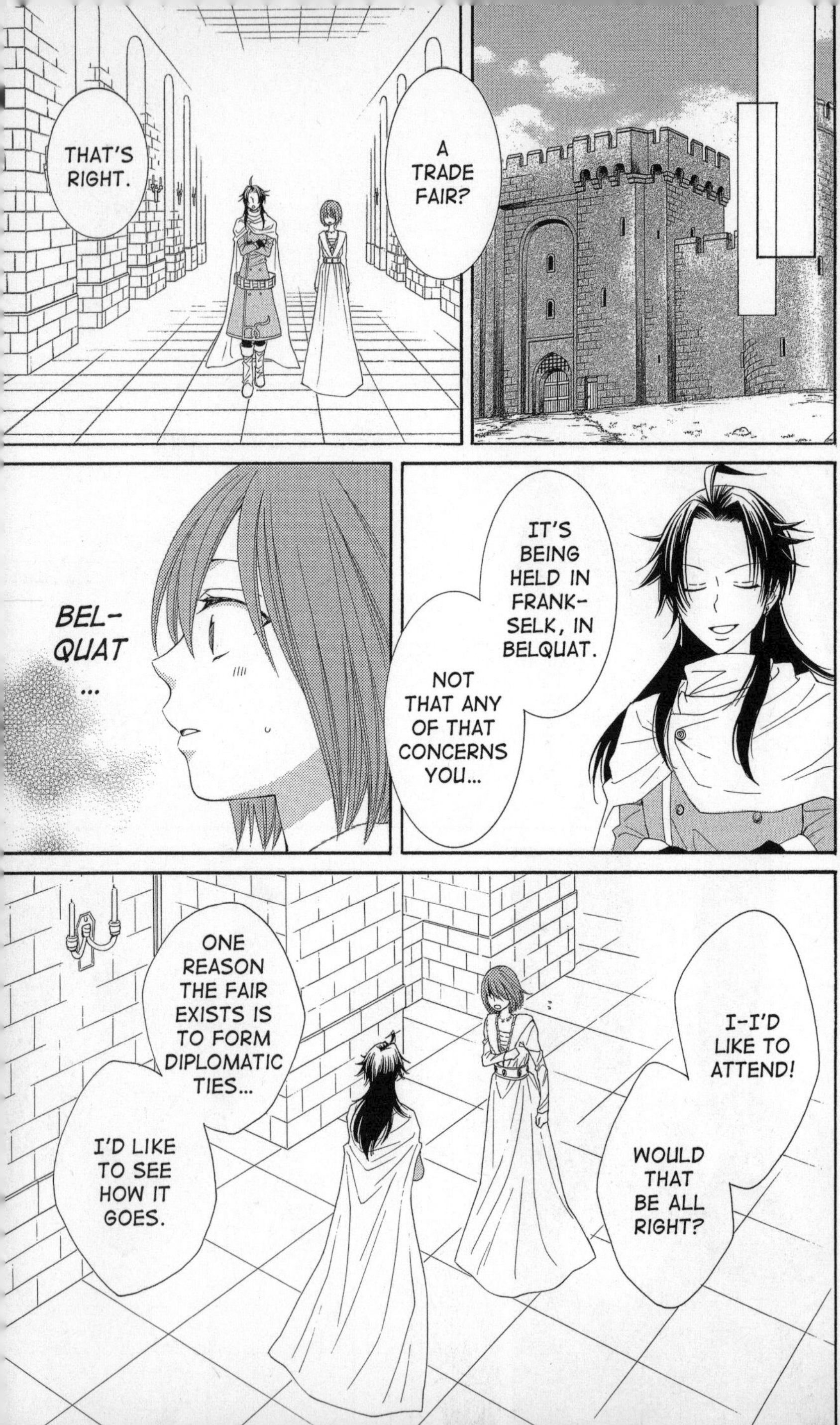
A TRADE FAIR?
THAT'S RIGHT.
IT'S BEING HELD IN FRANK-SELK, IN BELQUAT.
NOT THAT ANY OF THAT CONCERNS YOU...
BEL-QUAT ...
I-I'D LIKE TO ATTEND!
WOULD THAT BE ALL RIGHT?
ONE REASON THE FAIR EXISTS IS TO FORM DIPLOMATIC TIES...
I'D LIKE TO SEE HOW IT GOES.

PLEASE, ADEL.

SINCE YOU'RE SO PASSIONATE, I MIGHT CONSIDER IT.

W-WELL ...

PLEEEASE.

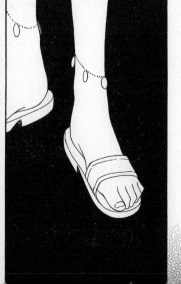

THANK YOU, ADEL!

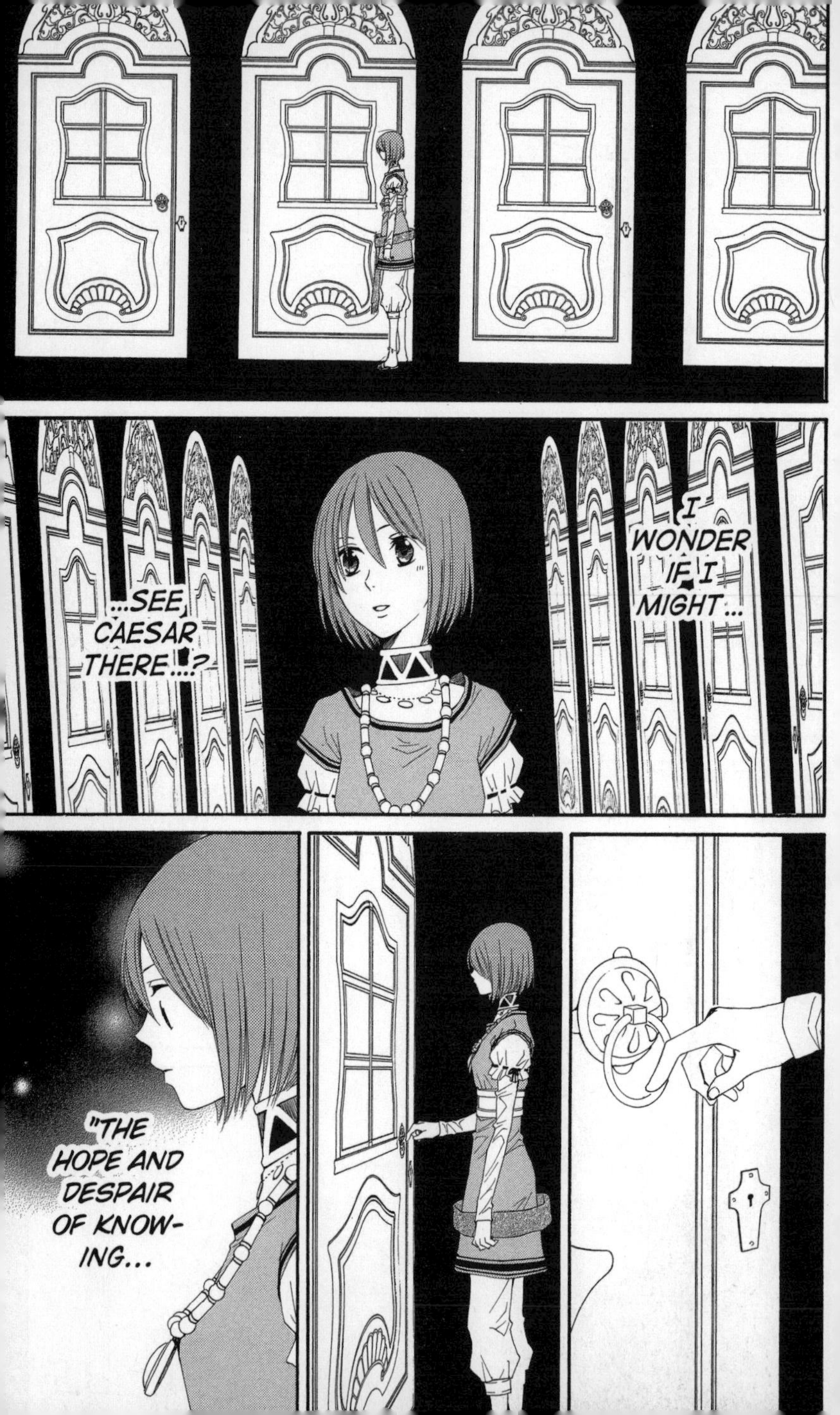
I WONDER IF I MIGHT...
...SEE CAESAR THERE...?
"THE HOPE AND DESPAIR OF KNOW-ING...

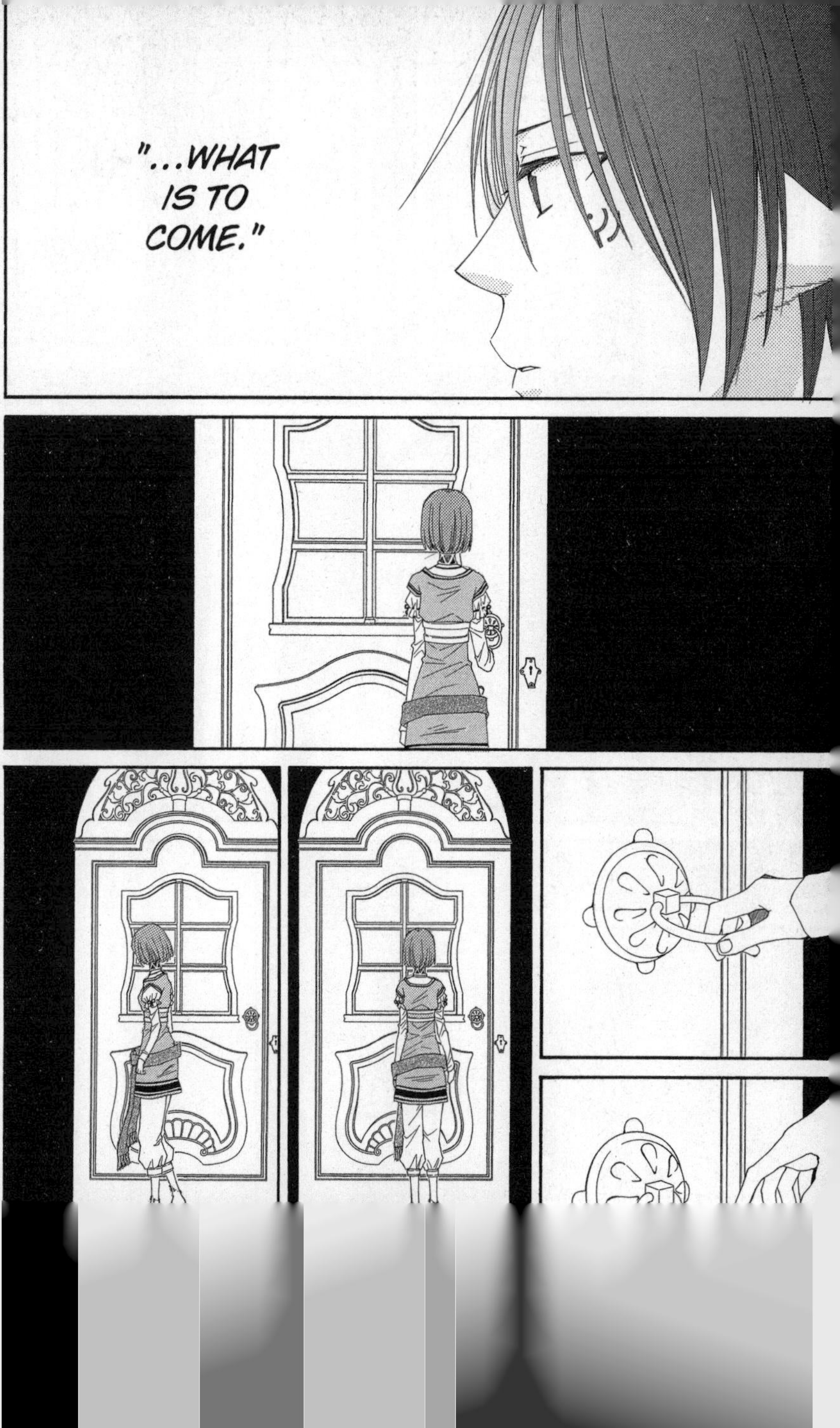
"...WHAT IS TO COME."

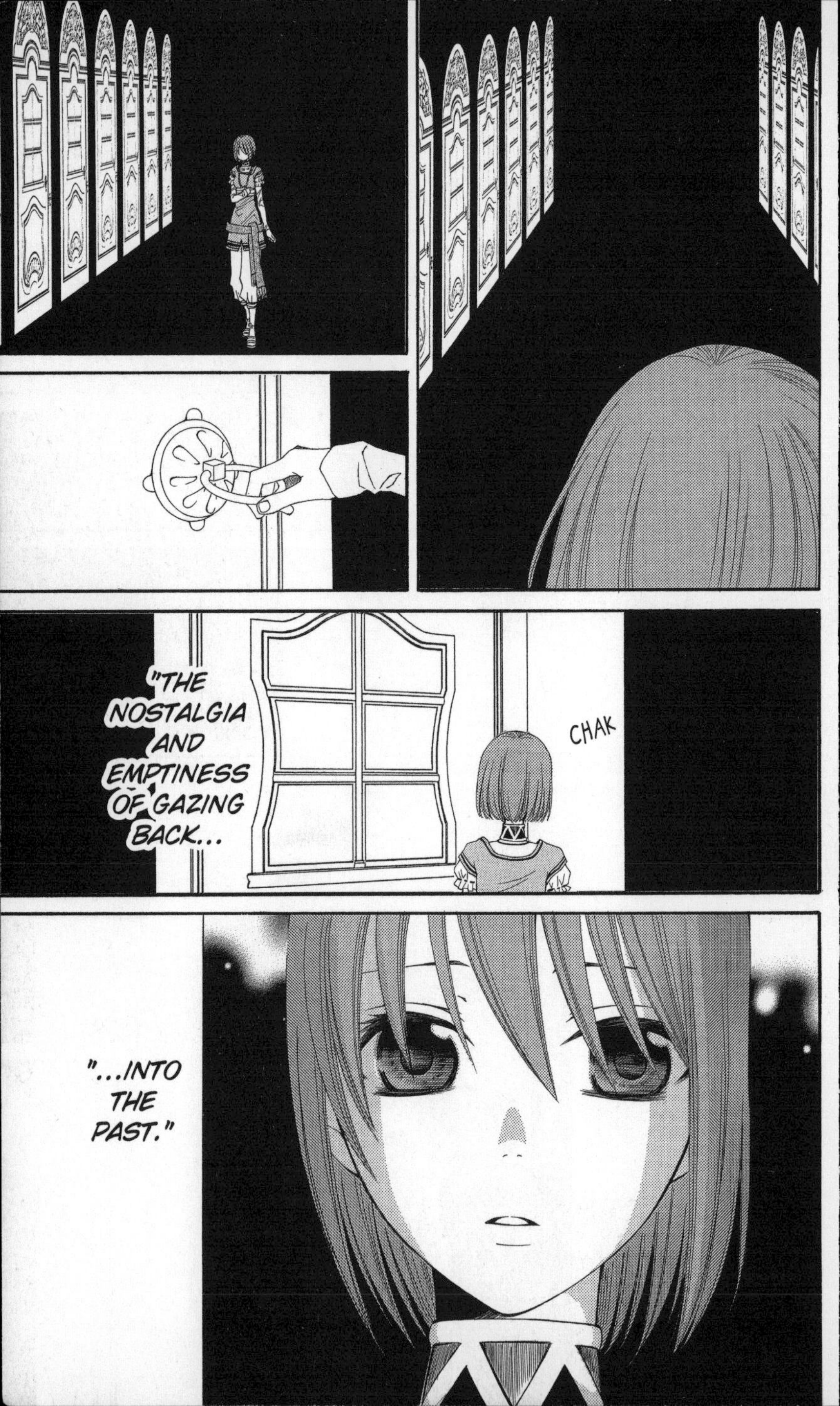
"THE NOSTALGIA AND EMPTINESS OF GAZING BACK...
CHAK
"...INTO THE PAST."

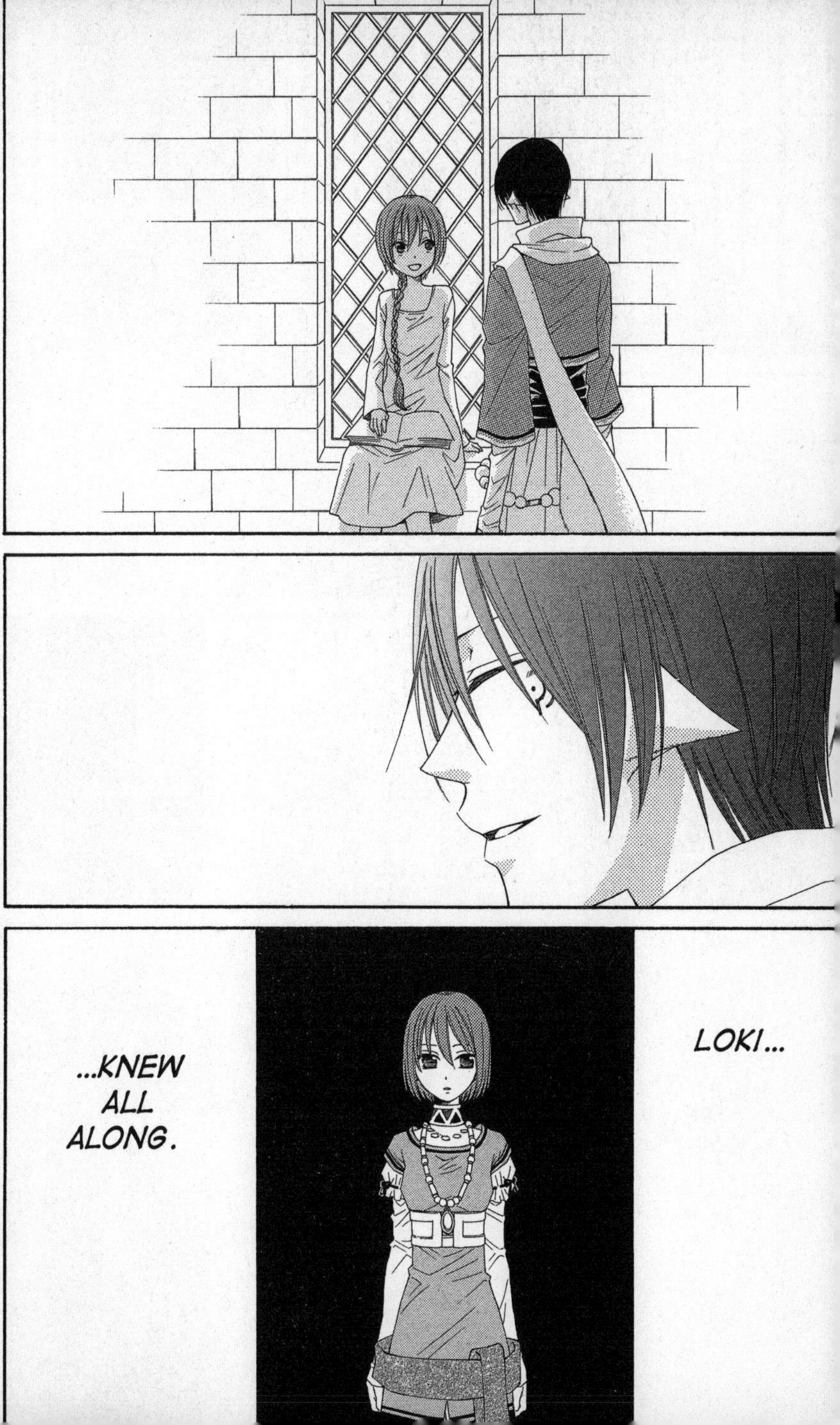
LOKI...
...KNEW ALL ALONG.

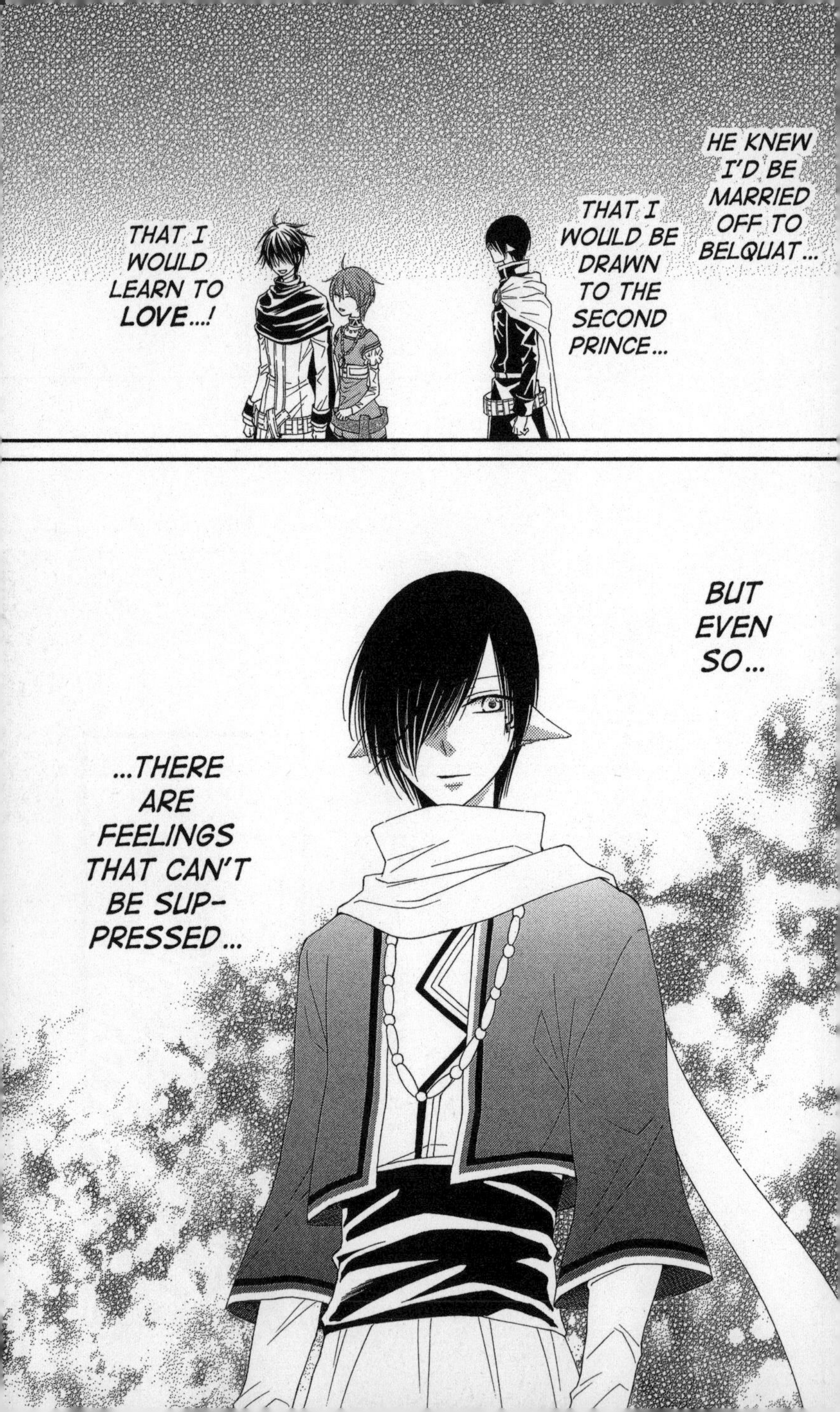
HE KNEW I'D BE MARRIED OFF TO BELQUAT...
THAT I WOULD BE DRAWN TO THE SECOND PRINCE...
THAT I WOULD LEARN TO LOVE...!
BUT EVEN SO...
...THERE ARE FEELINGS THAT CAN'T BE SUP-PRESSED...

Chapter 43

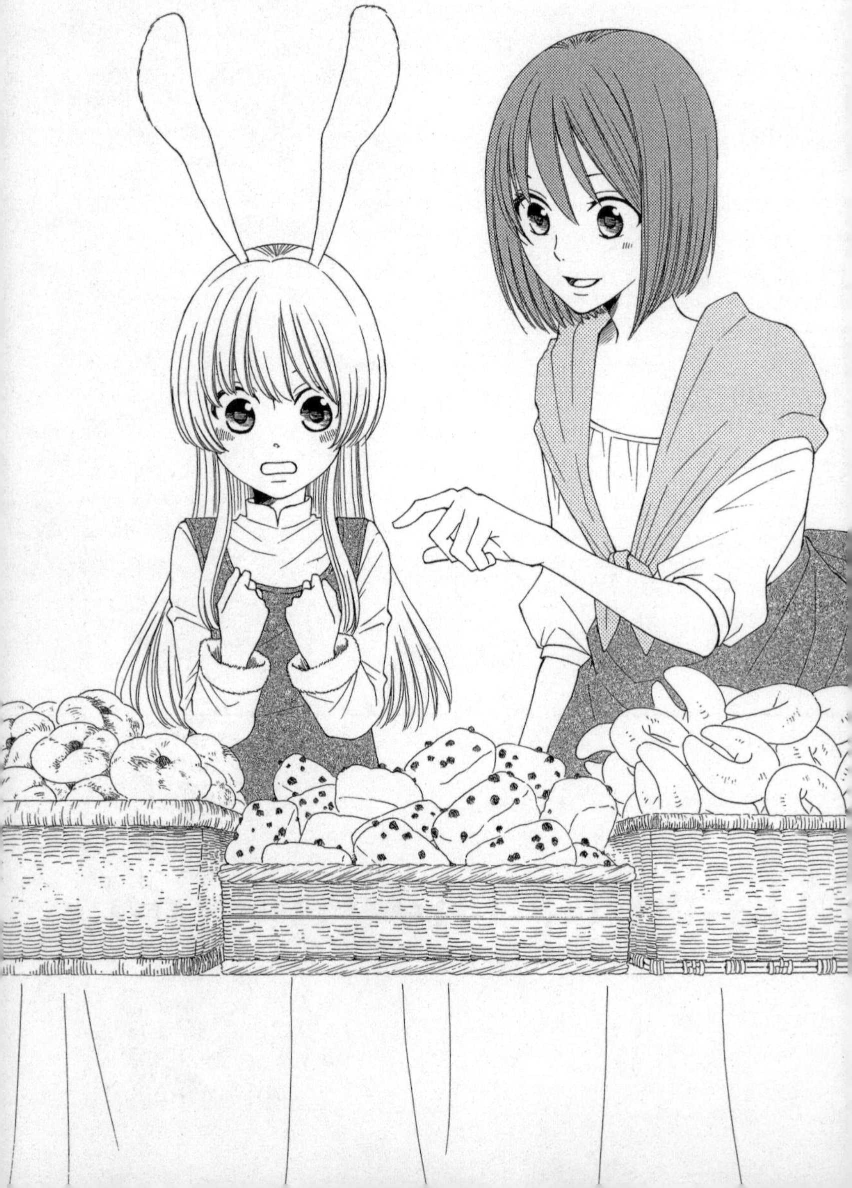

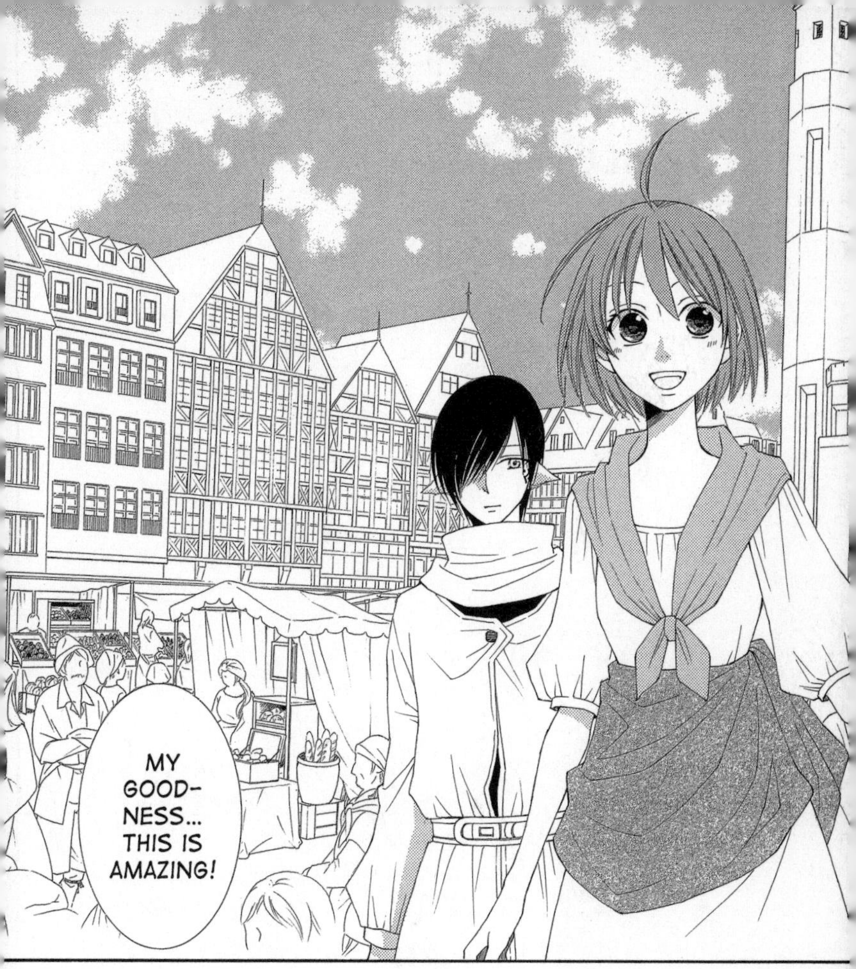
MY GOOD-NESS... THIS IS AMAZING!

Dawn of the Arcana

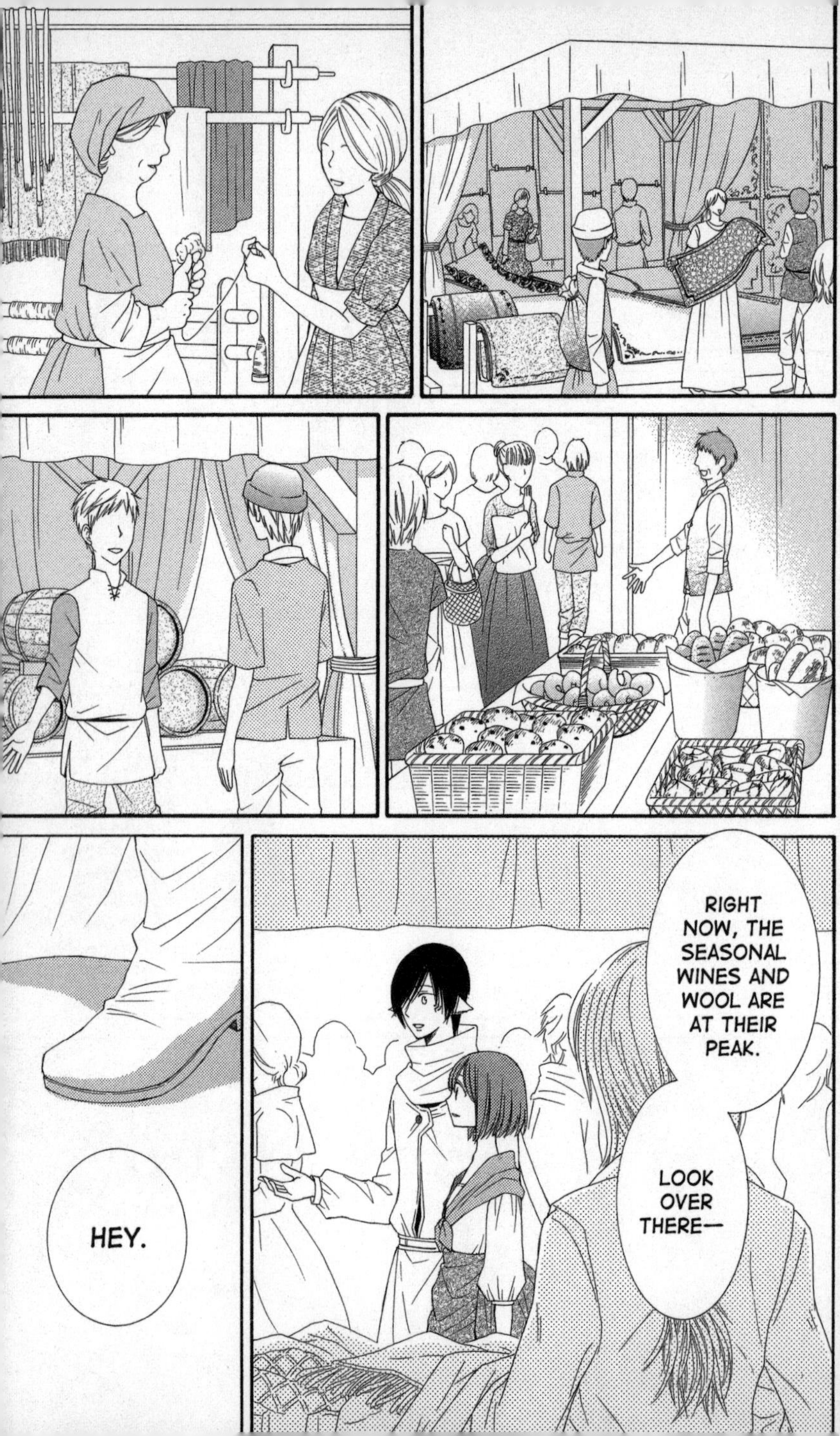
RIGHT NOW, THE SEASONAL WINES AND WOOL ARE AT THEIR PEAK.
LOOK OVER THERE—
HEY.

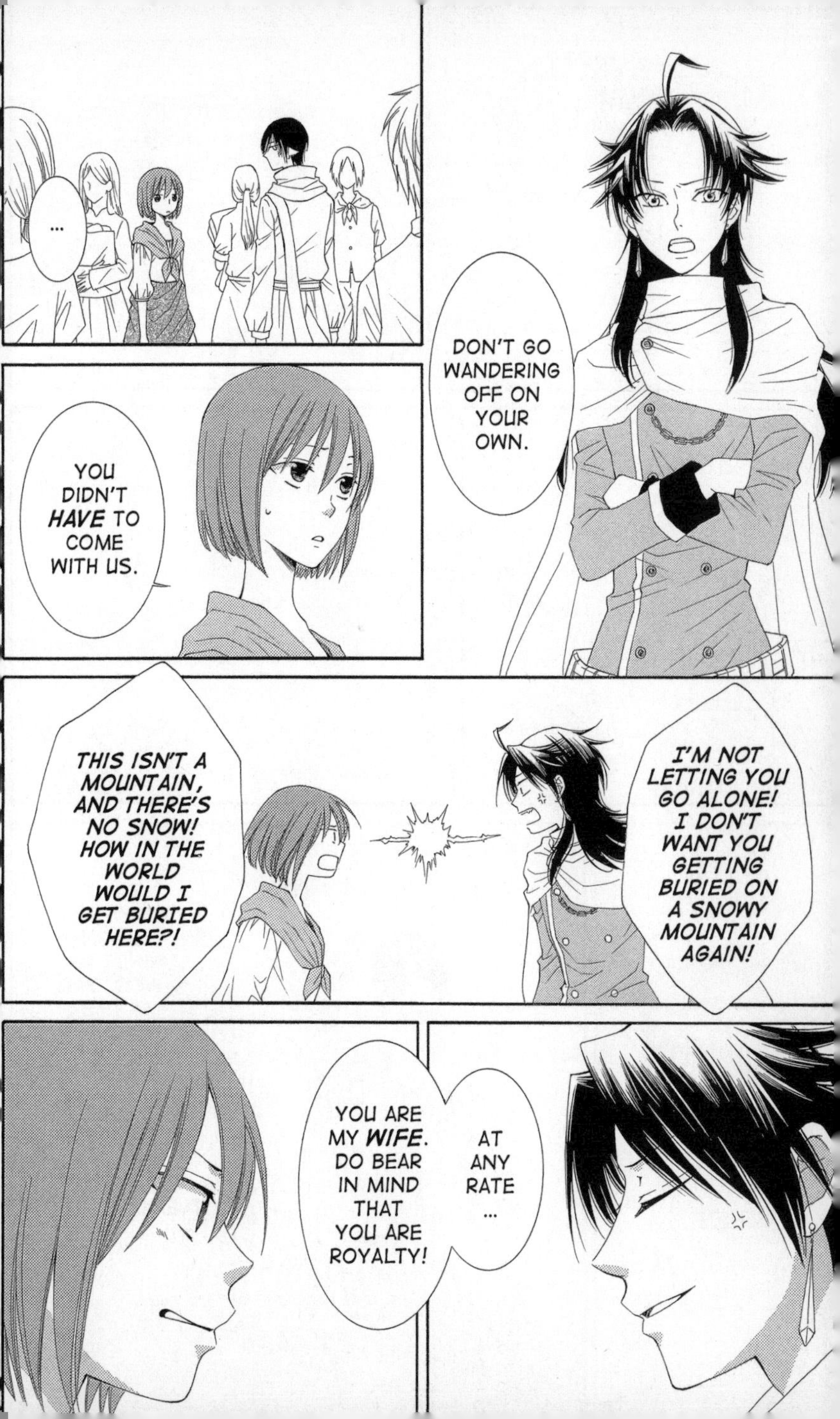
DON'T GO WANDERING OFF ON YOUR OWN.
...
YOU DIDN'T *HAVE* TO COME WITH US.
I'M NOT LETTING YOU GO ALONE! I DON'T WANT YOU GETTING BURIED ON A SNOWY MOUNTAIN AGAIN!
THIS ISN'T A MOUNTAIN, AND THERE'S NO SNOW! HOW IN THE WORLD WOULD I GET BURIED HERE?!
AT ANY RATE ...
YOU ARE MY ***WIFE***. DO BEAR IN MIND THAT YOU ARE ROYALTY!

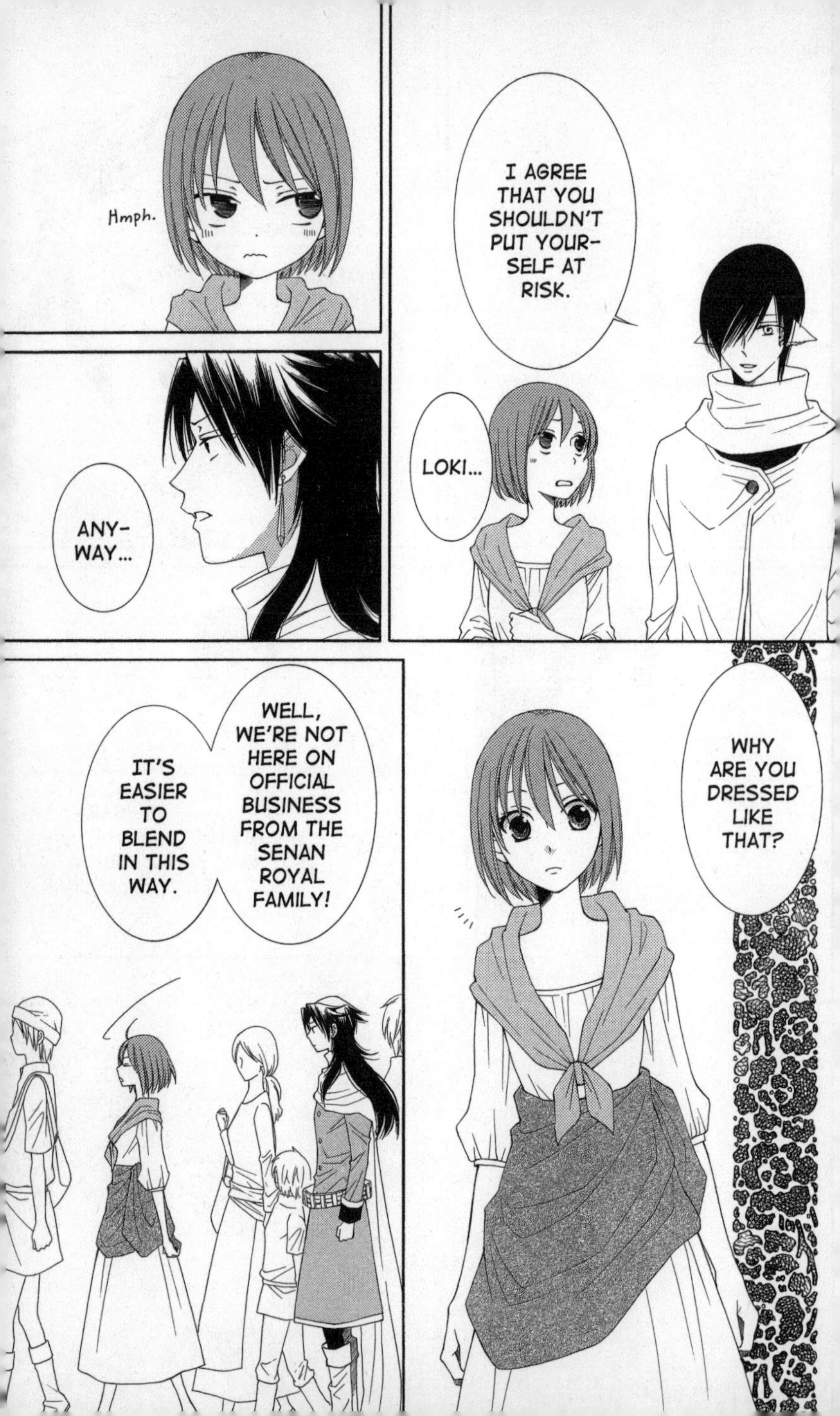
I AGREE THAT YOU SHOULDN'T PUT YOUR-SELF AT RISK.
LOKI...
Hmph.
ANY-WAY...
WHY ARE YOU DRESSED LIKE THAT?
WELL, WE'RE NOT HERE ON OFFICIAL BUSINESS FROM THE SENAN ROYAL FAMILY!
IT'S EASIER TO BLEND IN THIS WAY.

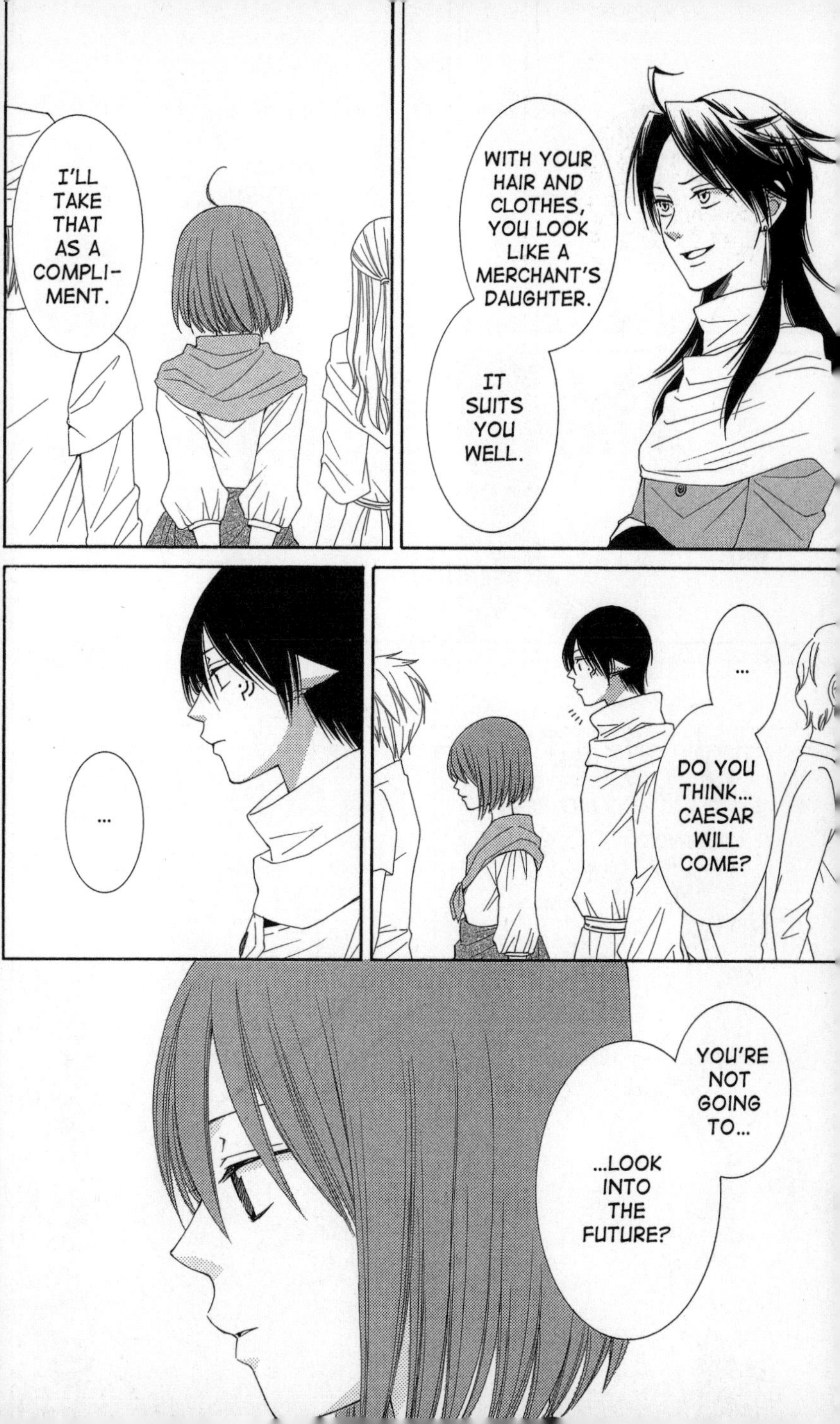
WITH YOUR HAIR AND CLOTHES, YOU LOOK LIKE A MERCHANT'S DAUGHTER.
IT SUITS YOU WELL.
I'LL TAKE THAT AS A COMPLIMENT.
...
DO YOU THINK... CAESAR WILL COME?
...
YOU'RE NOT GOING TO...
...LOOK INTO THE FUTURE?

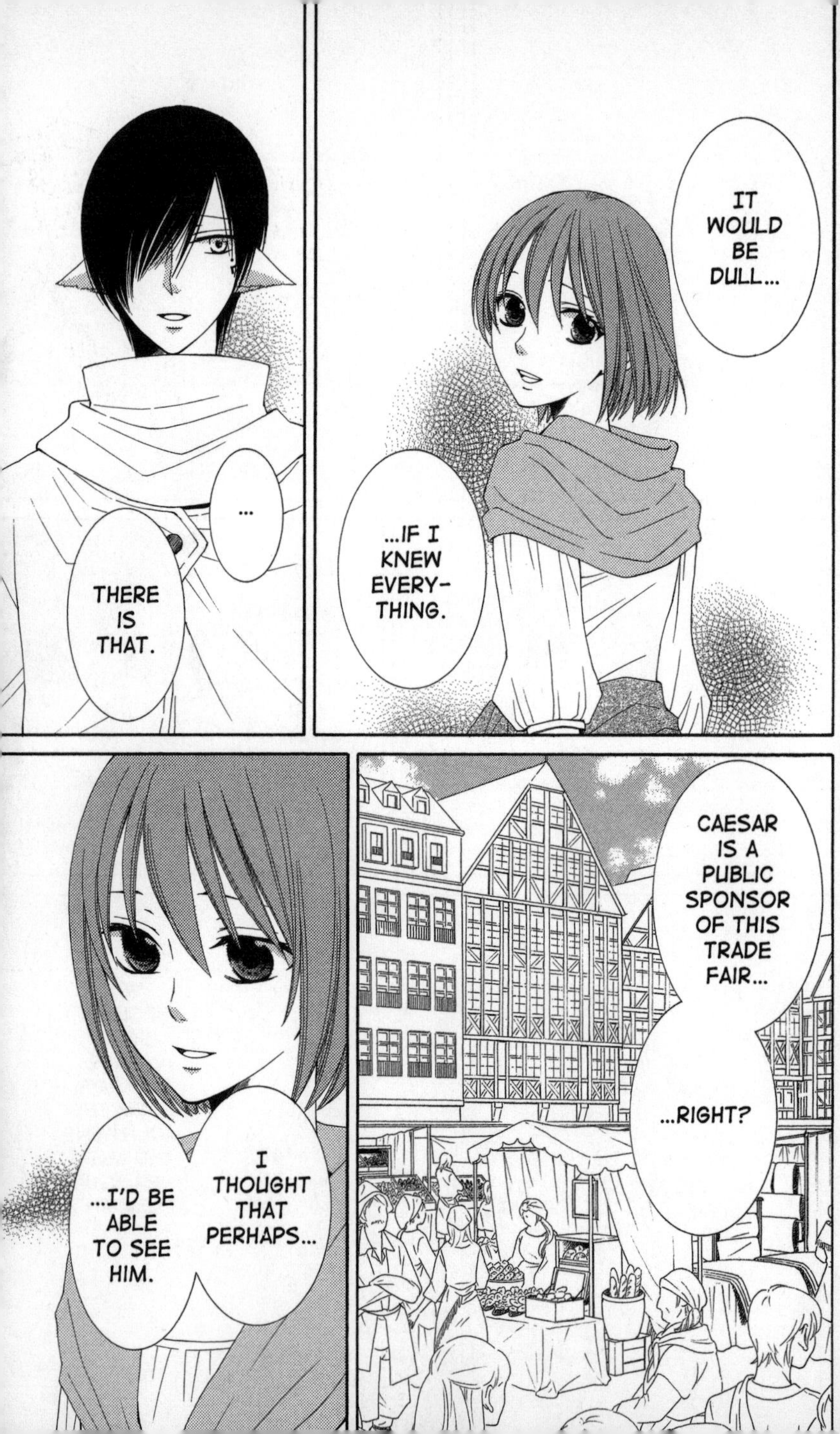
IT WOULD BE DULL...
...IF I KNEW EVERY-THING.
...
THERE IS THAT.
CAESAR IS A PUBLIC SPONSOR OF THIS TRADE FAIR...
...RIGHT?
I THOUGHT THAT PERHAPS...
...I'D BE ABLE TO SEE HIM.

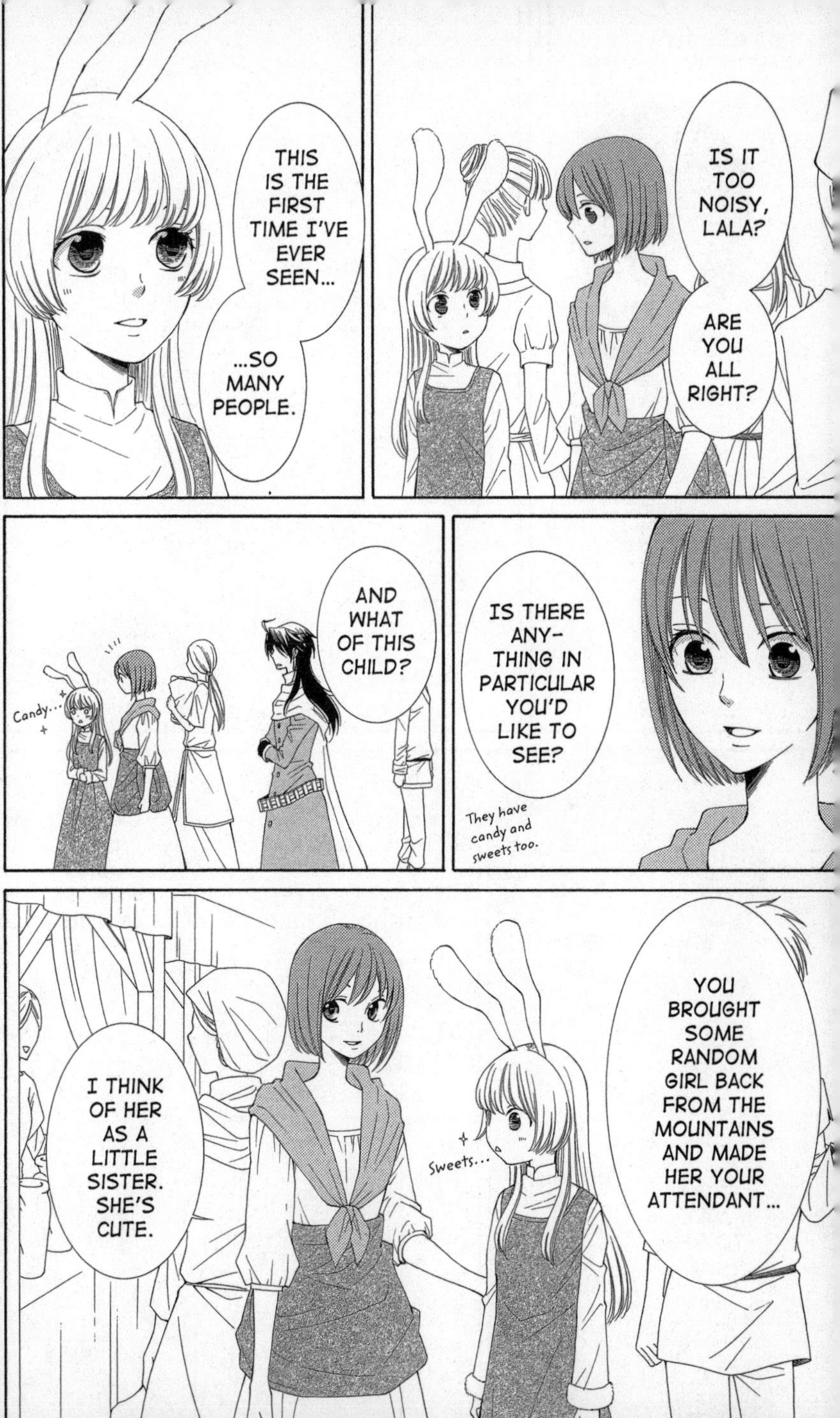
IS IT TOO NOISY, LALA?
ARE YOU ALL RIGHT?
THIS IS THE FIRST TIME I'VE EVER SEEN...
...SO MANY PEOPLE.
IS THERE ANY-THING IN PARTICULAR YOU'D LIKE TO SEE?
They have candy and sweets too.
AND WHAT OF THIS CHILD?
Candy...
YOU BROUGHT SOME RANDOM GIRL BACK FROM THE MOUNTAINS AND MADE HER YOUR ATTENDANT...
Sweets...
I THINK OF HER AS A LITTLE SISTER. SHE'S CUTE.

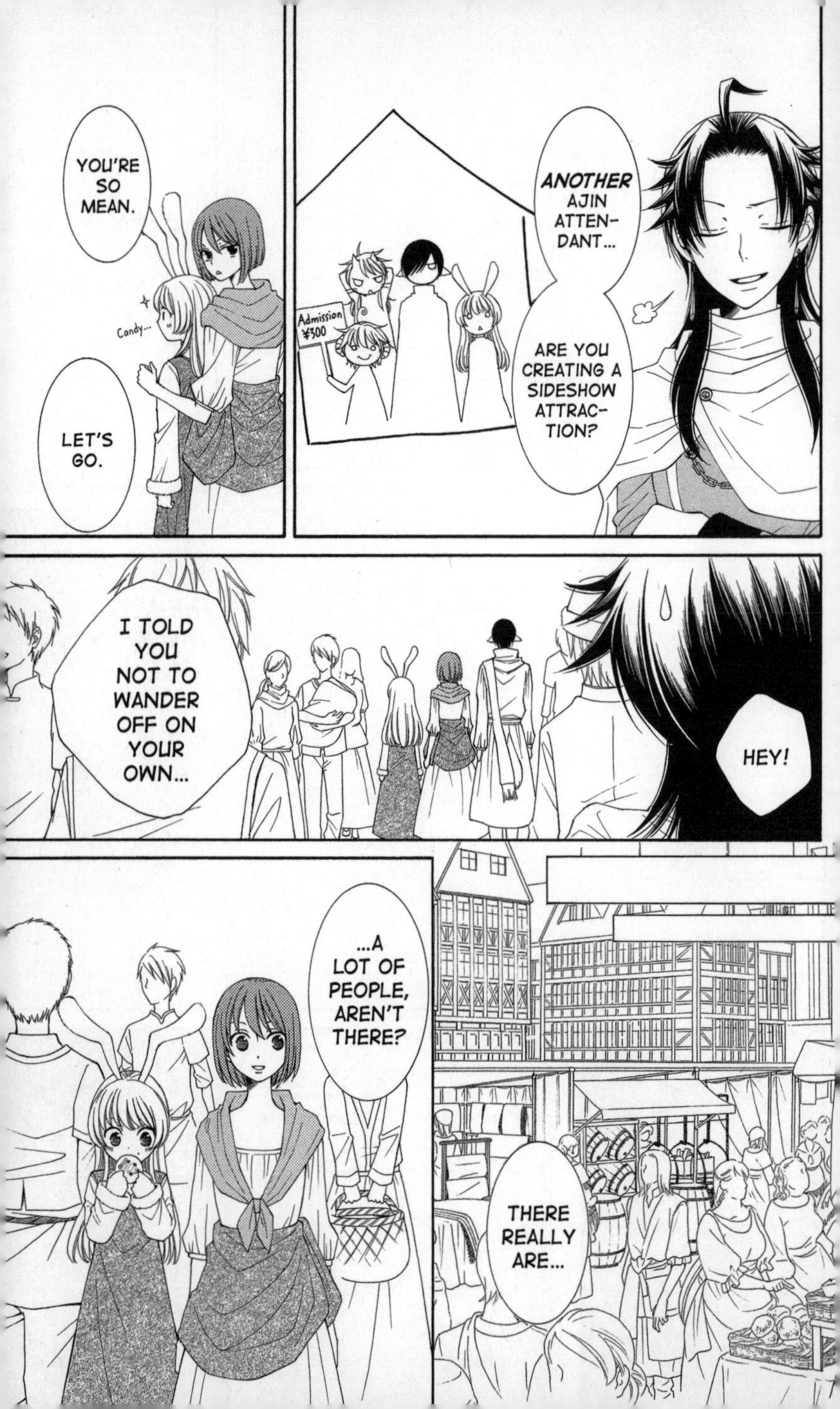
ANOTHER AJIN ATTENDANT...
Admission ¥300
ARE YOU CREATING A SIDESHOW ATTRACTION?
YOU'RE SO MEAN.
Candy...
LET'S GO.
HEY!
I TOLD YOU NOT TO WANDER OFF ON YOUR OWN...
THERE REALLY ARE...
...A LOT OF PEOPLE, AREN'T THERE?

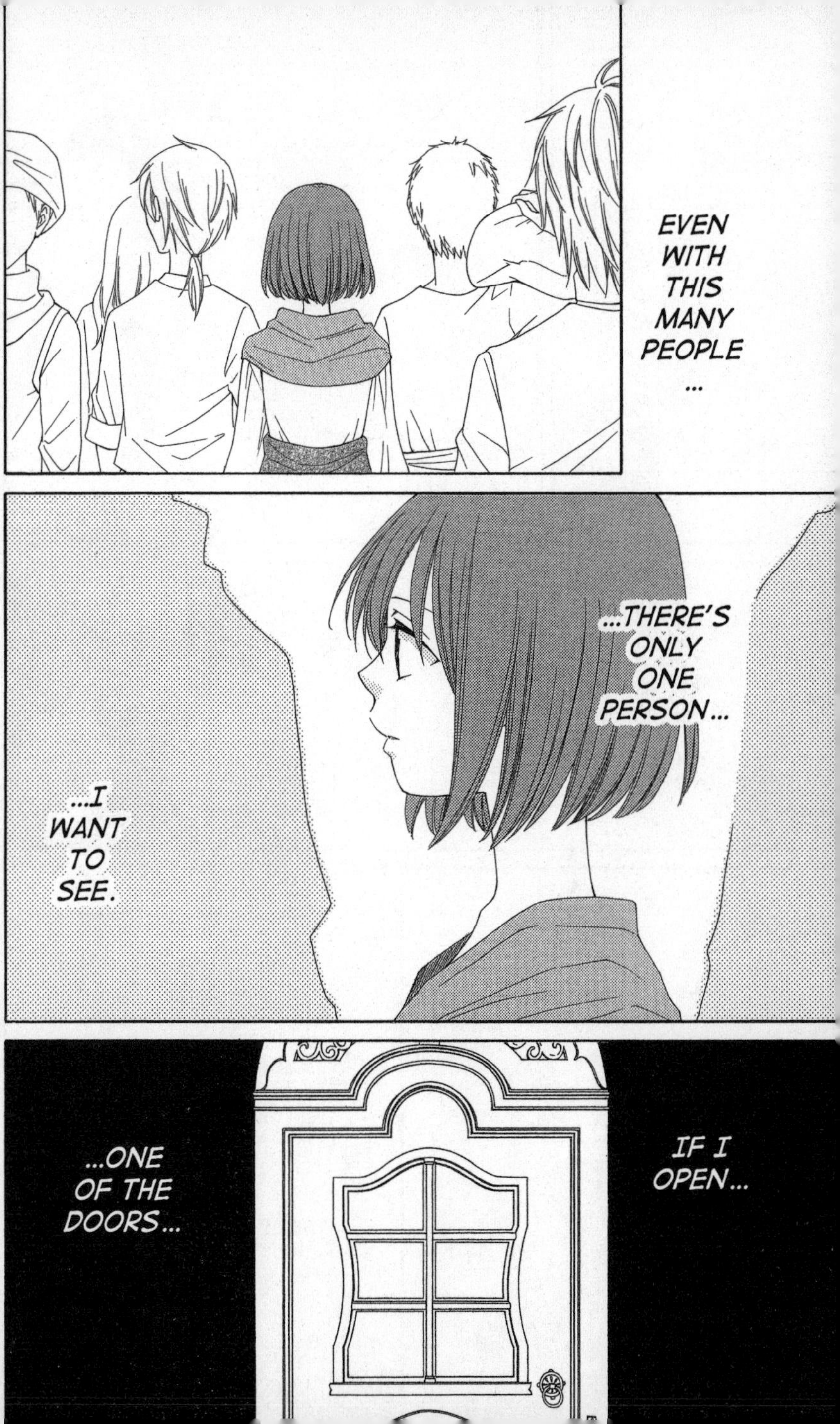
EVEN WITH THIS MANY PEOPLE ...
...THERE'S ONLY ONE PERSON...
...I WANT TO SEE.
IF I OPEN...
...ONE OF THE DOORS...

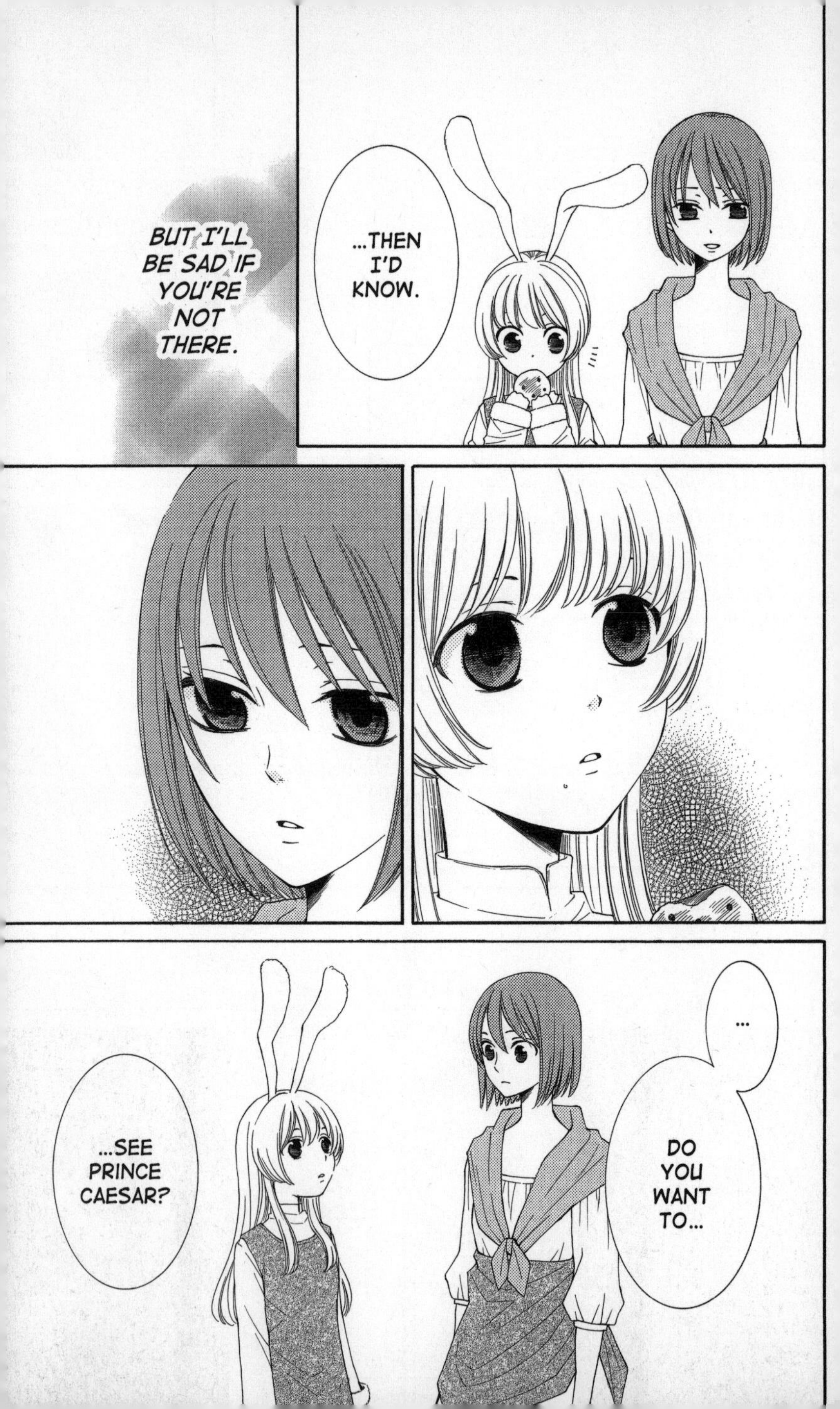
...THEN I'D KNOW.
BUT I'LL BE SAD IF YOU'RE NOT THERE.
...
DO YOU WANT TO...
...SEE PRINCE CAESAR?

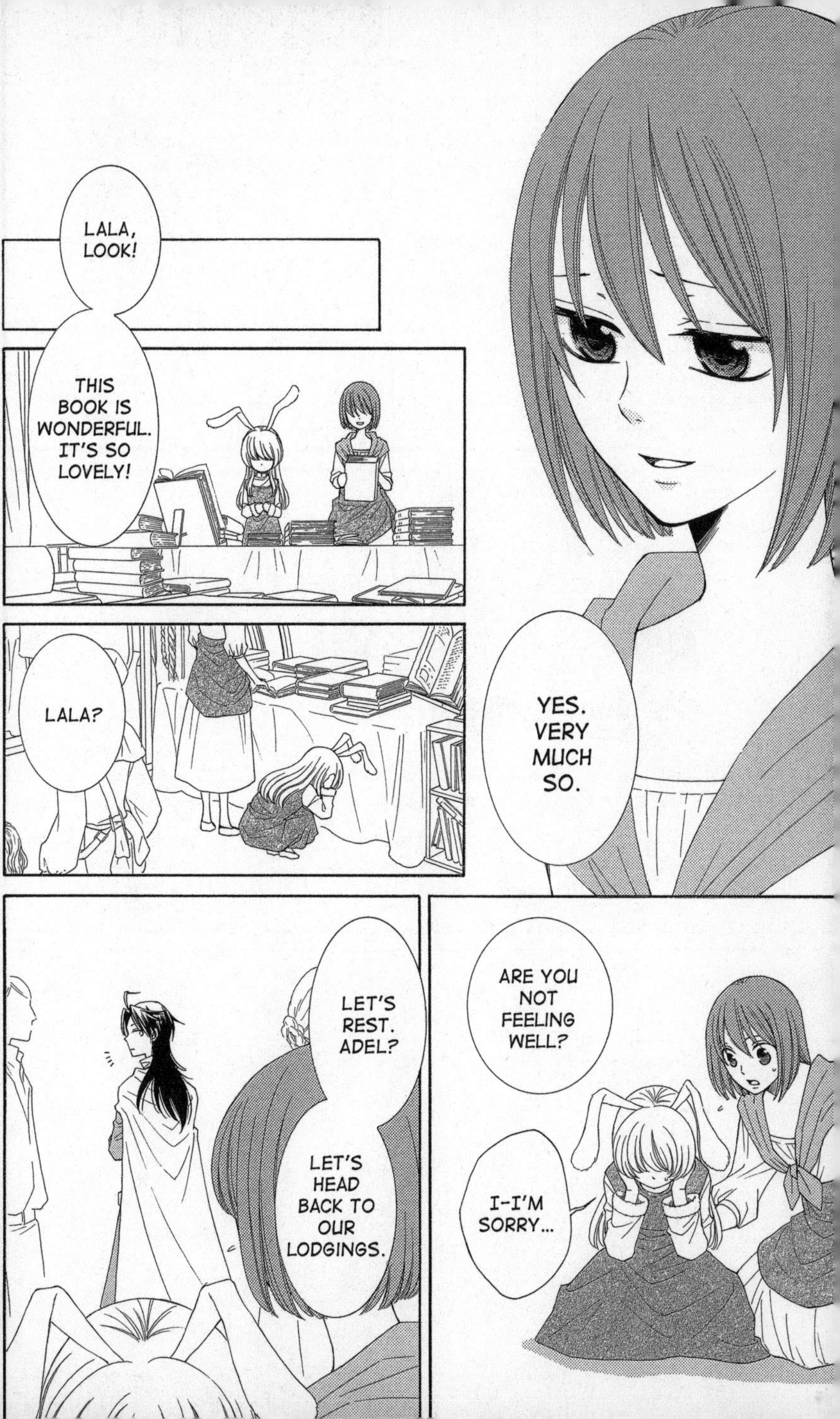
YES. VERY MUCH SO.
LALA, LOOK!
THIS BOOK IS WONDERFUL. IT'S SO LOVELY!
LALA?
ARE YOU NOT FEELING WELL?
I-I'M SORRY...
LET'S REST. ADEL?
LET'S HEAD BACK TO OUR LODGINGS.

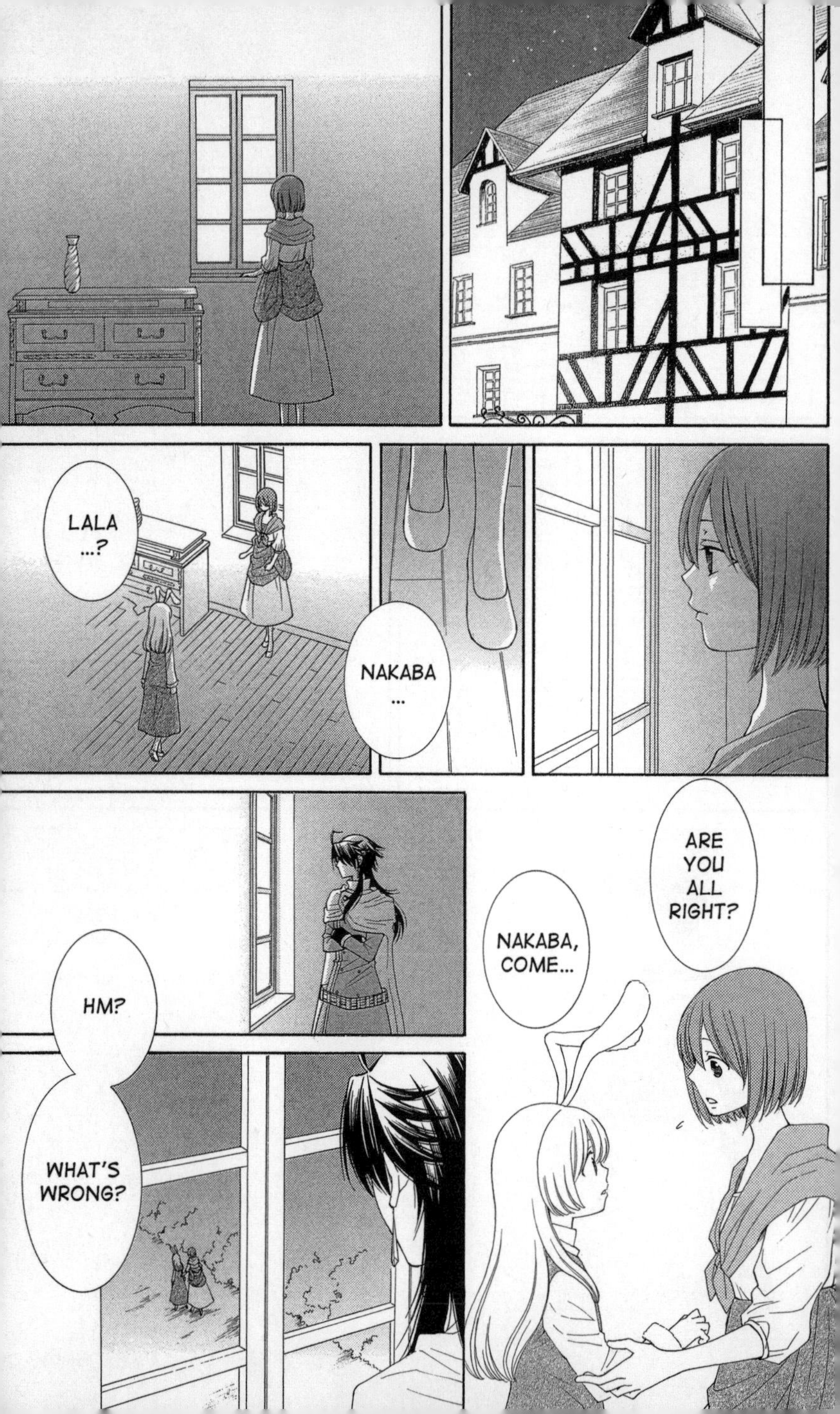
NAKABA ...
LALA ...?
ARE YOU ALL RIGHT?
NAKABA, COME...
HM?
WHAT'S WRONG?

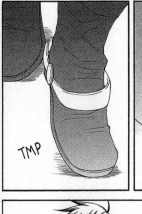

CHAK

TMP

WELCOME, YOUR ROYAL HIGHNESS!

WE'RE DELIGHTED YOU COULD MAKE THE TRIP HERE.

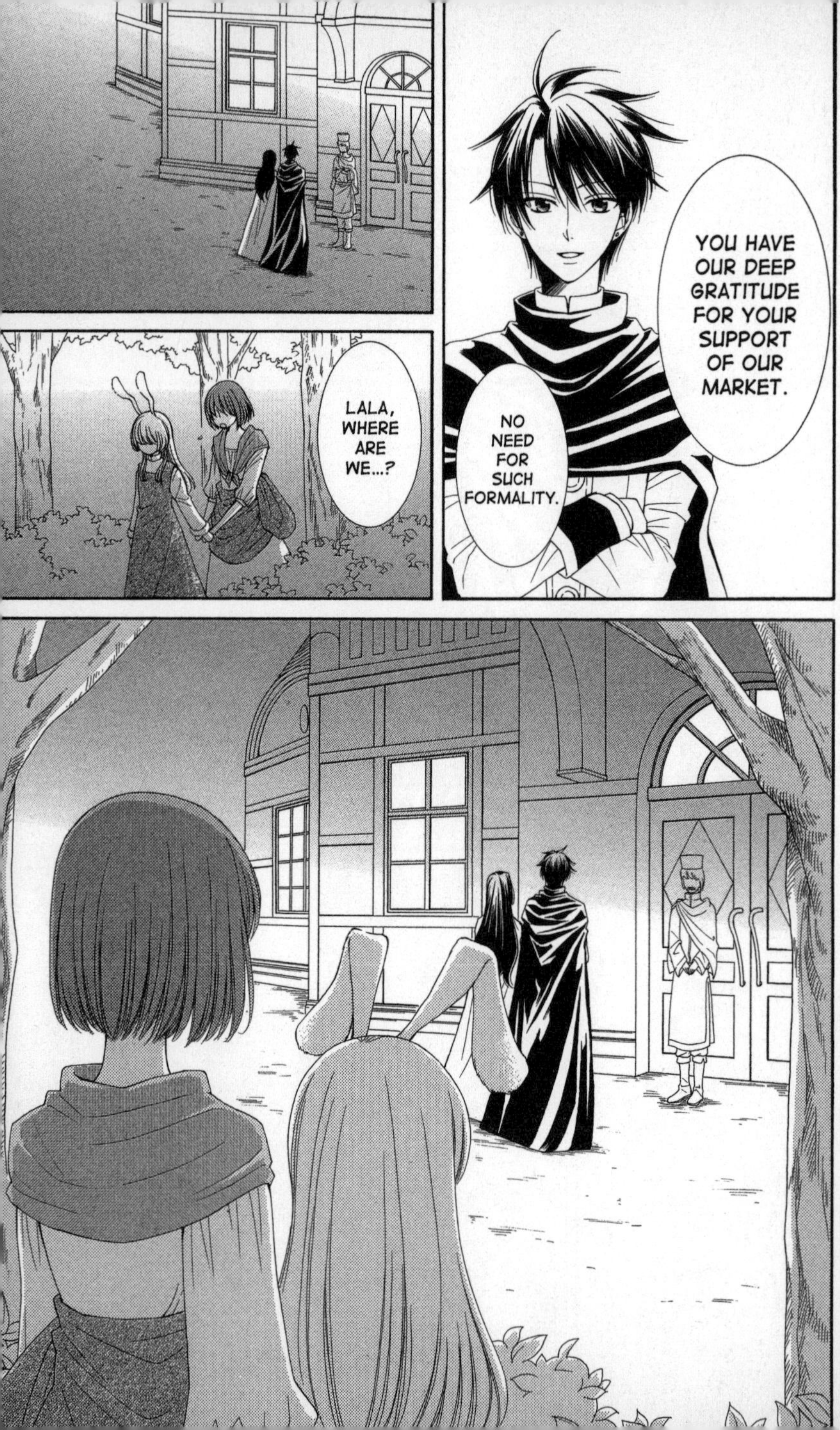
YOU HAVE OUR DEEP GRATITUDE FOR YOUR SUPPORT OF OUR MARKET.
NO NEED FOR SUCH FORMALITY.
LALA, WHERE ARE WE...?

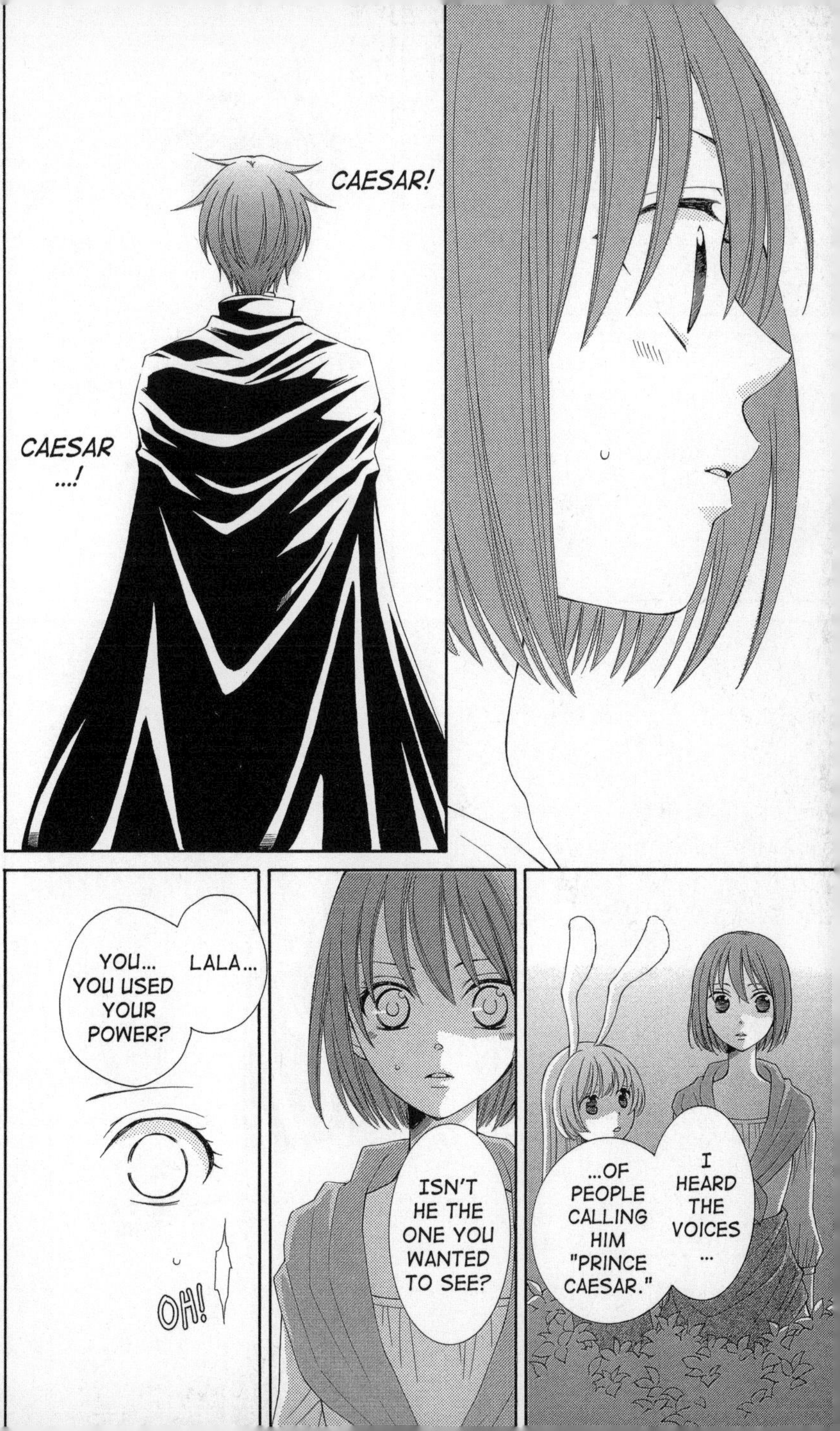
CAESAR!
CAESAR ...!
I HEARD THE VOICES ...
...OF PEOPLE CALLING HIM "PRINCE CAESAR."
ISN'T HE THE ONE YOU WANTED TO SEE?
LALA...
YOU... YOU USED YOUR POWER?
OH!

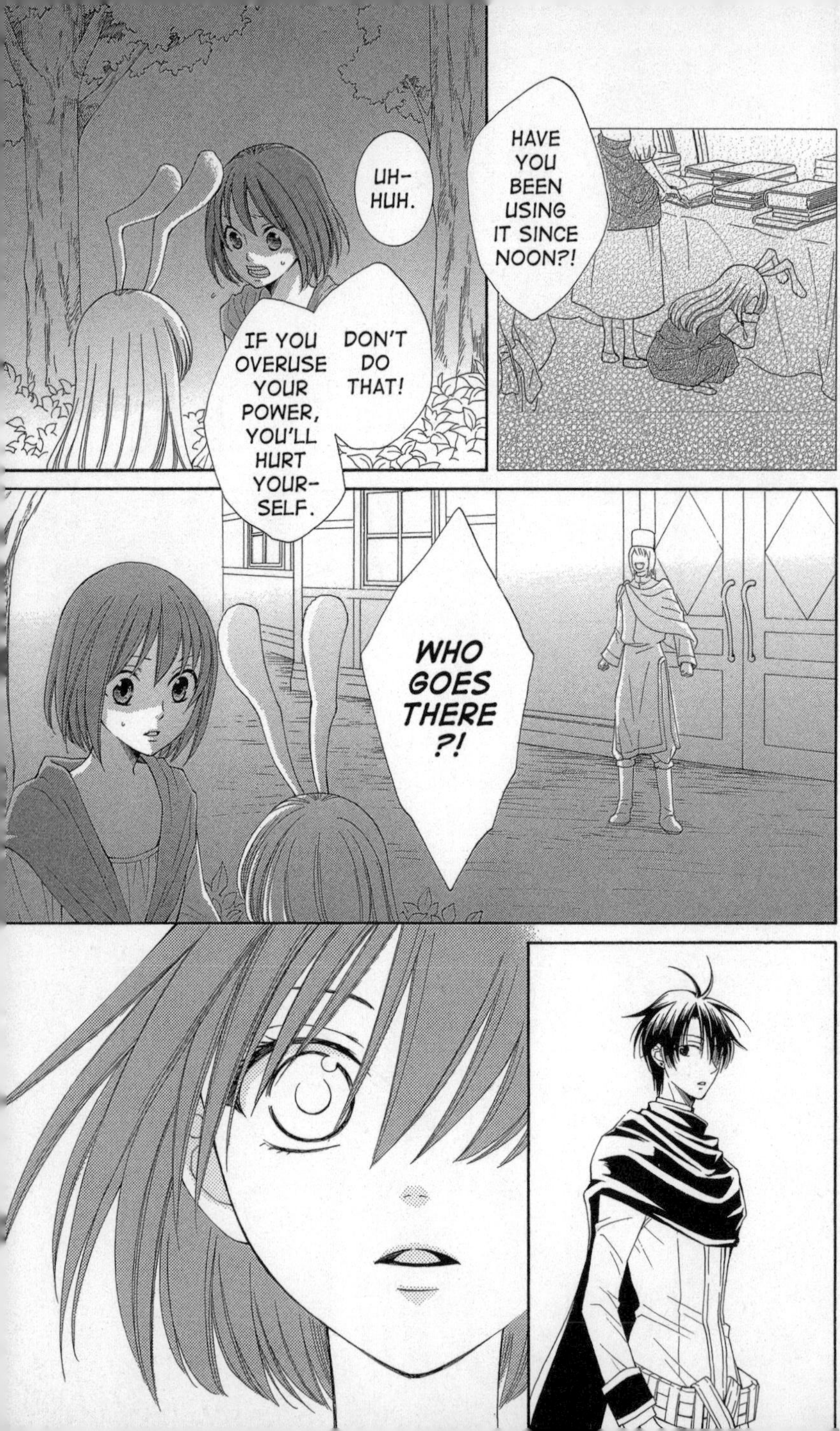
HAVE YOU BEEN USING IT SINCE NOON?!
UH-HUH.
DON'T DO THAT!
IF YOU OVERUSE YOUR POWER, YOU'LL HURT YOUR-SELF.
WHO GOES THERE?!

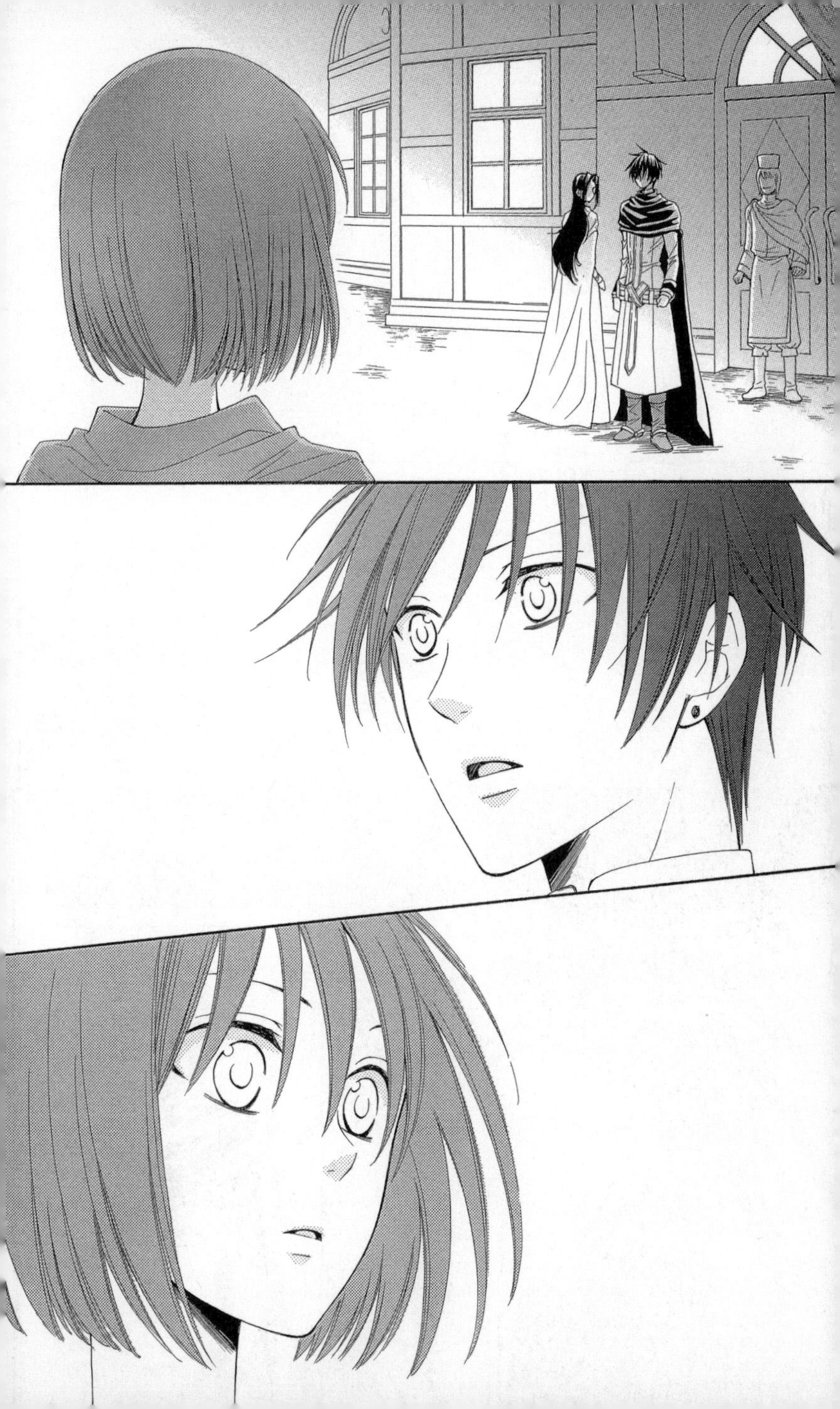

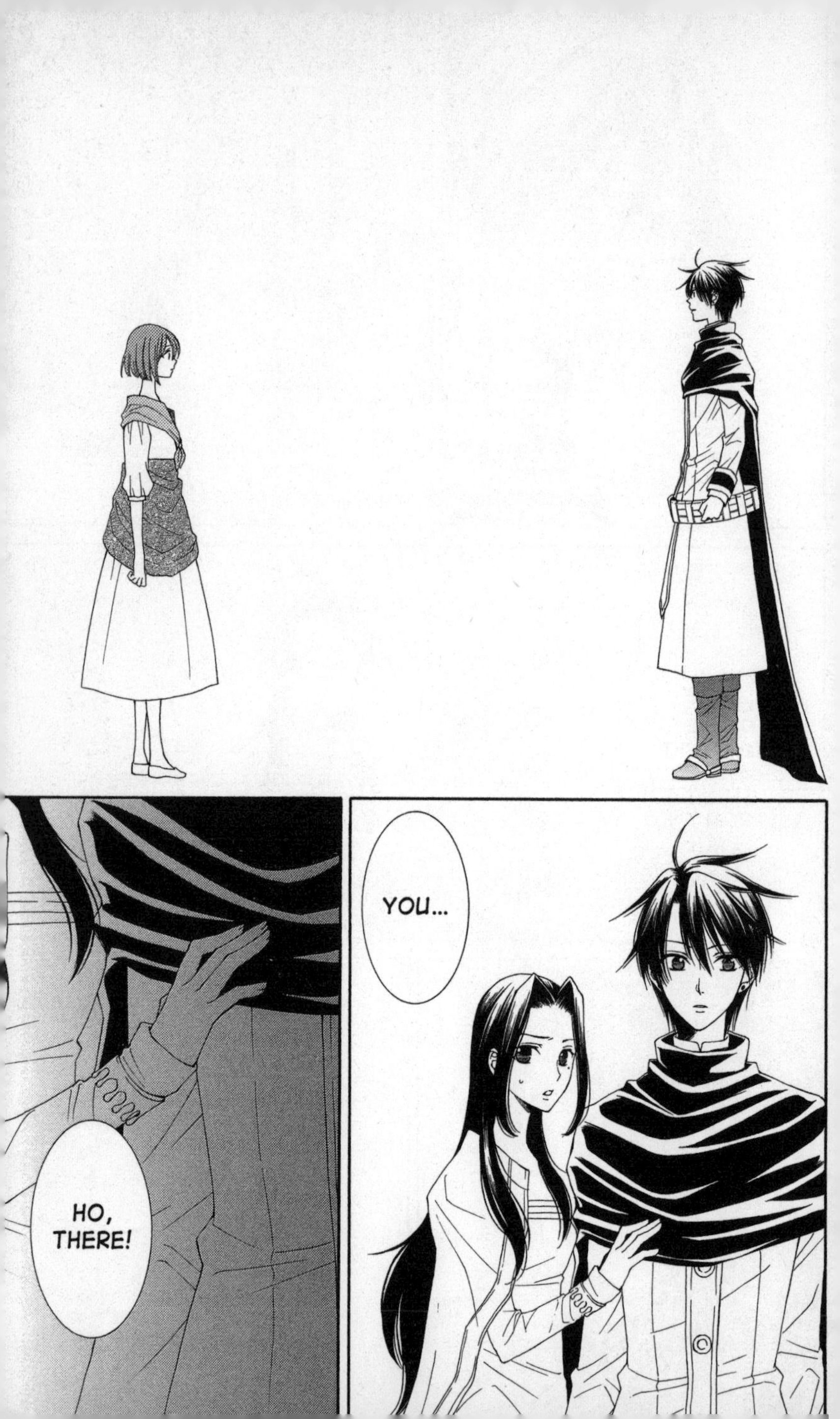
YOU...
HO, THERE!

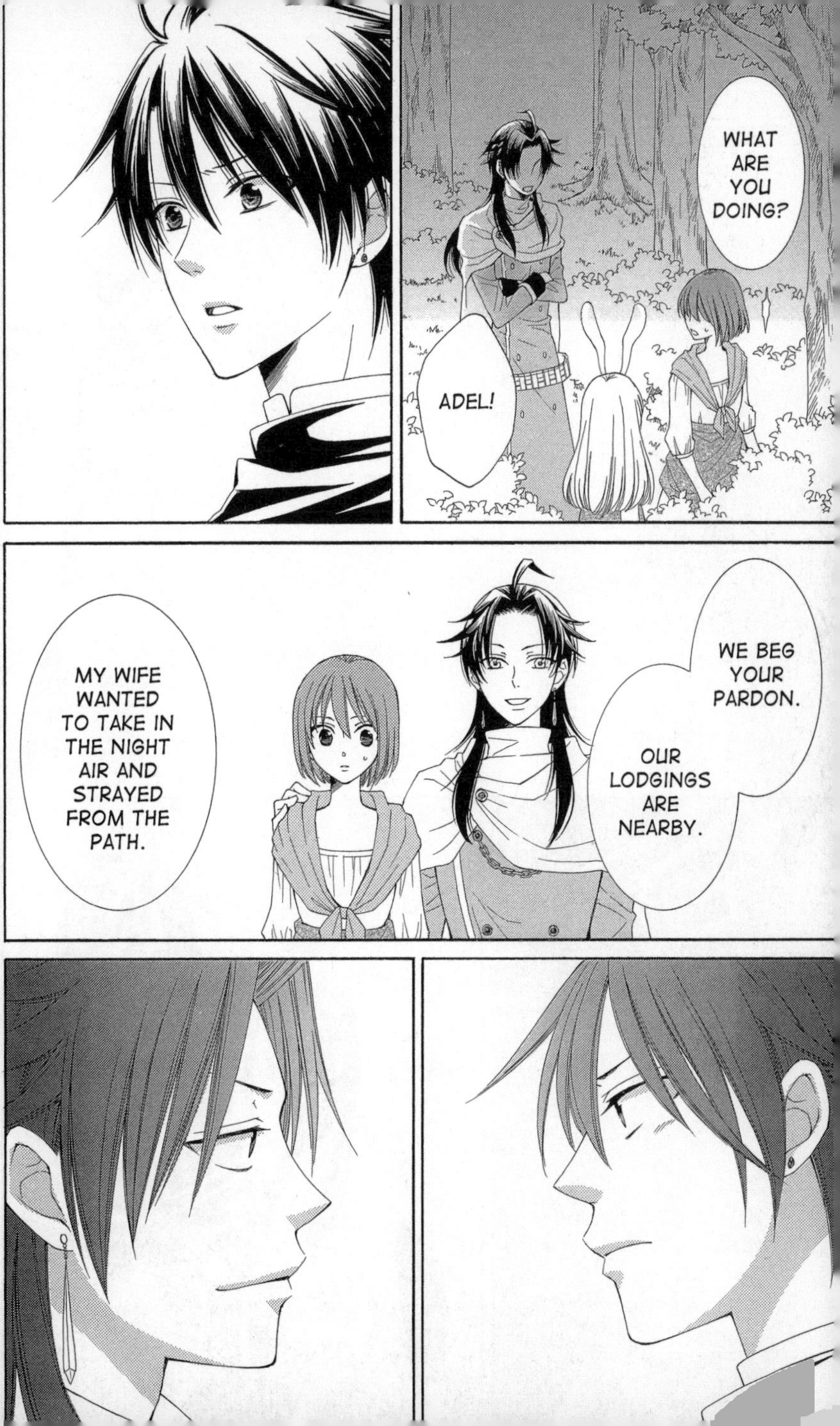
WHAT ARE YOU DOING?
ADEL!
WE BEG YOUR PARDON.
OUR LODGINGS ARE NEARBY.
MY WIFE WANTED TO TAKE IN THE NIGHT AIR AND STRAYED FROM THE PATH.

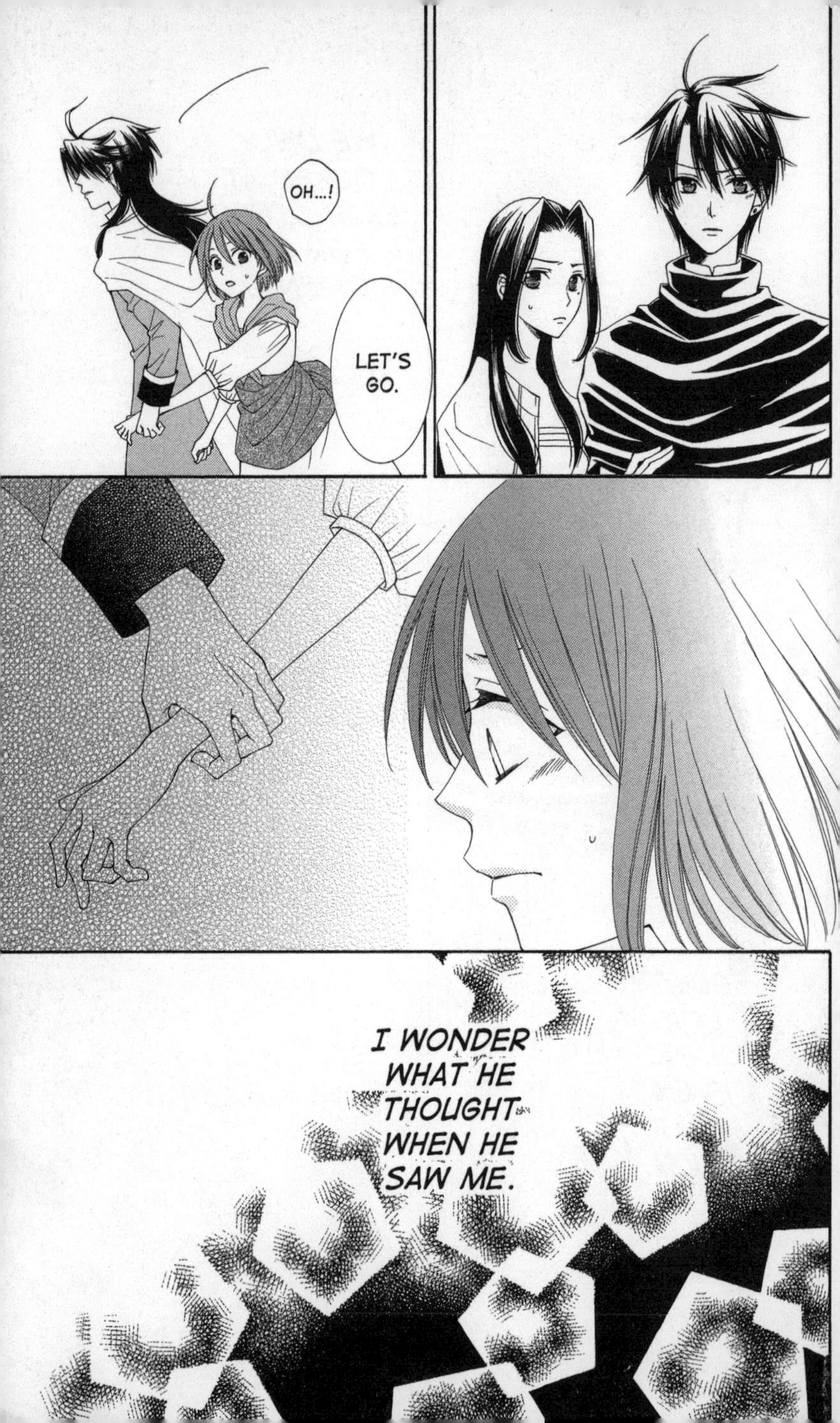
OH...!
LET'S GO.
I WONDER WHAT HE THOUGHT WHEN HE SAW ME.

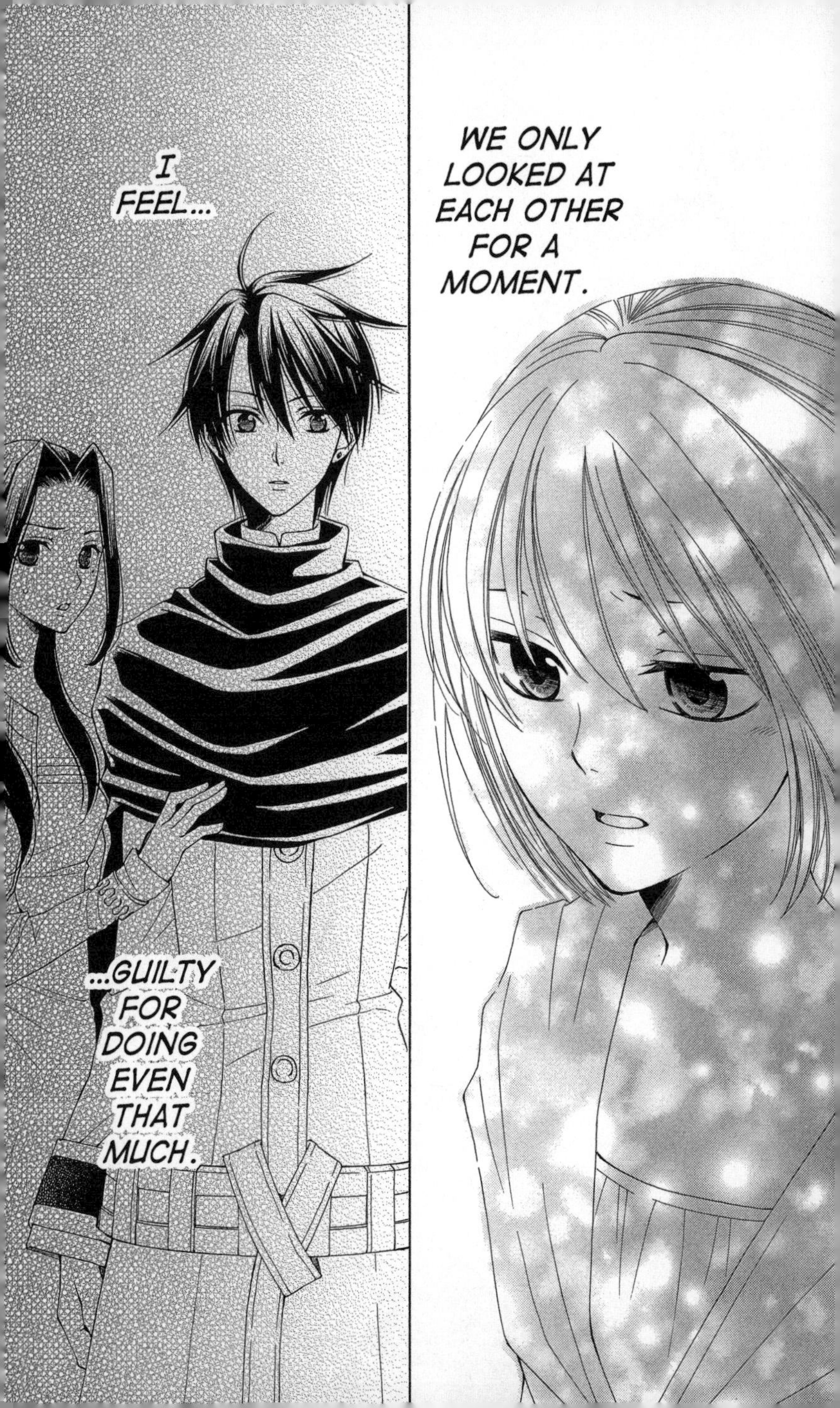

WE ONLY LOOKED AT EACH OTHER FOR A MOMENT.
I FEEL...
...GUILTY FOR DOING EVEN THAT MUCH.

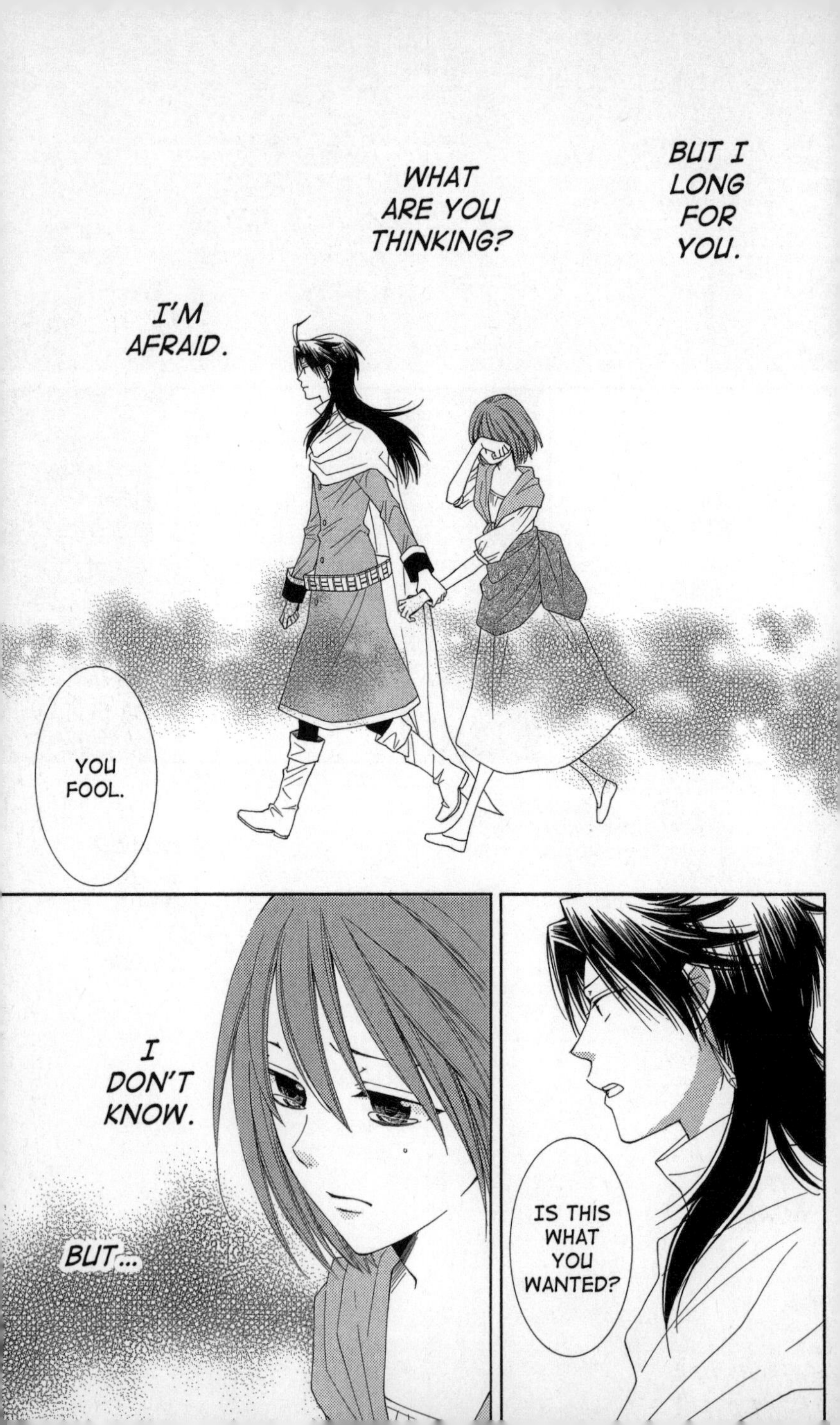
BUT I LONG FOR YOU.
WHAT ARE YOU THINKING?
I'M AFRAID.
YOU FOOL.
IS THIS WHAT YOU WANTED?
I DON'T KNOW.
BUT...

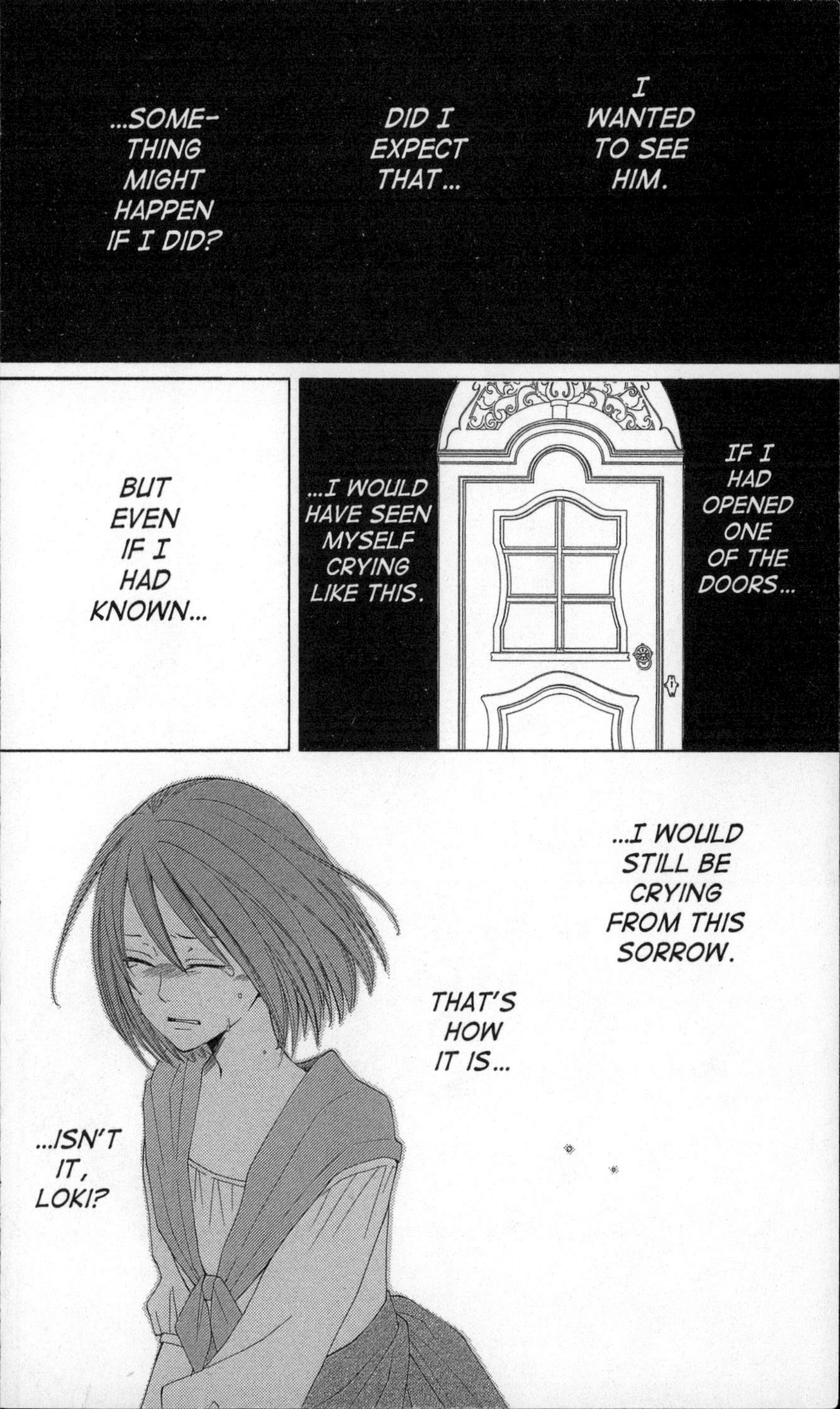
I WANTED TO SEE HIM.
DID I EXPECT THAT...
...SOME-THING MIGHT HAPPEN IF I DID?
IF I HAD OPENED ONE OF THE DOORS...
...I WOULD HAVE SEEN MYSELF CRYING LIKE THIS.
BUT EVEN IF I HAD KNOWN...
...I WOULD STILL BE CRYING FROM THIS SORROW.
THAT'S HOW IT IS...
...ISN'T IT, LOKI!?

Chapter 44

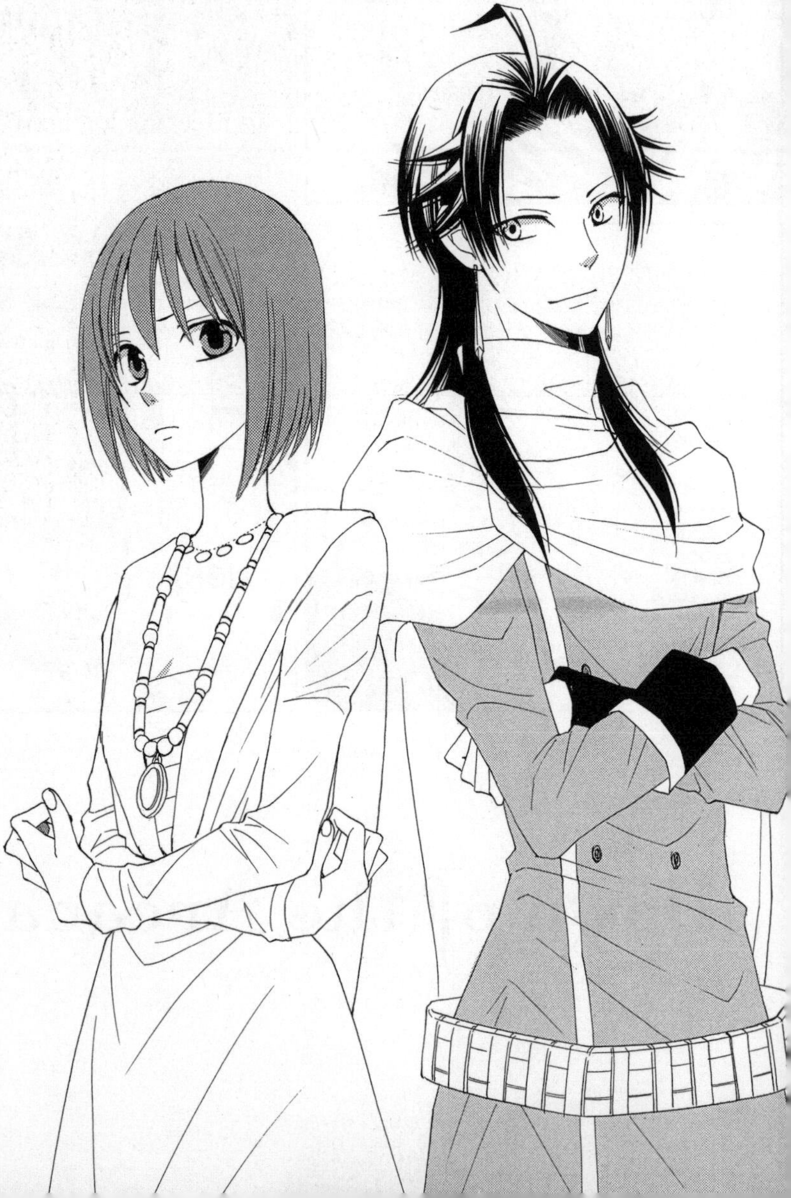

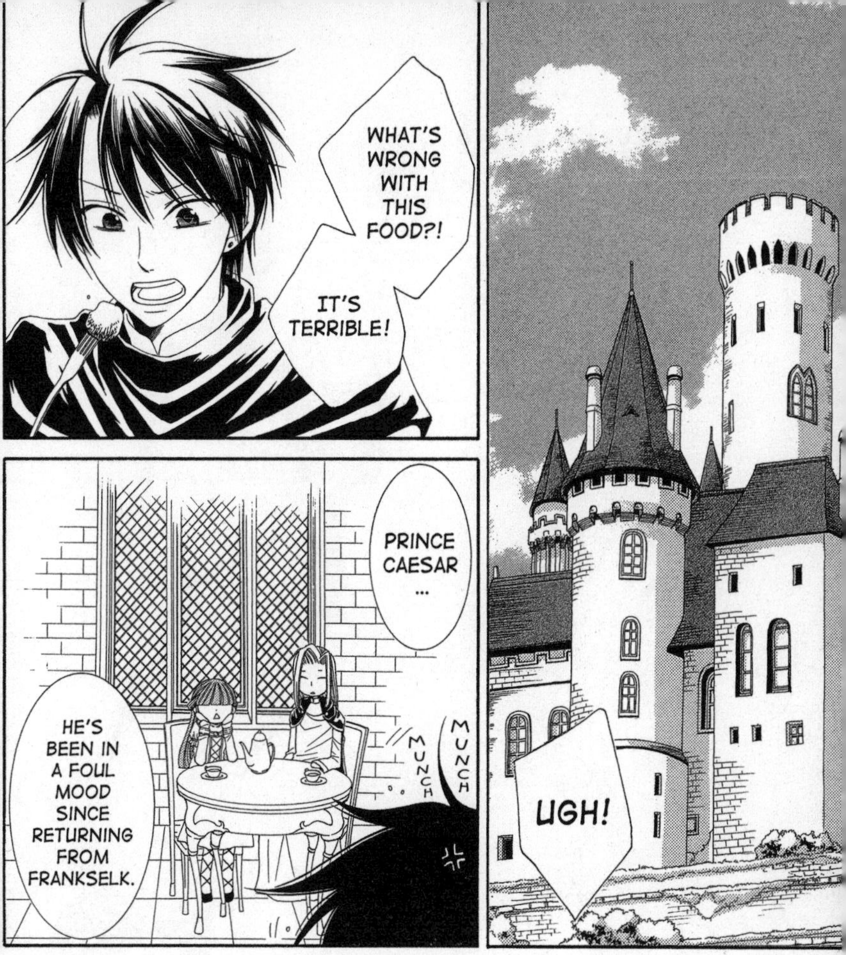
UGH!
WHAT'S WRONG WITH THIS FOOD?!
IT'S TERRIBLE!
PRINCE CAESAR ...
MUNCH
MUNCH
HE'S BEEN IN A FOUL MOOD SINCE RETURNING FROM FRANKSELK.

Dawn of the Arcana

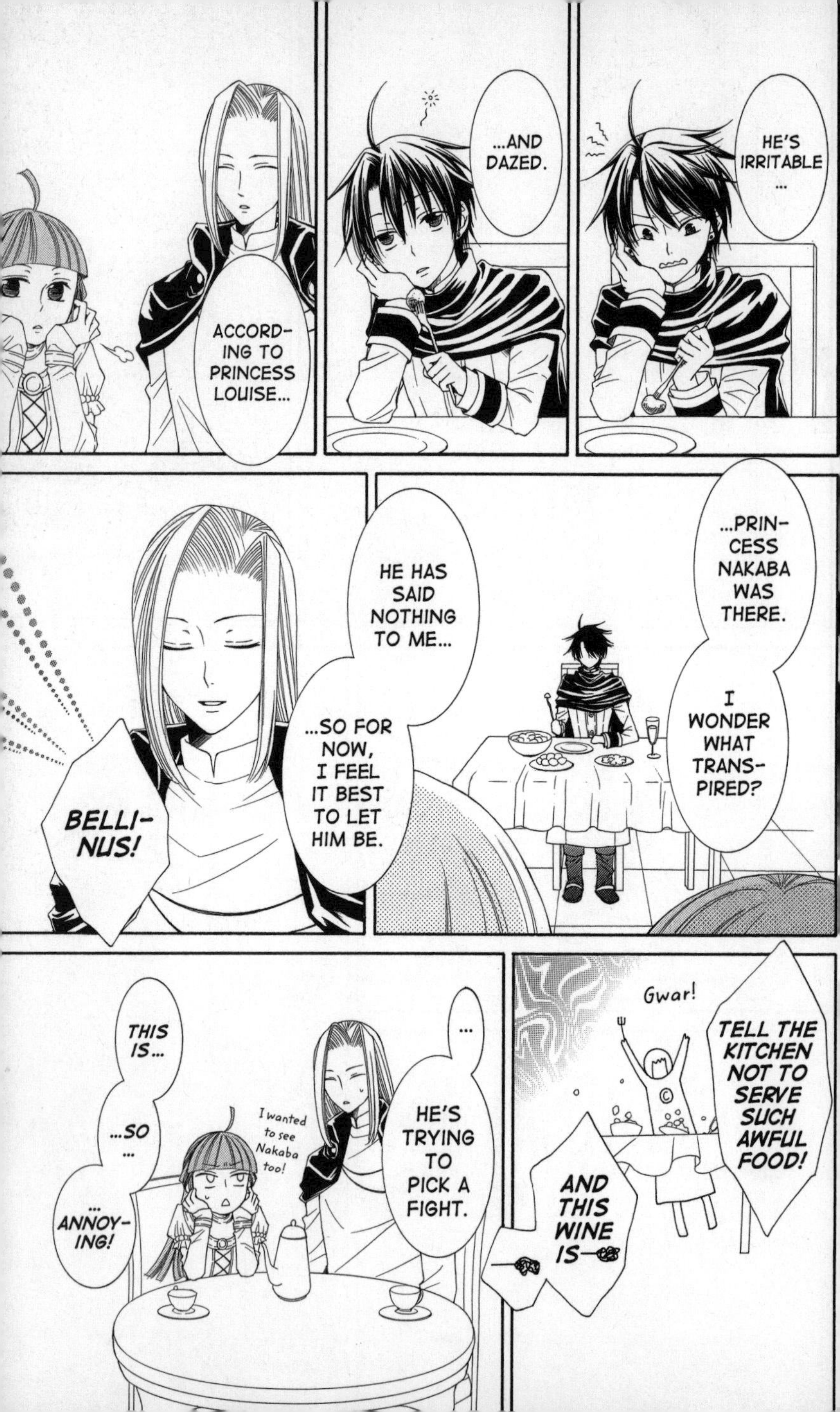
HE'S IRRITABLE...
...AND DAZED.
ACCORDING TO PRINCESS LOUISE...
...PRINCESS NAKABA WAS THERE.
I WONDER WHAT TRANSPIRED?
HE HAS SAID NOTHING TO ME...
...SO FOR NOW, I FEEL IT BEST TO LET HIM BE.
BELLINUS!
Gwar!
TELL THE KITCHEN NOT TO SERVE SUCH AWFUL FOOD!
AND THIS WINE IS—
...
HE'S TRYING TO PICK A FIGHT.
I wanted to see Nakaba too!
THIS IS...
...SO...
...ANNOYING!

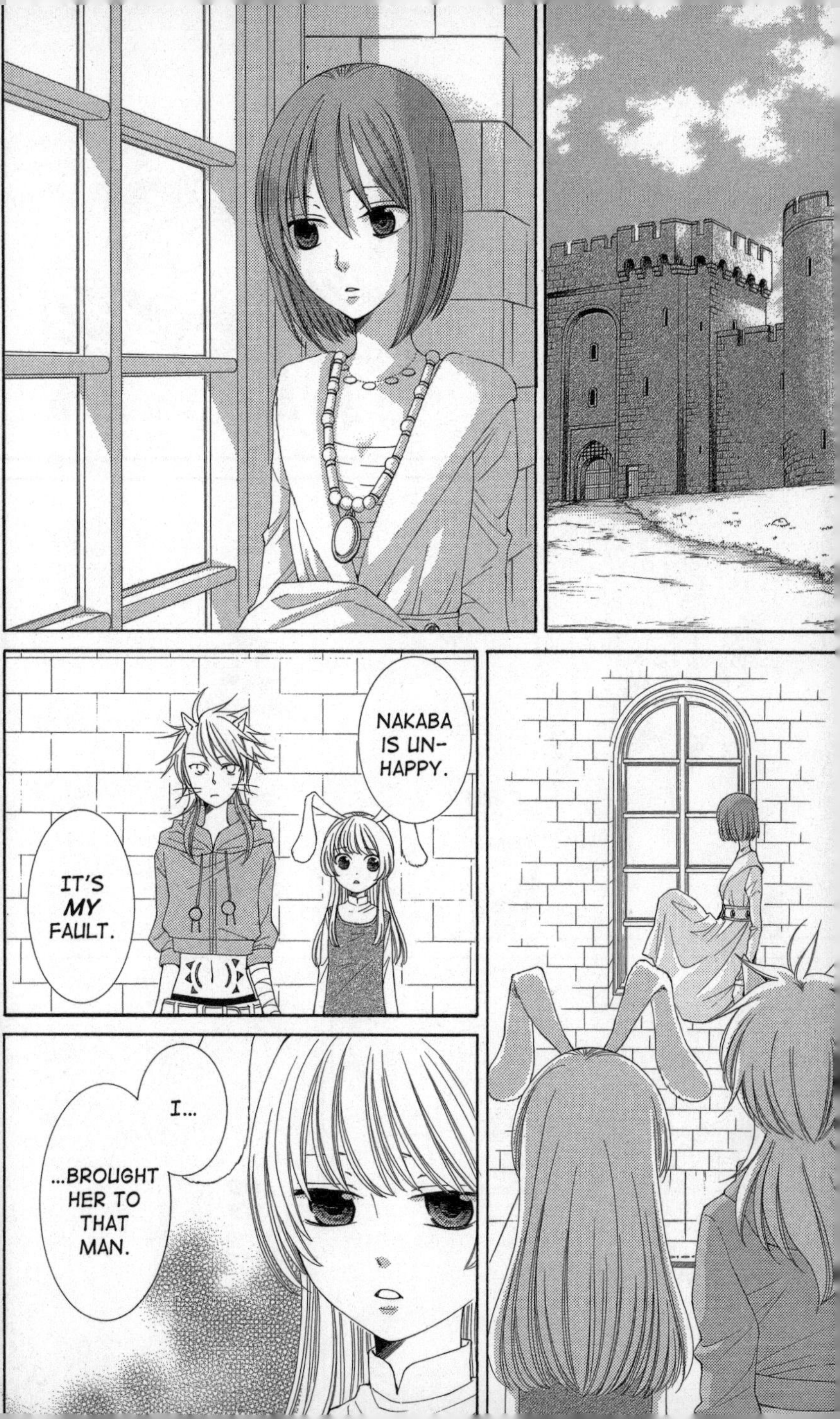
NAKABA IS UN-HAPPY.
IT'S *MY* FAULT.
I...
...BROUGHT HER TO THAT MAN.

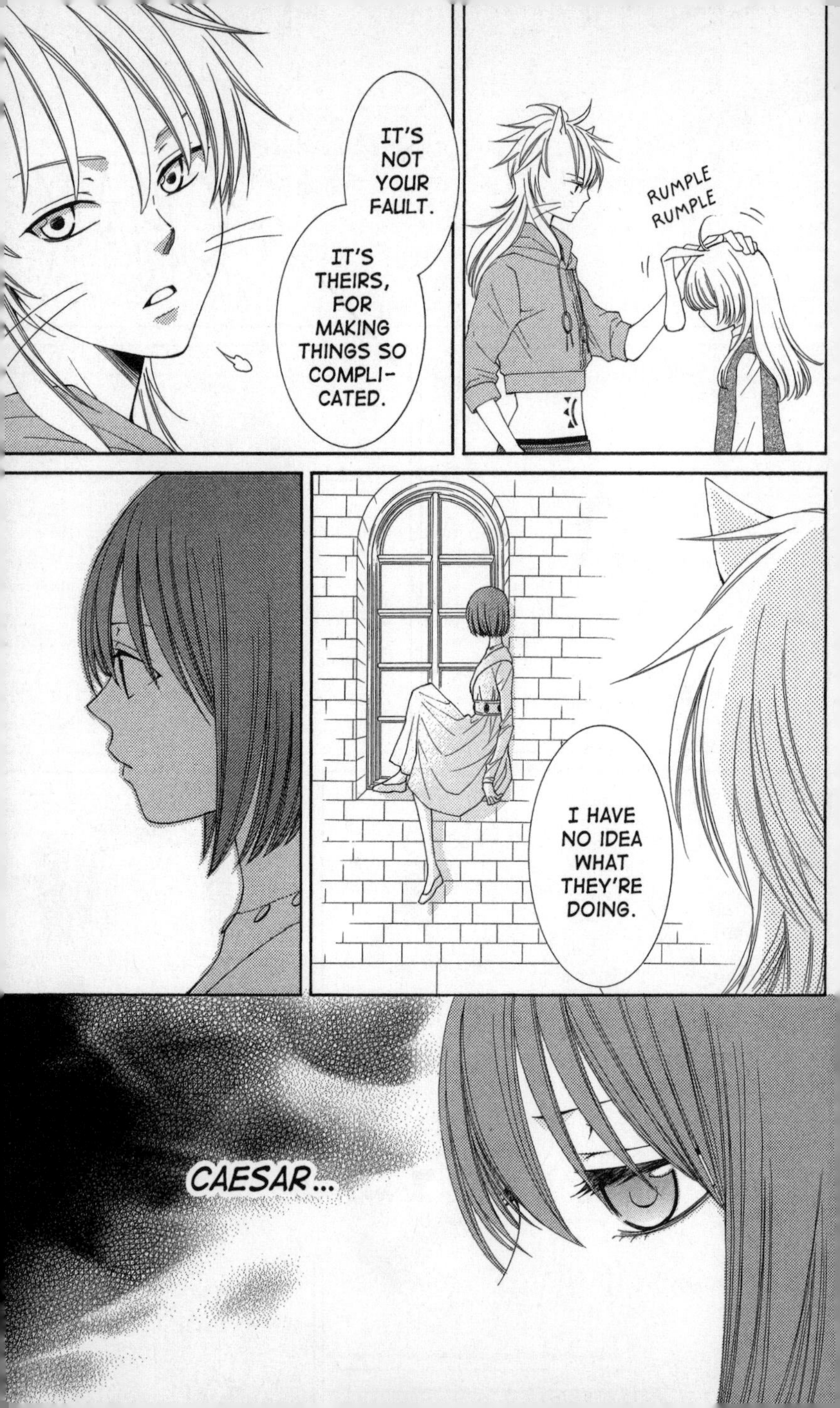
RUMPLE RUMPLE
IT'S NOT YOUR FAULT.
IT'S THEIRS, FOR MAKING THINGS SO COMPLI-CATED.
I HAVE NO IDEA WHAT THEY'RE DOING.
CAESAR...

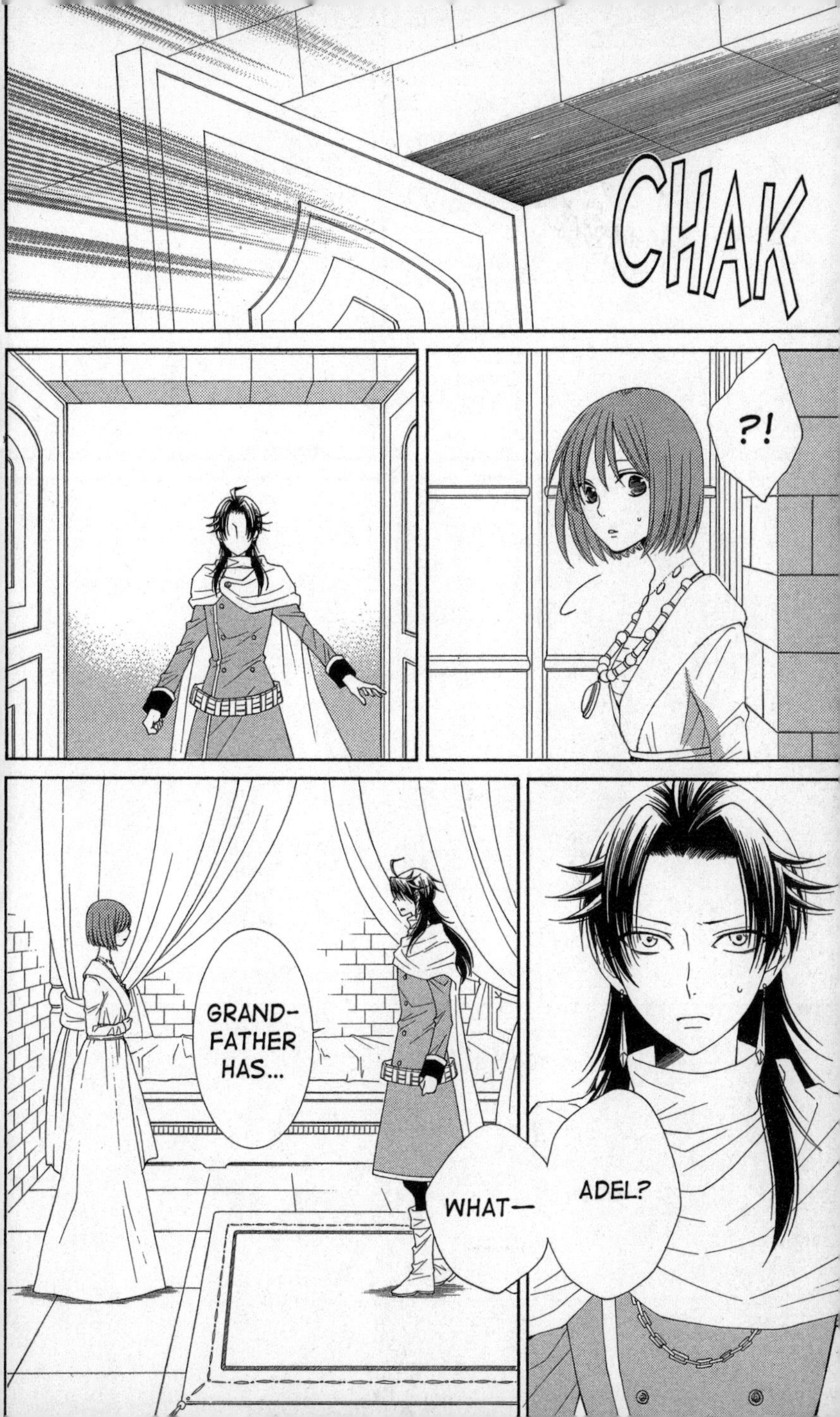
CHAK
?!
ADEL?
WHAT—
GRAND-FATHER HAS...

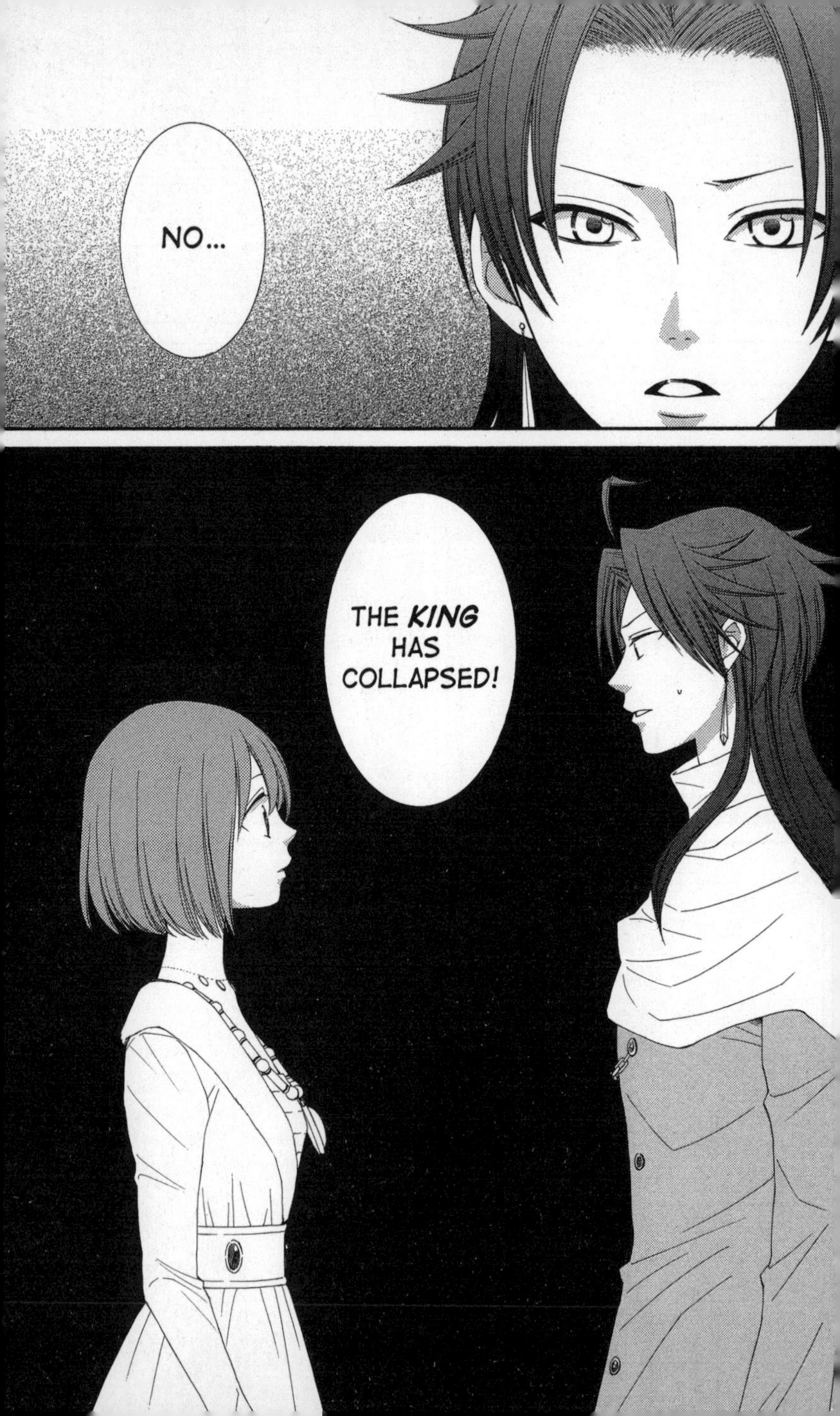
NO...
THE KING HAS COLLAPSED!

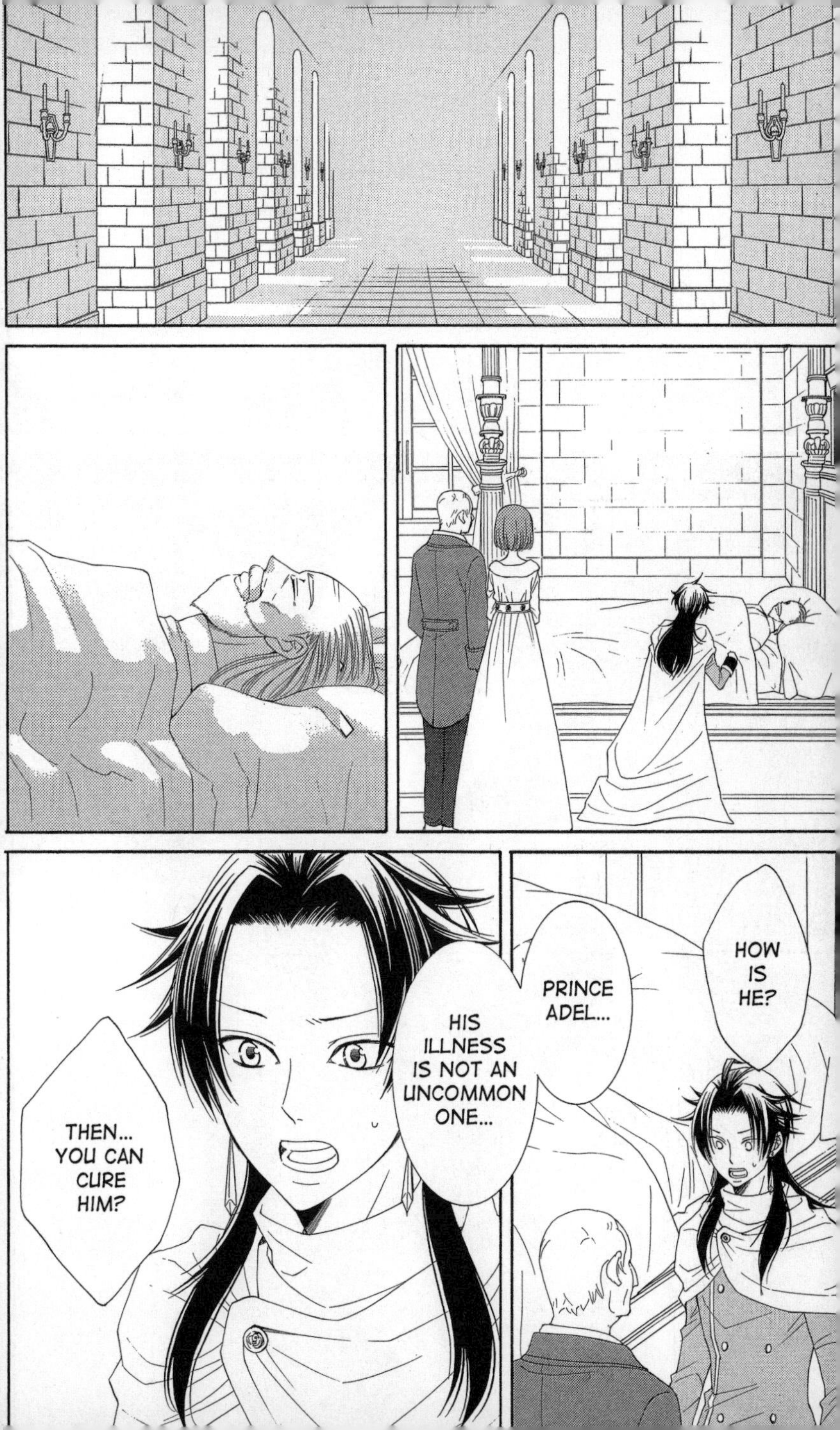
HOW IS HE?
PRINCE ADEL...
HIS ILLNESS IS NOT AN UNCOMMON ONE...
THEN... YOU CAN CURE HIM?

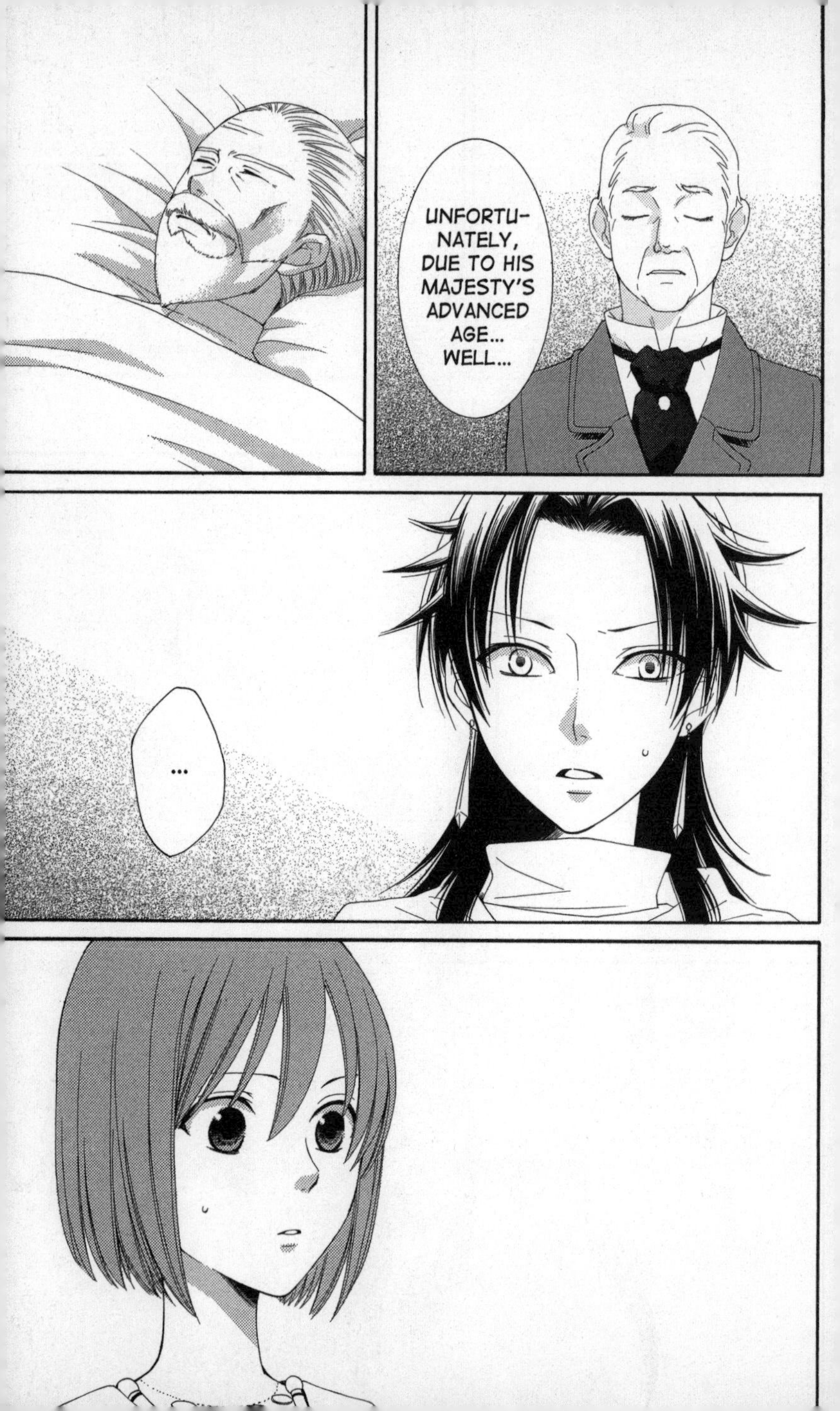
UNFORTU-NATELY, DUE TO HIS MAJESTY'S ADVANCED AGE... WELL...
...

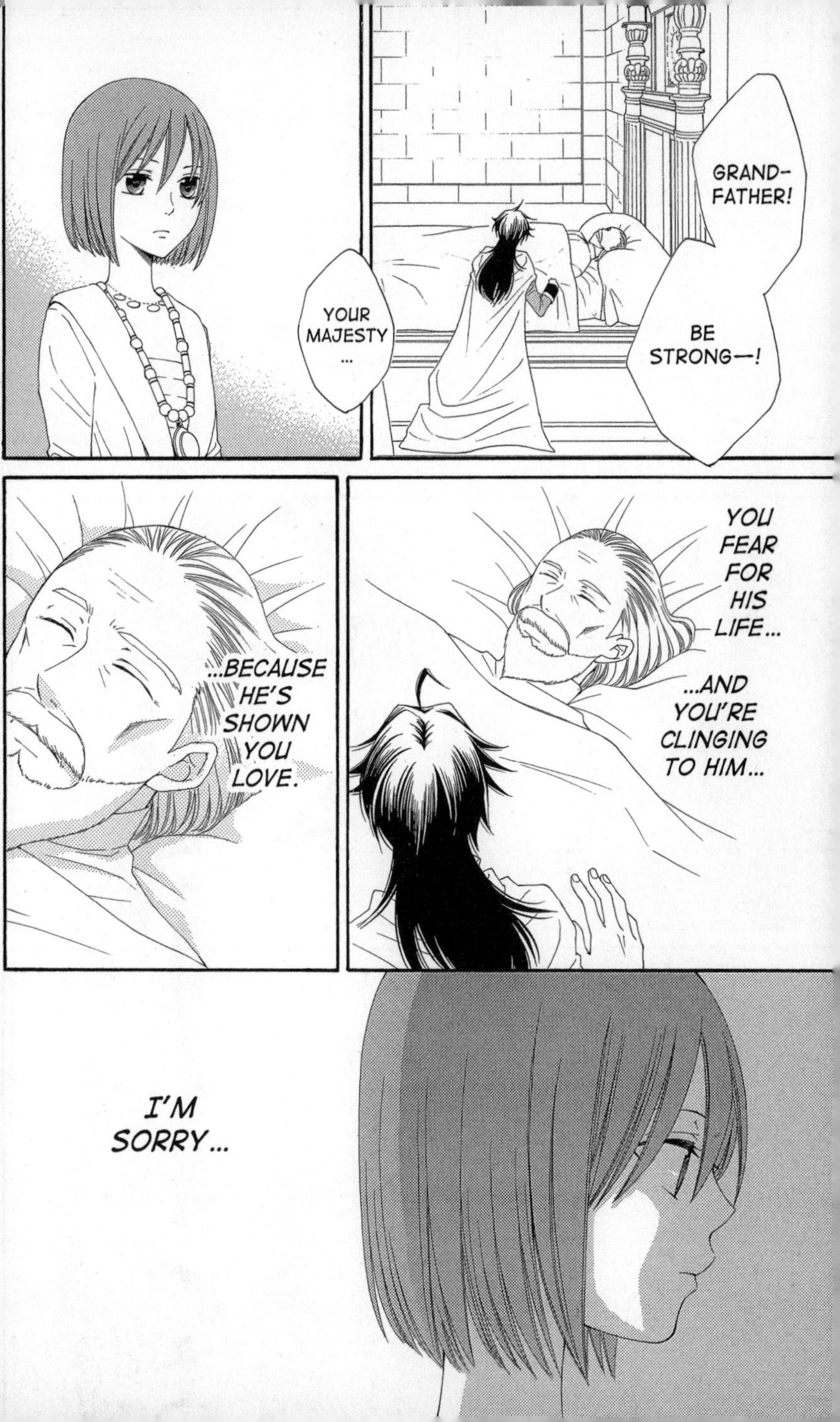
GRAND-FATHER!
BE STRONG—!
YOUR MAJESTY ...
YOU FEAR FOR HIS LIFE...
...AND YOU'RE CLINGING TO HIM...
...BECAUSE HE'S SHOWN YOU LOVE.
I'M SORRY...

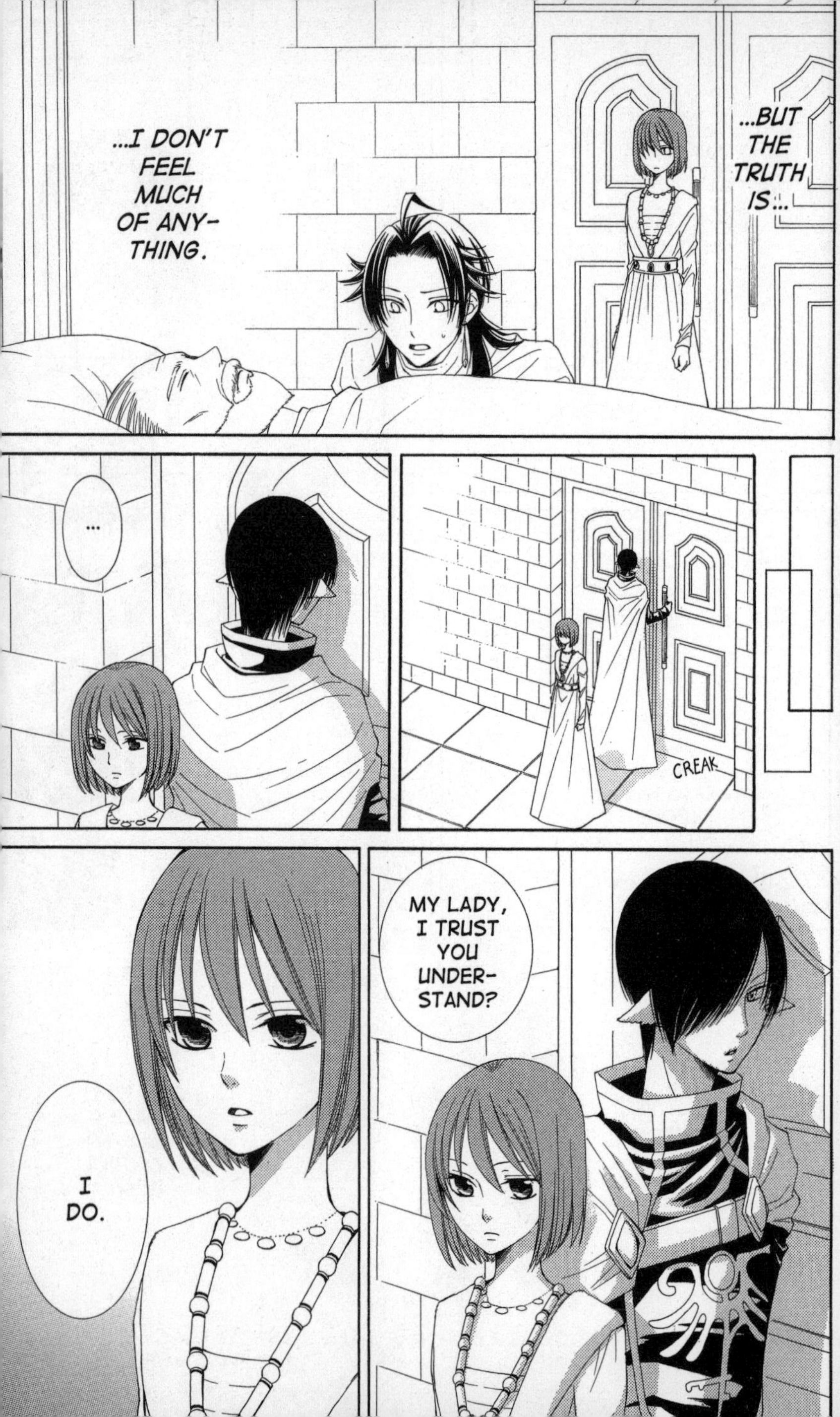
...BUT THE TRUTH IS...
...I DON'T FEEL MUCH OF ANY-THING.
CREAK
...
MY LADY, I TRUST YOU UNDER-STAND?
I DO.

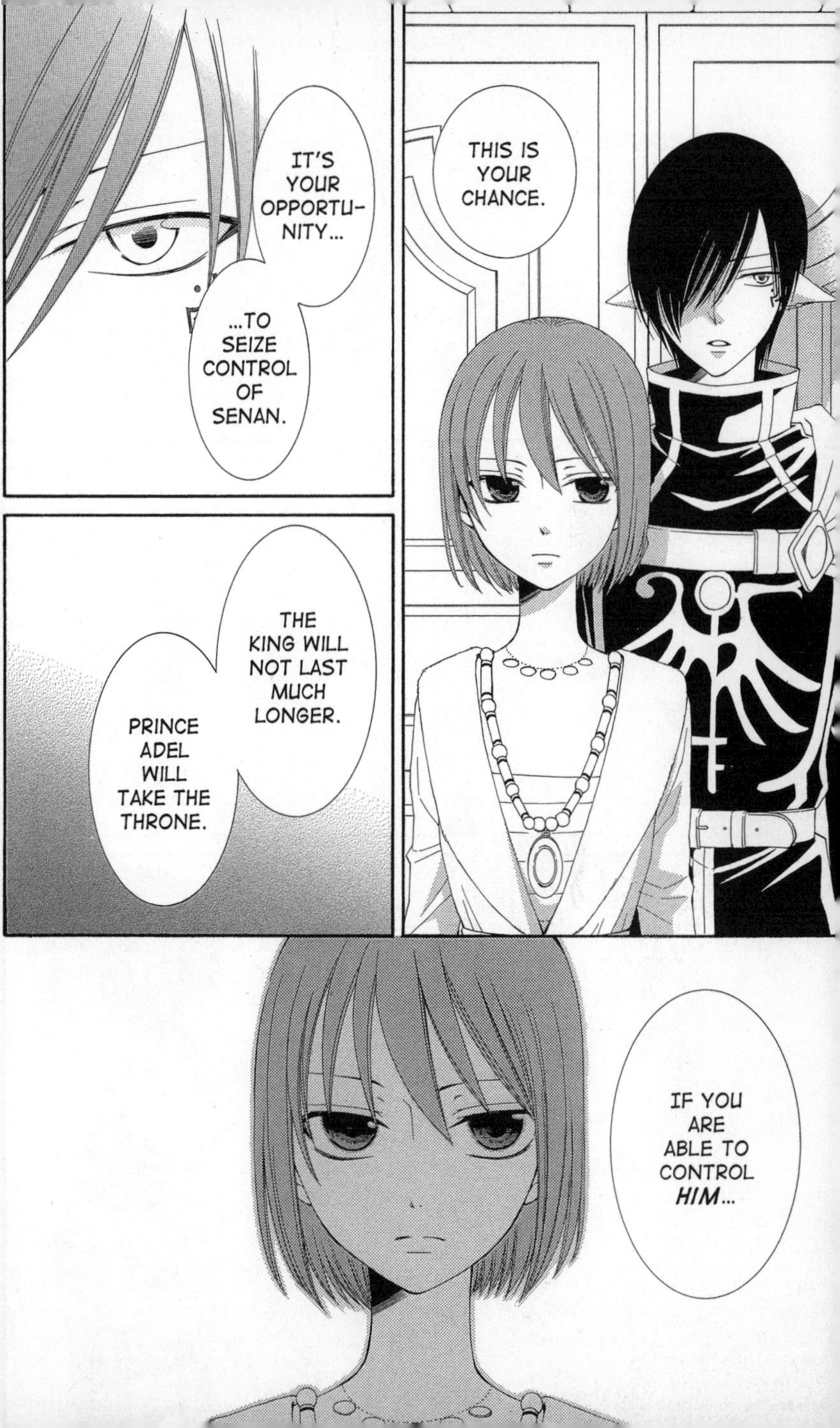
THIS IS YOUR CHANCE.
IT'S YOUR OPPORTUNITY...
...TO SEIZE CONTROL OF SENAN.
THE KING WILL NOT LAST MUCH LONGER.
PRINCE ADEL WILL TAKE THE THRONE.
IF YOU ARE ABLE TO CONTROL *HIM*...

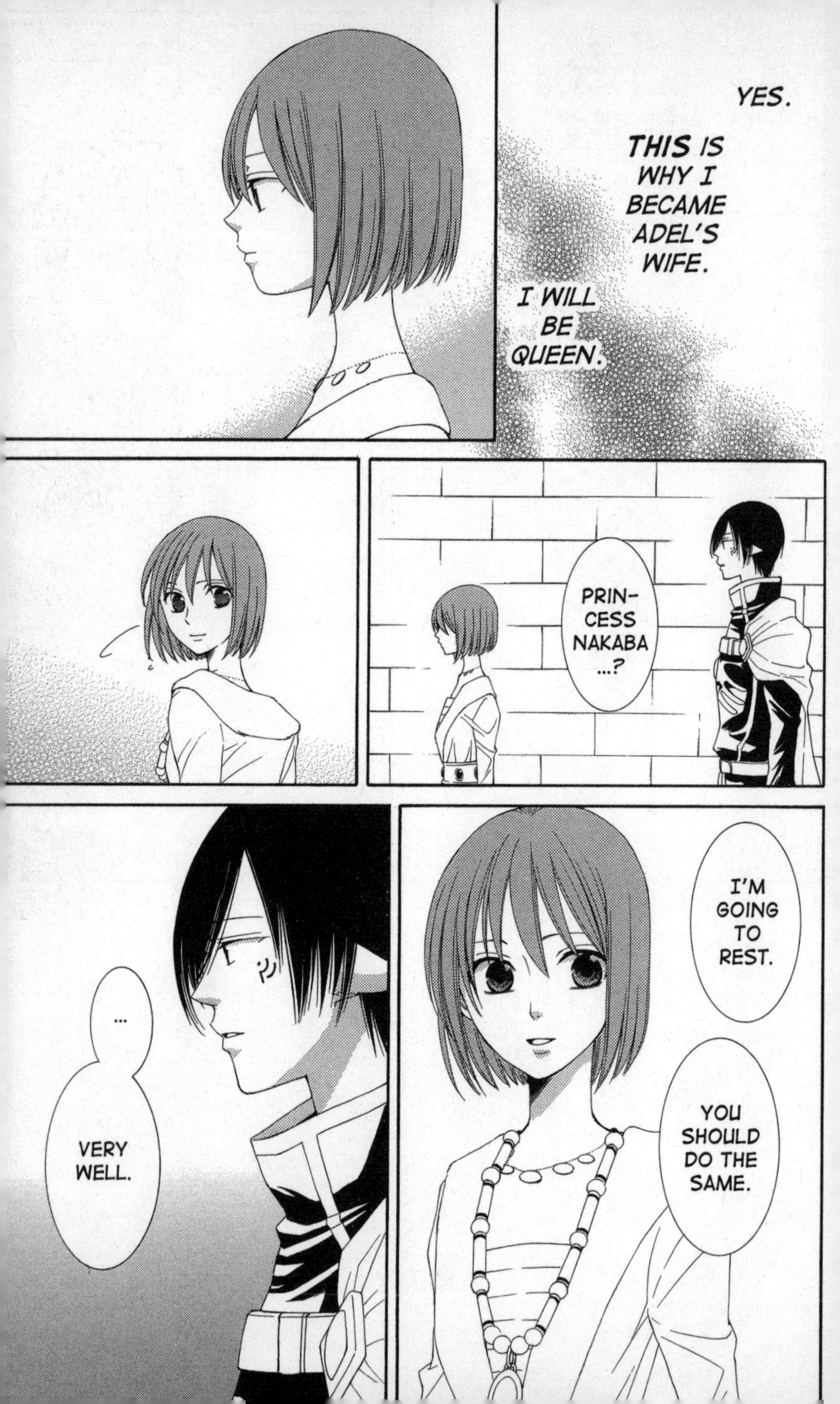
YES.
THIS IS WHY I BECAME ADEL'S WIFE.
I WILL BE QUEEN.
PRIN-CESS NAKABA ...?
I'M GOING TO REST.
YOU SHOULD DO THE SAME.
...
VERY WELL.

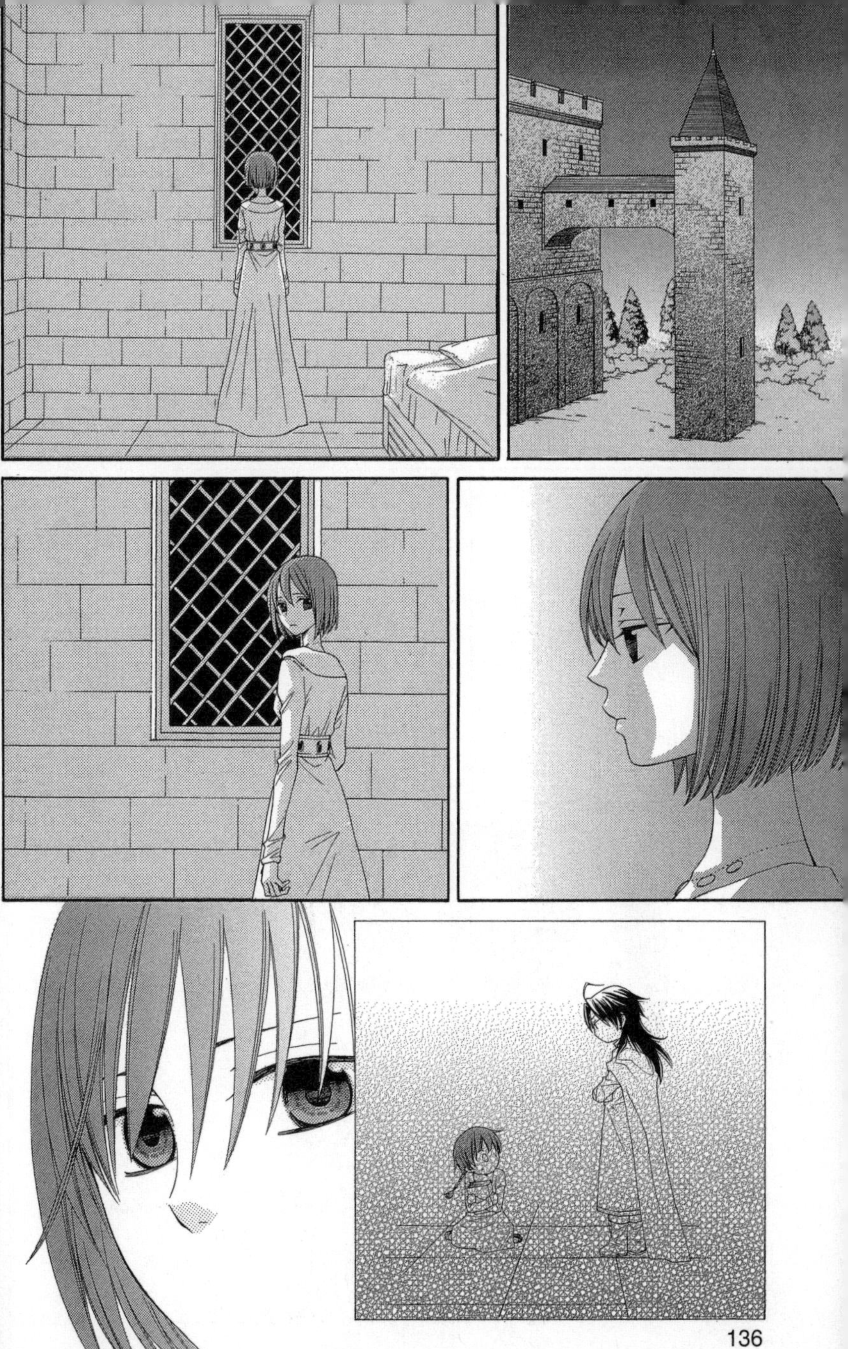

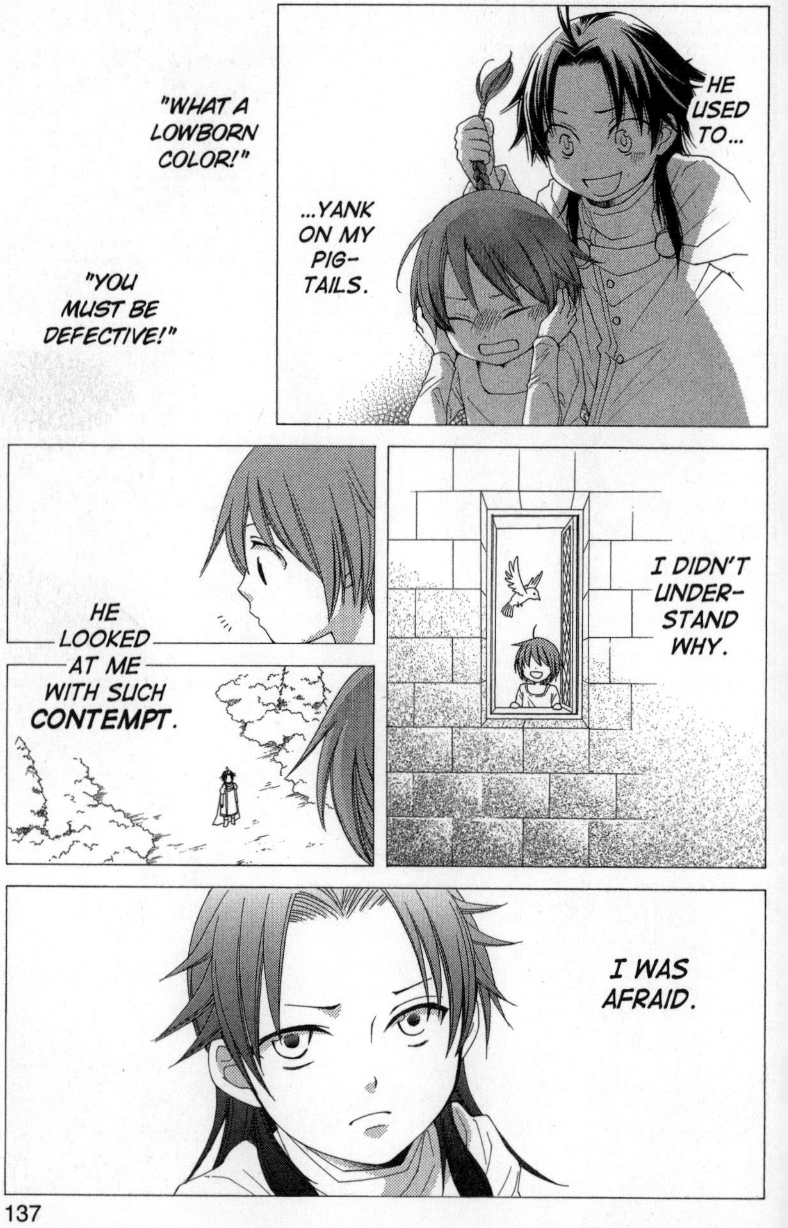
HE USED TO...
...YANK ON MY PIG-TAILS.
"WHAT A LOWBORN COLOR!"
"YOU MUST BE DEFECTIVE!"
I DIDN'T UNDER-STAND WHY.
HE LOOKED AT ME WITH SUCH CONTEMPT.
I WAS AFRAID.

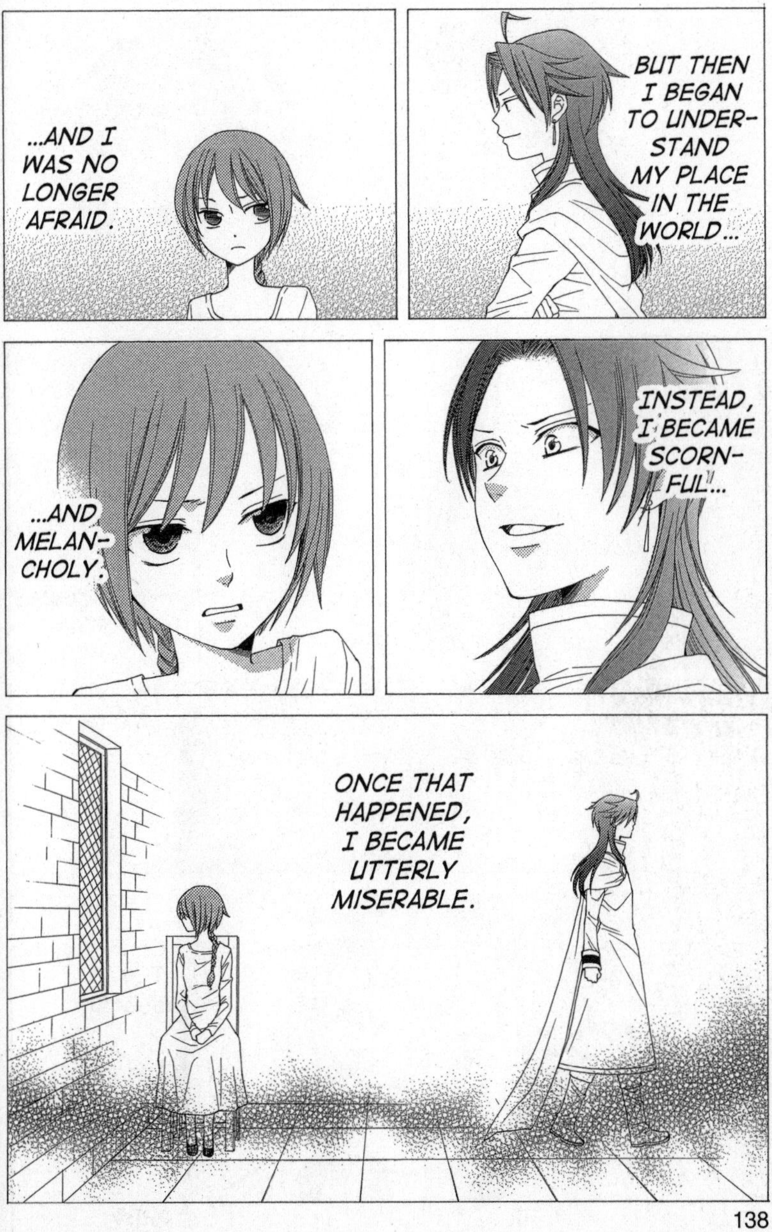
BUT THEN I BEGAN TO UNDER-STAND MY PLACE IN THE WORLD...
...AND I WAS NO LONGER AFRAID.
INSTEAD, I BECAME SCORN-FUL...
...AND MELAN-CHOLY.
ONCE THAT HAPPENED, I BECAME UTTERLY MISERABLE.

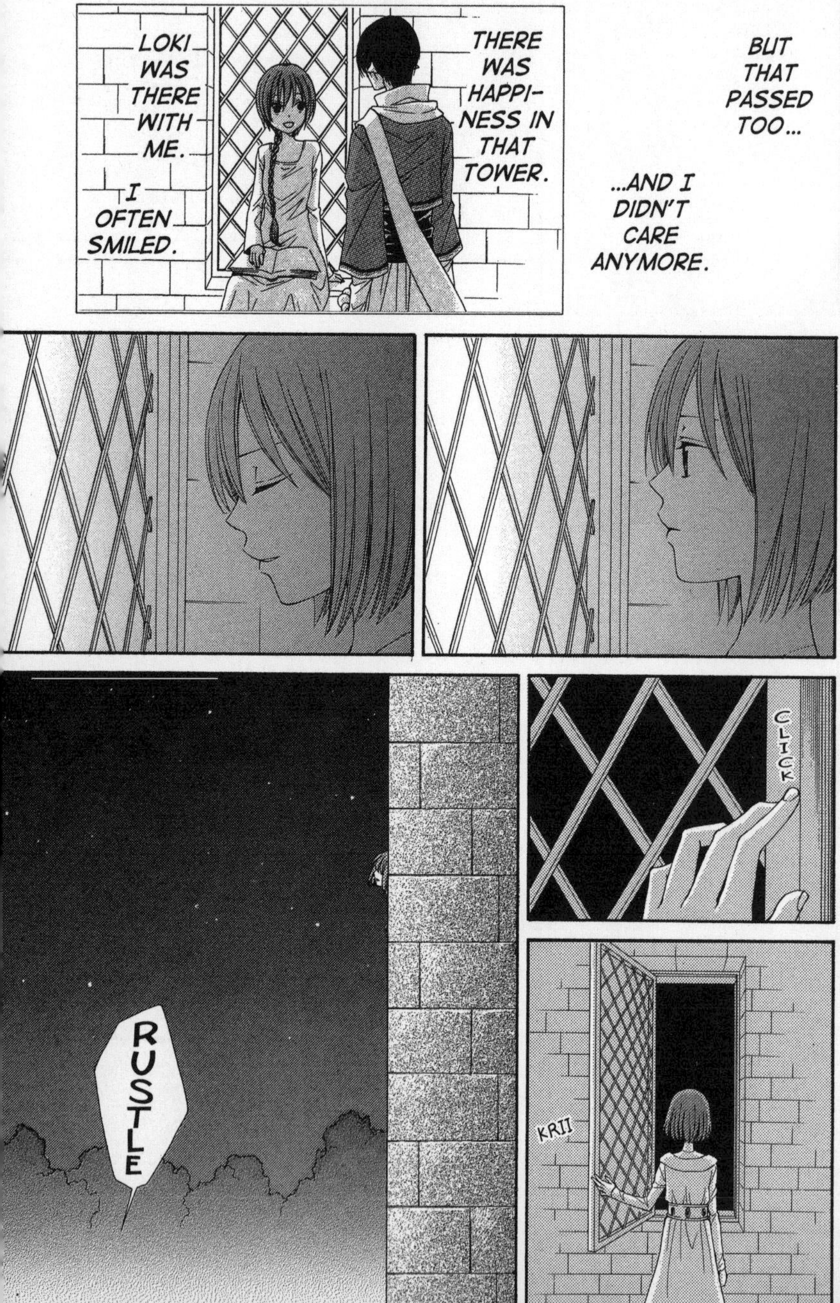
BUT THAT PASSED TOO...
...AND I DIDN'T CARE ANYMORE.
THERE WAS HAPPINESS IN THAT TOWER.
LOKI WAS THERE WITH ME.
I OFTEN SMILED.
CLICK
KRII
RUSTLE

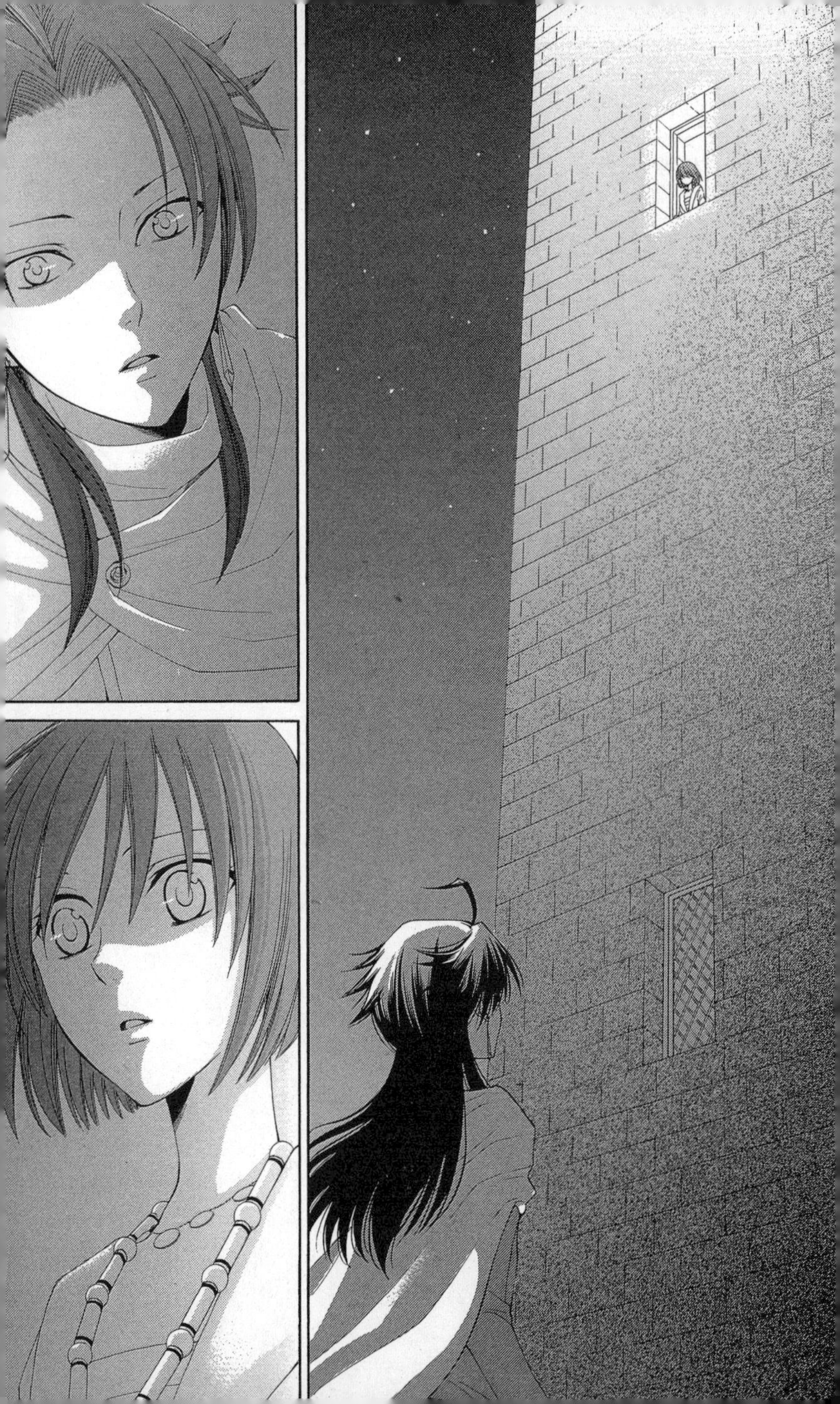

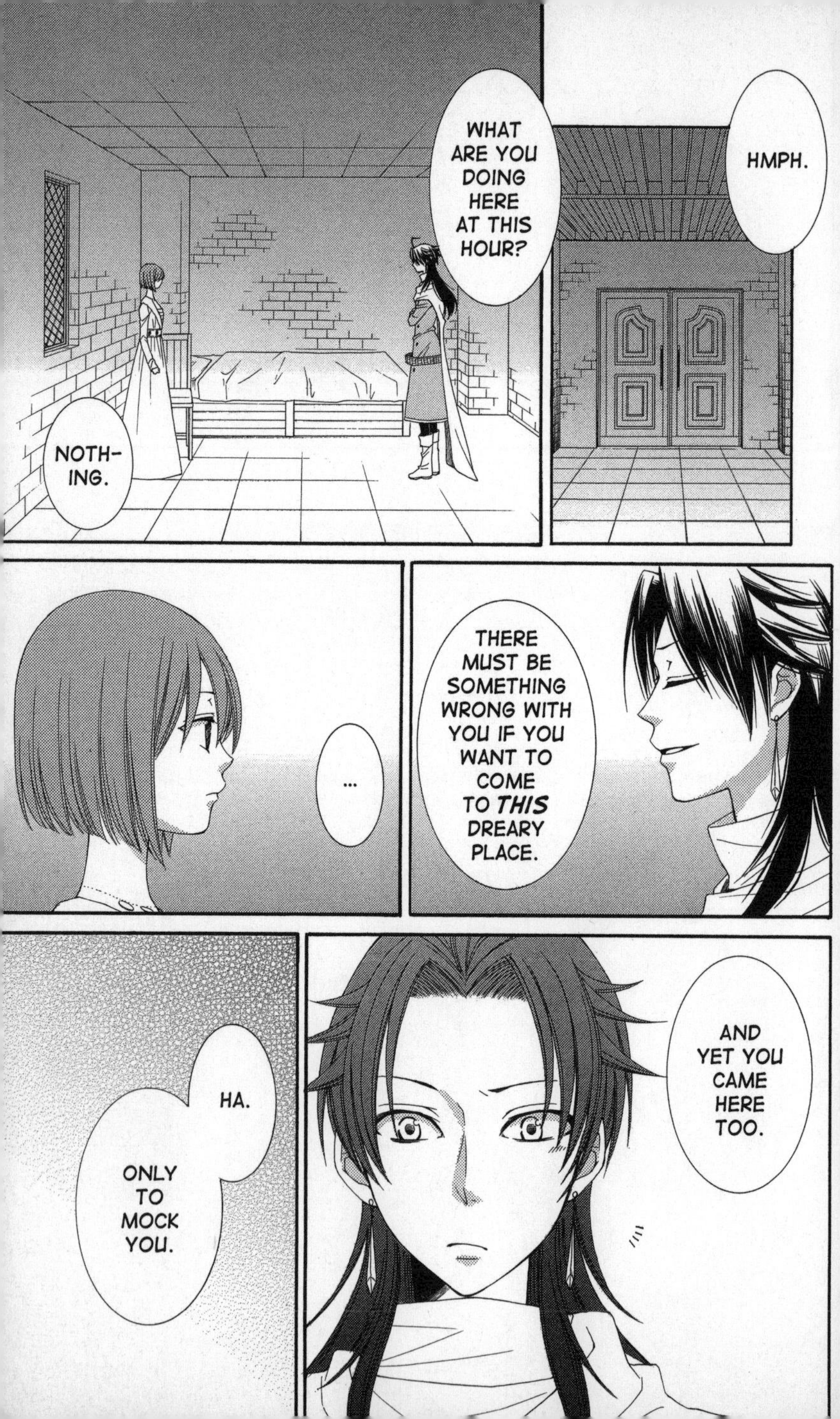
HMPH.
WHAT ARE YOU DOING HERE AT THIS HOUR?
NOTH-ING.
THERE MUST BE SOMETHING WRONG WITH YOU IF YOU WANT TO COME TO *THIS* DREARY PLACE.
...
AND YET YOU CAME HERE TOO.
HA.
ONLY TO MOCK YOU.

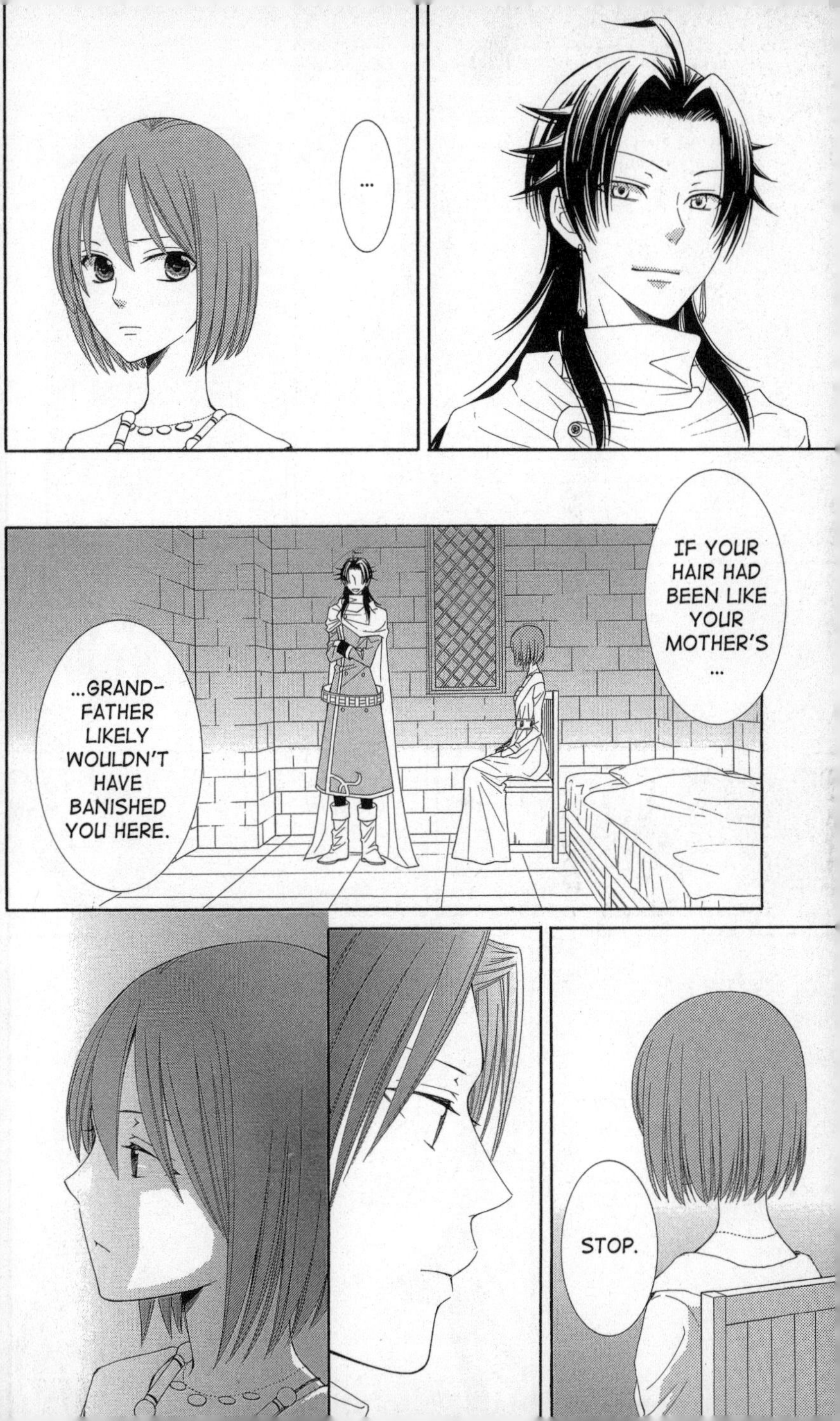
...
IF YOUR HAIR HAD BEEN LIKE YOUR MOTHER'S ...
...GRAND-FATHER LIKELY WOULDN'T HAVE BANISHED YOU HERE.
STOP.

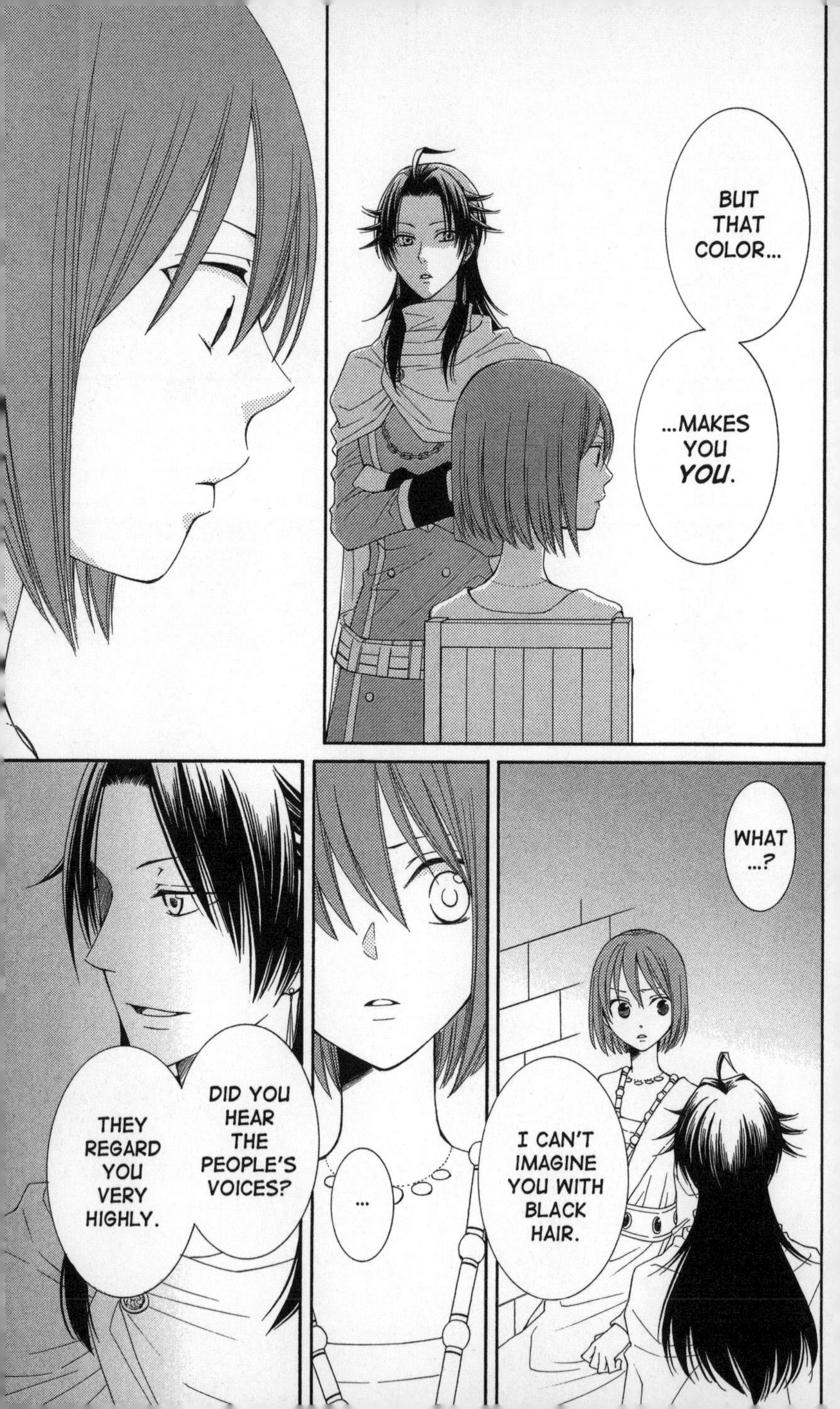
BUT THAT COLOR...
...MAKES YOU *YOU*.
WHAT ...?
I CAN'T IMAGINE YOU WITH BLACK HAIR.
...
DID YOU HEAR THE PEOPLE'S VOICES?
THEY REGARD YOU VERY HIGHLY.

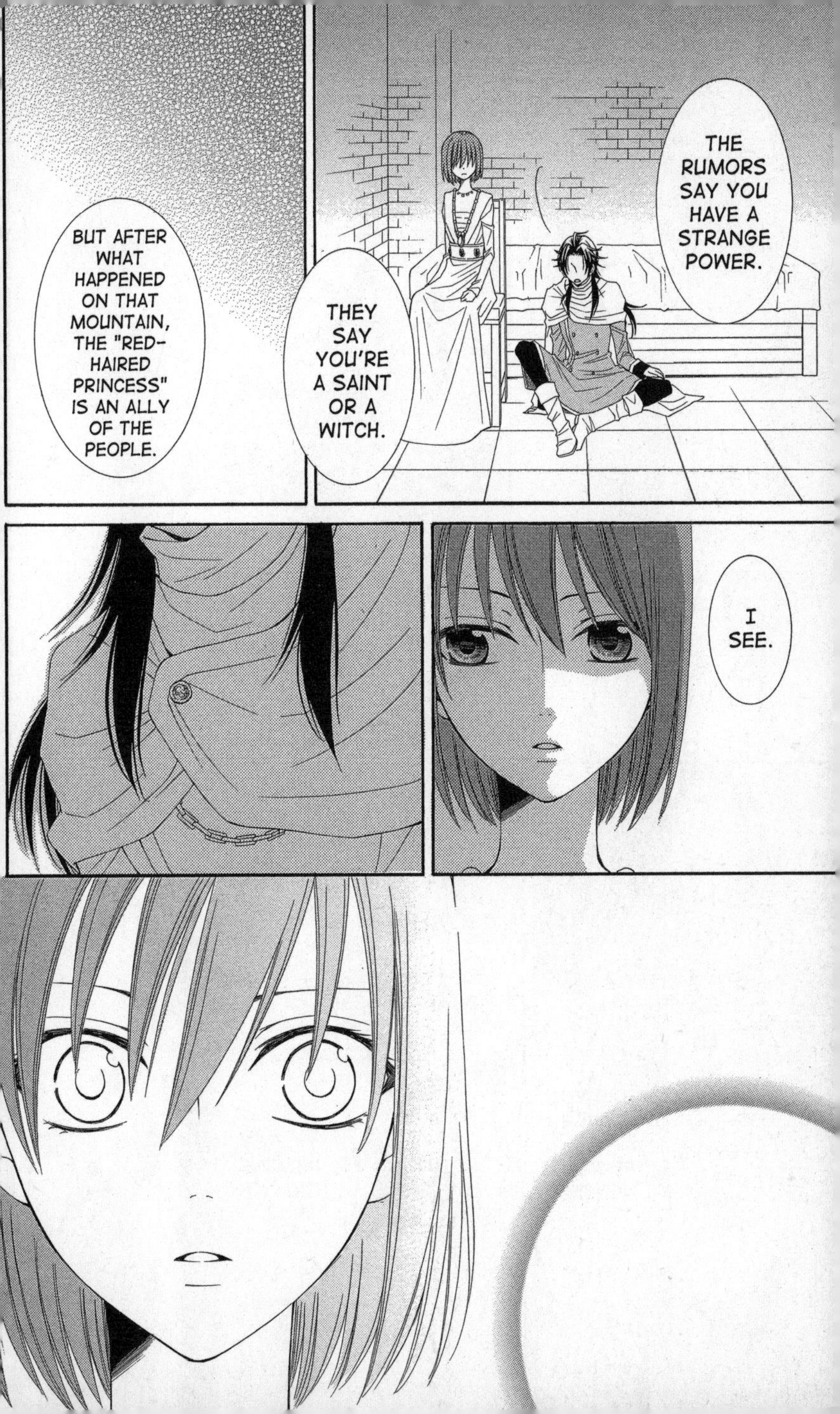
THE RUMORS SAY YOU HAVE A STRANGE POWER.
THEY SAY YOU'RE A SAINT OR A WITCH.
BUT AFTER WHAT HAPPENED ON THAT MOUNTAIN, THE "RED-HAIRED PRINCESS" IS AN ALLY OF THE PEOPLE.
I SEE.

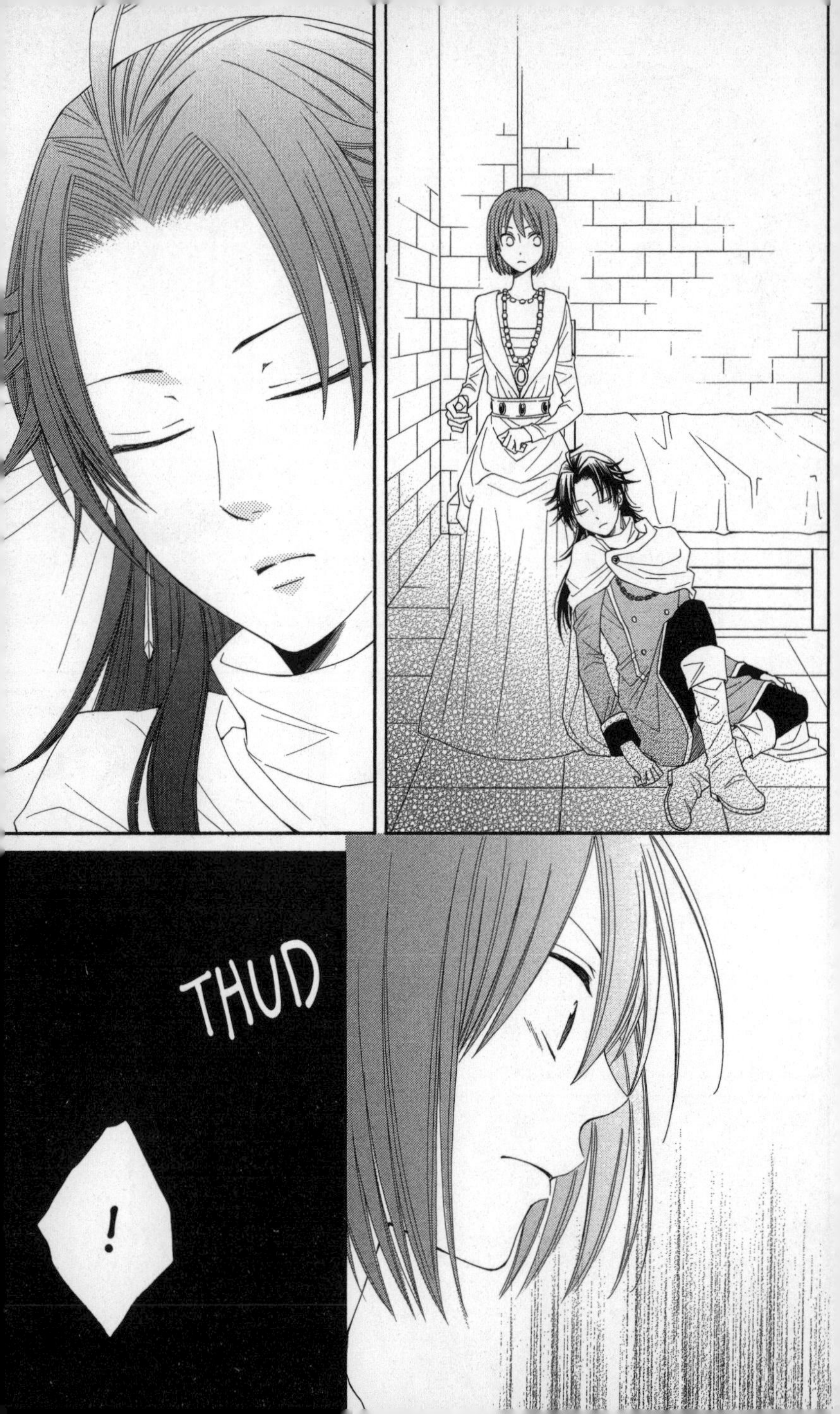
THUD
!

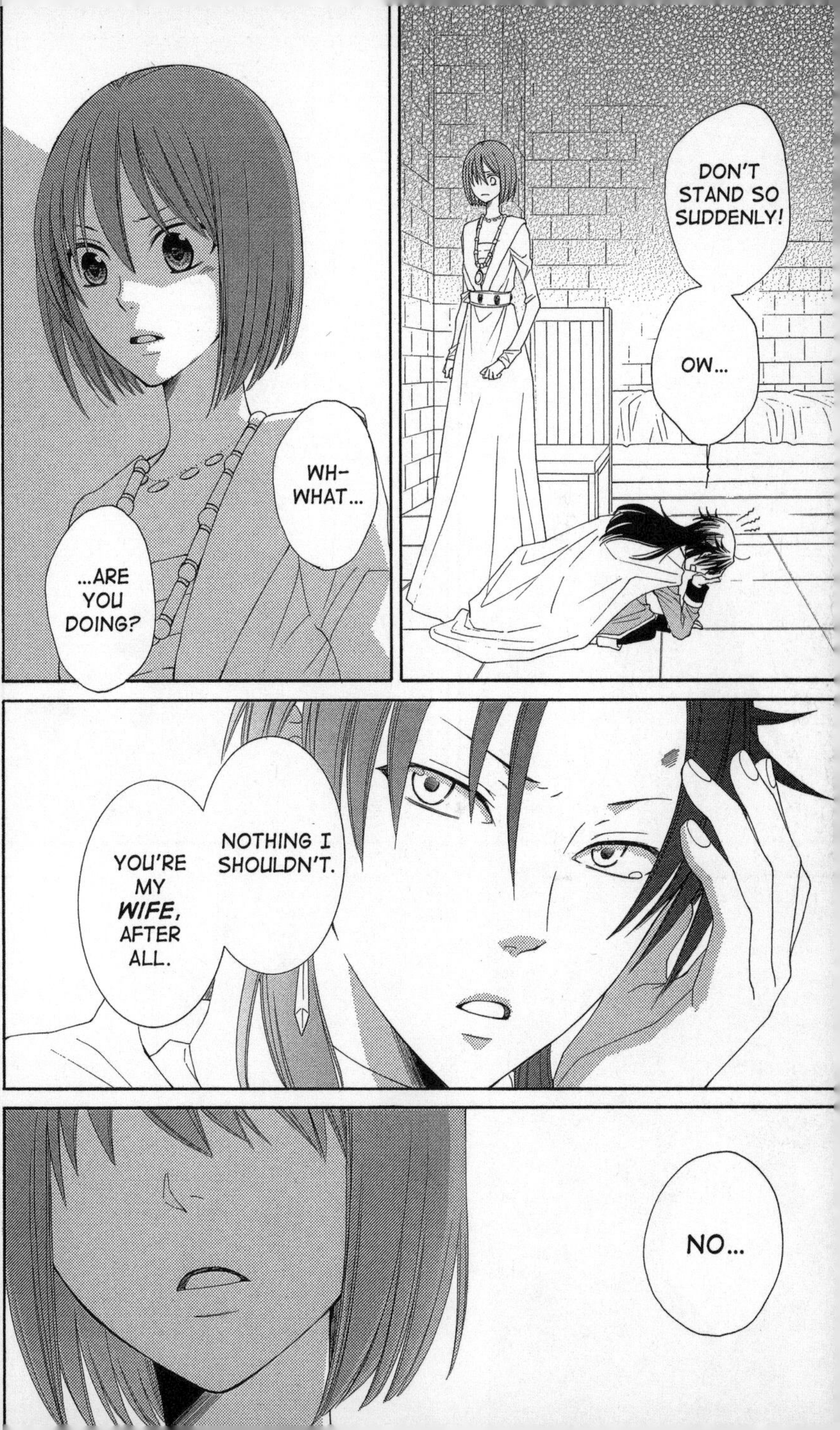
DON'T STAND SO SUDDENLY!
OW...
WH-WHAT...
...ARE YOU DOING?
NOTHING I SHOULDN'T.
YOU'RE MY *WIFE*, AFTER ALL.
NO...

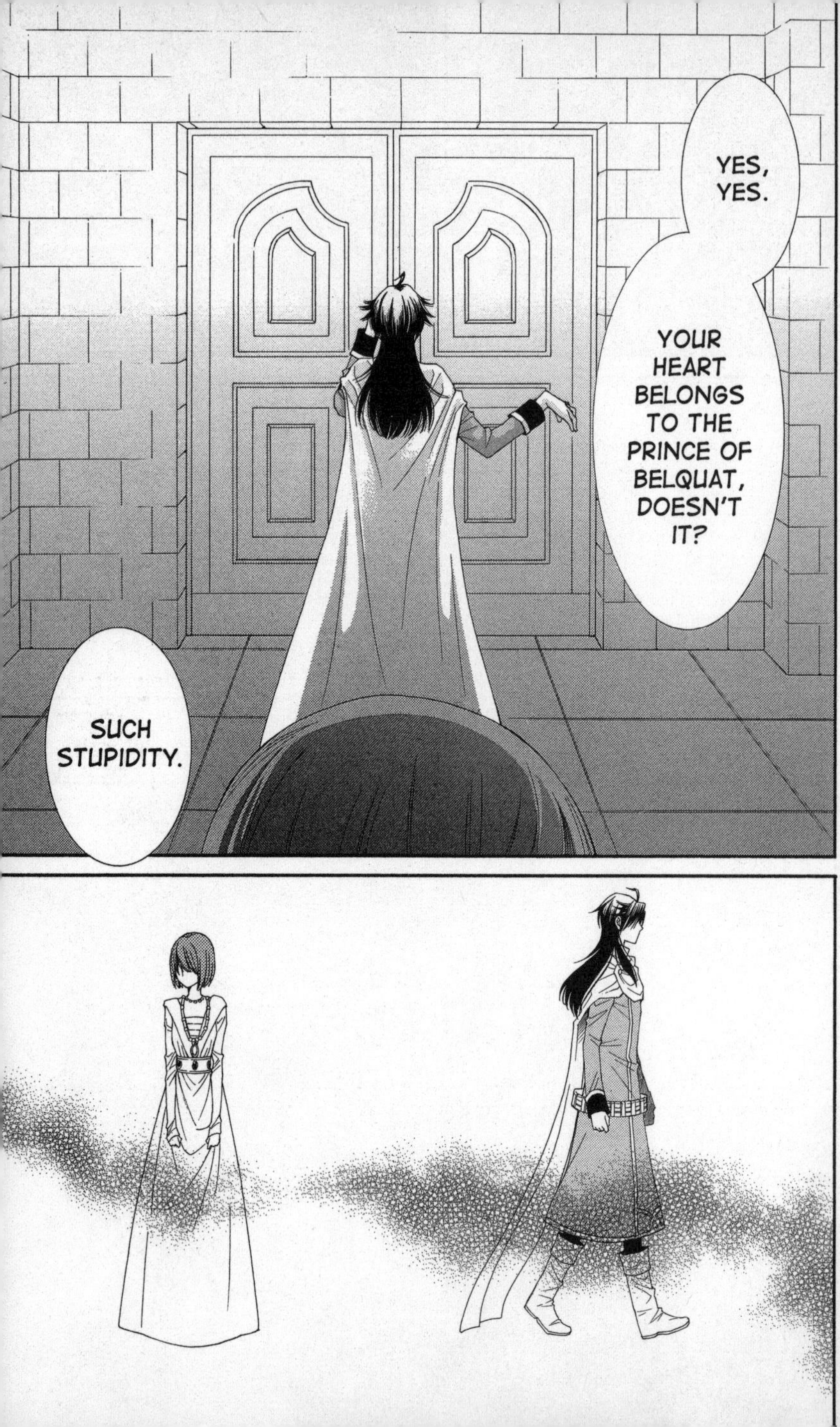
YES, YES.
YOUR HEART BELONGS TO THE PRINCE OF BELQUAT, DOESN'T IT?
SUCH STUPIDITY.

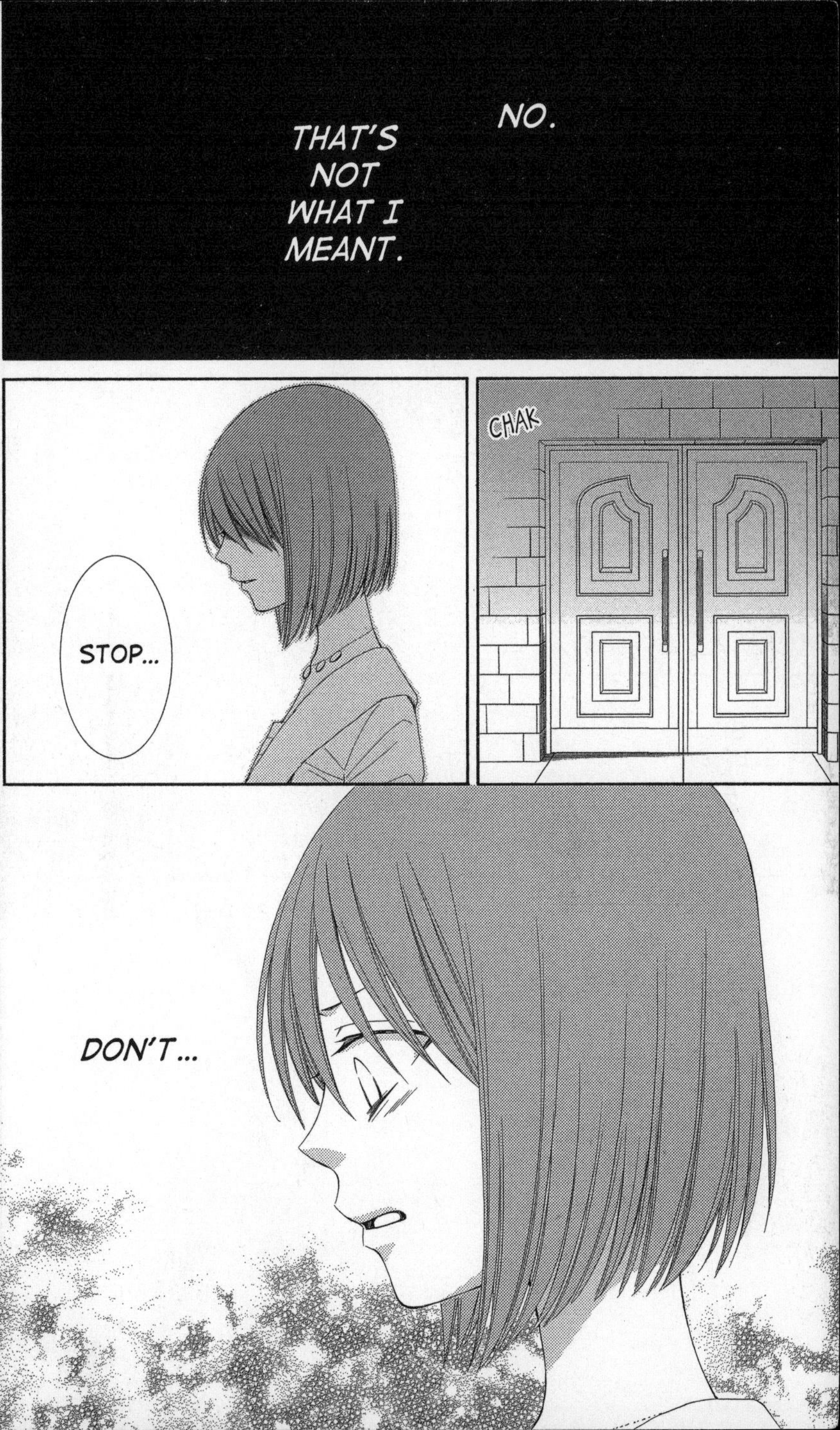
NO.
THAT'S NOT WHAT I MEANT.
CHAK
STOP...
DON'T...

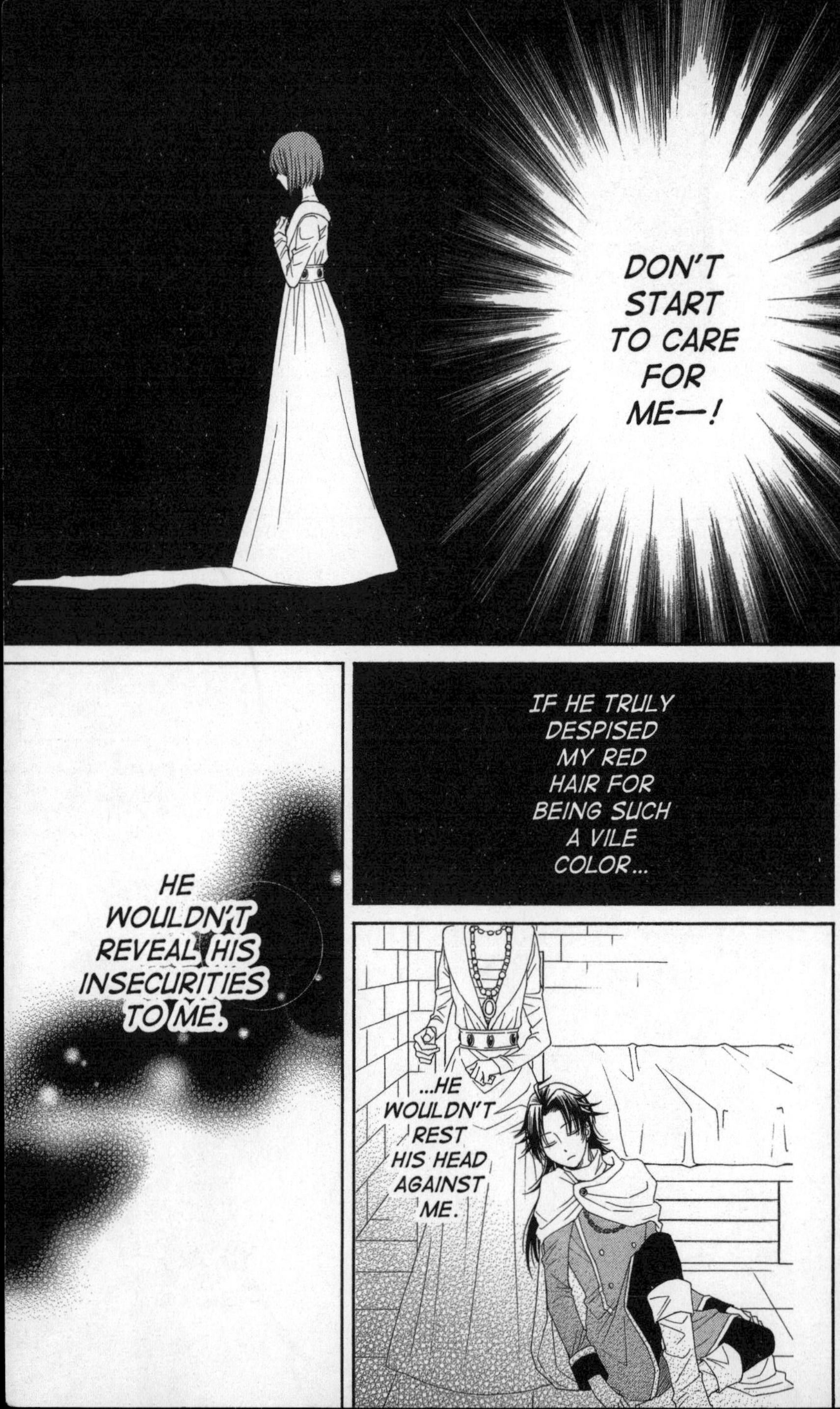
DON'T START TO CARE FOR ME—!
IF HE TRULY DESPISED MY RED HAIR FOR BEING SUCH A VILE COLOR...
...HE WOULDN'T REST HIS HEAD AGAINST ME.
HE WOULDN'T REVEAL HIS INSECURITIES TO ME.

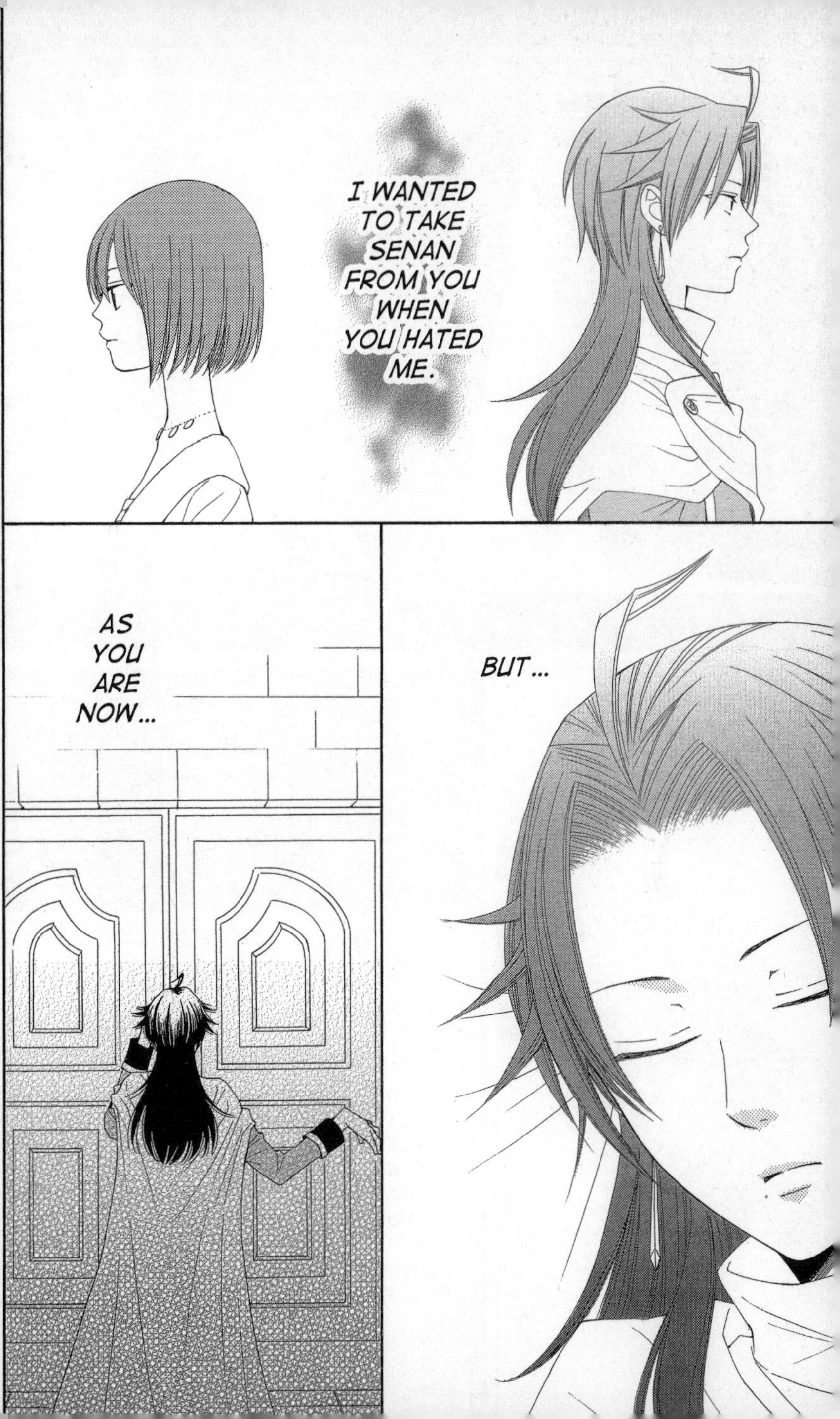
I WANTED TO TAKE SENAN FROM YOU WHEN YOU HATED ME.
BUT...
AS YOU ARE NOW...

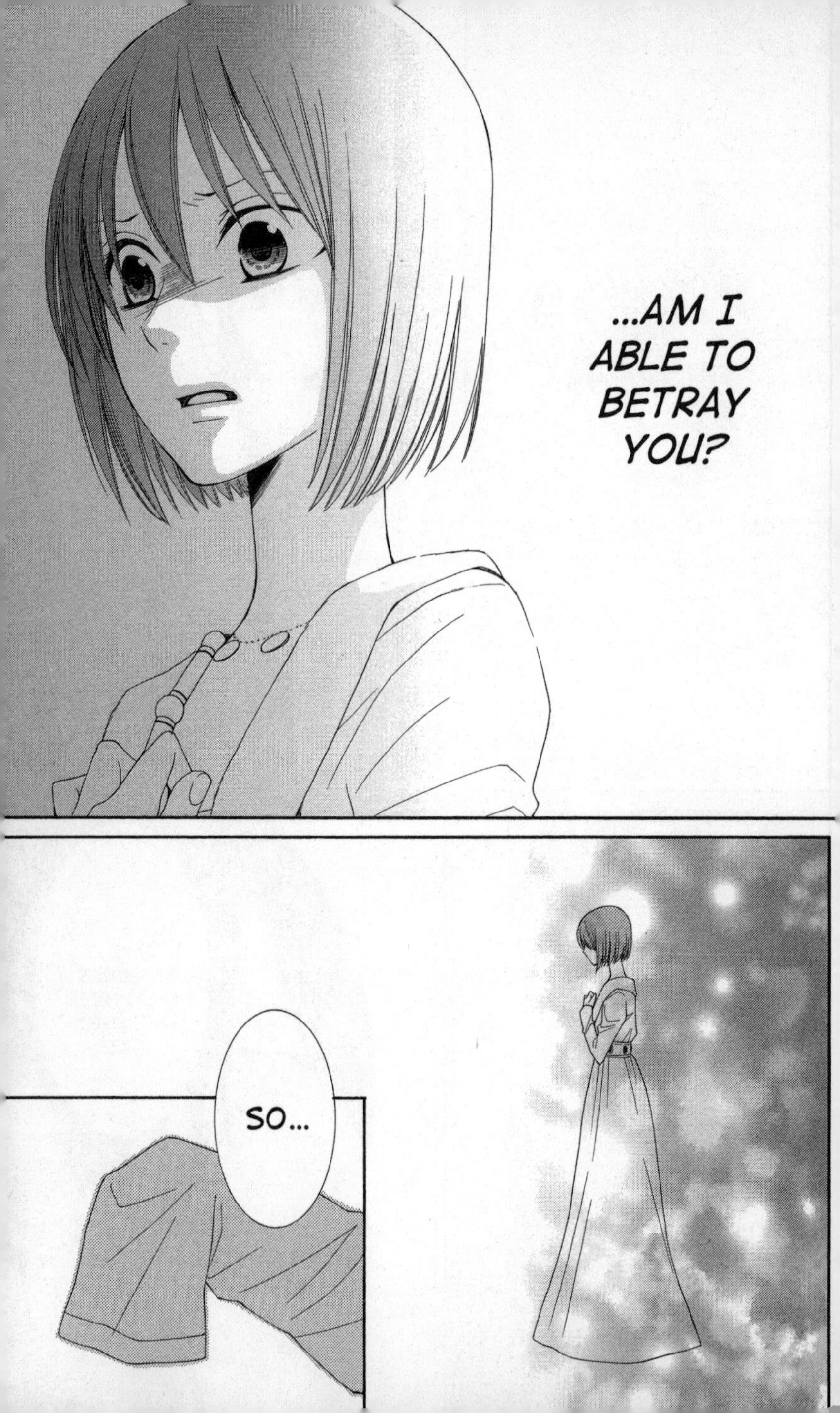
...AM I ABLE TO BETRAY YOU?
SO...

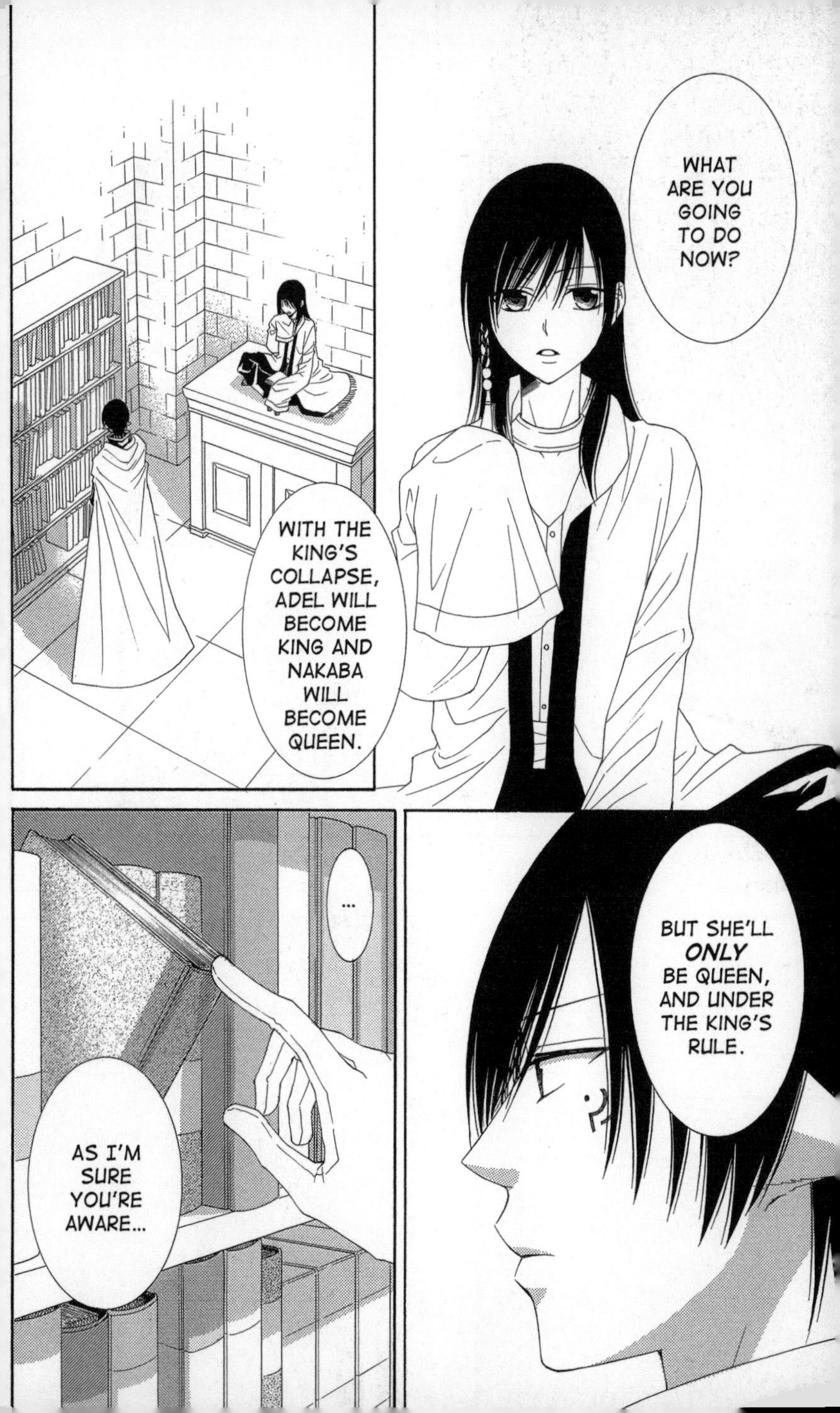
WHAT ARE YOU GOING TO DO NOW?
WITH THE KING'S COLLAPSE, ADEL WILL BECOME KING AND NAKABA WILL BECOME QUEEN.
BUT SHE'LL *ONLY* BE QUEEN, AND UNDER THE KING'S RULE.
...
AS I'M SURE YOU'RE AWARE...

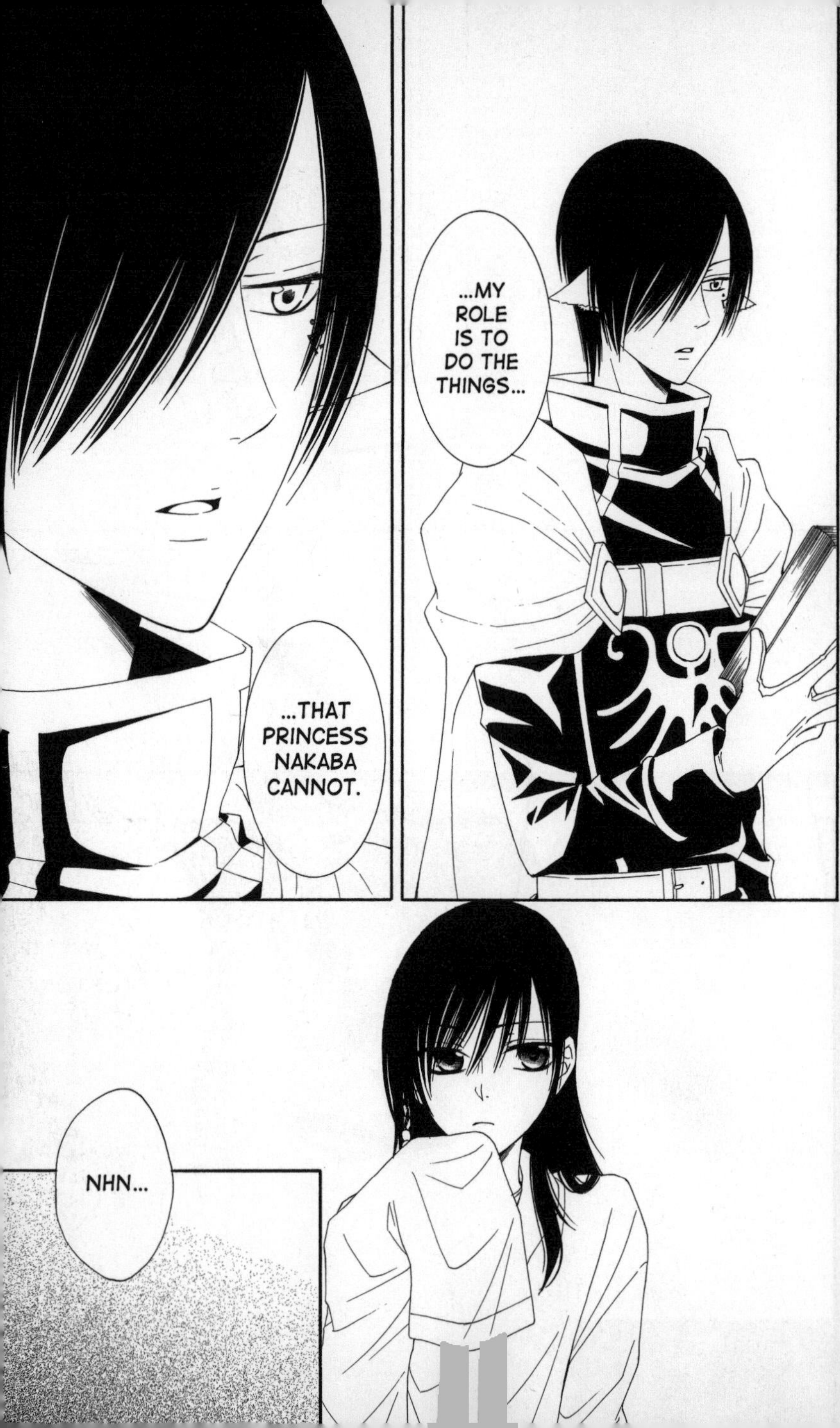
...MY ROLE IS TO DO THE THINGS...
...THAT PRINCESS NAKABA CANNOT.
NHN...

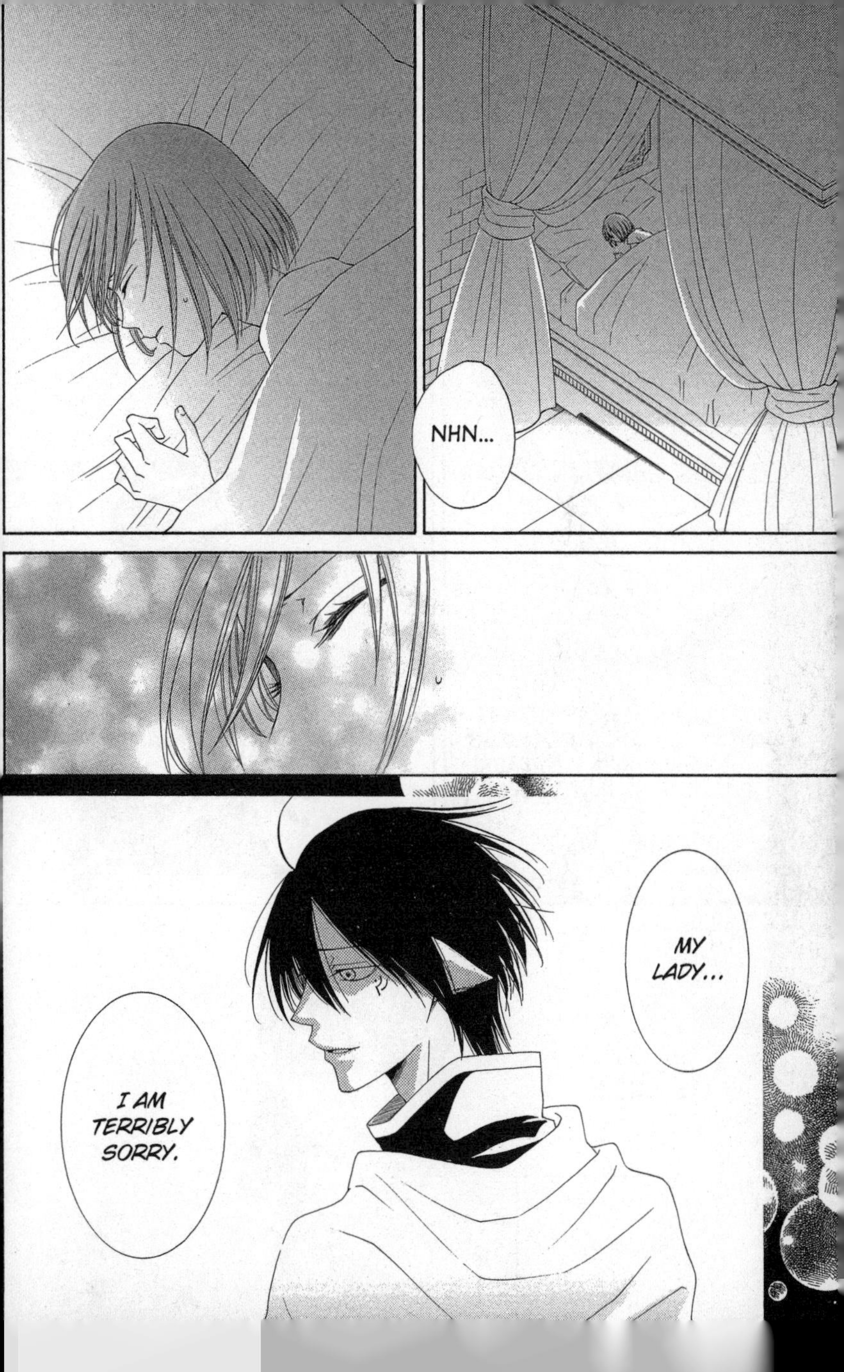
NHN...
MY LADY...
I AM TERRIBLY SORRY.

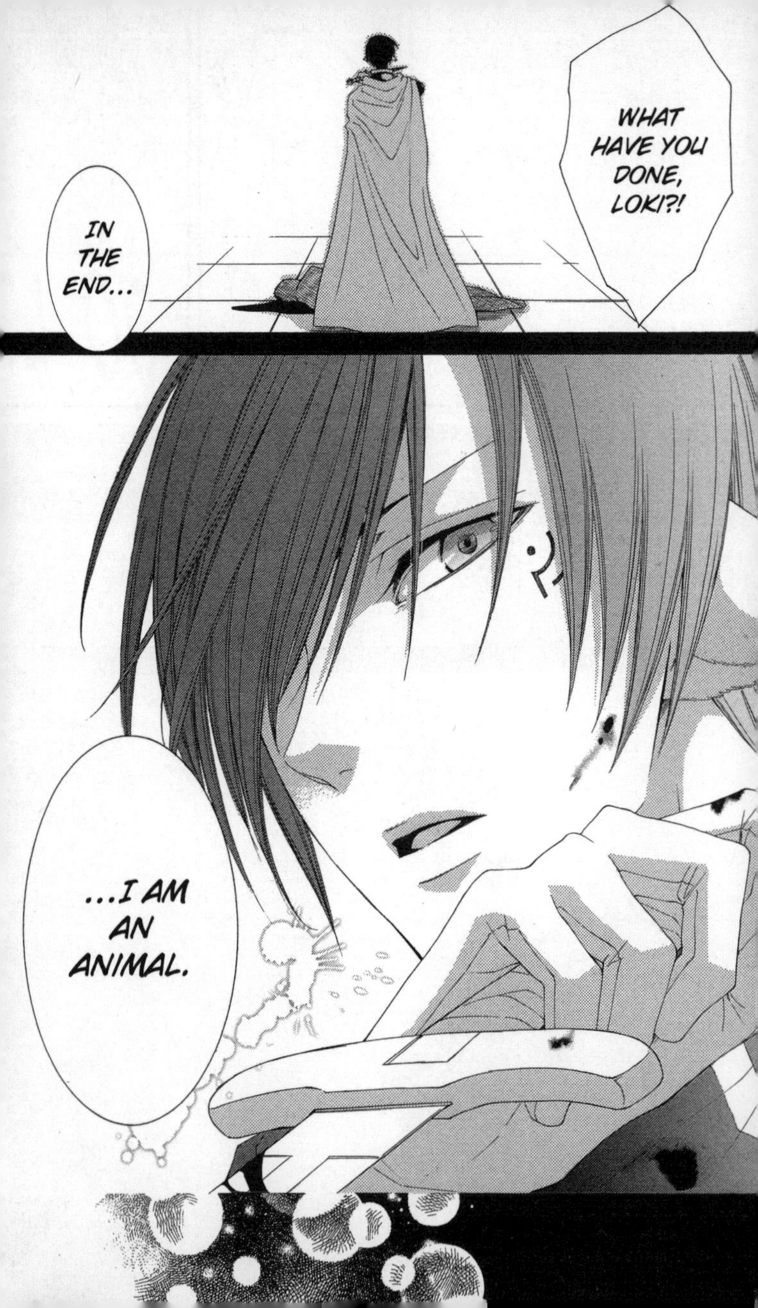
WHAT HAVE YOU DONE, LOKI?!
IN THE END...
...I AM AN ANIMAL.

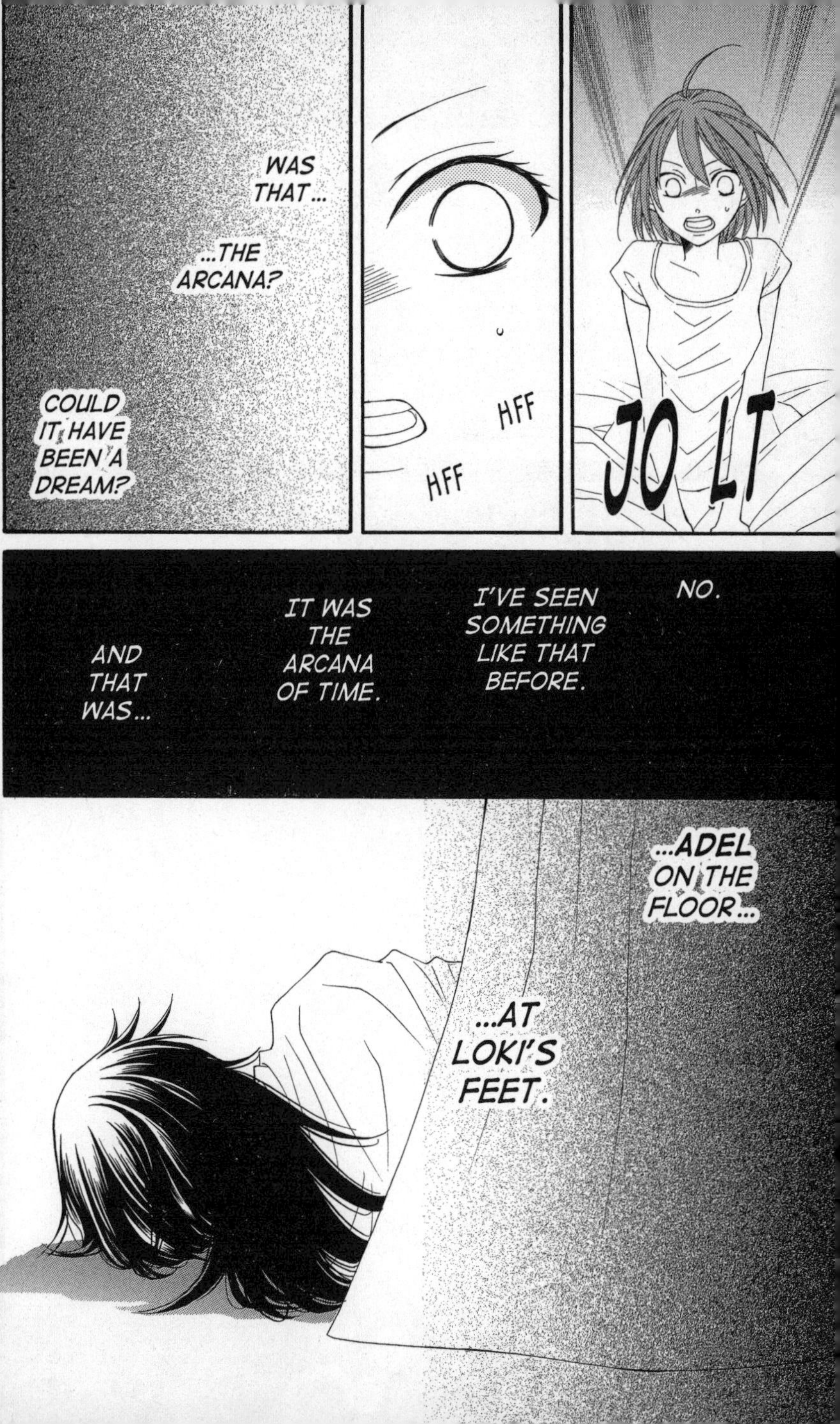
JOLT
HFF
HFF
WAS THAT...
...THE ARCANA?
COULD IT HAVE BEEN A DREAM?
NO.
I'VE SEEN SOMETHING LIKE THAT BEFORE.
IT WAS THE ARCANA OF TIME.
AND THAT WAS...
...ADEL ON THE FLOOR...
...AT LOKI'S FEET.

Chapter 45

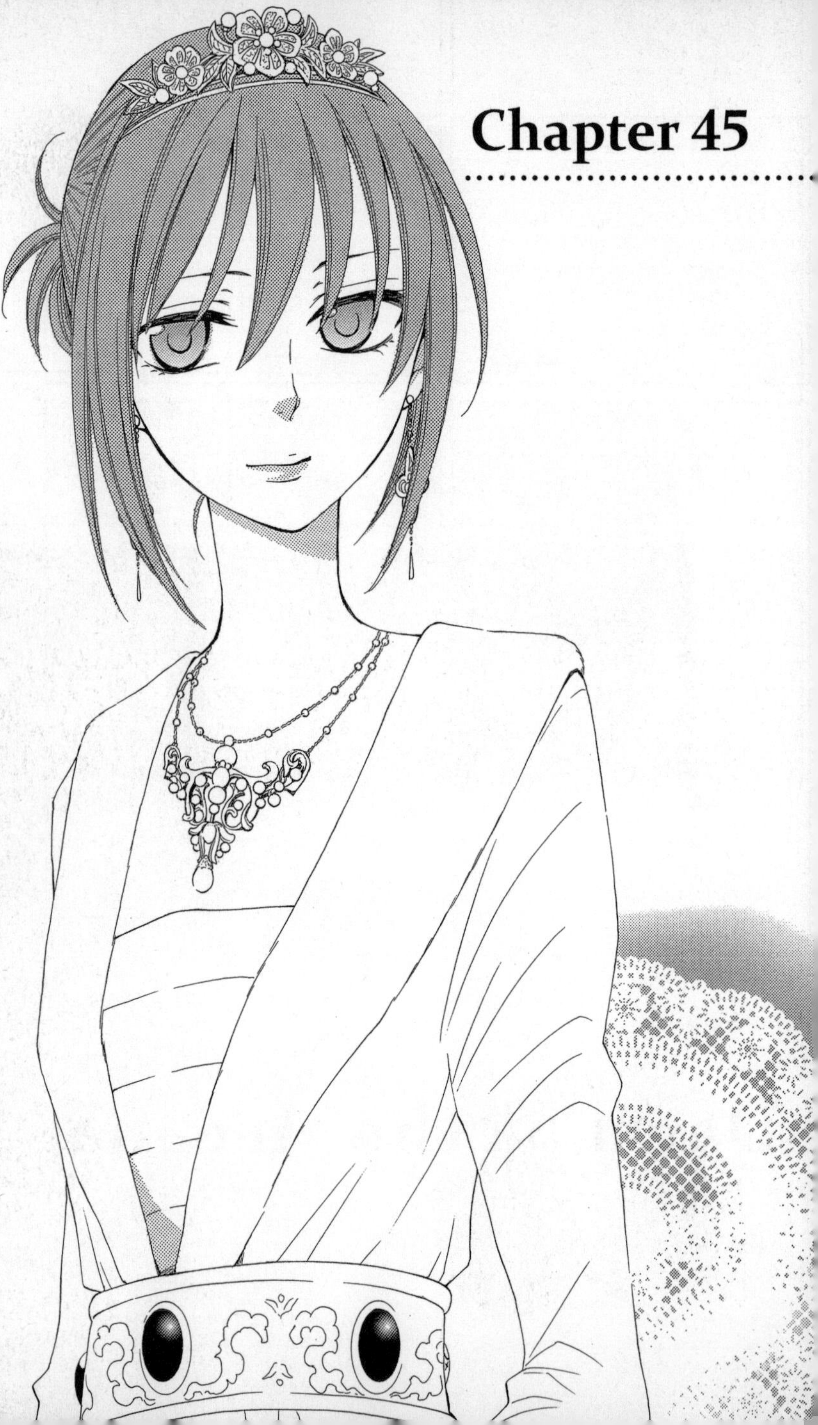

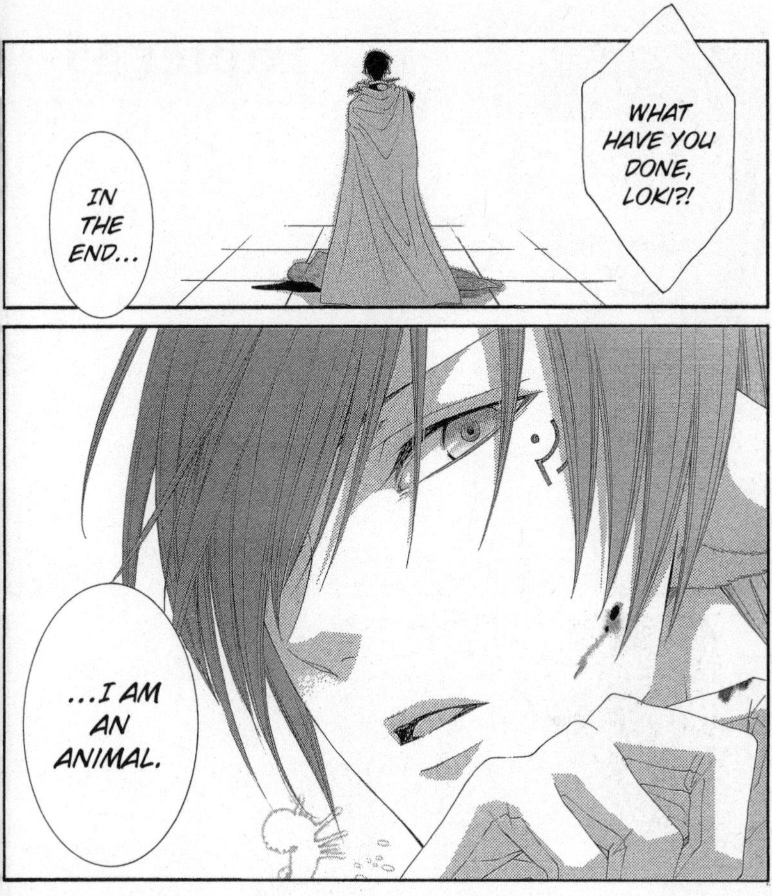
WHAT HAVE YOU DONE, LOKI?!
IN THE END...
...I AM AN ANIMAL.

Dawn of the Arcana

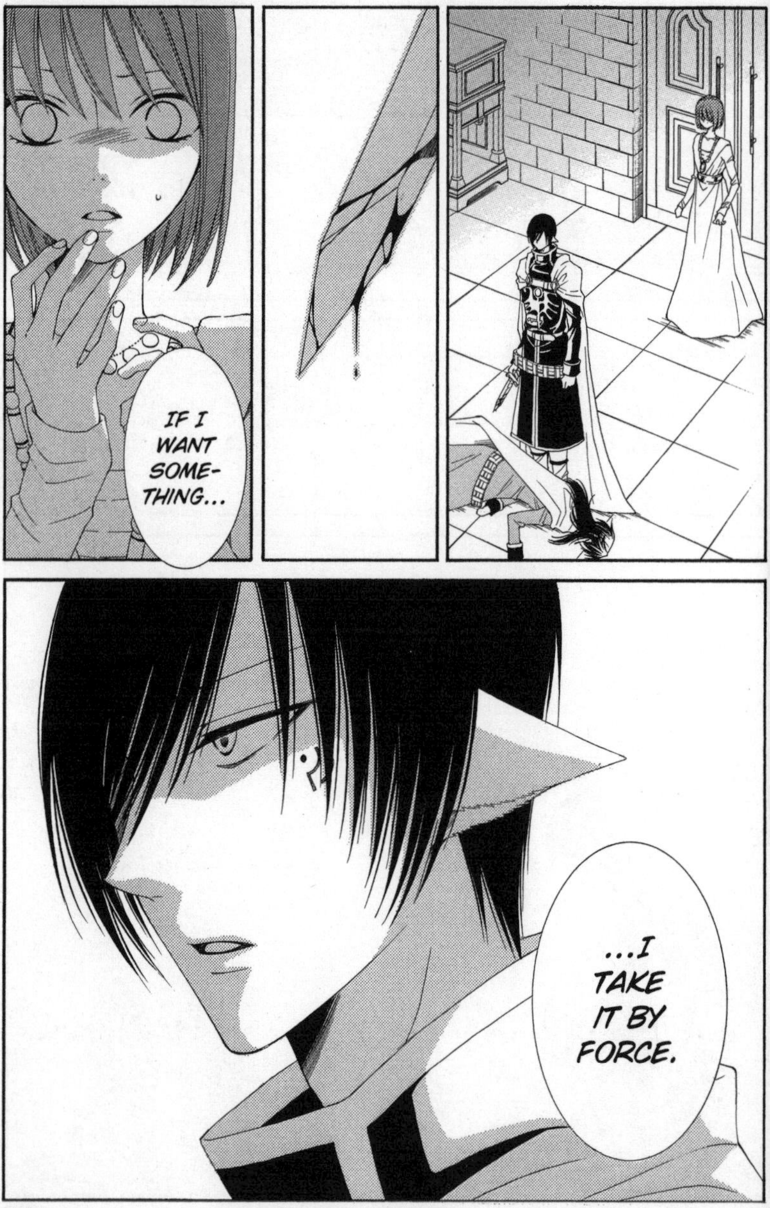
IF I WANT SOME-THING...
...I TAKE IT BY FORCE.

WHAT IS IT YOU WANT...?

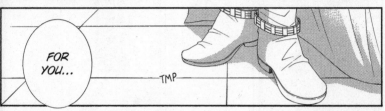

FOR YOU...

TMP

...TO BECOME THE RULER OF THIS COUNTRY.

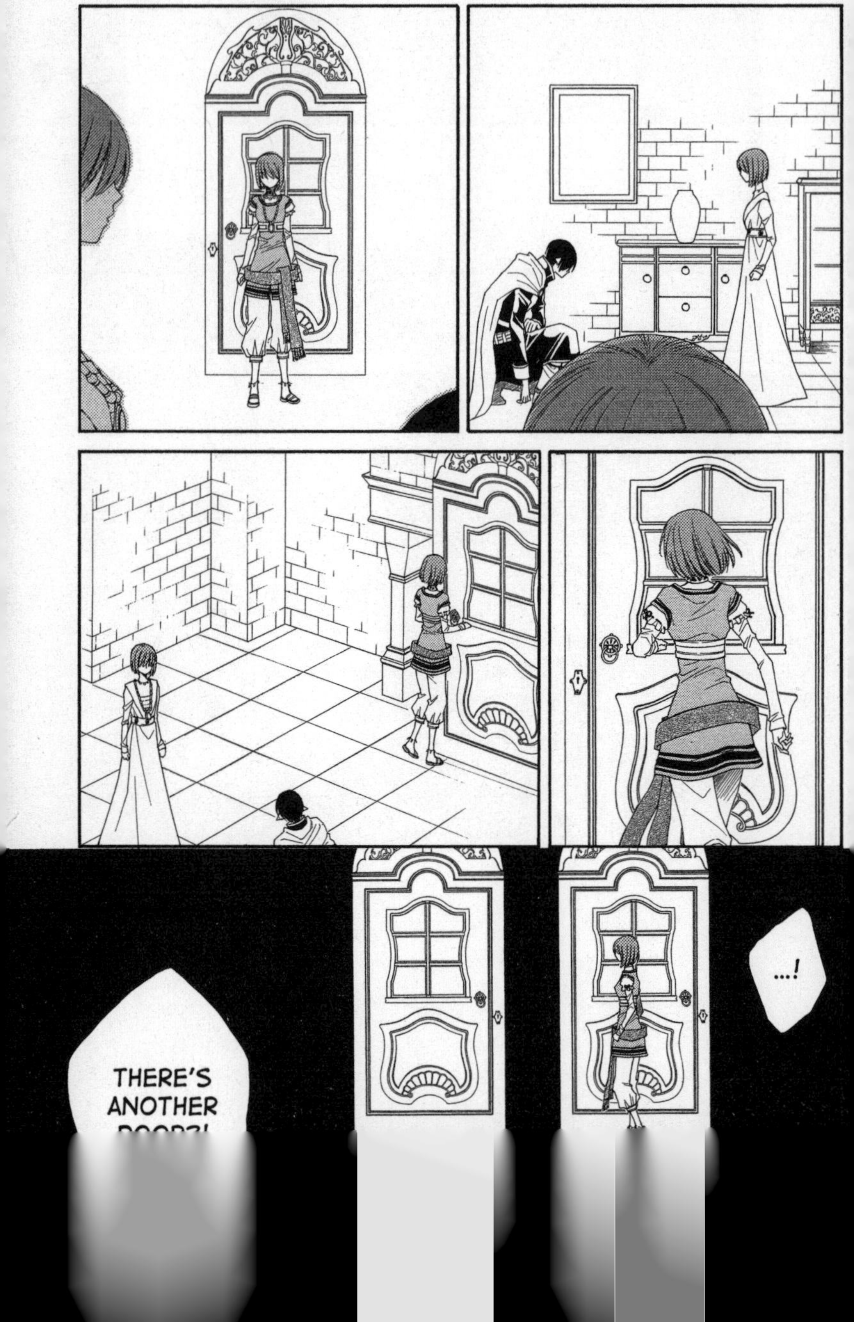
...!
THERE'S ANOTHER

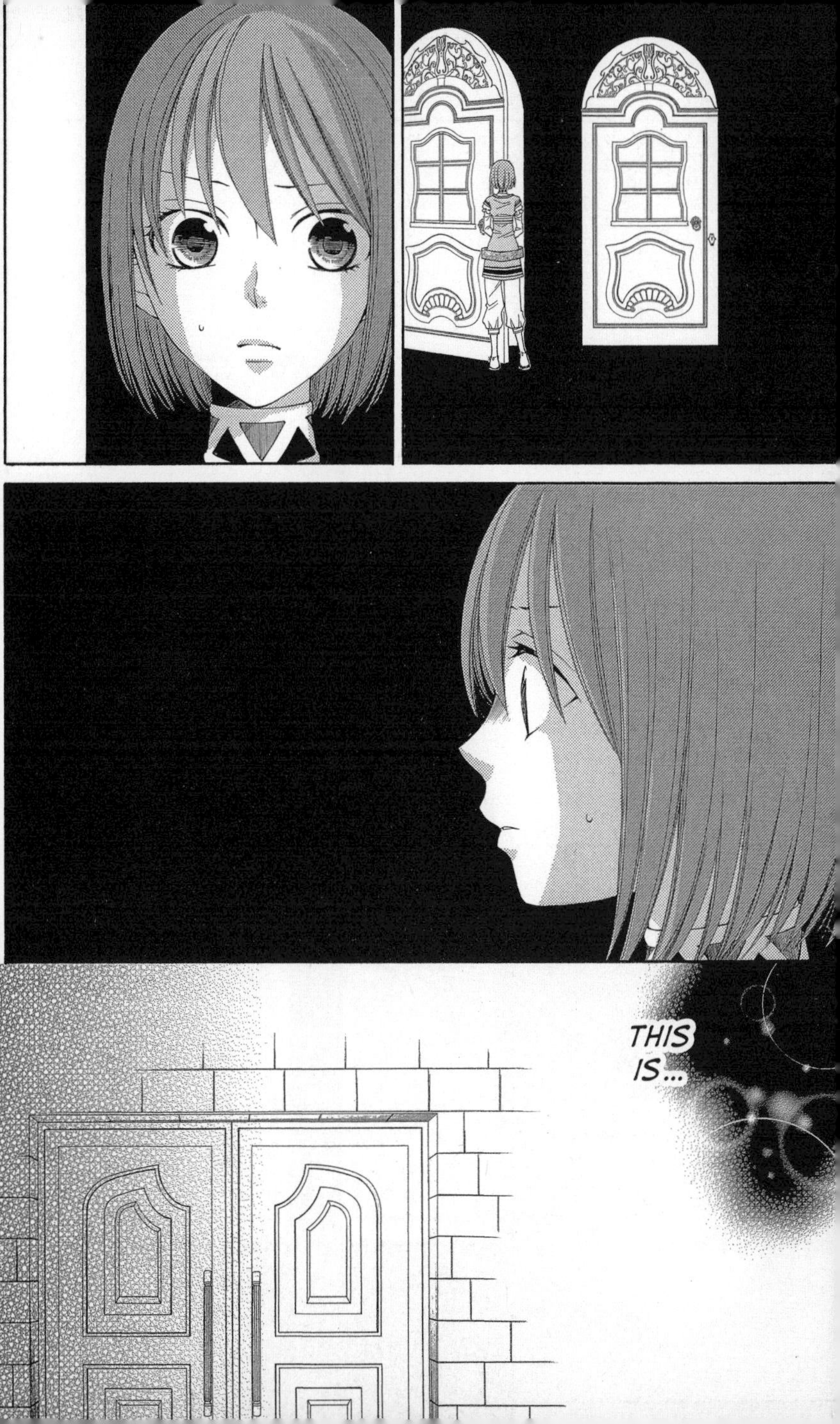
THIS IS...

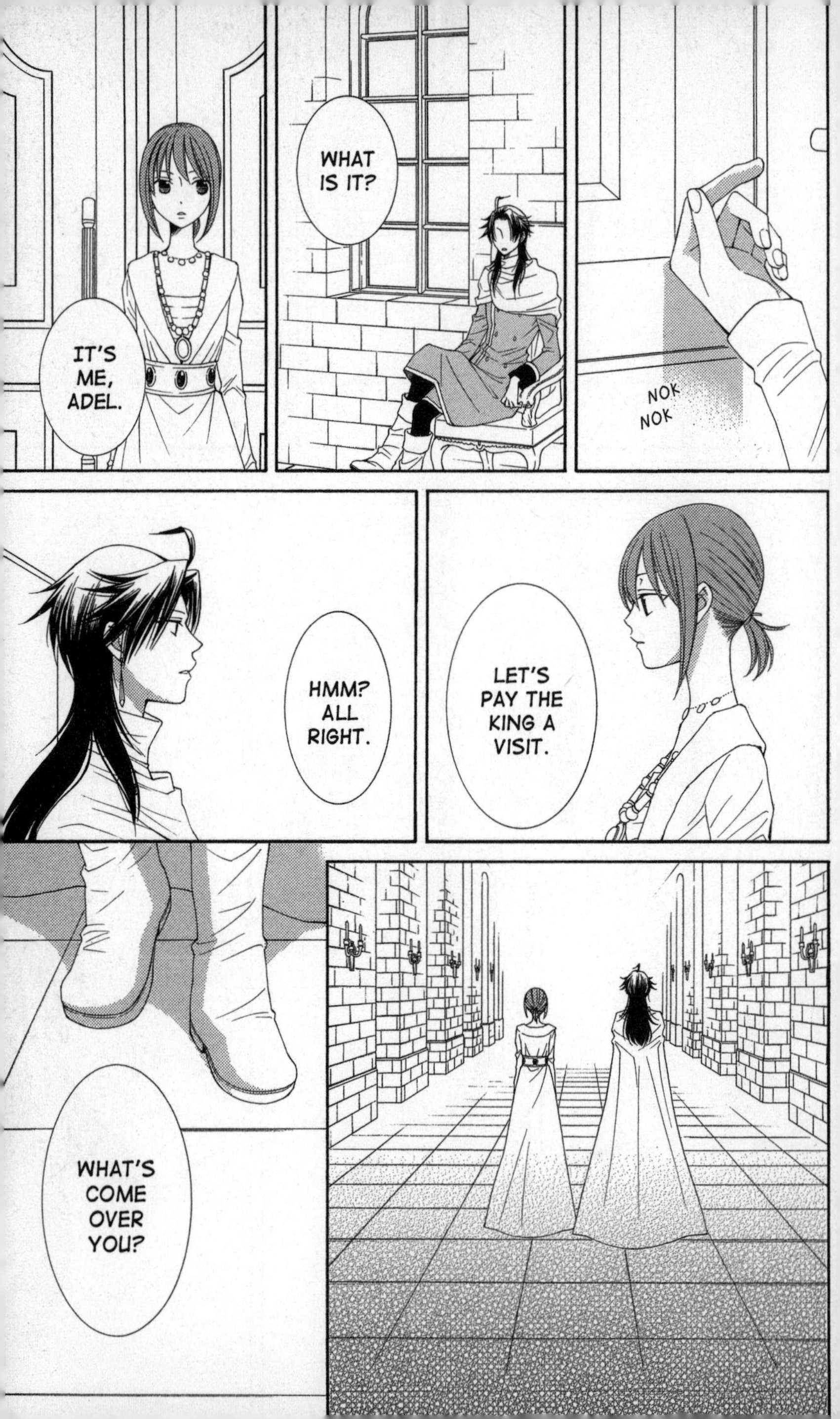
NOK NOK
WHAT IS IT?
IT'S ME, ADEL.
LET'S PAY THE KING A VISIT.
HMM? ALL RIGHT.
WHAT'S COME OVER YOU?

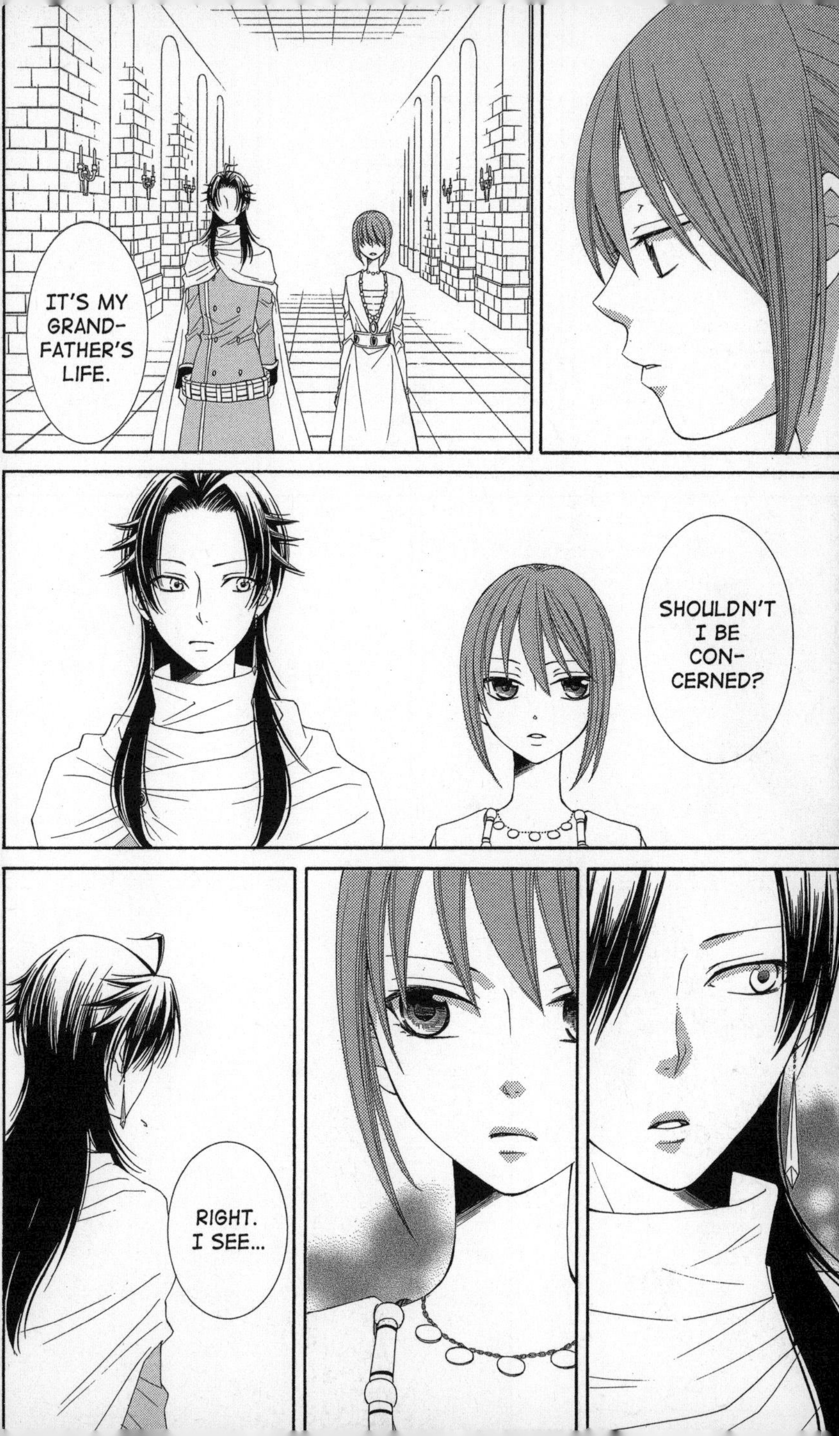
IT'S MY GRAND-FATHER'S LIFE.
SHOULDN'T I BE CON-CERNED?
RIGHT. I SEE...

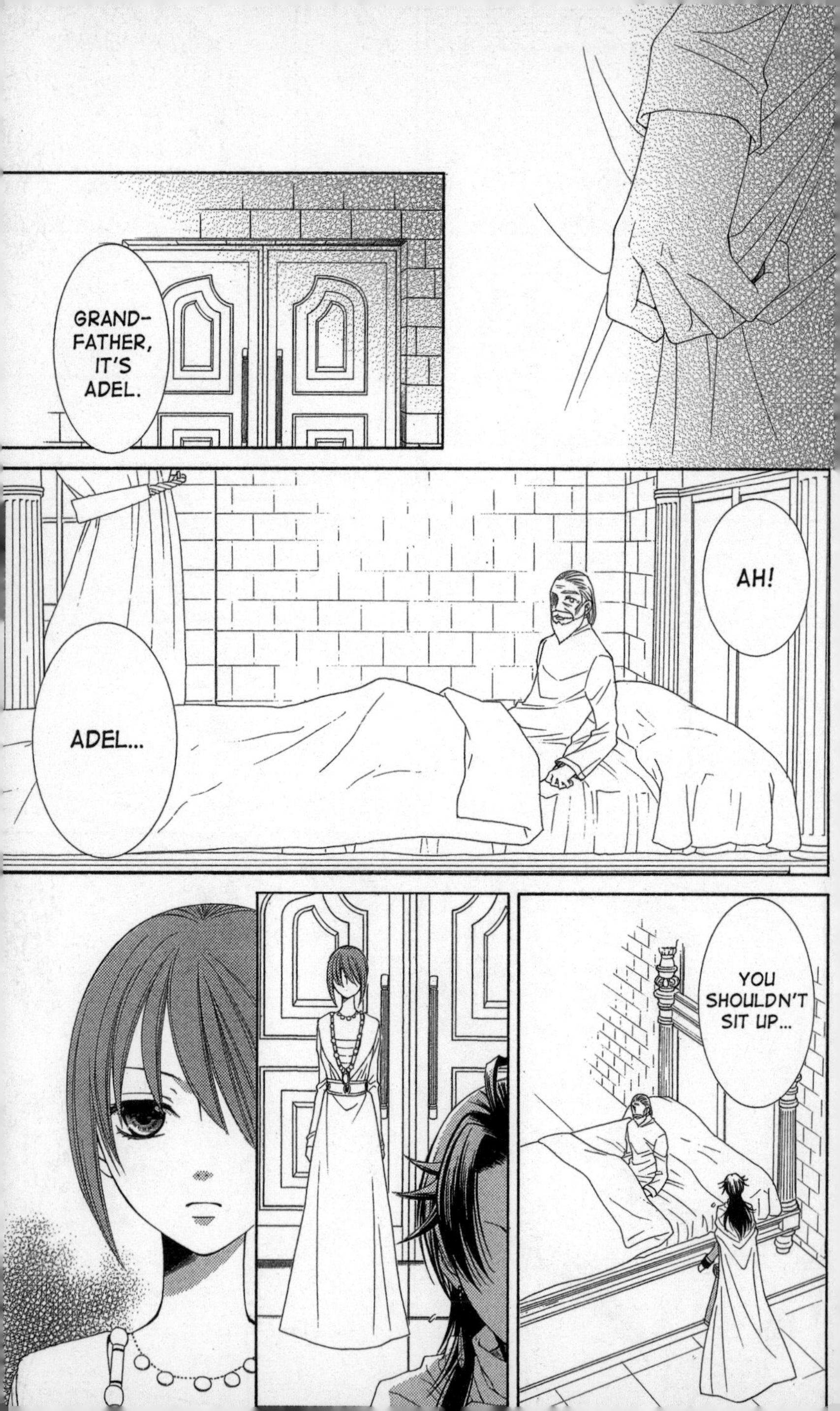
GRAND-FATHER, IT'S ADEL.
AH!
ADEL...
YOU SHOULDN'T SIT UP...

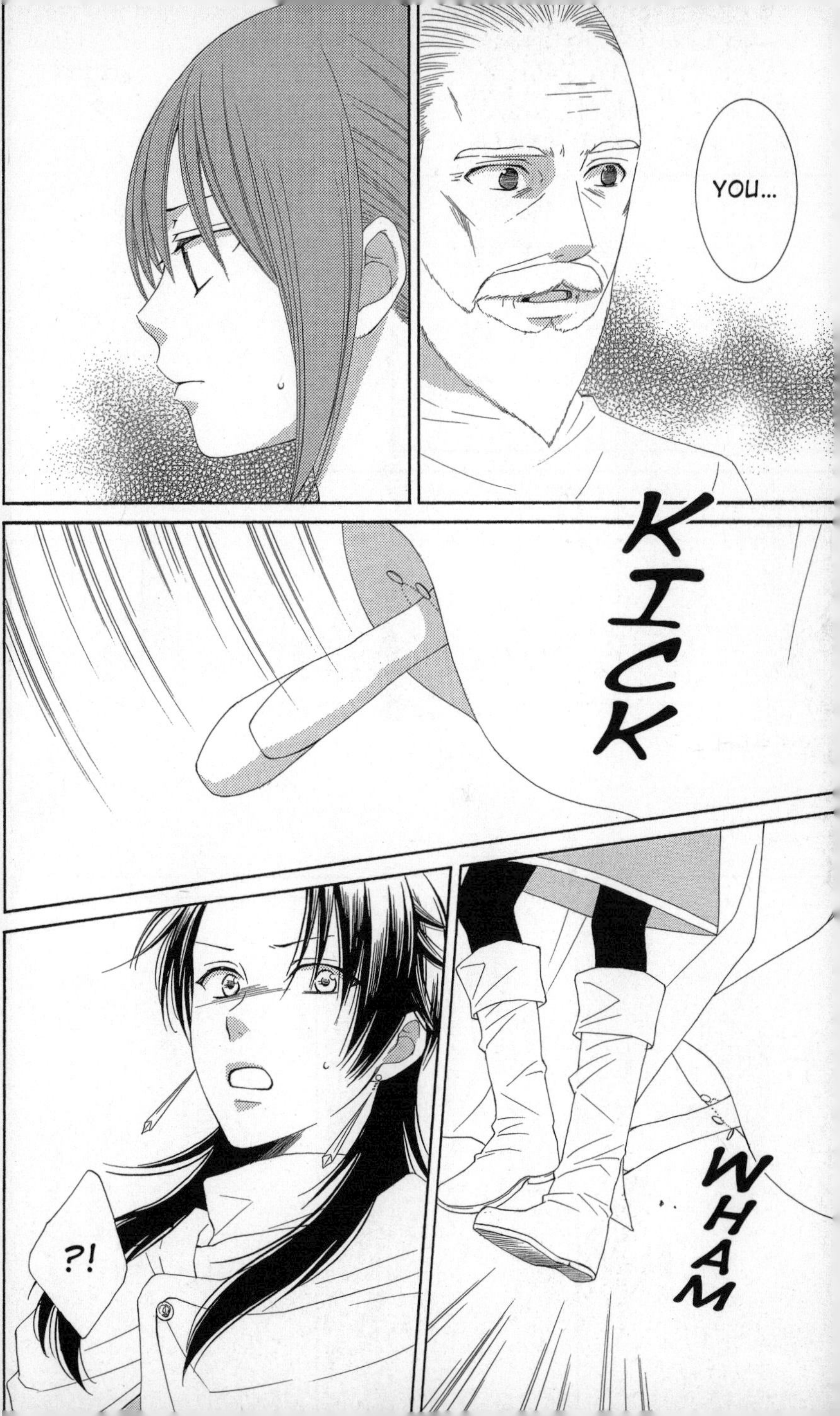
YOU...
KICK
WHAM
?!

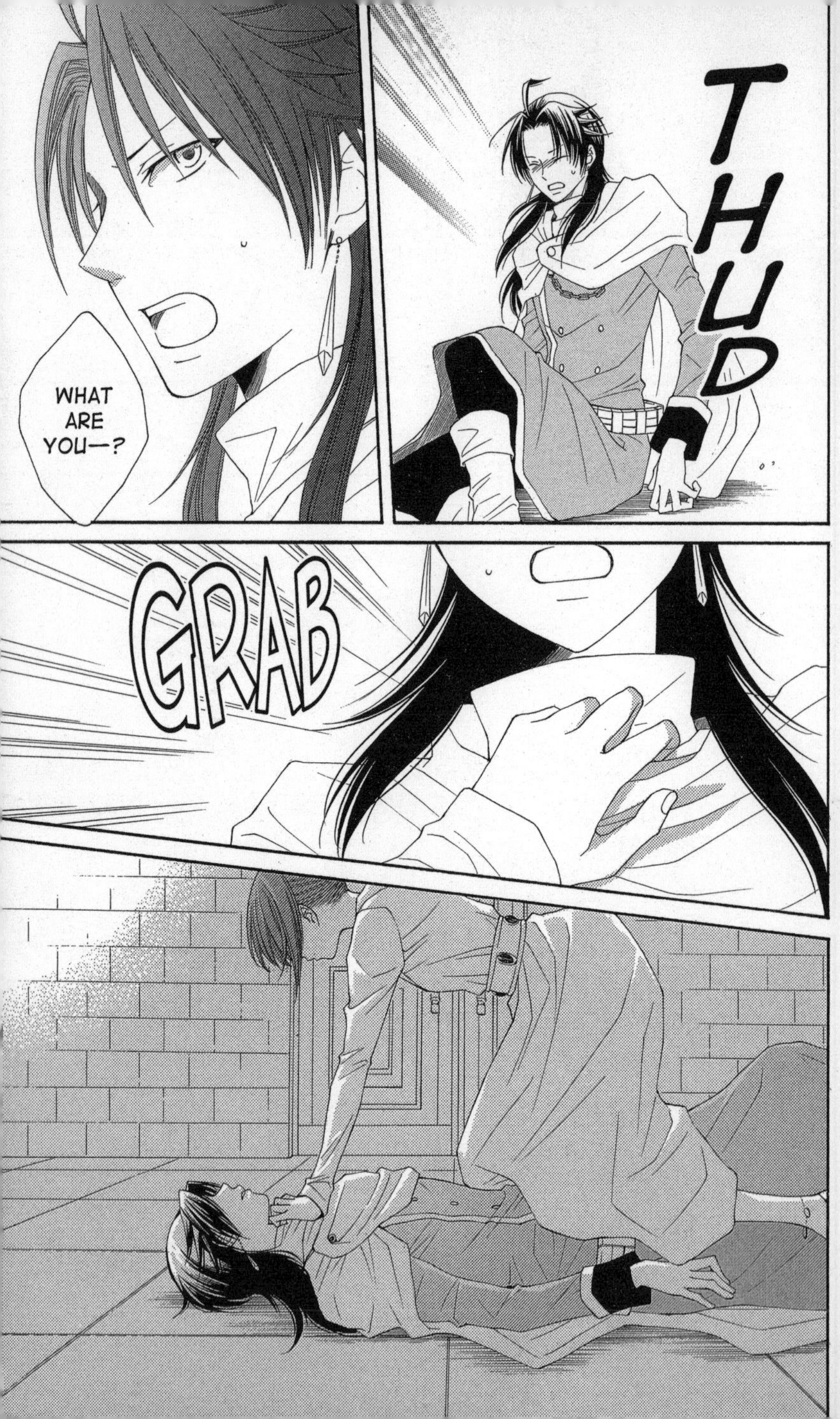
THUD
WHAT ARE YOU—?
GRAB

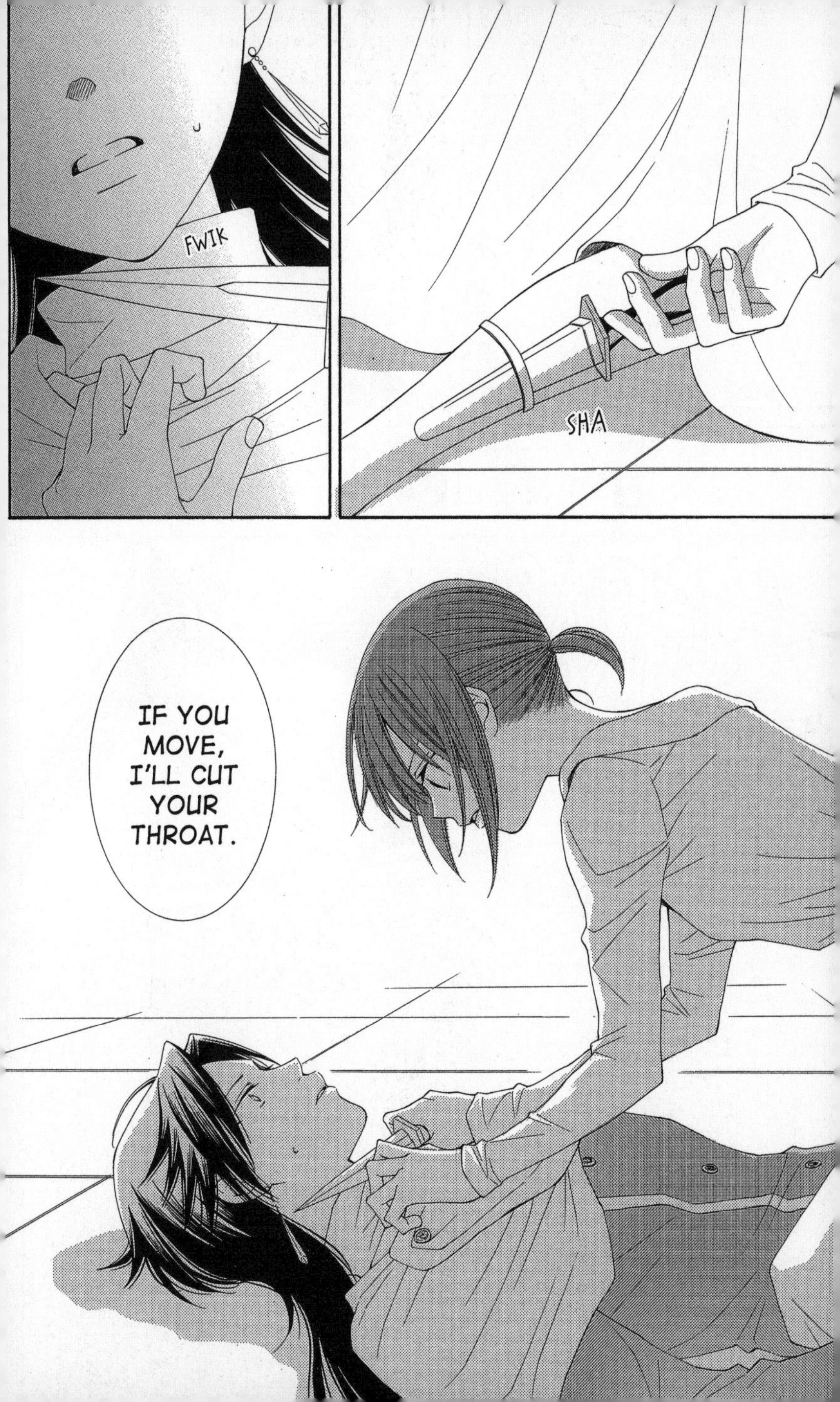
SHA
FWIK
IF YOU MOVE, I'LL CUT YOUR THROAT.

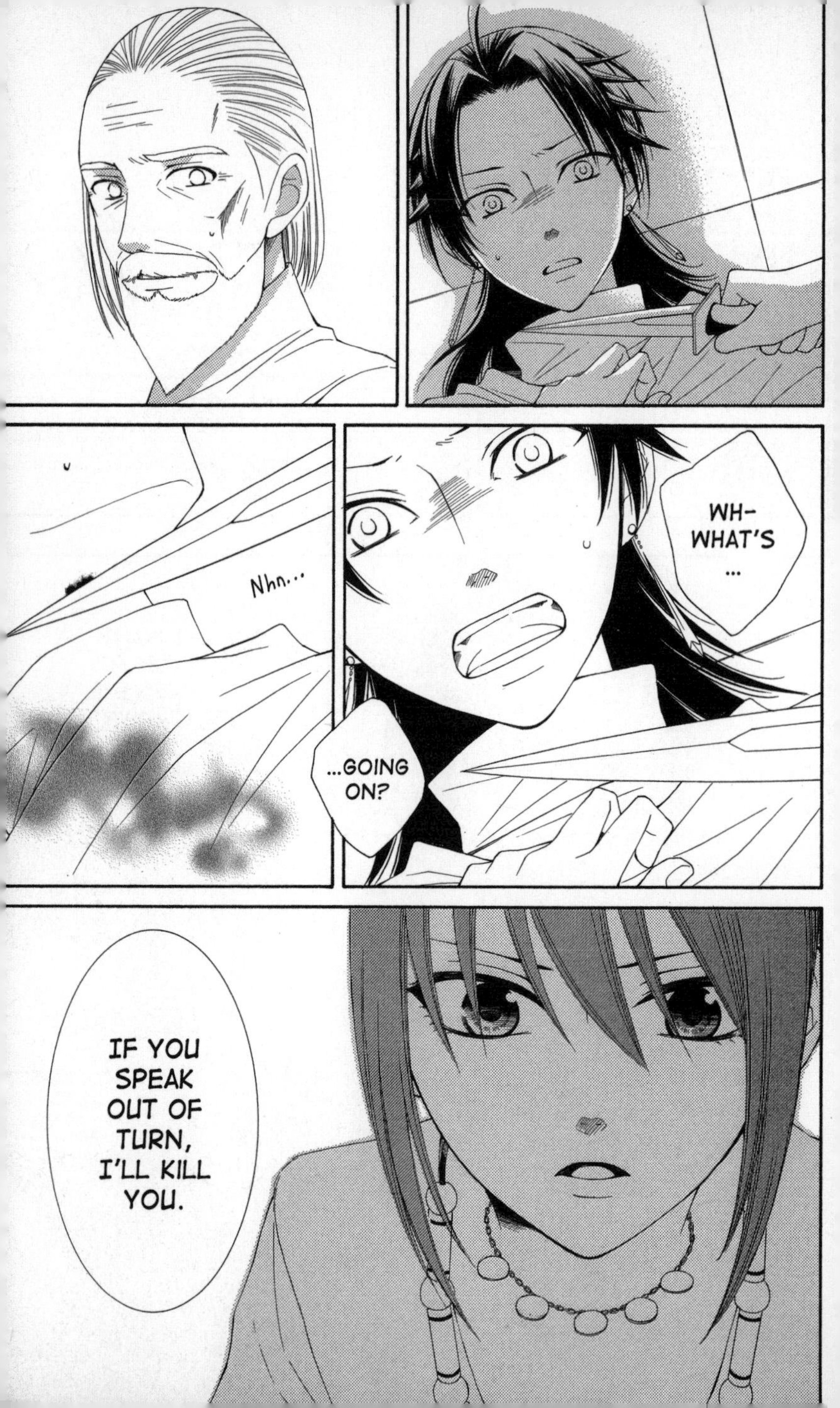
WH- WHAT'S ...
...GOING ON?
Nhn...
IF YOU SPEAK OUT OF TURN, I'LL KILL YOU.

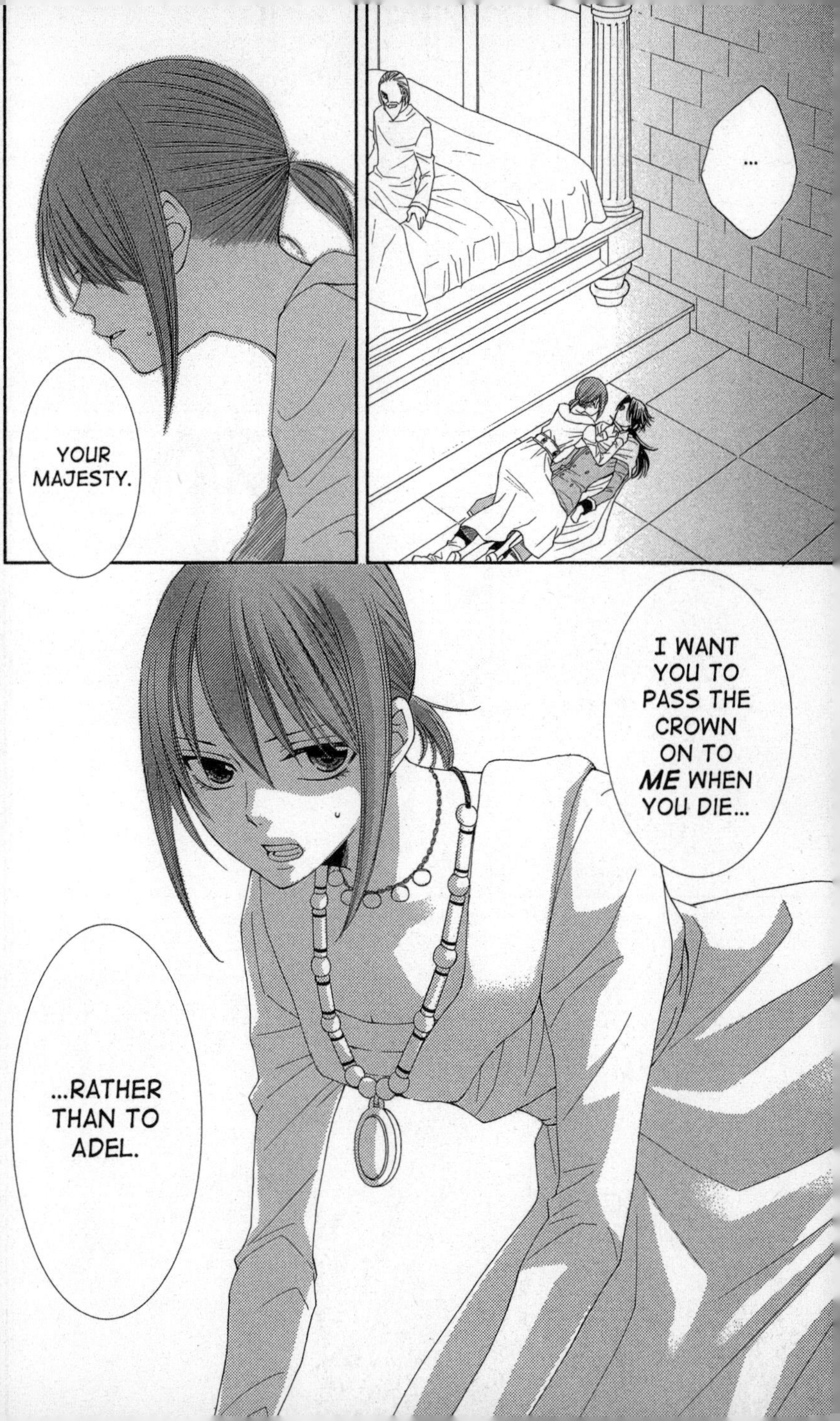
...
YOUR MAJESTY.
I WANT YOU TO PASS THE CROWN ON TO *ME* WHEN YOU DIE...
...RATHER THAN TO ADEL.

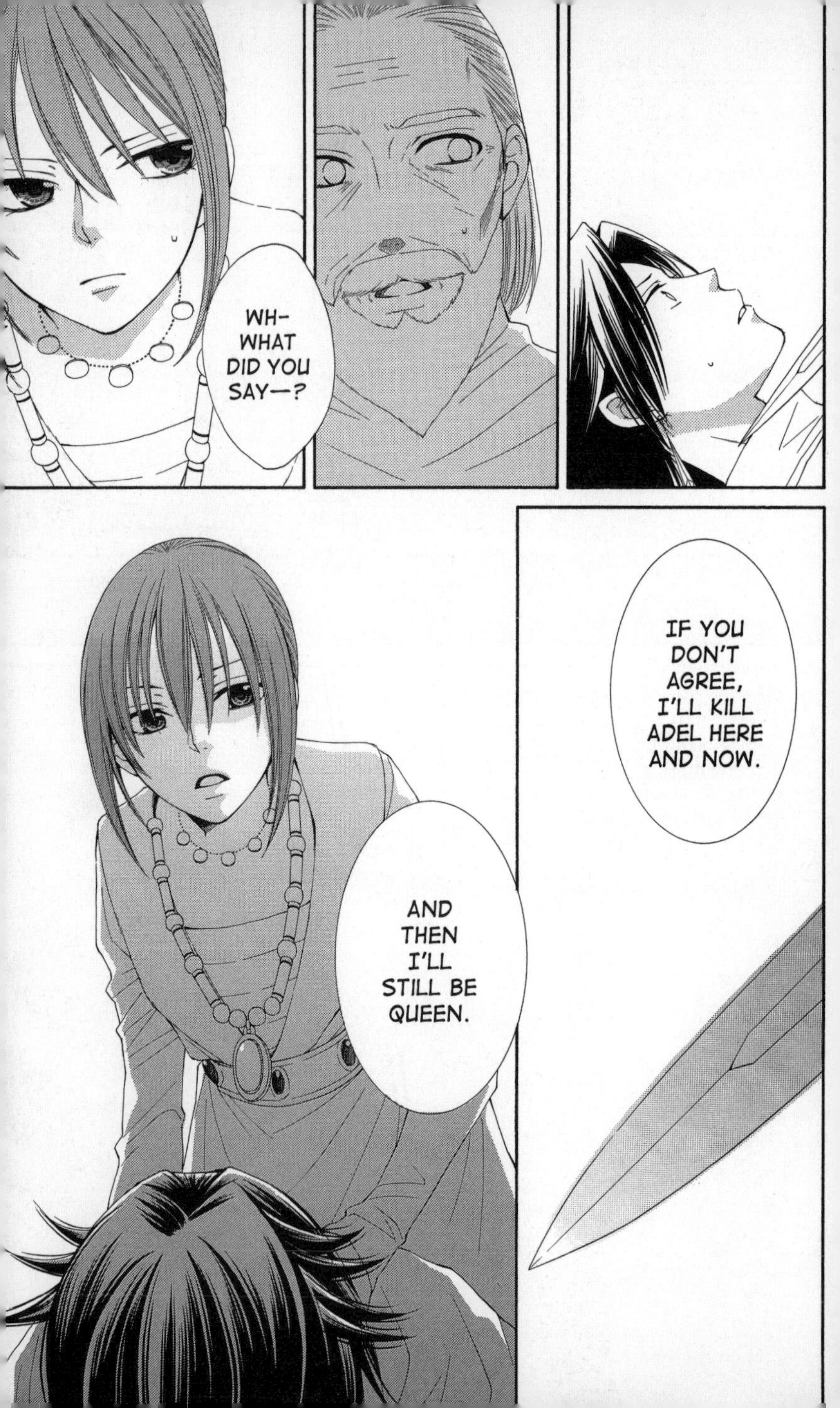
WH- WHAT DID YOU SAY—?
IF YOU DON'T AGREE, I'LL KILL ADEL HERE AND NOW.
AND THEN I'LL STILL BE QUEEN.

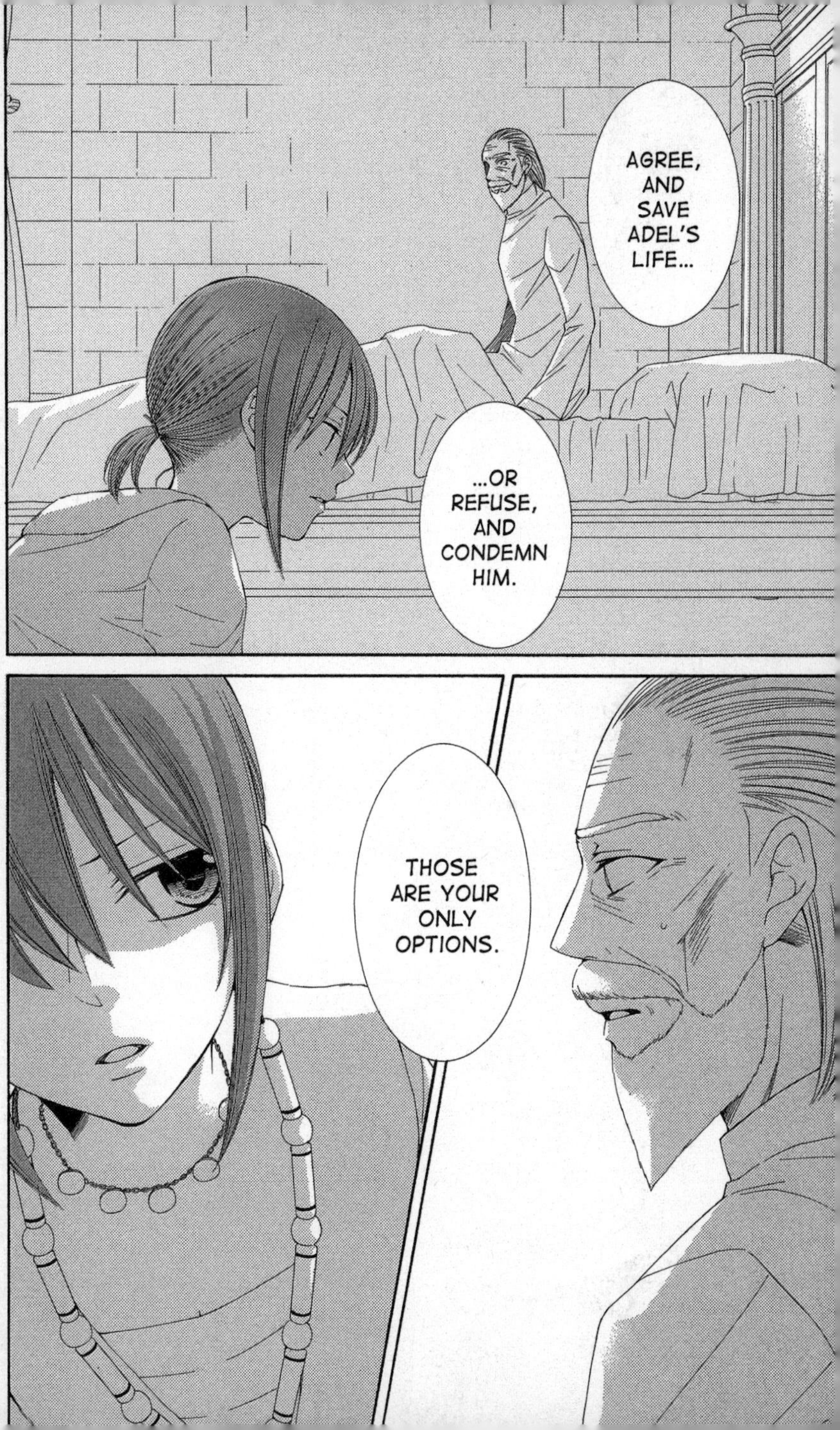
AGREE, AND SAVE ADEL'S LIFE...
...OR REFUSE, AND CONDEMN HIM.
THOSE ARE YOUR ONLY OPTIONS.

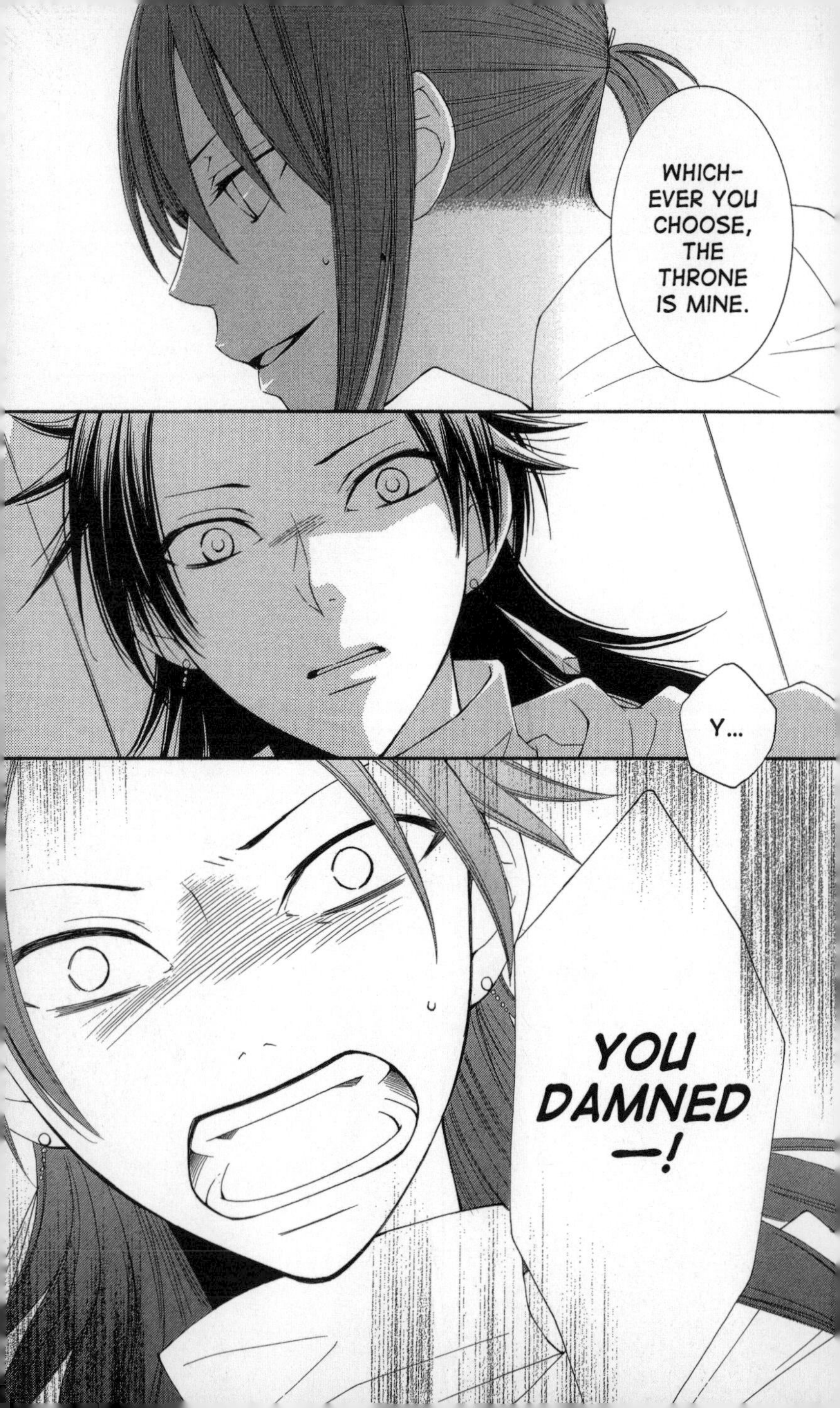
WHICH-EVER YOU CHOOSE, THE THRONE IS MINE.
Y...
YOU DAMNED —!

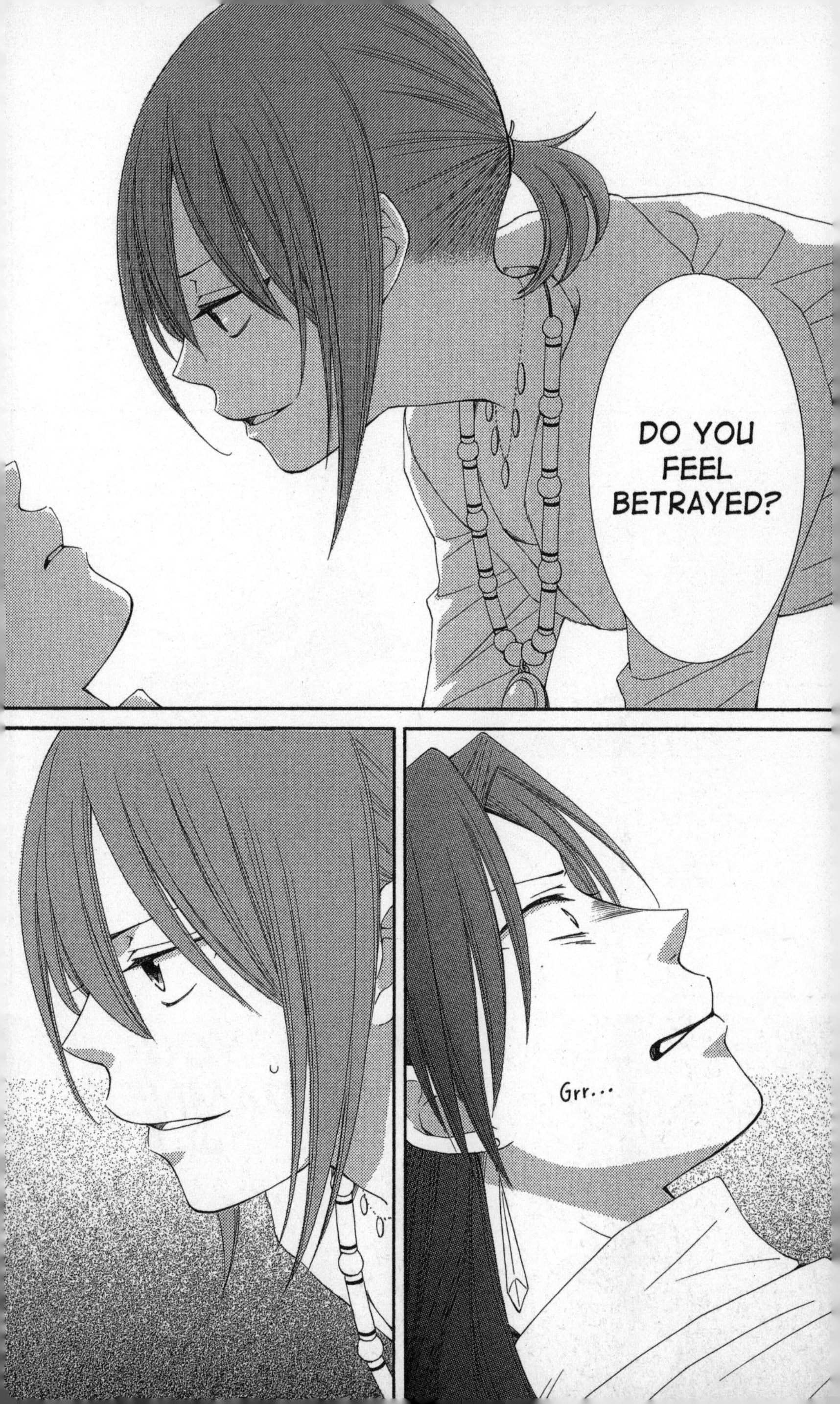
DO YOU FEEL BETRAYED?
Grr...

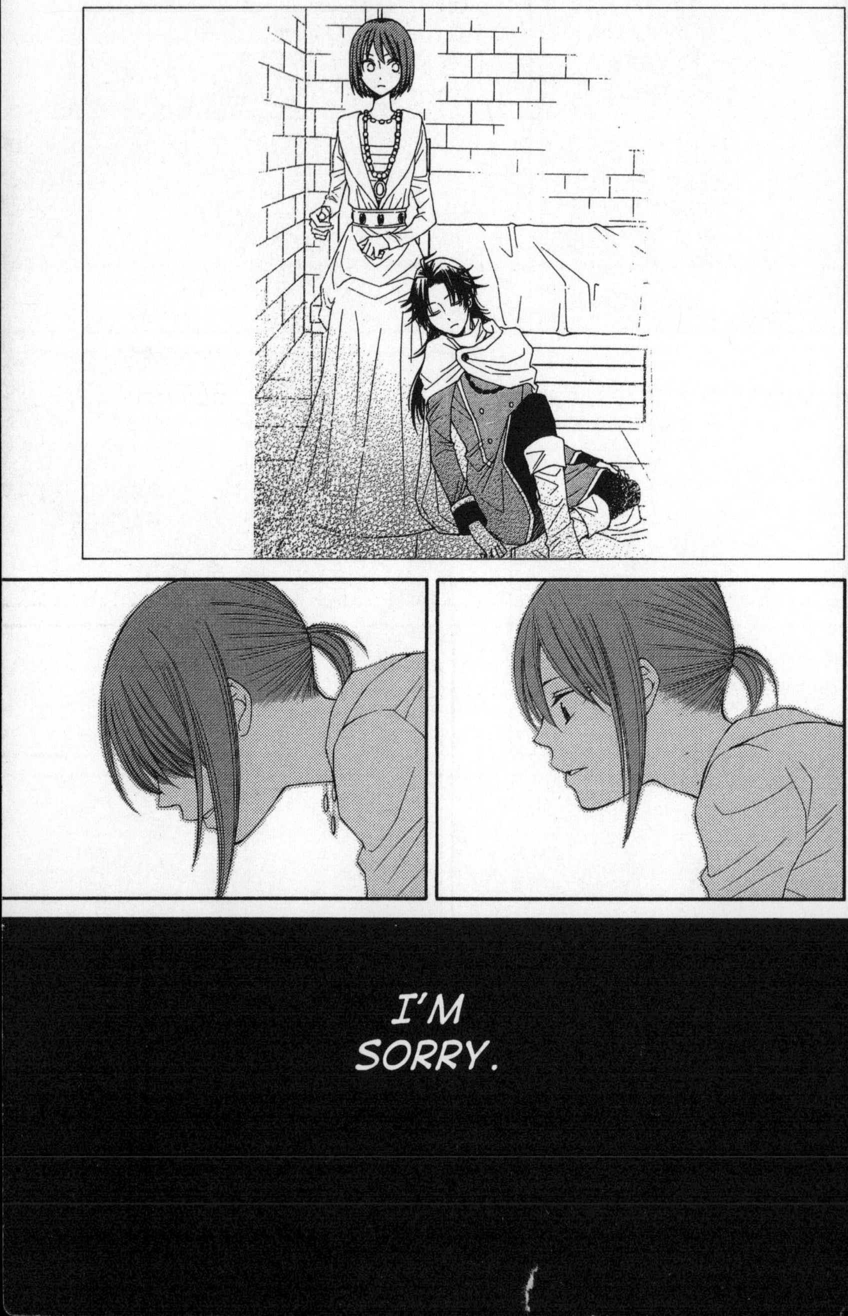
I'M SORRY.

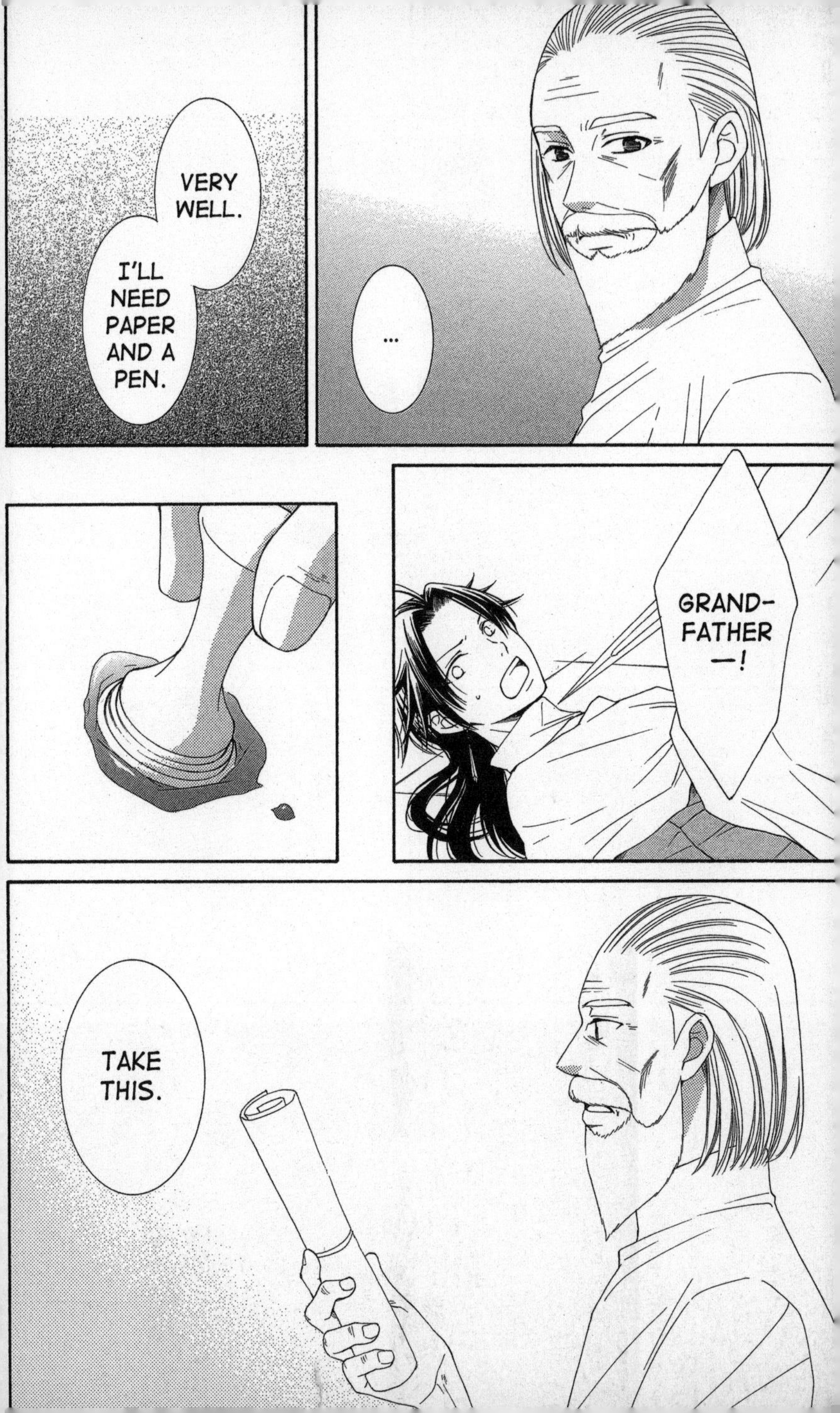
...
VERY WELL.
I'LL NEED PAPER AND A PEN.
GRAND-FATHER—!
TAKE THIS.

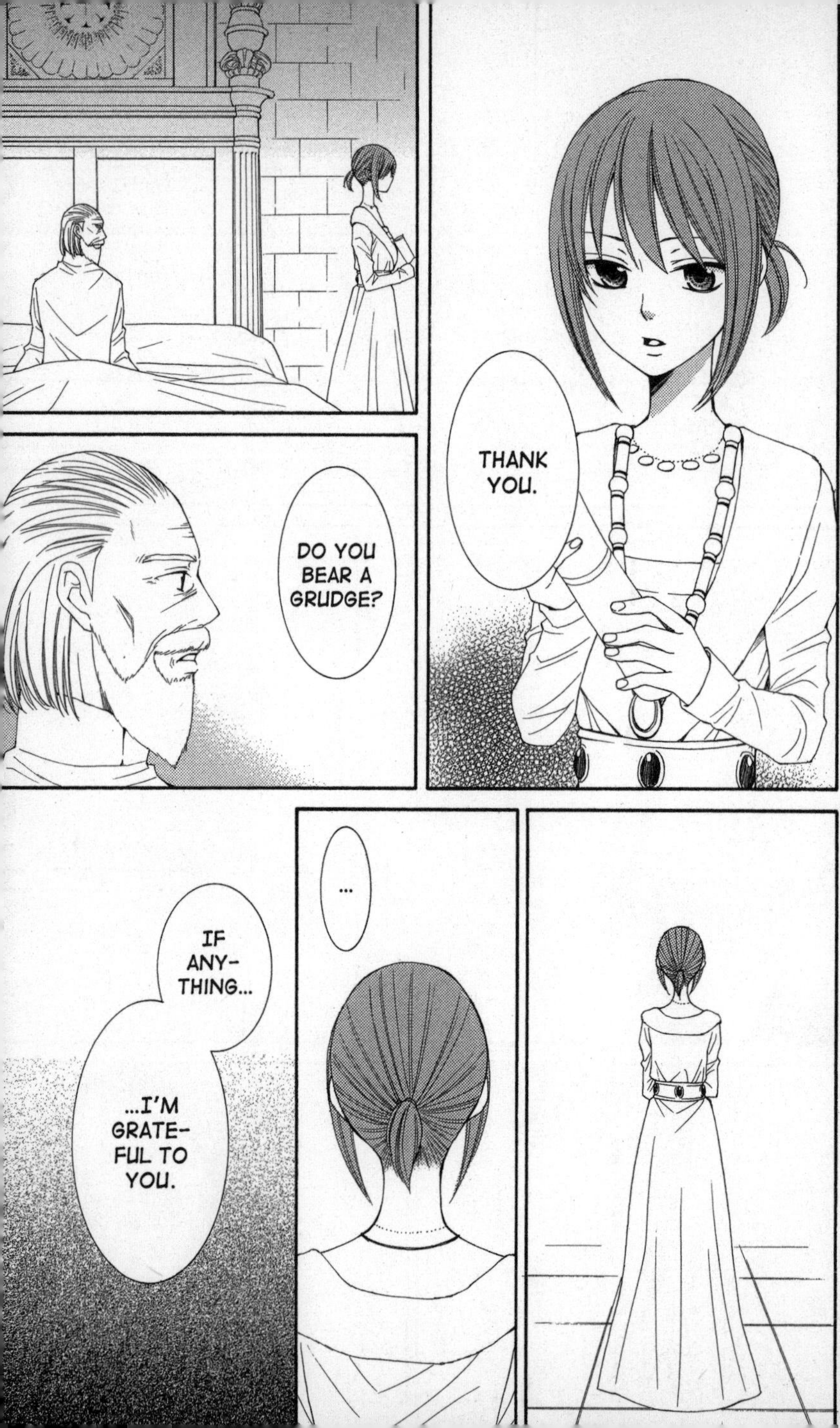
THANK YOU.
DO YOU BEAR A GRUDGE?
...
IF ANY-THING...
...I'M GRATE-FUL TO YOU.

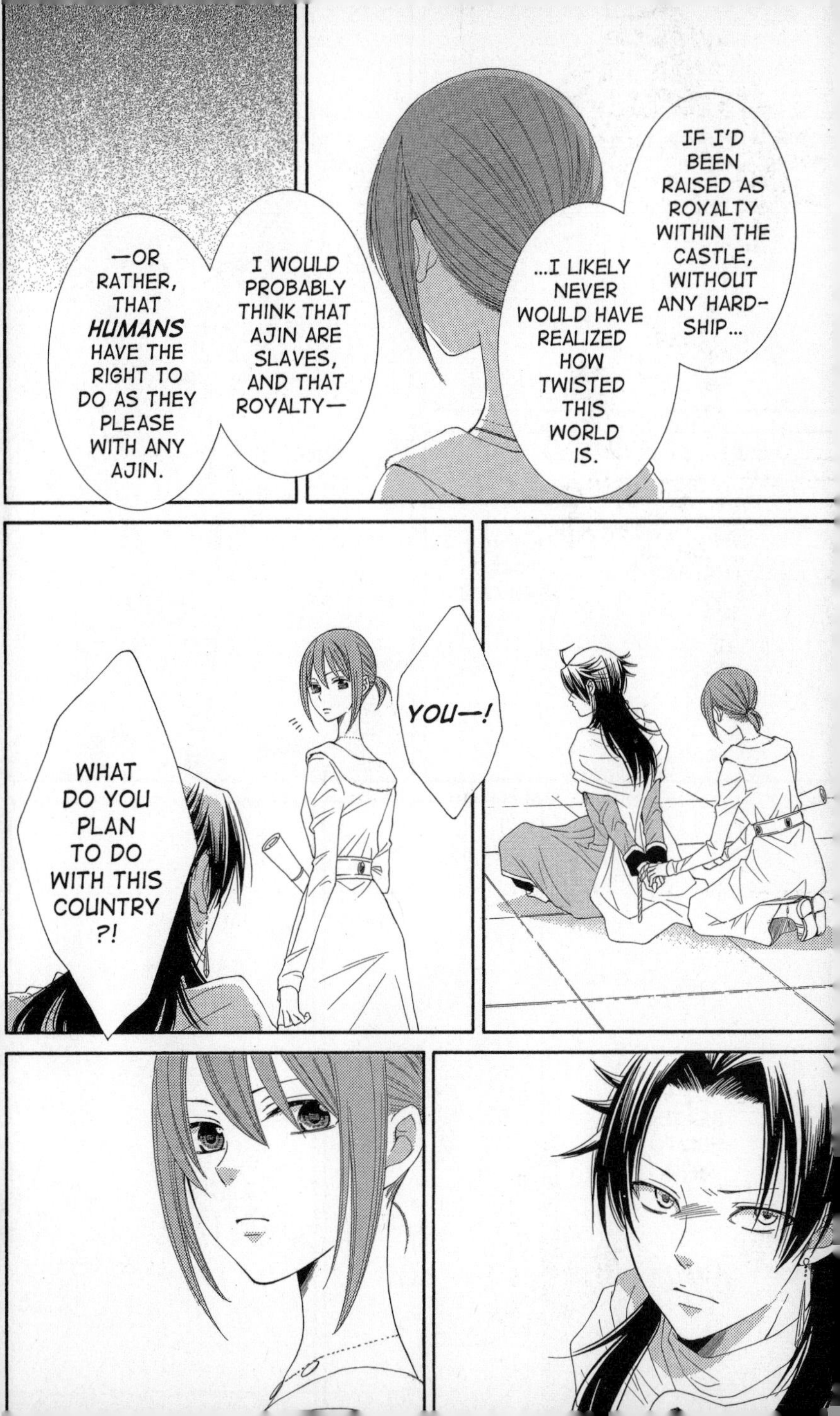
IF I'D BEEN RAISED AS ROYALTY WITHIN THE CASTLE, WITHOUT ANY HARDSHIP...
...I LIKELY NEVER WOULD HAVE REALIZED HOW TWISTED THIS WORLD IS.
I WOULD PROBABLY THINK THAT AJIN ARE SLAVES, AND THAT ROYALTY—
—OR RATHER, THAT *HUMANS* HAVE THE RIGHT TO DO AS THEY PLEASE WITH ANY AJIN.
YOU—!
WHAT DO YOU PLAN TO DO WITH THIS COUNTRY?!

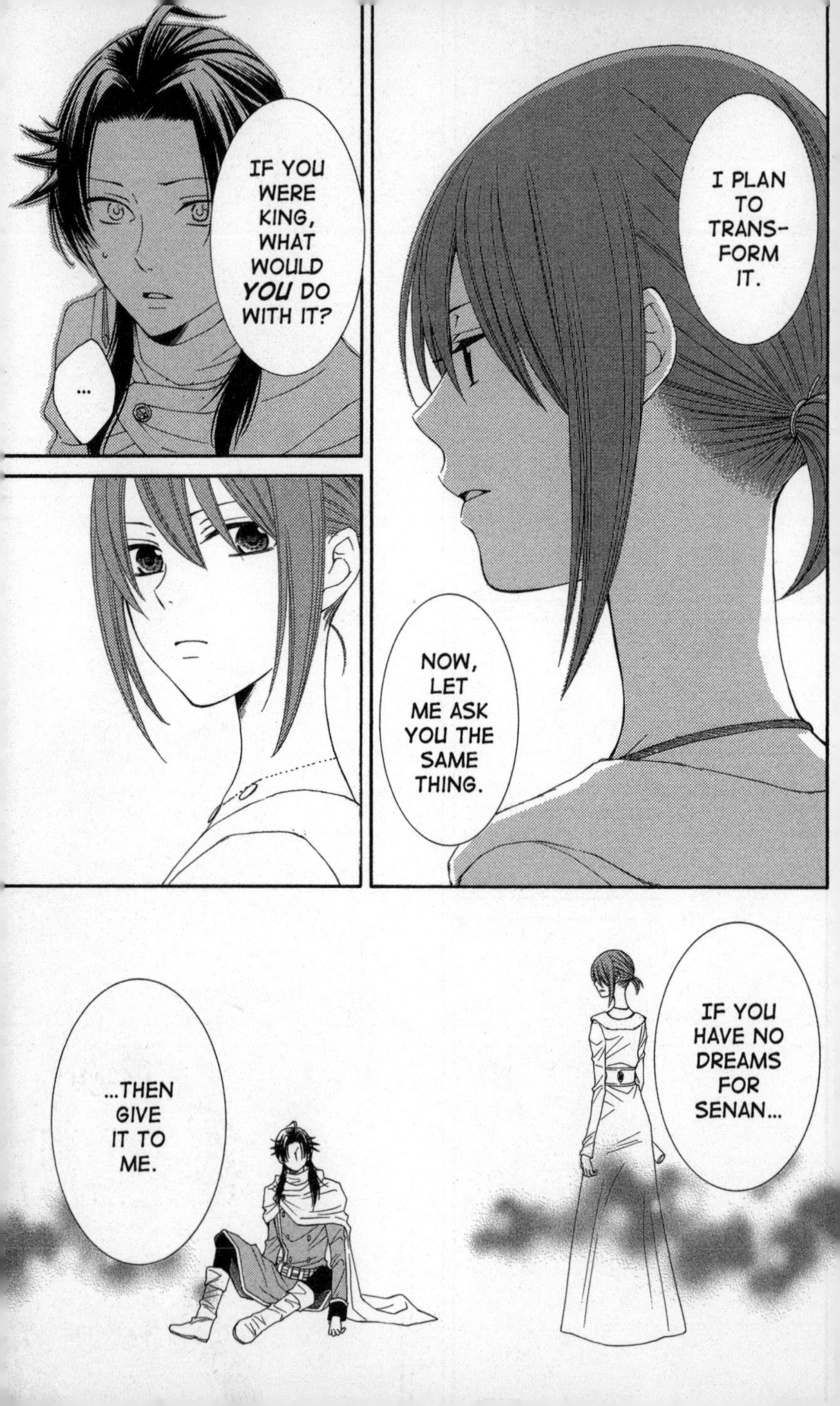
I PLAN TO TRANS-FORM IT.
NOW, LET ME ASK YOU THE SAME THING.
IF YOU WERE KING, WHAT WOULD *YOU* DO WITH IT?
...
IF YOU HAVE NO DREAMS FOR SENAN...
...THEN GIVE IT TO ME.

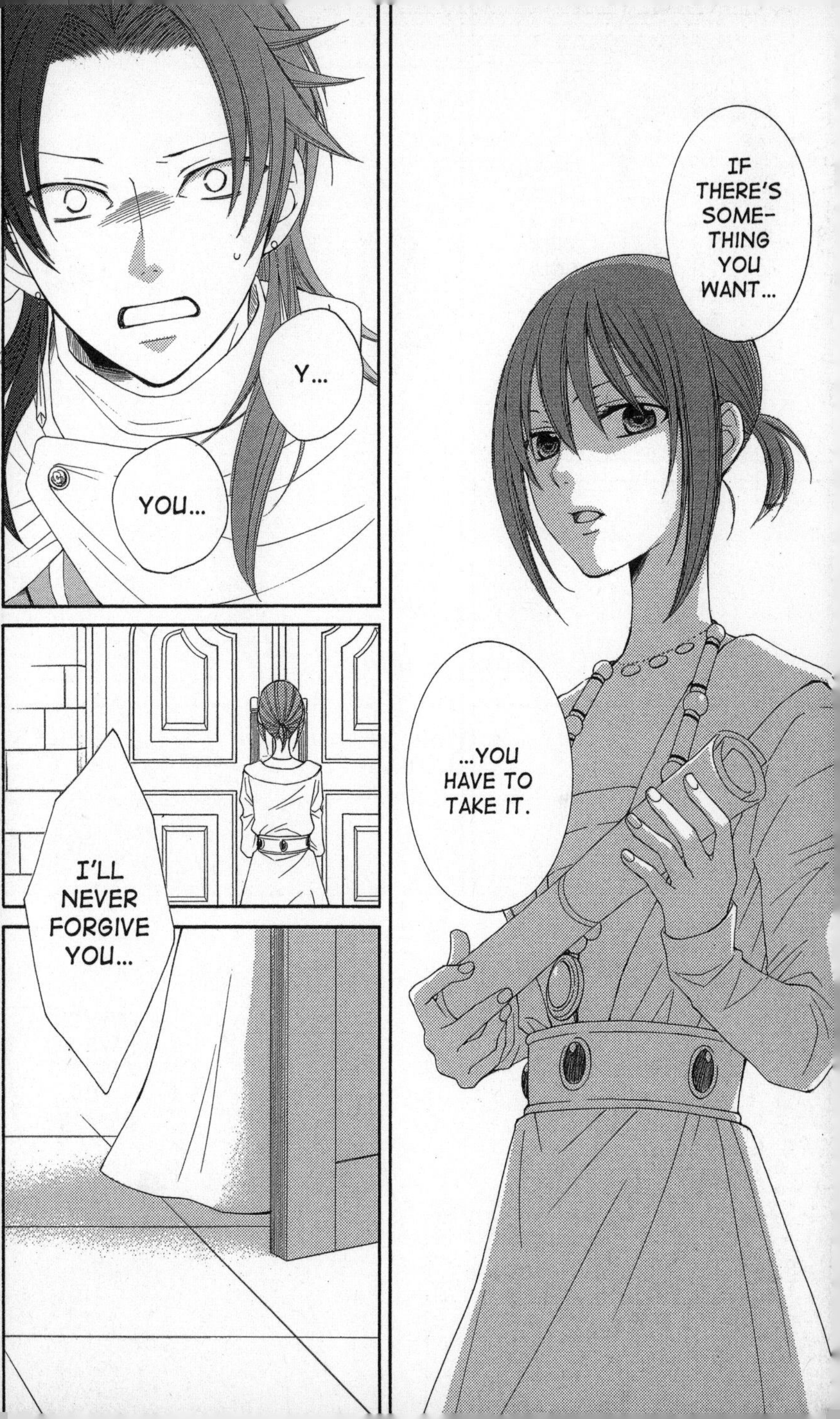
IF THERE'S SOME-THING YOU WANT...
...YOU HAVE TO TAKE IT.
Y...
YOU...
I'LL NEVER FORGIVE YOU...

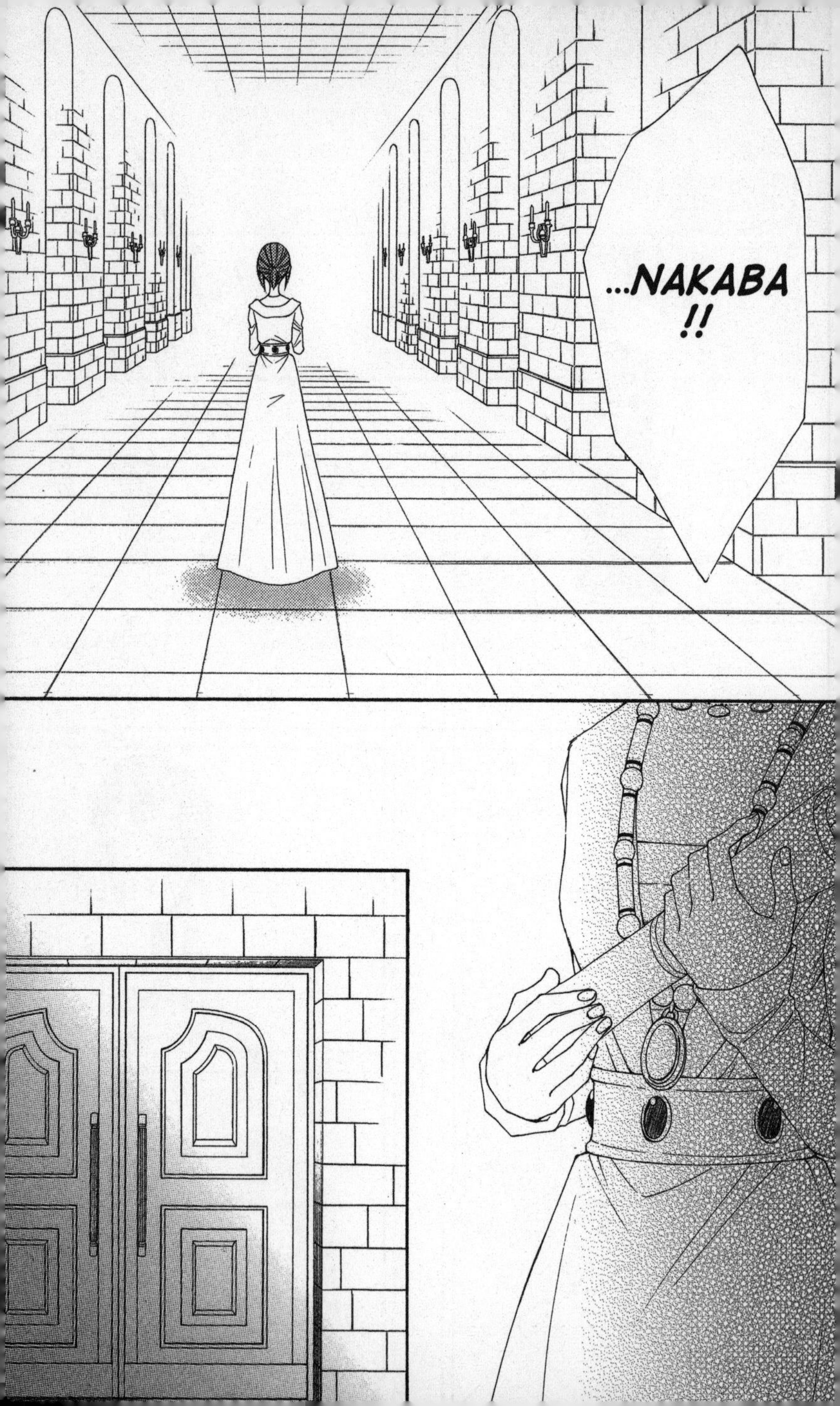
...NAKABA !!

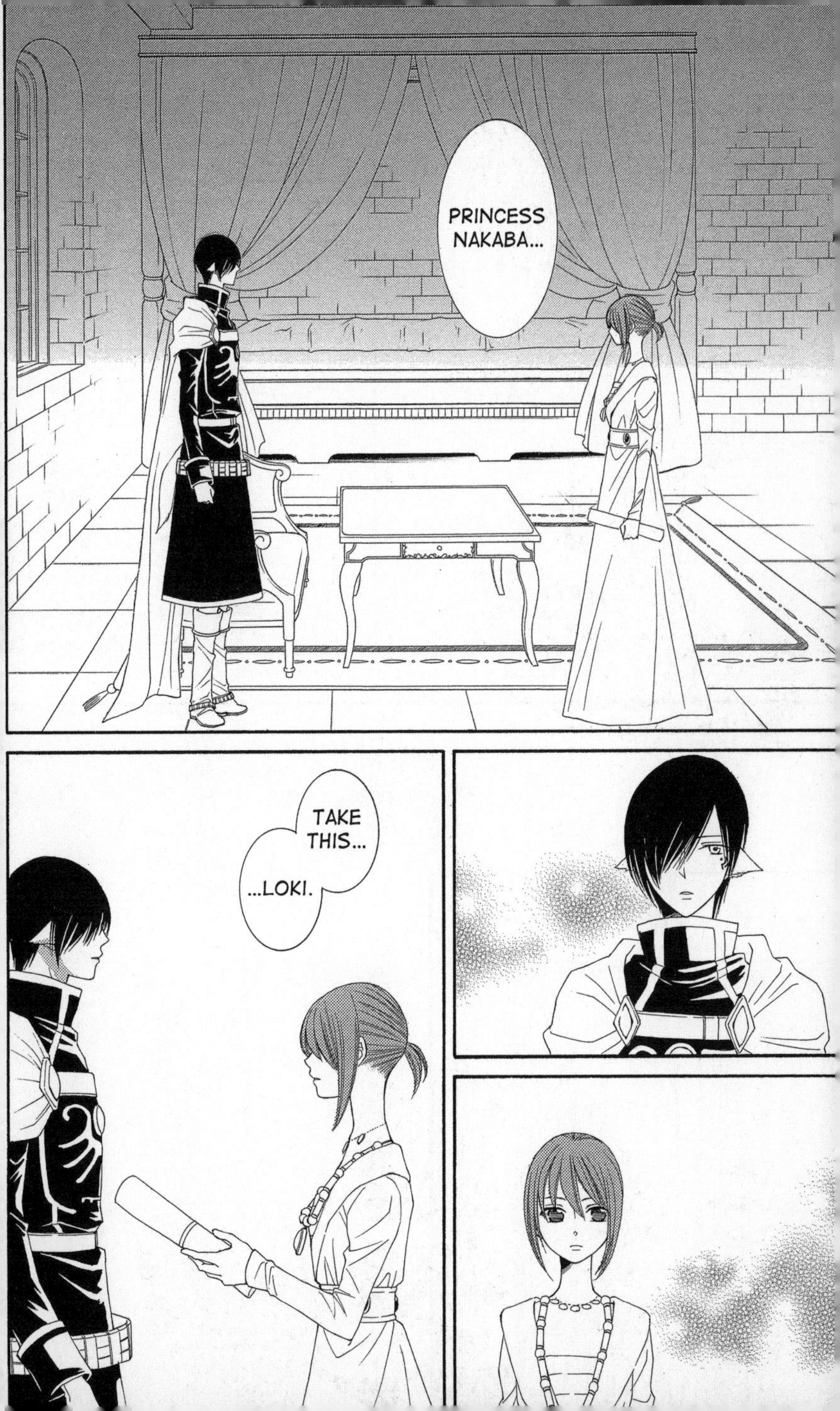
PRINCESS NAKABA...
TAKE THIS...
...LOKI.

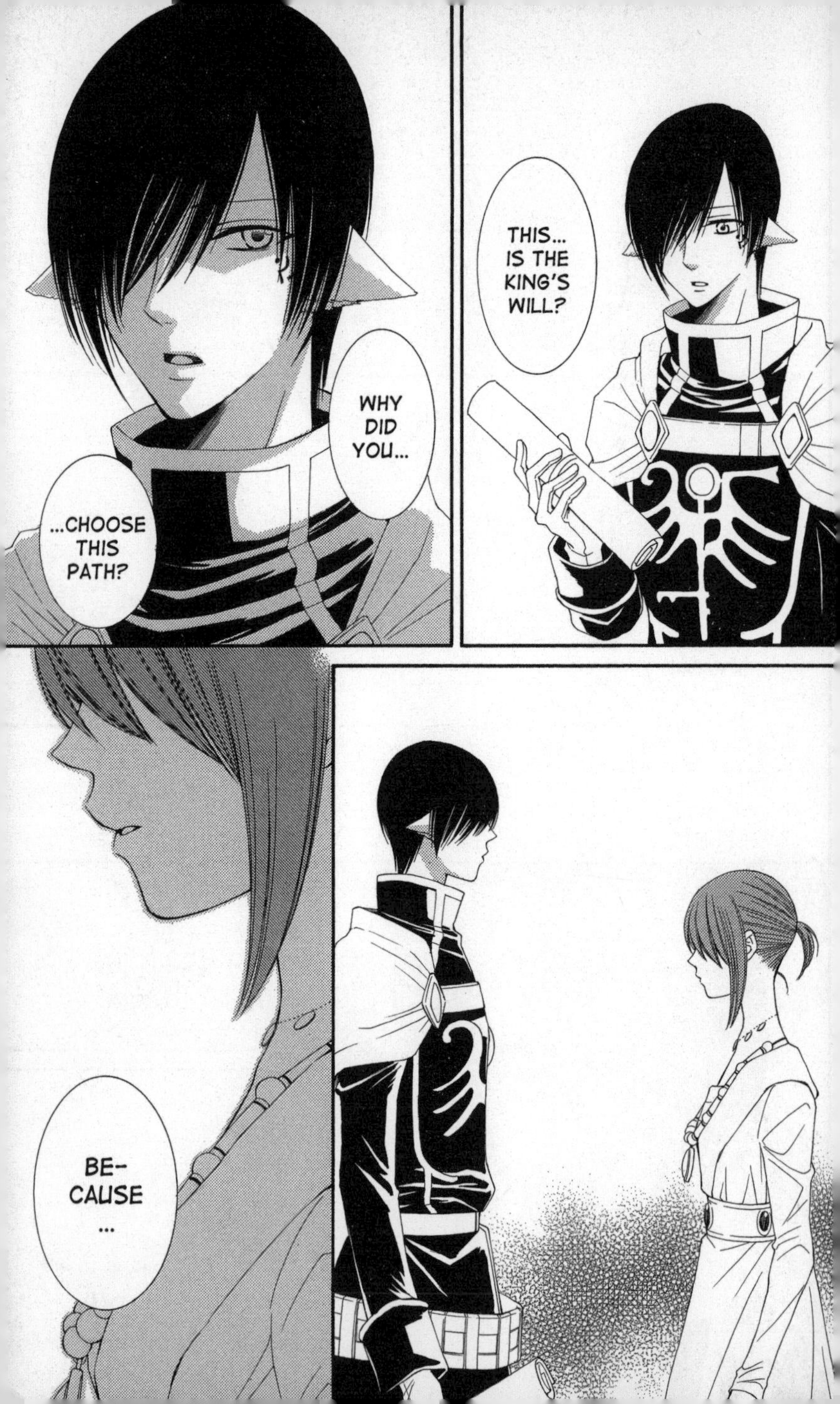
THIS... IS THE KING'S WILL?
WHY DID YOU...
...CHOOSE THIS PATH?
BE-CAUSE ...

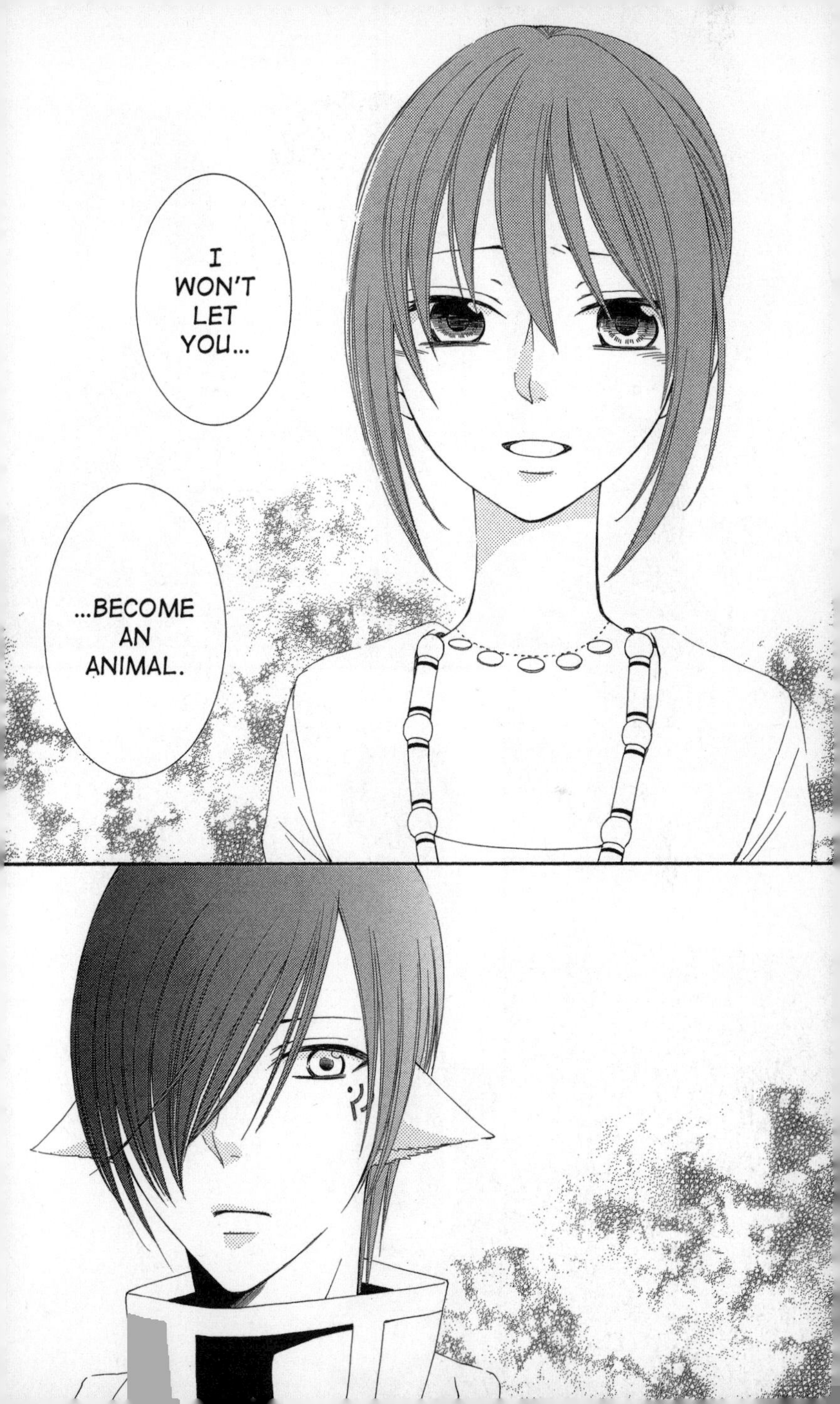
I WON'T LET YOU...
...BECOME AN ANIMAL.

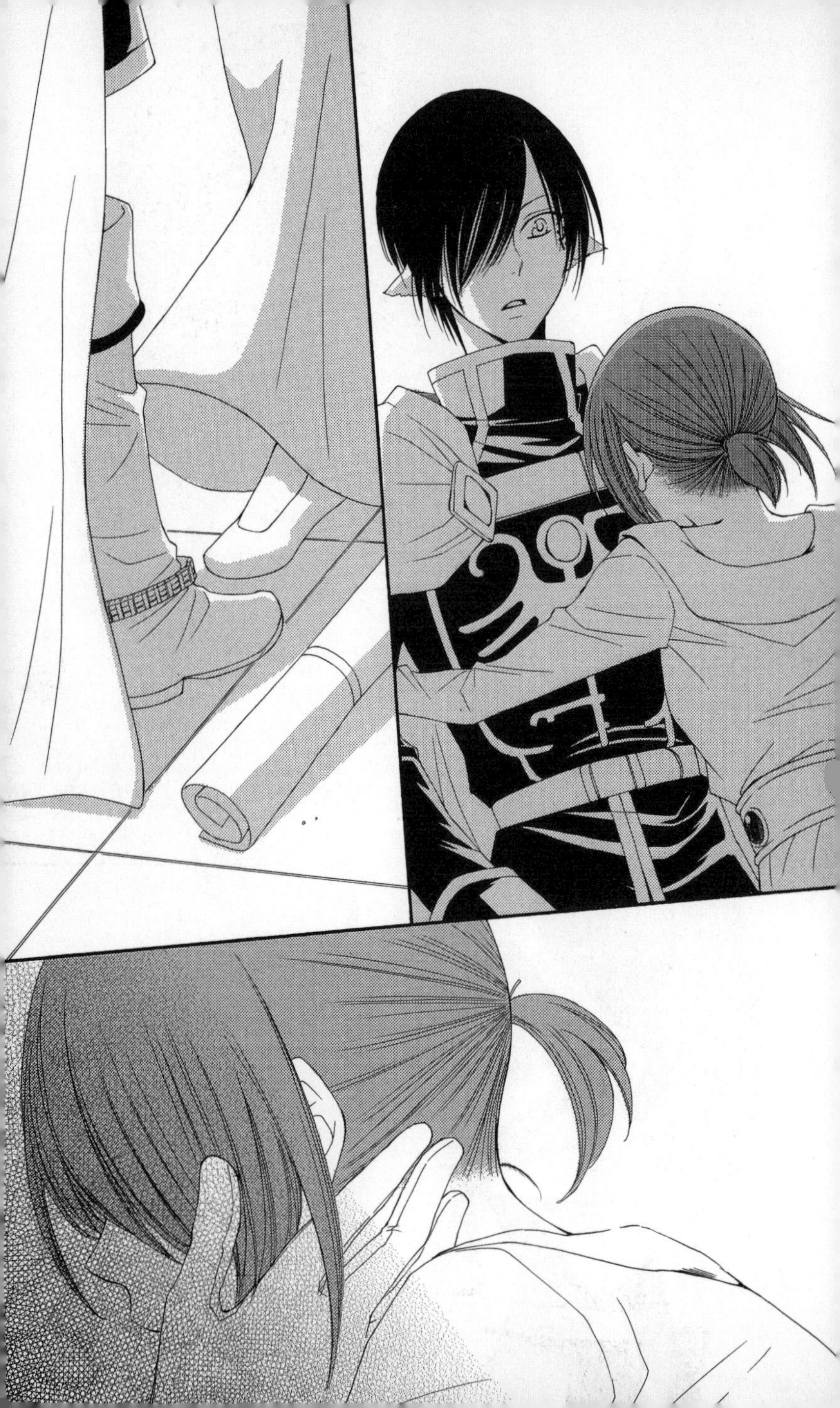

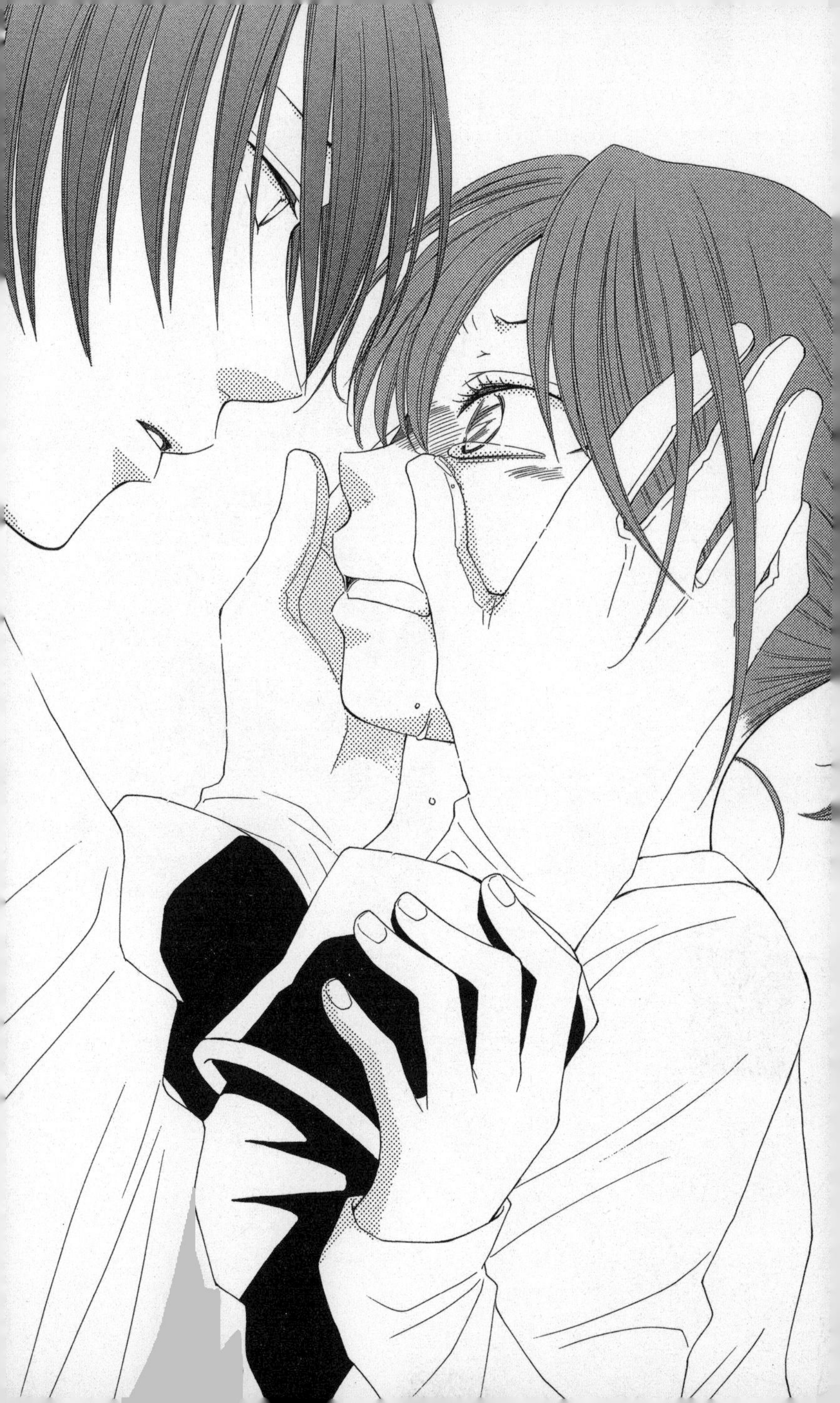

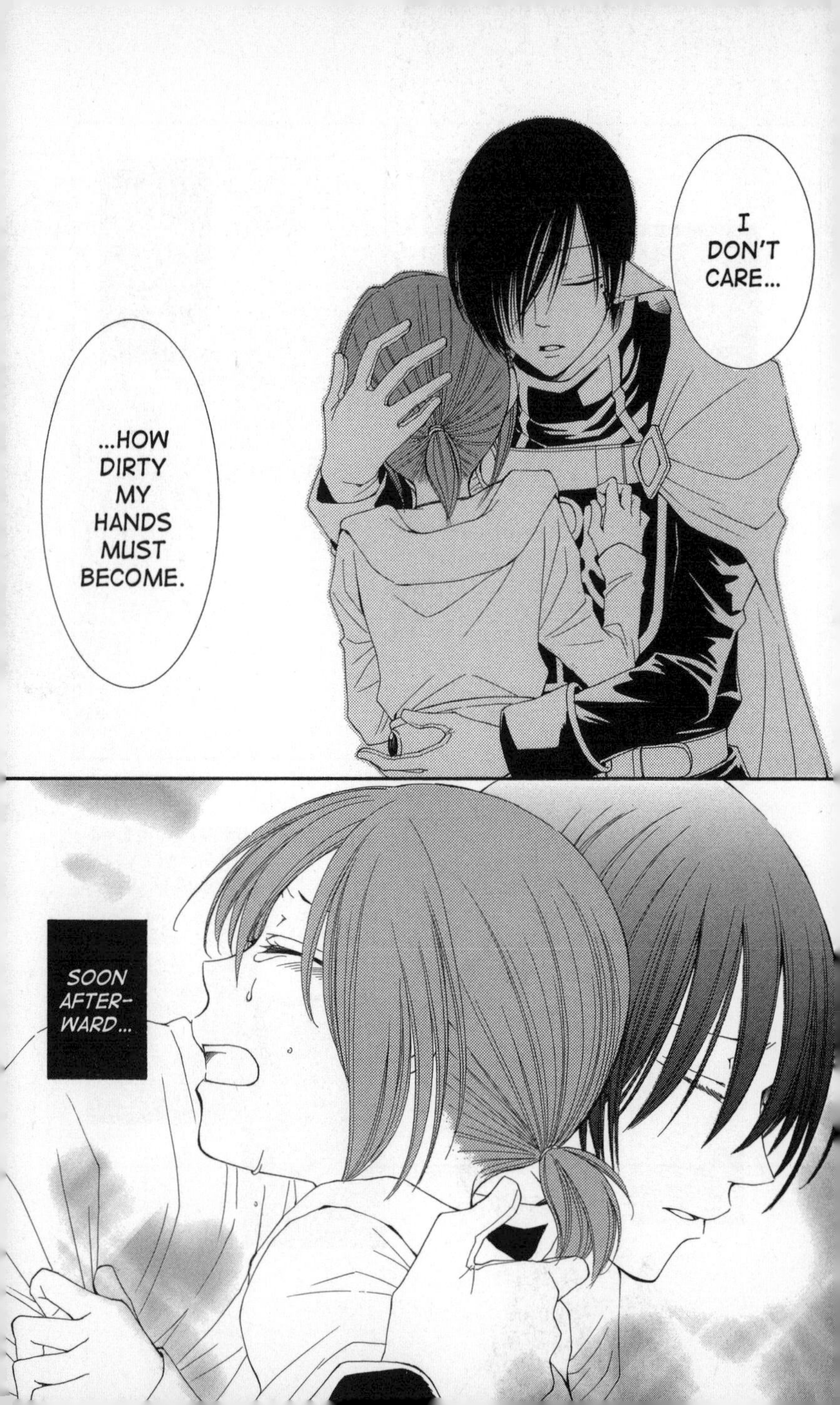
I DON'T CARE...
...HOW DIRTY MY HANDS MUST BECOME.
SOON AFTER-WARD...

...KING MORRIS OF SENAN PASSED AWAY.

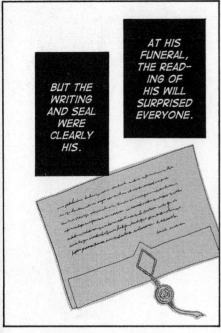

AT HIS FUNERAL, THE READ- ING OF HIS WILL SURPRISED EVERYONE.

BUT THE WRITING AND SEAL WERE CLEARLY HIS.

THOSE WHO'D EXPECTED ADEL TO BE THEIR NEXT KING...

...SET ASIDE THEIR CONFUSION FOR THE MOMENT.

AND I...

...TOOK
THE
THRONE.

DAWN OF THE ARCANA 11 (THE END)

Adel is on the cover this time. Surprisingly, a lot of people like him. I like him quite a bit myself.

–Rei Toma

Rei Toma has been drawing since childhood, but she only began drawing manga because of her graduation project in design school. When she drew a short-story manga, *Help Me, Dentist*, for the first time, it attracted a publisher's attention and she made her debut right away. Her magnificent art style became popular, and after she debuted as a manga artist, she became known as an illustrator for novels and video game character designs. Her current manga series, *Dawn of the Arcana*, is her first long-running manga series, and it has been a hit in Japan, selling over a million copies.

DAWN OF THE ARCANA
VOLUME 11
Shojo Beat Edition

STORY AND ART BY
REI TOMA

REIMEI NO ARCANA Vol. 11
by Rei TOMA
© 2009 Rei TOMA
All rights reserved.
Original Japanese edition published by SHOGAKUKAN.
English translation rights in the United States of America and
Canada arranged with SHOGAKUKAN.

English Adaptation/Ysabet MacFarlane
Translation/JN Productions
Touch-up Art & Lettering/Freeman Wong
Design/Yukiko Whitley
Editor/Amy Yu

Printed in the U.S.A.

Published by VIZ Media, LLC
P.O. Box 77010
San Francisco, CA 94107

10 9 8 7 6 5 4 3 2 1
First printing, October 2013

www.viz.com   www.shojobeat.com

This is the last page.

In keeping with the original Japanese comic format, this book reads from right to left—so action, sound effects, and word balloons are completely reversed. This preserves the orientation of the original artwork—plus, it's fun! Check out the diagram shown here to get the hang of things, and then turn to the other side of the book to get started!

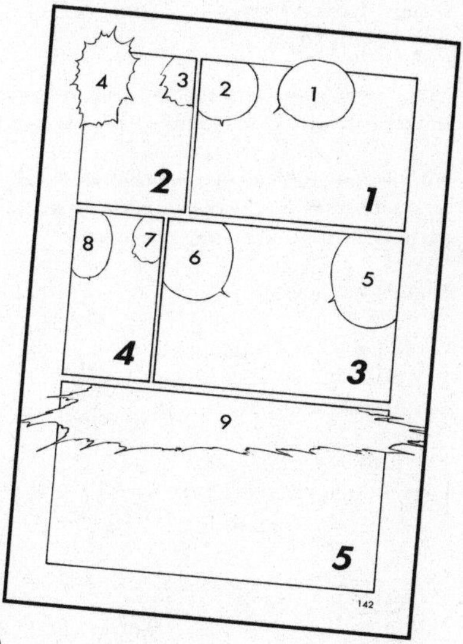
1
2
3
4
1
2
5
6
7
8
3
4
9
5
142

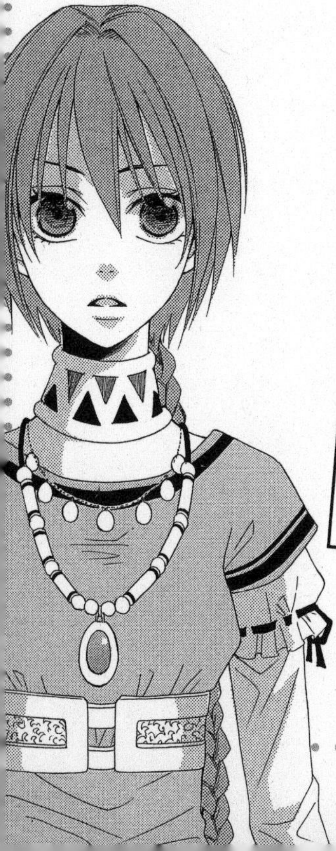

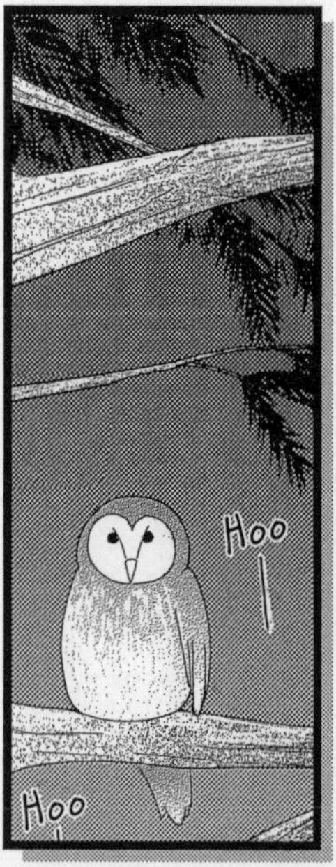
Hoo
Hoo

Chapter 41

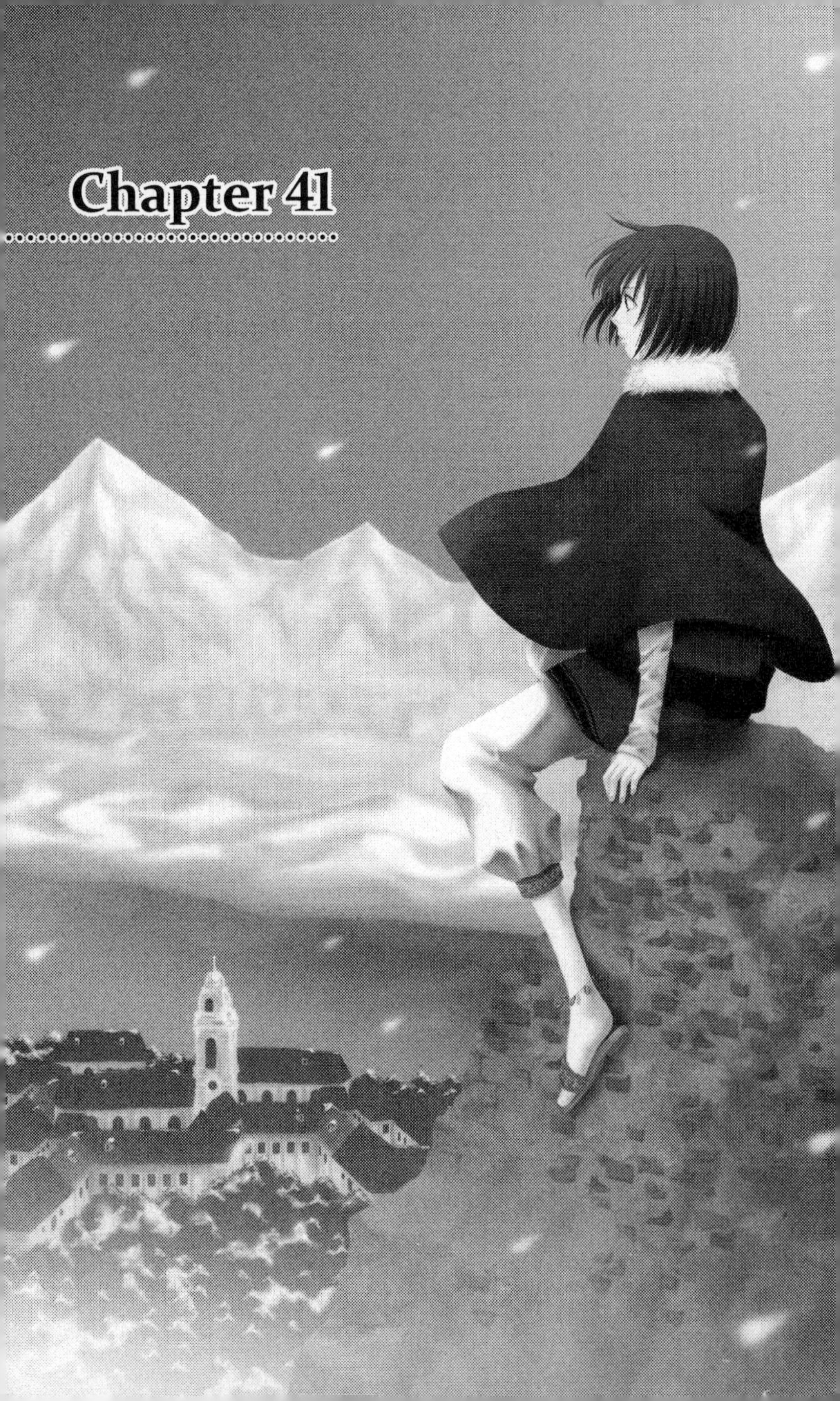

Dawn of the Arcana

Volume 11

CONTENTS

story

• Wed to Prince Caesar as a symbol of the peace between their two countries, Nakaba is actually little more than a hostage. Unbeknownst to King Guran, she is a survivor of the race he tried to destroy for fear of their power. Nakaba herself possesses the Arcana of Time, so she can see the past and the future. The political marriage between Nakaba and Caesar gets off to a rocky start, but as they grow to know each other, the gulf between them begins to close.

• In order to protect Nakaba, Loki kills Cain, Caesar's older brother. Realizing that pursuit from Belquat is inevitable, Nakaba and the others travel to Senan to seek refuge. There they receive orders from the King of Senan to go to Lithuanel to build diplomatic ties.

• Unfortunately, they are unsuccessful with their mission in Lithuanel. In order to change a world full of absurd wars and battles for the throne, Caesar heads to Belquat while Nakaba heads to Senan. They hope to become rulers of their respective countries and merge the two one day.

• When Caesar returns to Belquat, he does as his mother bids and marries Louise. Meanwhile, Nakaba returns to Senan and uses her Arcana power as a bargaining tool to marry Adel, who is next in line for the Senan throne.

• Nakaba then sees a vision of an avalanche in the mountains of Ulma. She manages to evacuate the villagers ahead of time, but she learns that a child who was born from a forbidden union between a human and a demi-human has been abandoned in a cave. She goes to save the child despite the approaching danger!

Neighboring Kingdoms

Senan
A poor kingdom in the cold north of the island. Militarily weak.

Belquat
A powerful country that thrives thanks to its temperate climate.

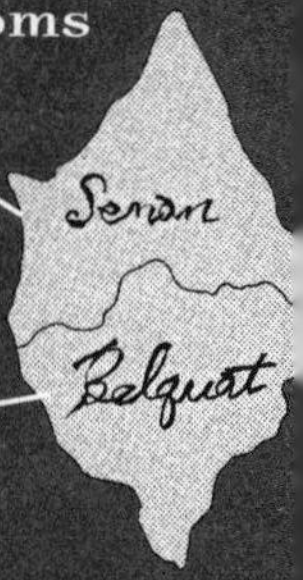
Senan
Belquat

characters

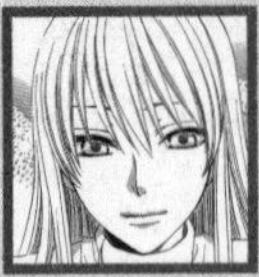

Sara
King Guran's concubine. Deceased.

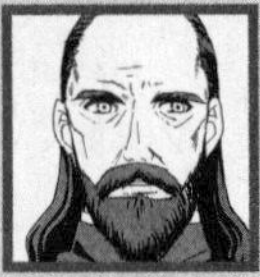

Guran
King of Belquat.

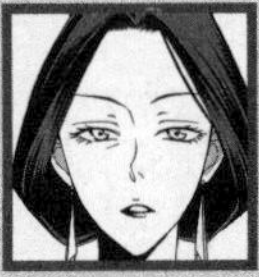

Rosenta
Queen of Belquat.

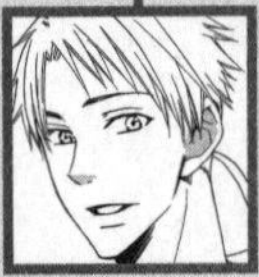

Cain
First-born prince of Belquat. Caesar's brother. He was killed by Loki.

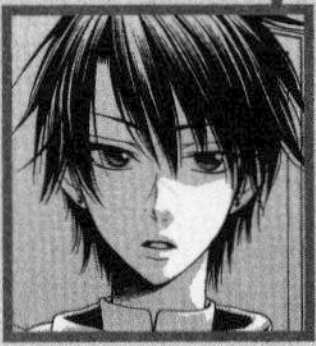

Caesar
The second-born prince of Belquat. He breaks up with Nakaba and marries Louise.

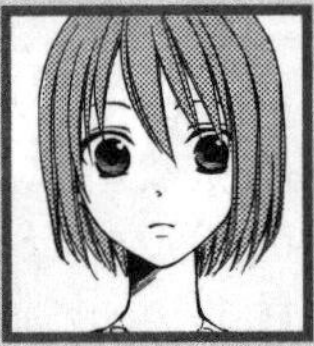

Nakaba
The princess royal of Senan. Strong of will and noble of spirit, she possesses a strange power.

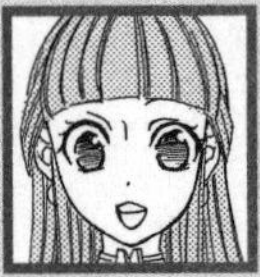

Lemiria
Bellinus's younger sister. Fond of her big brother.

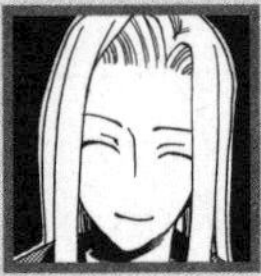

Bellinus
Caesar's attendant. Always cool and collected.

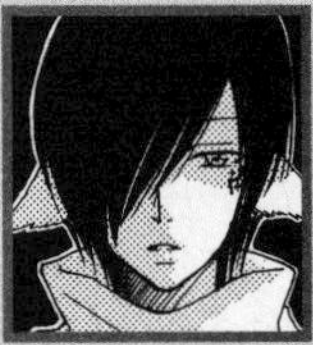

Loki
Nakaba's attendant. His senses of perception are unmatched.

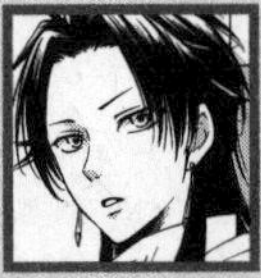

Adel
Successor to the throne of Senan. Married to Nakaba.

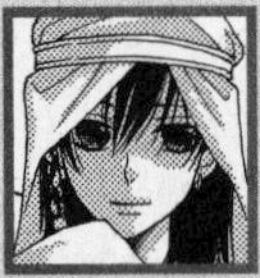

Akhil
Fifth-born prince of Lithuanel.

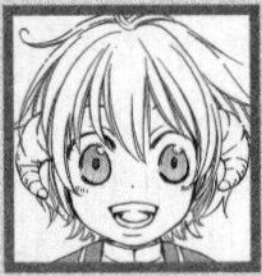

Rito
Nakaba's attendant.

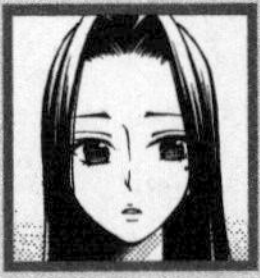

Louise
The daughter of a Belquat general.

Dawn of the Arcana

11

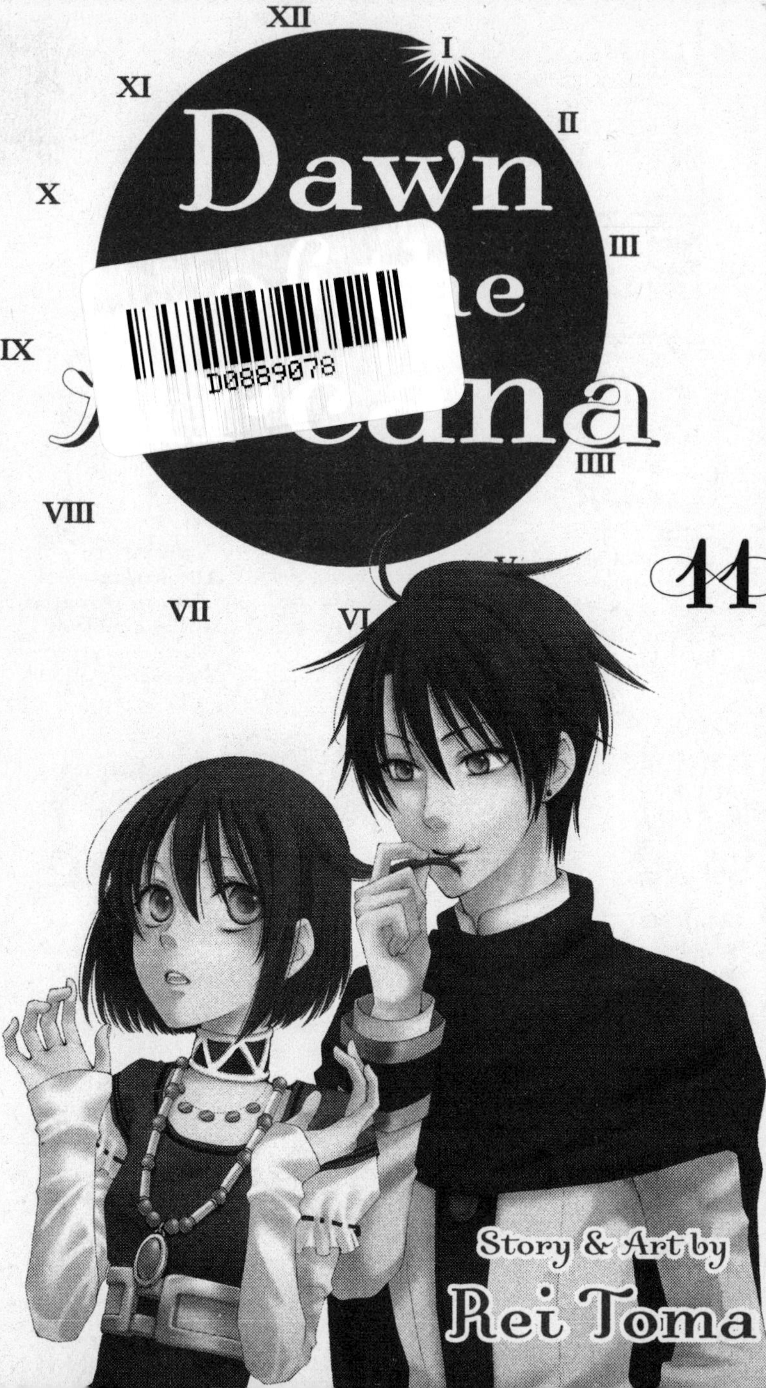

Story & Art by

Rei Toma